ARCHER'S DIGEST

SECOND EDITION

Edited By Jack Lewis

DBI BOOKS, INC., NORTHFIELD, ILLINOIS

(Formerly Digest Books, Inc.)

Production Editor
BOB SPRINGER

Research Editor
JACQUELINE FARMER

Art Director
JOHN VITALE

Staff Artists
LORIE DISNEY
SONYA KAISER
RICK RIVADENEYRA

Copy Editor
RUSTY SPRINGER

Production Supervisor
WENDY L. WISEHART

Production Assistant
JO ANNA SIMPSON

Associate Publisher
SHELDON L. FACTOR

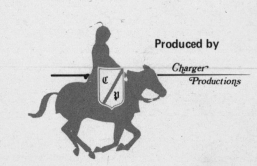

Produced by

Charger Productions

ISBN 0-695-80718-8   Library of Congress Catalog Card Number 77-148722

CONTENTS

Introduction

Since the first edition of this book appeared in 1971, there has been as wide a span in archery advancement as there has been between the Model T and the cars of today in the automotive field.

In this new edition of Archer's Digest, we have felt it necessary to bring things up to date, but still maintain the information that is the background of archery; what we have today, as in any type of development, is the ultimate product of what has gone before.

In the original edition, there was virtually no material on compound bows. Indeed, the catalog section contained only two models, one by Allen, the other, Tom Jennings' original offering based upon the Allen patents. Frankly, I was not certain at the time that the compound bow was not a temporary fad that would go away in a few months.

But with the aid of a host of contributors, including Dr. Sam Fadala, PhD, this oversight has been corrected and we have given the compound its just due in this update.

As stated in the last edition: I hope each reader will find information of value; something to help him on the target range and in the game fields.

Jack Lewis
Capistrano Beach, California

Chapter 1

YOU'VE COME A LONG WAY, BABY!

Through The Centuries, Archery Has Been A Way Of Life From Warfare To Olympic Sport!

THE oldest of projectile weapons — the bow — also was the most widely distributed in use. This weapon has been known since time immemorial, with evidence of its use as long ago as 7000 B.C.! References to the bow are recorded in the ancient military history of many lands, including China, Japan, India, Russia, Switzerland, France and England. In the storied days of Nimrod, archers were the vaunted pride of the Assyrian kings. More familiar to us, perhaps, are the legends of the famed long bowmen of Merrie England.

In view of the prominence which this weapon has achieved and the vast lore which has been built up about its use, it is interesting to note that undoubtedly the best bows ever made were the composite bows of the old Mohammedan nations. Small and light, they were designed to propel arrows with considerable force over great distances. The making of bows was a highly esteemed craft and many sultans prided themselves on their personal mastery of the craft. Mohammed himself raised proficiency in the use of the bow to the status of a religious duty.

Unfortunately for the military historian, the origin of the Turkish bow is lost far back in the dim reaches of antiquity. Interestingly enough, however, bows are pictured on the earliest pieces of pottery and are spoken of in the earliest written accounts. From all that can be learned, there was little change in the bows through the years. We know, of course, that both foot and horse archers made up an important part of all Ottoman armies.

The typical Turkish military bow was a composite affair of very flexible wood, horn and sinew, some thirty-six inches long, although the bows used by mounted archers were shorter. The frame or core of the bow was of wood, varying from some three-quarters of an inch thick at the center to a quarter of an inch or even less at the ends. Particularly tough wood was used for the limbs. After the three pieces of wood had been glued together they were heated and bent to shape. Very flexible horn and sinew then was applied and glued in place, first being softened in extremely hot water. Approximately three inches of wood were allowed to project beyond the sheathing of horn and sinew at each end of the bow. These projecting ends were large enough to allow the cutting of nocks to accomodate the bowstring.

The horn used in making Turkish bows was cut from the horn of a buffalo or an antelope and was usually about a quarter of an inch thick. The sinew, which was applied to the back of the bow, was taken from the great neck tendon of an ox or stag. It was shredded lengthwise

Most arrows had nocks that had their sides shaped so they had to be parted to fit into the Turkish bowstring.

and after being soaked in elastic glue was compressed into a long flat strip and carefully glued to the wood frame. It was always put on under great tension so as to cause the bow to take a most pronounced reverse curve. Unfortunately, the formula for preparing the glue used in the construction of these bows has been lost for many years. Similarly, although we know the composition of the bows, we do not know just how they were put together and we are unable to duplicate them even though we use approximately the same materials.

The bow was carried by the archer in a half case, often of richly decorated leather, suspended from the waist.

The string used on the Turkish bow was made up of sixty or so strands of tough silk thread, knotted at each end and tied securely to a loop of twisted sinew. This arrangement was necessary, since a loop of silk threads would soon have frayed and pulled apart. For approximately one and a half inches on each side of the center, the bowstring was bound with fine silk thread. Lashings of this thread held the strands of the string together at several points between the center and the ends.

War arrows measured slightly over two feet in length, as a general rule, with the balance about twelve inches forward of the inner end of the nock. The shaft was thickest at the balance, tapering to the ends. Most arrows had a nock so shaped that the sides had to be parted to admit the bowstring, after which they closed about it. This held the arrow in place, a rather valuable consideration, particularly for mounted archers.

Arrows were fitted with either feathers or thin parchment, the former almost always used for military purposes. In some instances the feathers were arranged in a spiral fashion in order to cause the arrow to rotate along its axis and so keep it more true in its trajectory.

Some arrows were fitted with heads with movable barbs. In flight, these folded back against the head but swung out at right angles when an attempt was made to withdraw the arrow from the flesh. This type of head also was employed extensively by ancient Japanese archers.

Since Turkish bows were very short, great strength and skill were required to bend them. This was particularly true of the heavier bows used by the foot archers

which sometimes required a pull of nearly 160 pounds. In bending these bows in olden times, the archer spread his feet slightly apart with one end of the bow, the bowstring already attached, against his leg, just below the knee. The belly of the bow pressed against the back of the other leg just above the rear of the knee. The free end of the bow was then pulled forward with one hand and the free loop of the bowstring placed in the nock with the other hand. The bow had to be kept from twisting during this maneuver, else it would splinter. This all required not only a strong wrist but strong arm muscles as well. Few if any modern archers are equal to the task of bending an ancient Turkish bow and must use mechanical assistance to accomplish the job.

For shooting at extreme ranges Turkish archers at times used an arrow several inches shorter than usual, but bent the bow to the same extent as for a longer arrow. In order to keep the arrow properly guided in such cases, since the head was well back of the inside of the bow, a grooved horn guide was employed. Roughly six inches long, it was attached to a ring which was worn

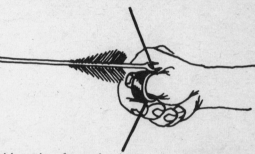

In this ancient form of archery, a thumb ring often was worn to protect the thumb from chafing by the string. Today, similar devices are being used in competition.

on the thumb of the hand holding the bow. This allowed the bowstring to be pulled back to its limit.

The Turkish bow was held in the center and Turkish archers used the "Mongolian release" in which the arrow is placed to the right of the bow and the thumb passes around the bowstring and under the forefinger.

A thumb ring is worn to protect the thumb from the pressure and from the chafing friction of the bowstring. Use of the thumb ring and this manner of release allowed the pressure of the bowstring to be concentrated at a point close to the nock of the arrow, making the arrow release, speed and trajectory much better than would be possible when three or four fingers were used to draw the bowstring. It also allowed the feathers to be placed much closer to the nock without the danger of being crushed. This in itself permitted longer and steadier flight. The part of the thumb ring which bore on the bowstring was always wider than the rest. The rings were usually made of ivory, jade, horn or bone.

The range of the Turkish bow was tremendous indeed, distances of 600 to 800 yards having been regularly accomplished. Mohammedan archers considered themselves rank amateurs if they could not exceed 600 yards. Consider for a moment the fact that the famed English long bow had a range of some 250 yards and the military crossbow of medieval times had a range around 380 yards and you will have some idea of the power of the Turkish weapon.

Mohammedan military leaders were great believers in mobility and fire power and they used their archers, particularly their horse archers, with deadly effect. Well mounted on small but rugged horses and clad in light flexible mail, they were more than a match for the heavily armored knights and men-at-arms from Europe. Either afoot or mounted, the well trained Sons of the Prophet usually gave an outstanding account of themselves. — *Robert H. Rankin*

BANZAI BOWS

The Samarai Used Bows For Centuries After Others Had Firearms!

MENTION of ancient Japanese arms most usually calls to mind, as far as most people are concerned, the famed samurai sword. It may come as something of a surprise to you to learn that the Japanese were well known for their prowess with the bow. Bows were used by all nobles and peasants alike. Instruction in the use of the weapon began at an early age and was continued on through adult years.

It is probable that the Japanese were easily the equal of the storied English long bowman and the famous Turkish archers. In early times, the bow was deemed of even greater importance than the sword. Indeed, the Japanese terms for bow and arrow and for war were synonymous. Even after the sword became the principal weapon and the symbol of rank, proficiency in the use of the bow was much sought and was regarded as an indication of the individual's military ability.

The best archers in Nippon journeyed to Kyoto to demonstrate their skill. There, at Sanju-San-Gen Do temple, a covered gallery was erected for their use. With a length of 132 yards, this structure was only twenty-two feet high, a fact which required tremendous strength on the part of the bowman to achieve a trajectory flat enough to allow the arrow to reach the mark. It is recorded that in 1696, one Wasa Daicheri shot 8,133 arrows in twenty-four hours (this is at the rate of about five a minute), of which 3,213 reached the mark!

The Japanese war bow was long. In fact, some were as long as eight feet, but this was the exception, the average being around seven feet. Bows were made of a piece of deciduous wood sandwiched in between two especially selected pieces of bamboo, with the bark outward, all held together with fish glue. It was nearly uniform in section throughout its length and at intervals was tightly bound with cane.

The bow was curved at either end and, when strung, it reversed itself. There were no notches for the string. Instead, the ends were cut back for a short distance to form shoulders. The string went about the projecting ends and was held in place by the shoulders. Strings were of sinew or of bundles of silk thread treated with lacquer.

The handle of the bow was well below center, in some instances as much as two thirds of the way down. This was necessary, because the average Japanese is short and the bow was used from a kneeling position when the archer was not mounted. All in all, these war bows were powerful and effective.

Another type of Japanese bow, resembling a Tartar bow in shape, was made of several different varieties of bamboo glued together. A metal sleeve covered the belly. The string striking against this produced a characteristic sound which often was used for signaling.

Ceremonial bows, intended only for parades and court functions, were highly lacquered and ornamented.

This heavy arrowhead for warfare, shaped much like the European halberd was of 18th Century Japanese vintage.

This barbed arrowhead was called the "watakusi," translated to mean "tear flesh." This was due to the difficulty in removing it from a wound it had caused.

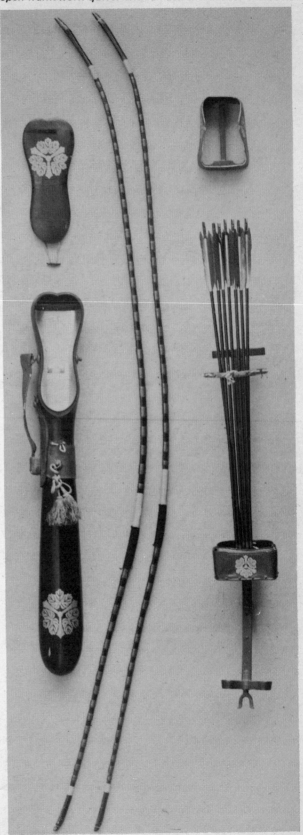

Japanese tackle from late 18th Century includes: (from left), arrow case or yadzutsu of black lacquer bearing owner's crest; pair of Japanese bows, unstrung; an open framework quiver with an attachment for the bow.

These bows were in two sections, joined in the center by a metal sleeve which formed the handle. In addition to these, there were hunting bows of various lengths, some as short as two feet. These smaller bows were made of horn or whalebone.

Arrows for the war bows averaged forty inches long and weighed around half a pound. Practically all were feathered, usually in a straight line with the shaft. Some, however, had the feathers arranged spirally about the shaft to cause it to rotate in flight and thus assist in keeping it on course.

For the practical purposes of war, arrow heads differed greatly from those used for ceremonial purposes. Among the war arrows was the hiki-ya. This had a large hollow head with openings cut in the sides. Air rushing through these while the arrow was in flight caused a whistling sound. Arrows of this type were used for signaling purposes. The wata-kusi, "tear flesh," had a head with movable barbs. These laid close to the shaft when the arrow was in flight but swung out at right angles when an attempt was made to pull it out of the flesh. The yanagi-ha, "willow leaf," had a head with straight sides and was diamond shape in section. It was an extremely efficient general purpose missile. The karimata, "forked arrow," was a two-prong design with sharp cutting edges. These heads varied in size from one to six inches between the prongs. They were used to cut ropes and armor lacing. Another lovely number, a variation of the karimata, was known as the "bowel raker" and was reputed to cause a horrible death.

Ceremonial arrows had heads which were large, heavy, elaborate — and quite useless as weapons. They often were made by famous artist-armorers.

It is rather interesting to note that the length of the bow and arrow was related to the particular warrior who was to use them. The unit of measurement for the war bow was the distance between the tips of the thumb and little finger of the spread right hand of the archer. Twelve to fifteen of these units was considered the proper length of the bow. The unit of measurement for war arrows was the width of the right hand, across the palm. Here again, twelve to fifteen of these units were reckoned to be the proper length for the arrows.

Several kinds of quivers were used. One consisted of an open box to which a framework was attached to support the shafts of the arrows. The heads rested within the box contained a small drawer in which spare bow strings were carried. Another type of quiver was a closed

The forked arrow or "karimata" was used for cutting ropes or lacings of warrior's armor during the 18th Century.

The "yanagi-ha" or willow leaf arrowhead was the most common type of fighting arrow, varying in size, shape.

wooden container with hinged lids at the top and on the sides. This type kept the arrows safe from the elements but it was awkward to get the arrows. Quivers were highly lacquered and richly decorated.

Archers of higher rank wore gloves resembling gauntlets. The second and third fingers were of softer leather and were usually of a different color than the rest of the glove. The right thumb had a double thickness of leather on the inside to take the wear of the bow string. Lower ranks wore an abbreviated glove on the right hand only. This consisted of a thumb and two fingers. These attached to a broad band which tied about the wrist. At times all degrees of archers wore a mail covered glove on the left hand to protect the hand holding the bow.

The flaring neck guard of the characteristic Japanese helmet, in the case of archers, sometimes was hinged on the right side so that it could be folded back out of the way when the bow was being used. Many mounted archers, as well as other mounted warriors, frequently wore a horo. This was a long, wide piece of cloth attached at the top to the rear of the helmet and at the bottom to the waist. It was ornamented with the chop mark or crest of the wearer. As the archer rode along this bellied out behind and protected the back from arrows.

In any discussion of Japanese military history and weapons, it is well to note that the feudal era in Japan did not come to an end until comparatively recently; in the late 1800s, as compared to the early 1400s in Europe. Although firearms were introduced into Japan as early as 1543 by Portuguese traders, they were not well received in the feudal society. In fact, firearms were not developed to any great extent in Nippon until the end of the Nineteenth Century. This resulted in the Japanese passing directly from the use of the primitive matchlock to the modern breech-loading percussion rifle, both of which were copied in toto from western models without any developments in between. One of the reasons for this was that the samuari, the Japanese warrior knights, with their peculiar code of ethics and honor, regarded the use of firearms as ungentlemanly! Consequently the bow was a major weapon until the very dawn of the present century!

With the advent of Commodore Perry and the opening of Japan to world trade and western culture, that nation was thrown overnight from medieval times into the modern world. – *Robert H. Rankin*

11

You've Come A Long Way, Baby

THE ENGLISH LONGBOW
On This Bow The British Empire Was Built

The Battle of Poictiers in 1356 saw the longbow at its height as an instrument of combat. In this battle, some 6000 English archers defeated three times their number.

When mounted men began to utilize the bow for combat, it was necessary to shorten its length. This is evidenced in this ancient drawing, which was made in the year 1544.

OF ALL THE vast armory of weapons which man has used throughout the centuries, one of the most legendary is the English longbow. Undeniably it was a great weapon. However, some military historians question some of the prowess assigned to it.

This famed English weapon had its inception in Wales. During the Welsh campaigns of Edward I, in the latter half of the Thirteenth Century, the native archers wrought such havoc among the ranks of the English that Edward made peace with them and enlisted them in his own army. The Welsh bow was short and rather thick and was, at times, used as a club when combatants closed on each other in hand to hand fighting.

The English immediately improved upon the Welsh weapon, developing it into the storied longbow. Some six feet long, on the average, it was made of yew by choice. However, ash, elm or witch-hazel also were used. In fact, yew was considered so superior and was used up so rapidly that it became necessary to forbid its sale outside England. Furthermore, it was required by law that any merchant ship coming to England from abroad had to bring along four bowstaves for every ton of merchandise carried.

For a long time during this period, the Lombards supplied the English with quite respectable quantities of high quality bowstaves. Apparently unable to stand prosperity, they began sending along bowstaves of poor quality, meantime increasing the price. As a result, it was decreed by the English government that the Lombards must supply ten good bowstaves free of charge along with every butt of wine shipped into England. Since this wine business was a most important part of the Lombard trade, this was punishment indeed! Incidentally, little yew grows wild in England today, so extensively was it used during the days of the longbow.

The arrows used with the longbow were commonly called clothyards. The arrow was as long as the distance measured between the outstretched hand and the ear. This was approximately the length of measurement used by weavers and cloth merchants.

Arrows usually were made of ash, oak or birch, and were winged with gray goose feathers. However, the feathers of the peacock and of swans also were used for the purpose. The head of the arrow was of steel. It was, of course, of prime importance that all arrowheads be of the best materials and workmanship. In this connection, in the year 1405 some faulty arrowheads were delivered for military use. Thereupon a royal decree provided that "All head for Arrows...after this Time to be made, shall be boiled or brased, and hardened at the Points with Steel." In order to insure that responsibility for poor materials and workmanship could be promptly fixed, the decree went on to say that "Every Arrow head...be marked with the Mark of him that made the same."

The longbowmen stood with his side to the target, the bow held straight out with fully outstretched arm. Using the tips of the first three fingers, he drew the string back to his ear. The arrow was held steady between the first and second fingers of the other hand, its head lying on the hand, against the bow. Medieval manuscripts on the subject of warfare refer to both left and right-hand archers.

Many years of hard training were required to develop a good longbowman. English youths were given their first bow while quite young and archery was practiced on every village green. Practice was required by law and a fine was imposed for shooting at a target less than two hundred yards distant. Any longbowman worthy of the name could shoot between twelve and fifteen aimed arrows a minute. It was a common saying of the time

Originally, English longbows were fashioned from yew and measured six feet in length. Today, because of the wide use of this type of wood, there is little yew in England.

that a longbowman carried the lives of twelve of the enemy at his belt, that being the number of arrows in his quiver. So powerful was this weapon that its arrows pierced mail easily and it, along with the crossbow, was responsible for the change to plate armor.

The longbowman, himself, wore little armor, usually only an iron or steel skull cap or helmet and a stout leather jacket. In addition to his bow he usually was armed with a sword or dagger. These were most useful in finishing off the enemy wounded.

Although the longbow was a superior weapon for its time, it is well to note that many English victories of this particular era were also due, in no small measure, to tactics, organization and patriotism. The kings of England had begun to realize the weakness of armies composed of a comparatively few nobles or knights and a host of untrained serfs, the latter fighting only because they had to. English rulers began more and more to place their reliance upon trained free men, paid for their services to the crown. Consequently it wasn't too difficult at all to come by numbers of trained longbowmen ready to sign up for long terms of service, since they knew that they would be paid a wage in addition to anything they might come by in the way of plunder. At the same time, these Englishmen were developing a great sense of national pride and were ready to fight for it. It is indeed significant that, at a time when the ranks of the armies of Europe were made up largely of serfs, Englishmen were regarding military duty as an obligation of all free men, an obligation not at all restricted to the knightly class.

The battles of Crecy, Poictiers and Agincourt often are pointed out as the three great battles in which the longbow reached it greatest heights. At Crecy, in 1346, the English forces under Edward III consisted of some 4000 men-at-arms, 10,000 or so archers, and 5000 foot troops. The French, under Philip, had nearly 12,000 armored horsemen, at least 6000 crossbowmen, and 20,000 foot troops.

Edward dismounted his horsemen and placed them in the center of a crescent-shape formation the ends of which, pointing toward the enemy, were composed of longbowmen positioned behind pointed stakes. In an exchange of fire between the longbowmen and the crossbowmen, the latter were completely routed. The French knights were so scornful of their fleeing crossbowmen that they cruelly rode them down as they galloped into a charge against the English. As the French

headed for the dismounted English knights, they came under a heavy cross-fire from the longbowmen. On-coming night finally put an end to a total of sixteen foolhardly attacks. Thousands of French were killed, including 1500 knights and members of noble families. Only fifty Englishmen were killed. Overnight, England became a military power to be reckoned with, mainly because of carefully planned use of the longbow.

Ten years later, in 1356, Edward, the Black Prince, with only 6000 men defeated almost three times that many French, led by King John and his son, Philip. A mere handful of longbowmen, craftily placed to pour in flanking fire, easily fought off all attacks. Then an English counter-attack by what amounted to little more than a so-called corporal's guard of longbowmen and mounted knights resulted in the complete collapse of the French. When the fighting was over, 2000 French knights and nobles were dead, plus thousands of common soldiers. Furthermore, the king, his son, and 2000 knights were captive.

In the combat at Agincourt, fought in 1415, some 40,000 French attacked about 10,000 English, including 6000 longbowmen, under the leadership of Henry V. The longbowmen had a field day and the French suffered a horrible bloody defeat. Although less than two hundred English were killed, French losses totaled thousands, including at least 5000 of noble birth. Among the nobles killed were the Constable of France, three dukes, five counts, and ninety barons. Thus a few commoners armed with the longbow practically wiped out the French aristocracy.

The longbow for many years was superior in accuracy, range and rate of fire to the crude early firearms. It was not until around the mid-1500s that it finally was displaced. A shortage of trained archers was one of the major causes contributing to the abandonment of the longbow when it did occur. It took years of hard training, as has been noted, to develop a good longbowman. The steadily growing use of firearms for sport in times of peace at length resulted in a shortage of young willing to train as archers. Consequently when war came there were few archers and although the firearms of the day were inferior to the bow they were used in ever increasing numbers. In an effort to reverse the tide, Henry VIII prohibited the use of guns except by special permission of the Crown. He also decreed that every man under the age of forty had to provide himself in use of the bow. All such efforts were futile and at length were given up.

The end of the longbow, as noted above, came to an end about the middle of the Fifteenth Century. However, it took many years for the fact to be recognized, so slowly does the mind of some military leaders adjust to new weapons and new tactics. By this time France had developed an efficient standing army. In addition, her gun founders had developed the culverin, a comparatively light, long barrel, muzzle-loading cannon, into an effective field piece. Among other things, they mounted the piece on wheel instead of on a cumbersome sled and provided it with a screw arrangement which allowed rapid changes in elevation. They had also improved the quality of their gunpowder.

At the battle of Formigny, in 1450, a small force of 4000 French, including some well trained artillerymen, bloodily routed a host of more than 7000 English. Skillful employment of the culverins cut the longbowmen to pieces and rendered the survivors easy prey for the French horsemen. Nearly 3000 English were killed, as contrasted to only twelve French dead. The lesson was repeated two years later at a placed named Castillon. There French cannon all but annihilated an attacking force of 6000 English and their Gascon allies, including a large force of longbowmen.

Yet the lesson had to be repeated again and again until it was finally admitted that reeking, noisy firearms had supplanted the bow and arrow. — *Robert H. Rankin*

You've Come A Long Way, Baby

THE CROSSBOW

Yesterday's Weapon Of Terror

EVER since warfare began, the introduction of an efficient new weapon often has raised a storm of protest and a cry of dismay. The rifle, machine gun, submarine, torpedo, airplane and nuclear warhead, to name a few, have all in their time been decried as far too ruthless. But regardless of prohibitions and international agreements, so-called terror weapons have always been used — especially when one of the belligerents found that he couldn't win any other way.

Interestingly enough, the military crossbow of the Middle Ages once was considered too cruel and inhumane for general use in war. In 1139, high church officials, meeting in council in Rome, prohibited the use of this weapon, except against infidels, under pain of excommunication. It was declared that the crossbow was a weapon hateful to God and therefore unfit for use against Christians. Then, at the close of the 12th Century, Pope Innocent III confirmed this prohibition.

Nonetheless the crossbow was far too effective a weapon to be discarded. The missile fired by the crossbow could punch through the heaviest armor at considerable distances and it made a horrible wound. It was widely used throughout Christendom, except for a few isolated spots. For instance, Conrad III, King of Germany, prohibited the use of the crossbow within his kingdom. This was the exception and not the rule. Some folks, however, apparently never quite forgot the Church's ban against the weapon. When Richard I of England was killed by a crossbow bolt during the siege of a castle near Limoges, France, it was whispered about that his death was due to the wrath of Heaven because he used crossbowmen in his army.

Surely such a weapon deserves to have its history reviewed, if only briefly.

Known variously as *arbalest*, *arbelast*, and *arblast*, the crossbow, according to some military historians was invented by Zaphyrus, a resident of the Greek city of Tarentum, as early as 300 B.C. Our concern, however, is with the military crossbow of the Middle Ages.

This weapon appears to have been introduced into England by the Normans during their invasion in 1066. During the next few hundred years, it gained military popularity both in England and in Europe. However, it never did achieve the popularity in England accorded the famed longbow. The longbow was, of course, a much faster shooting weapon than the crossbow. Used against moving targets, it was a wonder to behold. Be that as it may, the crossbow fired a heavier missile and had greater range. Furthermore, it did not require the skill and strength necessary to use the longbow properly. The crossbow was particularly effective against, or in defense of, fortifications of all kinds.

Although all nations of any consequence developed their own crossbowmen and considered them elite troops, the Genoese became widely famous as makers and users of the weapon. They hired out extensively as mercenary troops at fancy fees. They were so adept at their profession that their mere presence among the ranks of the enemy was often cause enough to strike stark terror into the hearts of defending forces.

But what of the weapon itself? Basically the crossbow consists of a heavy bow mounted across a stock at a right angle. A groove or channel runs lengthwise of the top of the stock. The bolt or quarrel, as the short arrow is known, moves along this groove. Near the rear of the stock is a simple trigger-tripped mechanism for holding and releasing the bowstring.

Early crossbows were lightweight, hand-drawn affairs with bows of wood, horn, or whalebone. Composite bows, built up of the same materials, were introduced from Asia by the Turks during the Crusades. These found considerable favor in Europe. At the highest period of its development, steel bows were used for military crossbows.

The average military crossbow with steel bow weighed in the neighborhood of fifteen pounds. Siege crossbows, designed to be mounted on stands or up on a parapet, often weighed eighteen pounds or more. These bigger jobs had a bow at least three feet long, one inch thick and two and a half inches wide at the center. They had a range of around 450 yards! The range of the average military crossbow of that era, however, was some 380 yards. The usual rate of fire of the crossbow was a bolt per minute. Accuracy was very good. Consider that a bolt aimed at the forehead of a man fifty yards away would strike not lower than his chin. Now that is pretty accurate shooting!

Based upon accepted practice of the time, the use of the crossbow was according to the following "man-

These bolts for the crossbow — or quarrels, as they are called — were made in Germany during the late 16th, early 17th Centuries. Note wood fletch, heavy heads.

ual of arms": (1) take crossbow from shoulder; (2) unhook windlass from belt; (3) attach windlass to stock and bowstring; (4) wind back bowstring; (5) secure bowstring in trigger nut; (6) disengage windlass; (7) return windlass to belt; (8) seat bolt in groove; (9) take aim, and (10) fire.

The bolt, or quarrel, had a butt end approximately the same thickness as the bowstring. Of wood, the bolt tapered forward to an increased diameter, over which an iron head fitted. Only the head of the bolt rested on the stock, thus reducing friction to a minimum. No degree of artistry was lavished on the bolts; they were expendable. Just as long as they were true in flight and did their job, they were acceptable. Military bolts often were fletched or winged with thin strips of wood, leather, or horn. The wings were fitted to the top and sides, but not the bottom, of the bolt. Military bolt heads were of solid metal with a hollow end fitting over the foreshaft. Bolts varied in length, thickness, and weight, but all of them packed a mean wallop. Bolts with sharp pointed heads were used against light armor. Bolts with square heads and short blunt prongs were used against heavy armor. The prongs helped to keep the bolt from glancing off the armor and concentrated the impact in one spot. They were much feared.

The bolt rested in the groove running lengthwise of the stock, with the butt of the bolt seated firmly against the bowstring. The groove sometimes was lined with metal or horn. In any event, it was highly polished. It had to be as smooth and as straight as possible to insure accuracy.

The string of the bent bow was held by a notched, revolving nut secured by a trigger. This nut was grooved to hold the butt of the bolt against the bowstring and to prevent the bolt from falling out of the stock groove when the crossbow was elevated or depressed. Pulling the trigger moved its fore end out of a slot in the underside of the nut, allowing it to rotate and release the bowstring.

Inasmuch as the steel bow of a crossbow could not be bent by hand and since the bowstring always was shorter than the bow, some means had to be devised to string the bow. A so-called bastard or false string was used for this purpose. This bastard string was long enough to be easily attached to each end of the bow. It was then pulled back until the bow was bent enough for the bowstring to be attached, after which it was removed.

Early bows, and even some later light ones were attached to the stock by lashings of cord or sinew. The bow passed through a hole or a mortise at the fore end of the stock. It was held in position by a saddle, a piece of hard wood extending out over the back of the bow for a short distance on each side of the stock. Through another hole in the stock, some dis-tance back from the inside of the bow, dampened cord or sinew passed several times and wrapped around the saddle on each side of the stock. This lashing was drawn tight and was wrapped about itself tightly. As the cord or sinew dried it tightened, making a secure fastening.

Heavy bows passed through a mortise in the fore part of the stock and were held in place by bow-irons, one on each side of the stock. The base or curve of the stirrup and the center of the bow passed through the mortise and through the irons and were held fast against the stock by the irons which were themselves tightened by and held fast to the stock by wedges. The stirrup mentioned here was of a rough "D" shape, with the bar or straight part of the "D" foremost. In bending heavy bows, as will be described later, the crossbow was placed with the forepart of the stirrup on the ground. The foot of the crossbowman was thrust through the stirrup to hold and steady the weapon while the bow was bent.

Early bows and even later light bows were bent by hand. For heavy bows several different methods were employed.

In the so-called cord-and-pulley method a hook on one end of a cord was fastened in a ring on the bowman's belt. The cord then passed through a pulley and hooked to a ring at the top rear of the crossbow stock. An open hook or claw on the pulley engaged the bowstring. The bowman placed one foot in the stirrup of the grounded crossbow, bent his knees and stooped enough to engage the bowstring. He then straightened up to bend the bow.

In the belt and claw method, a long metal hook was attached to the crossbowman's belt. To bend the bow, he placed one foot in the stirrup, engaged the bowstring with the hook, then pushed the crossbow away from his body. This method was much used with lighter military crossbows during the 14th Century.

Some heavy crossbows were bent by the screw and handle method. A long metal screw passed through the butt of the stock. A claw or hook on the fore end engaged the bowstring. A revolving nut, fitted with handles, worked on the rear of the screw shaft to draw it back until the bowstring could be caught by the trigger mechanism.

These bolts, also of German origin, were formed so that the heavy head directed flight for horrendous injuries.

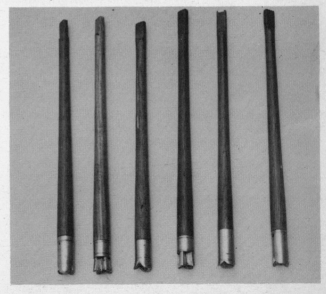

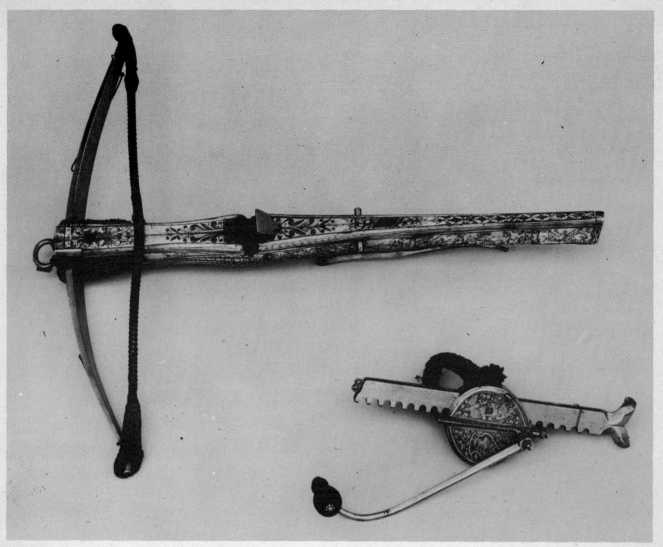

This German crossbow, circa 1550, is highly decorated. Also shown are rack, pinion and cranequin to bend bow.

On light and medium size crossbows a goat's foot lever often was used. This was handy and easy to use. So much so, in fact, that it was often employed by mounted crossbowmen. This device consisted of a long handle or lever fitted with a movable claw which caught the bowstring. The lever was fitted with a two-prong fork which passed easily over the stock and was kept from slipping by a pin protruding on each side of the stock. The lever was simply pulled back to bend the bow. When the string was caught in the nut of the trigger mechanism, the device was removed and hung on the belt. In some instances the device was permanently attached to the stock by pins passing through the prongs into the stock.

The windlass was another mechanism sometimes used. This was an arrangement of pulleys on each side of the stock, fitted with hooks, and connected to a removable windlass which was attached to the rear of the stock. Turning the handles of the windlass pulled back the pulleys, which were hooked to the bowstring. The windlass was very powerful and was much used with large, heavy crossbows.

The cranequin or ratchet winder was still another device used to bend the bow on medium and heavy crossbows. Rugged and fairly simple, it was heavier and slower than the windlass. It generally was used by the military on the big crossbows mounted on battlements.

This device, usually removable, consisted of a large cog turned by a smaller cog which was attached to a crank. The cogs were housed in a low cylindrical box attached to the stock by thick cords. A long toothed bar or ratchet, fitted with a hook or claw to engage the bowstring, moved back and forth through the box, the teeth on the bar engaging those on the big cog. Turning the crank drew back the bar, bending the bow.

When firearms first were introduced, they were no serious threat to the crossbow, what with their limited range, inaccuracy, unreliability, and slowness. In fact, as is generally known, the value of the early firearms was largely one of morale — the discharge of smoke and flame, accompanied by a deafening noise, being terrible to behold!

Gradually, however, as firearms were improved they replaced the crossbow. By 1525, the latter had been abandoned by practically all armies. Interestingly enough, the crossbow had some influence on the design of shoulder guns. Among other things the shape of the stock and the trigger of the early guns were very similar to those of the crossbow.

You've Come A Long Way, Baby

BOWS OF OLD CATHAY

The Chinese Invented Gun Powder, But Favored Bows For Warfare

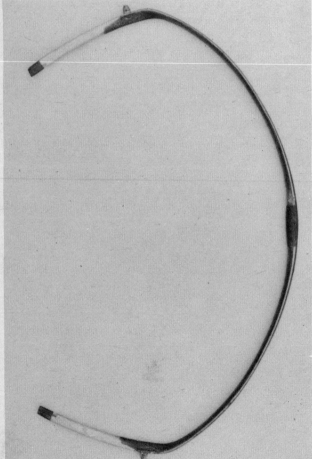

THERE is a popular myth to the effect that long ago the classic Chinese had risen far above war. Among other things it is related that, although they invented gunpowder, the Chinese choose to use it largely for fireworks, declining to use it for the purpose of slaughtering their fellow men. This fiction has been repeated by many respected historical writers who could be expected to know better!

Actually, such things as weapons, fortifications, and siegecraft were brought to a high degree of development in old China. It was only in later years that the art of warfare declined. Consider for instance that under such rulers as Wu Ti, who reigned 140-86 B.C., the Chinese conquered far-flung territories. Consider, too, that the oldest military work in existence, and certainly one of the finest dissertations on military principles ever written was produced about 500 B.C. by Sun Tzu. This work in fact deals with fundamentals which are timeless and it is read with profit and with interest by military planners today.

The low estate into which Chinese military affairs eventually fell is due far less to philosophic and pacifist tendencies than to a pure love of war for war's own sake, a characteristic which at length led to pre-occupation with the pure theory of living rather than to a practical concern for the development of weapons and tactics.

Left: This unusual bow of Chinese origin is horn-backed, using a single long strip of horn for the full length. Middle area is covered with sharkskin. The bow is said to have been used by warriors during the Boxer Rebellion. (Below): This bow of Manchu tupe of the 18th Century has its back painted and the ends or tips are protected.

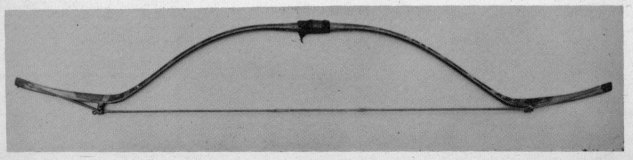

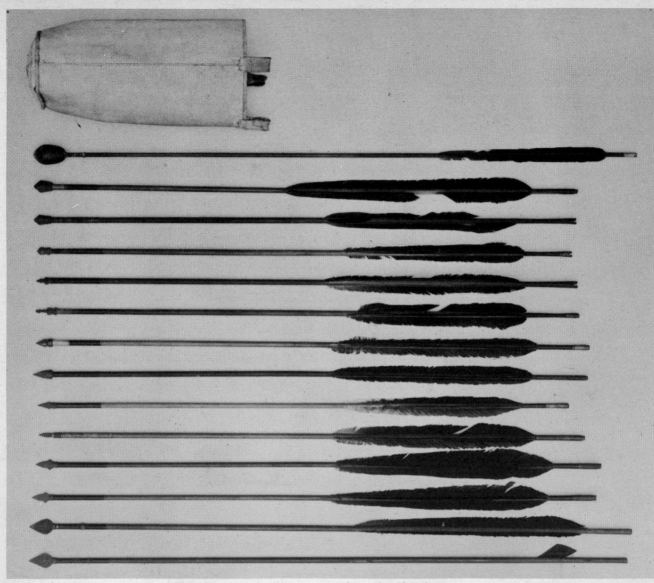

This selection of military arrows from the 19th Century features, at bottom, a whistling arrow that was used for signaling. Bag-shaped quiver is made of white leather.

Finally, after the conquering of vast areas, there was but little demand for the development of a vigorous strategy; the point having been reached where there was far more wealth within the empire than without. Consequently there was little incentive to develop aggressive tactics It is not at all surprising, therefore, that apathy set in and the military decline of China was speeded along on its way.

One of the oldest and most interesting of the old Chinese weapons is the bow. This is a composite design made up of a main core or frame of bamboo to which are glued pieces of deciduous wood, horn and sinew. The characteristic Chinese bow has a sharp bend near each end. Wood was glued to the bamboo at the handle and on the bends. Horn then was glued to the belly and sinew was glued to the back. The ends and the handle were covered then with leather or sharkskin. A small narrow block of wood was doweled and glued on the belly of the bow, about nine inches from each end. The bowstring rested on these when the bow was not in use.

Generally speaking, these bows were large and powerful. Military bows had a pull of from 70 to 100 pounds, with bows of 150 pounds pull frequently being encountered.

Arrows were of various lengths, but usually varied from around three and one-half feet to slightly over four feet. Military arrows were fitted with socketed iron heads. Whistling arrows, used for signaling, were originated by the Chinese and were used extensively by them as well as by the Japanese. Whistling arrows had a large hollow head with openings cut in the front and sides. The air rushing through these openings produced a weird whistling noise. Feathers were, in most instances, placed in a spiral. This caused the arrow to rotate, thus increasing its power.

Bow cases and quivers were of cloth or leather, or a combination of these. These articles were usually very highly decorated and were worn suspended from the belt of the warrior.

Bowstrings were of two kinds. Heavy strings for the big bows were made of twisted sinew, while strings for the lighter bows were composed of elaborately wound and knotted cotton threads.

Like the Japanese, the Chinese also used a sectional bow which could be folded or even taken apart. The Chinese version consisted of two pieces, hinged in the middle. Each half was built up of wood, horn and sinew, much in the same manner as the larger bows. These sectional bows were rather weak. They were most often used for parades and for amusement.

In drawing and loosing the bowstring, the Chinese, in common with other Asiatic people, used the thumb. A

Shown here out of proportion, this is a brocade-covered case for an archer's ring. It is divided into upper and lower sections so that it will handle two different rings.

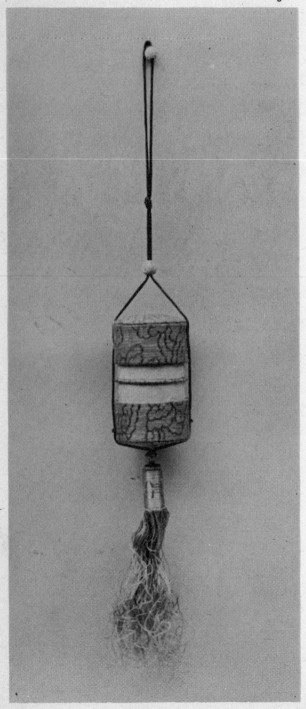

so-called archer's ring was used to protect the thumb from the chafing of the string as it was drawn and released. These archer's rings were made in various shapes from a number of materials, including horn, bone, ivory, stone and tortoise shell. Jade was most often used by the Chinese. These rings were often carried in highly decorated ivory or cloth cases suspended from the belt.

Any review of Chinese bows should include mention of the repeating crossbow, a weapon which was unique to China. This weapon, which permitted the discharge of ten bolts or arrows in less than twenty seconds, was ideal for stopping mass attacks. It was similar in appearance and in basic action to the conventional crossbow. A strong bow, made of a single stout piece of bamboo or

This is an archer's ring of the type described in the text. It is a D-section type fashioned of green jade.

This ring is of white jade with green spot in texture.

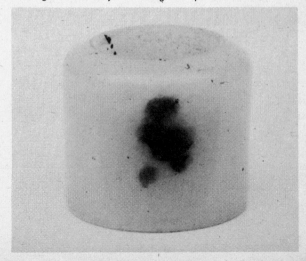

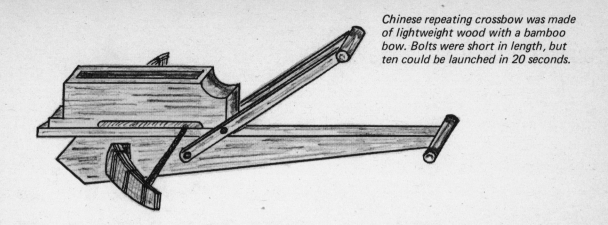

Chinese repeating crossbow was made of lightweight wood with a bamboo bow. Bolts were short in length, but ten could be launched in 20 seconds.

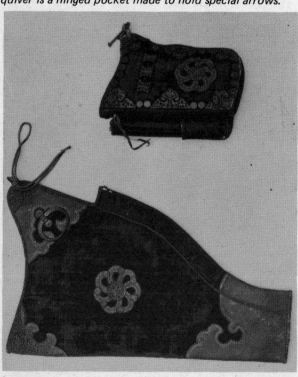

Of brown leather trimmed with black with bronze fittings, this bow case is of early 19th Century. On back of the quiver is a hinged pocket made to hold special arrows.

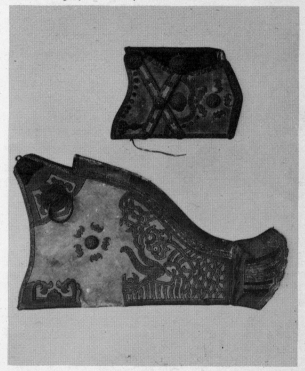

This Chinese bow case and quiver of late 18th Century boasted brass mountings. It was covered with black velvet and gray leather by an unknown Chinese artisan.

of several flat bamboo strips lashed together, passed through an opening in the fore part of the stock. It was lashed and wedged securely in place. This bowstring was of twisted sinew.

A long, oblong, box-like magazine was fitted to the top of the stock and was so arranged that it slid readily back and forth along the length of the stock. A lever hinged to either side of the stock also was attached to either side of the magazine. The magazine held ten or twelve bolts or arrows, each approximately fourteen inches long, stacked one on top of the other.

Pushing the lever forward shoved the magazines along the top of the stock, causing the bowstring to be caught in a notch above the trigger. The forward movement of the magazine was continued until the rear of the bolt or arrow cleared the bowstring, at which point it dropped

into a lengthwise groove in the top of the stock. The lever and magazine then were pulled back, bending the bow. Pulling the lever back still further released the bowstring to discharge the bolt or arrow.

The effective range of this unique weapon was reckoned at some eighty yards. The bamboo bolts or arrows were fitted with steel heads, but had no feathers. In such, as they were light in weight and had little penetrating power, the heads often were treated with highly poisoned ointment.

Interestingly enough, China's military know-how deteriorated so greatly that bows were being used as a principal weapon as late as the Boxer Rebellion (1900), a time when, in western civilizations, the magazine rifle and the machine gun were being used in increasing quantities. — *Robert H. Rankin*

OUT OF THE STONE AGE

This Tribe's Hunters Still Kill Jaguar With Arrows Tipped With Shark Teeth

DEEP in the southernmost jungle reaches of Peru live a handful of people, who, until only a few years ago, existed as remnants of the Stone Age.

These people, the last of the nearly forgotten and still little known Anerakaire Indians, had been recognized as a vicious, warlike tribe and were generally shunned by even the Peruvian army. However, it was in the mid-1950s that members of a missionary group, the Wycliffe Translators, moved into this remote area and made friends of the people.

Today, these Indians are dressed largely in clothing donated by contributors to the missionary organization. No longer do the women dress in skirts made from woven bark similar to the tapa cloth of the South Pacific. The men wear denim jeans instead of loin cloths. There are even a few shotguns in the tribe, which makes for easier hunting. The ground now is tilled with steel tools rather than crude stone implements as was done a decade ago.

But this tribe, little changed otherwise in many centuries, still lives largely by hunting. And the primary tool of the hunt is the bow and arrow, crude in design and workmanship by even pagan standards. Yet, with these weapons, the men of the tribe are able to furnish meat by shooting parrots — a primary item of diet — out of trees, killing tapir at short ranges, and there have been numerous jaguar killed with arrows even in recent years.

These bows are fashioned from palm wood, usually from the spine of the frond. Normally, this wood becomes quite brittle when dead, but the natives apparently have some specific manner of curing it, since the fibrous material retains its resilient qualities for years. Although steel-bladed knives now are used by the natives, those bows that were made prior to the arrival of the missionaries still show the marks of the stone-headed axes that were used in their manufacture.

The bowstring is crude even by the standards of the North American Indian, who used hide or sinew. The

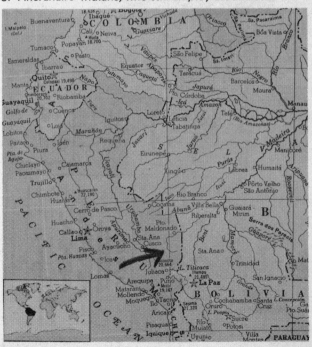

Arrow on map indicates the position of Stone Age colony of Anerakaire Indians, who still employ crude bows.

Crudeness of the fletch used on the arrows is shown in this photo of work.

long bows measure more than five feet in spite of the diminutive stature of the people, and the bowstrings are fashioned from fibers found in local plants. These strings are tightly twisted and appear to be tough and service-able.

The arrows reflect a bit of genius in their design and manufacture. The shaft proper usually is nearly half an inch in thickness and is selected for its straightness from a type of heavy grass that grows in the marshes. It resembles a reed, but there is no visible joint, although it is hollow and tube-like. Quite light, these shafts make up for this lack of weight in length. Most of the arrows, overall, are in the neighborhood of four feet long.

Several materials are used for arrowheads, but hard palm wood is by far the greatest choice. These heads, long and narrow, may measure as much as eighteen inches, and often have harsh rows of barbs carved in the sides. For smaller barbed heads, the teeth of the South American killer fish, the piranha, are used. Sharp and jagged, these teeth are set into the palm wood extension and are considered excellent for downing birds and small game, since the sharpness and angle make it difficult for game to shake out the arrows and escape.

The native engineering know-how, handed down from father to son, for making of these arrows is impressive. Local beeswax, gathered from the hive, is used to cement the long palm wood extensions to the reed-like shafts. Then the connection is bound with row upon row of various colored thread. Each man seems to attempt to vary the design in this binding probably so that he can reclaim his own arrows — or perhaps to determine who shot a killing arrow, if there is question.

The rear of the arrow, where one would expect to find a nock, is similarly bound with colored thread. Most of this, in recent years, has been furnished by the missionaries. In earlier times, however, the thread was manufactured by the women from the wild cotton plants that abound in the local jungles. Some of these

This odd-looking monkey often is tamed as a pet by the South American Indians, but more often ends up as the main course in a meal of meat taken with native bows.

cotton plants grow as high as fourteen feet, enough to make a Louisiana plantation owner turn green with envy.

In regard to nocks for these arrows, there are none. Instead, the nock end is simply a flat surface and the shooter holds this flatness against the fiber bowstring with thumb and forefinger, maintaining this hold until the bow is at full draw and he releases his arrow. By modern NAA standards, accuracy is to be desired, but these natives — through an intimate knowledge and daily use of these weapons — have become experts in their use.

As stated earlier, these Indians are not at all backward about stalking the dangerous jaguar with these seemingly inadequate implements of the kill. However, it should be pointed out that most killing shots are made at extremely short ranges — and sometimes the jaguar wins.

Specifically, there are two tribes of the Indians. One is this group now being educated by the Wycliffe Translators: there are approximately 125 in the village, all living in a single community house built of palm fronds.

Another tribe, still warlike, is located about fifty miles away, deep in the jungles. The number of persons belonging to this group numbers slightly over a hundred.

The tribe encountered by the Wycliffe Translators lives primarily off of the land, existing on the meat brought in by the male hunters armed with these bows and arrows and the few shotguns. The diet is supplemented by bananas, roots, a variety of pineapple, sugar cane and citrus fruits. Oranges grow wild in the jungle expanses, and a tree can be in full production in little more than a year. As indicated earlier, cloth is woven from the wild cotton and from the barks of trees.

The three arrowheads at left from this lost tribe of Indians are of carved palm wood, while the one on the extreme right has been fashioned of piranha teeth.

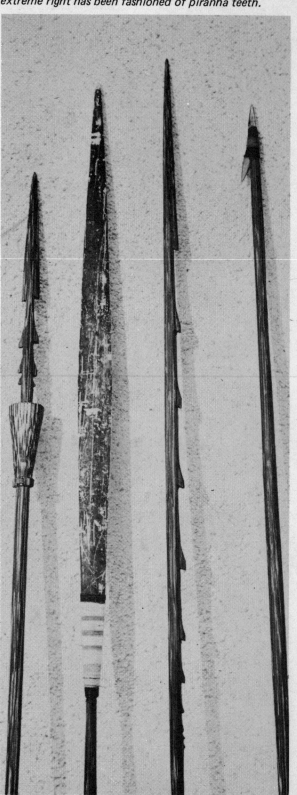

There isn't much style indicated in manner in which the bow is strung: just brace it and tie the string.

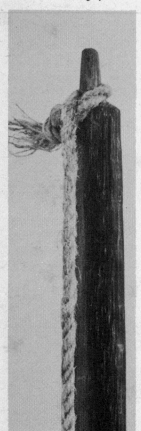 

Although shotguns are being introduced for hunting food among Indians, this huge jaguar was killed with native arrow, which had one of the crude heads of palm wood.

The entire tribe lives under the single roof of the community house, which is about 150 feet in length. Within, the interior is divided up into crude stalls and entire families live in these small areas — along with their dogs, a few chickens and the parrots, which have been tamed by the Indians as pets.

There are three fires in the crude shelter and the cooking for all the natives is done over these. Originally, earthenware pots were used, but the missionaries have introduced them to iron kettles, which have been accepted as being more practical and less breakable.

Supplementing their diet are fish from the nearby streams and rivers. The Indians have found the leaves of a particular tree which, when crushed and sprinkled in the waters upstream, rouse the fish to wild rushes. When the fish swim unwarily downstream to avoid the apparent narcotic effect of the juices from these leaves, the Indians are standing in the water with spears and arrows to literally harvest them.

Today, this tribe is located some five hundred miles from the nearest civilized settlement, other than the base camp of the missionary group. The translators spend approximately seven months at a stretch with the Indians, then return to this base camp with tape recordings and attempt to translate the Indian dialect and put it into books that ultimately will be used to teach them to read and to write.

There is no trail leading from this base camp to the tribal headquarters, and it would take months to hack a trail through the jungles. However, one Ted Long operates the Jungle Aviation and Radio Service, transporting missionaries into the village via amphibian aircraft. Landings are made on one of the deeper streams in the vicinity.

The natives of this particular tribe, while less than a decade away from the Stone Age, are rapidly becoming civilized. Probably the greatest single influence on their civilization was the introduction of the steel machete in 1952, when the first missionary arrived. Since then, they have sought modern conveniences, finding that three times as much ground can be cultivated with steel tools.

The stone axe and the bone knife are rapidly disappearing. As more firearms are introduced, chances are that the skill of making bows and arrows also will die. But perhaps not; they already have learned that the missionaries can trade such items for more practical goods such as shotgun shells. These items could eventually become big in the tourist trade! *–Jack Lewis*

You've Come A Long Way, Baby

ARCHERY IN MODERN RUSSIA

The Soviets Like To Win At Whatever They Enter And They Are Making Mammoth Gains

SOME years ago, during the III International Youth Competition held in Moscow's stadium "Avanguard," a score of Muscovites saw a sport which was most prodigical to their eyes. This sport gained such a number of curious and fascinated fans that the Czech, Jan Dobiash, immediately set up a "special seminar" for the bewildered inhabitants of Soviet Russia's capitol. Of course, the object of the massive bewilderment, curiosity, and interest was nothing less than the sport of — archery.

"Archery, as a sport, occupies a lesser than humble place in our country," admit the co-authors of the scanty, little pamphlet *The Bow-String Sings* — a booklet which undertakes the task of revealing the mysteries of the noble sport of *Toxophilus* to the Soviet citizen.

Although the Soviets claim to have had official status ("official" competitions and the like), given to archery only since 1959, they proudly proclaim that "we are not afraid to affirm that this sport will have a great future in the Soviet land." They further assert with their usual economical-political motto that "we have fallen behind in this sport from the West, but we will catch up — and this is certain — we will catch up, and catch up soon." To justify this claim they exemplify the "phenomenal" rise in popularity of the sport of canoeing in the Soviet Union. Only a few years back this sport was virtually unknown in the USSR.

This is quite true with archery also. The demand for archery equipment has become so great lately that several State factories began to manufacture archery's basic essentials: Bows and arrows. And so, since the spring of 1959, a sports equipment factory in the city of Lvov manufactures bows for Soviet "pros," while another state plant in Krasnopoliansk produces bows with less pressure designed for the beginner. But naturally, two factories which produce archery equipment merely as a side-line are not sufficient to provide for a country of over two hundred million popu-

lation. This is the reason why the authors Roman Grigorevich Berkovsky and Sergei Prokofievich Urchuk of *The Bow-String Sings* suggest home manufacture of bows and arrows. They list the following wood to be used for bows:

(1) Yew-tree (evergreen) — Found in the Crimea, the Caucasus and Central Asia; (2) Juniper-tree — In the central part of the USSR and in the Far East; (3) maple (sycamore) — in the western Ukraine, European part of the Soviet Union, and the Caucasus; (4) Rowan-tree — central Russian Republic; (5) White acacia — South Ukraine; (6) Beech-tree — the Crimea and the Caucasus; (7) Forest nut-tree — throughout Russia; (8) Mulberry-tree — in the republics of Central Asia; the Caucasus, and the Crimean region of the Ukraine; (9) Ash and elm — European part of the USSR.

For arrows they suggest duralumin tubing of one-quarter inch diameter.

One of the reasons, then, that archery in the Soviet Union takes up a "lesser than humble place" may be this acute lack of inventory in archery equipment.

But for skilled archers, *per se*, the Soviet Union cannot be said to be lacking. The first indication of this became apparent during that "epoch-making" III International Youth Competition of 1957 in the Avanguard Stadium. During the archery finals — with Finland, Poland, and Czechoslovakia participating — the first place was cupped by Finland. To demonstrate that the Soviet Union also had its competent archers, the Buriat-Mongolians came to Moscow especially for this event to display their skill and virtuosity with the bow and arrow — their traditional, ethnic weapons.

The methods of shooting did not at all resemble the modern, classic and accepted manner, though a great deal of accuracy and speed of the arrow was shown. It was on this occasion that the Swede, Lars Ekegren, the former general secretary for FITA

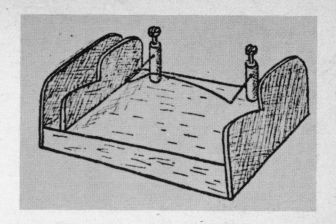

Illustrations on this page have been taken from official Russian handbook on archery, printed in this decade. It shows archery is undeveloped sport in that nation.

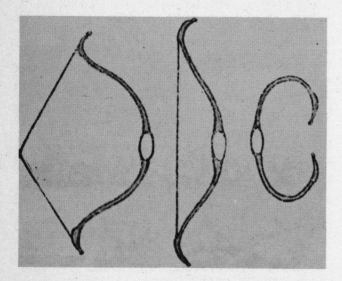

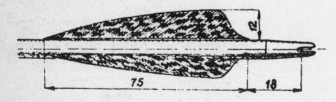

free people, untouched by the "blessings" of collectivism.

Held in spring, the festival is open to male participants of all ages. Young girls and unmarried women, however, may attend. Following tradition, the archers usually bring their own arrows but use only one, communal bow.

Competitions during this festival — the primary one is held in the capital city of Ulan Ude — are held in this manner: The archers are to shoot down two targets made of sheaves of stems from a tubular plant (*suur*) at a distance of five markings (*zurkhai*). There is a stipulation, however. The *suur* may not fall on the marking! Usually the archers compete in two or more groups, and the arrows are shot by the competing sides in turn. Results of the competition

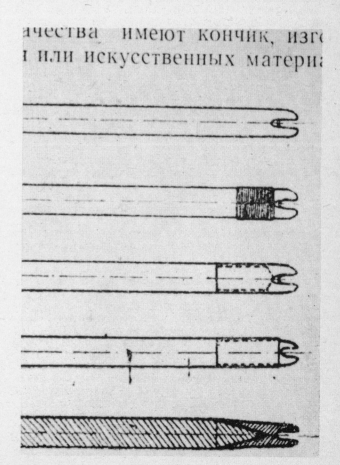

(International Federation of Target Archery), duly impressed, said, "The Buriat-Mongolians shoot from their national bows and are governed by inner feelings, but should they utilize the contemporary bows and universal methods, then they would become totally unsurpassed archers."

Who are these people that fascinated the archery official? The Buriats are of Mongolian stock and can be found around Lake Baikal. Previously they used their bow and arrow (*nomo* and *godli*) for hunting squirrel, sable, and ermine; but the major object for their hunt was the wolf which they shot from horseback. Strong tradition and a sense of national pride have retained the Buriats' claim to skillful art of archery to the present. The skill is passed from father to son.

Even now, many Buriats have kept their *nomo* and *godli*, and they use these during the annual folk sport festival *Sur-Kharban*, which, according to the Buriat ethnographer M. N. Khangalov, is the tradition remaining from the *Zegete-Aba*, the period of group hunt of the Buriats, when they still were nomadic,

Whistling arrowhead of Russia's nomadic Buriat tribes.

are judged by two elders who sit on a small mounting. Should the arrow find its destination, the Buriats exclaim *"bara!"* or *"ukhain bara!"* which in English finds its equivalent in "hooray!"

What is the Buriat *nomo* like? It is a composite bow, one that contains two or more layers of material. These are birch, horn of elk or maral (a type of Siberian stag), tendon, and raw horsehide. Formerly the entire process of bow manufacture took two years.

The bow's frame is of Siberian birch and ranges from forty-two to sixty-three inches in length. On the belly or inner side of the bow a backing of a wide strip of elk or maral horn is affixed. Prior to the pasting, however, the horn is steamed in a huge cast-iron kettle of boiling water. Then the horn is cut length-wise and affixed with a paste prepared from the bile of sturgeon. Preference usually is given the elk horn because it tends to be less branchy than the maral's. When neither elk nor maral is available, the belly backing is that of the long horn of the Mongolian yak (*khainaka*).

On the outside part of the bow (*ara tala*), gradually, layer by layer, threads of finished tendon of elk or maral — providing they are sufficiently long and strong — are glued on. Now, the reason it takes such a lengthy period to manufacture the bow lies in the gluing-up process of layers, a process which is resumed only after the previous layer has dried; this may take from four days to a week. When finally all the gluing is accomplished, the tendon layers may accumulate a thumb's thickness.

At both ends of the bow are the grooves (*khershelee*) which hold the raw horsehide bowstring (*khubshe*). The distance between the string and the bow's arm (*bariul*) amounts to about ten inches. Although the bow's frame consists of whole birch, its horn part has four horn billets, with the junctions covered by leather. On the opposite side of the *khershelee* (groove) a wooden support (*tebkhe*) is mounted. The *tebkhe* serves the function of preventing the bow from turning itself out, sagging, or the like; and instead, after the brace, it returns to its natural position.

Pine wood serves as material for the arrow shaft. Possibly just for the sake of decoration a wooden, cone-like object (*bolsu*) is speared on the shaft. The arrows are bearded with feathers (*ude*), and the heads range from blunt to metal tips (*zebe*), the latter particularly used by warriors.

During their nomadic period, the Buriats — in addition to being bowhunters — also were bow warriors. Each warrior carried forty-four arrows, of which only four had *zebe*, in a wooden quiver (*khobto*). This fact may account for the many Buriat myths and legends where the arrow figures prominently with the hero's actions. Here the arrow is spoken to, commanded, cajoled, and exalted. Various supernaturalistic powers were attributed the arrow.

For example, in the myth of "The Iron Hero" the hero, as he braces the bow to its maximum, says, "Go thou, my arrow, into the side of my enemy, tear around through his heart, lungs and liver. Come out then, break his forearm, and crack his spinal column at the neck, then come back to me." A further feat of the arrow in Buriat mythology is its ability to cut trees. (Interested readers may look up Jeremiah Curtin's *A Journey In Southern Siberia*, 1909, for additional *nomo* and *godli* myths in Buriat literature.)

There are numerous other ethnic groups in the USSR which have a traditional background in archery. Well known are the Bashkirs, a Tartar-Turcic people, who gained fame in the Battle of Nations at Leipzig in the days of October 16-18, 1813. Although some 22,000 Russians fell at the hands of Napoleon's armies, the Bashkirs did considerable damage to the enemy by attacking on horseback and employing their bows and arrows.

A form of archery has long existed in the Caucasus mountains with the Georgian people. An interesting example of bowhunting can be found with the Khanti and Mansi people of Northern Siberia. Their arrows were fletched with feathers of either an eagle or a hawk. When the arrows were shot, their noise resembled the whistle of a hawk, consequently the frightened ducks fell down upon the water, hid their heads in it, and thus were shot down quite easily. A similar intimidation technique was used on wild hares.

The Nanayans and the Ulchians used their bows for a dual purpose: For hunting and as ski poles. Bows often were made from whale bone by the Ulchians. Among others who employed bows for hunting are the Dolgans and Orochians.

It is interesting to observe, then, that with such a rich background in archery, this sport in the USSR is standing on such weak legs. Up to the present there are but a handful of fledgling archery groups in the Soviet Union, and these have originated in the cities of Moscow and Lvov. Only recently a few archery sections were formed in the "sport collectives" of Kiev and Riga. Only two archery instruction booklets exist: The aforementioned *The Bow String Sings*, and a translated pamphlet from the Czech *Bow and Arrow* by Frantishek Gadash and Irdzi Viskolich. This seems to be rather *less than a small amount*, considering that the Soviet Union claims to publish more books than the West, and comparing this amount to the Western scope of over 500 sources on archery even thirteen years ago. (In his bibliography, *Compendium of Works on Archery*, George S. MacManus Co., Philadelphia, 1950, Clement C. Parker lists some 573 sources on archery, with most in the English language.)

Notwithstanding the limited archery literature in the Soviet Union it tries to soft-sell the reader on archery and its physical and moral attributes — facts of universal acceptance in the West. The authors display such naivete as to suggest for the archer 'not to wear a necktie on the archery range," and "during cold weather one should don woolen socks and long underwear."

Soviet archery "experts" are not only well suited for long underwear, but they seem to be good for many a tall tale.

Earlier this year, for example, the FITA headquarters in Great Britain received a most magniloquent letter from a comrade L. Makarov, Head Trainer of the Federation of Archery of the USSR. After much anachronistic and misleading data, comrade Makarov finally made the statement that archery in the Soviet Union is fully in accordance with FITA regulations. Only we must note that the Soviet physical culture journal *Teoria i Praktika Fizicheskoi Kul'tury* (Theory and Practice of Phyical Culture) just recently voiced its lament that the Soviet Union still encounters difficulties in standardizing its sports — due to the various ethnic categories. And this certainly is true of their archery! – *Igor K. Kozak*

Chapter 2

LONG BOW,
RECURVE or **COMPOUND?**

**The Experts Take A Look At The
Possibilities And Leave The Choice To You!**

(The late Howard Hill needs no introduction. It was he who probably was most responsible for exposing the American masses to archery and bowhunting through his films, public appearances and books.

But Hill had some definite ideas as to what constituted the right kind of tackle. Prior to his death, we asked permission to use a passage from his book, "Hunting The Hard Way," to express his preferences in tackle. He was a firm exponent of the venerable longbow.)

A bow for hunting must be durable, steady, accurate, gentle in the hand, and smooth on the draw, yet with enough speed of cast and follow-through to throw a heavy arrow. Of these qualities, durability and steadiness are the most important. If a hunting bow is not durable, it is likely to break while the archer is making a shot at game.

If a hunting bow is sensitive and unsteady, it is all but impossible for anyone to shoot it accurately. Most shots in the bush are made quickly, oftentimes while in a precarious shooting position, while the archer is excited, or while

The bamboo longbow that Hill favored in his heyday has an odd, antiquated look in age of fiberglass, alloys.

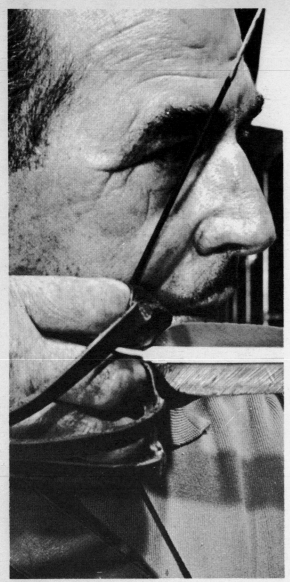

Howard Hill displays the concentration which he used to become one of the top archers of all time, using a bow of his own design that predated modern recurve styles.

under definitely adverse weather conditions. Then, too, the hunting archer does not get shots often enough to be warmed up, and he is usually carrying a bow that is heavier to pull than the one he ordinarily shoots while practicing. Considering all the difficulties which confront the hunting archer in the field, it is imperative that he recognize what he needs in the way of a weapon and unerringly select the proper one for his needs.

A straight-end longbow that follows the string slightly, with good cast, carries a heavy string, is pleasing to draw, and is comfortable to the hand, can be shot much more accurately under hunting conditions than a sensitive bow. It also has much more durability.

Among the hundreds of hunting archers I

know, there have been perhaps twenty-five who were really successful bow-and-arrow hunters. Every one of these during his years of hunting has tried short bows, as well as short recurved ones, some composite and some self-wood, yet all were forced to admit they were unable to shoot these sensitive bows under hunting conditions with any appreciable degree of success. All the successful hunters I know now use the straight-end longbow, at least for big game hunting.

In 1938, with a couple of friends, Fred Woodley and Bob Faas, I planned a three-weeks hunting expedition into British Columbia. I built a five-foot four-inch bamboo bow for myself. It was of six pieces of bamboo laminated, had recurved ends and a sinew back, and pulled eighty-five pounds.

The bow was so fast it made little difference whether I was seventy or forty yards from the target. The difference in the trajectory at seventy yards was no more than eighteen to twenty inches higher than when shooting at forty yards. The bow had speed and carry-through to burn. It mattered not whether I was shooting the heavier broadheads or the lighter blunt-pointed ones, the bow drove them through the air with exceptional speed and flatness of trajectory.

Finally the day came that found us seven hundred miles up the Fraser River in North British Columbia. Beyond, few white men had ever gone. It was wild and untamed country. There were lots of bear, moose, deer — and more grouse than I had ever seen before. In the bottom land there were hundreds of ruffed grouse, while high on the ridges and mountains there was an abundance of blue grouse and fool hens.

I had gone less than a mile when I ran into a flock of twenty or more fool hens. They flushed from the ground and lit in a thicket of dense spruce trees.

I felt this was going to be easy picking for me and my new bow. It was hard for me to take a natural stance or to shoot without having to squat, stoop, or kneel, because the birds were perched high in the branches of the thick spruce.

After an hour of shooting, gathering arrows, and shooting again, I had shot thirty-eight times, had lost every blunt-point in my quiver, and had a bag of four hens. I had done the poorest shooting I have ever seen any decent archer do. I felt like wrapping the bow around the nearest tree, but, instead, I went on the double back to camp, got "Gran-pa," my treasured old straight-end longbow, and a new supply of blunts and came back to the spot where I had left the fool hens.

They were gone, but I ran into a big full-grown mother with twelve young about the size of fry chickens. They lit in another patch of spruce. In less than twenty minutes, I had made

Although the feat has been repeated since, Howard Hill was the first man in modern archery history to down an elephant with an arrow. Draw of bow was 100-plus pounds.

eleven shots, had bagged nine birds, had found the two arrows I missed with and was hunting again.

During the remainder of the trip, I never strung that recurved bow again. While on the Canadian hunt, I killed a moose, two deer, more than a hundred grouse, several ducks, a bald eagle and lots of squirrels and rabbits, all with reliable old "Gran'pa."

This experience convinced me of one thing: I am not a good enough archer to shoot a recurved bow successfully under hunting conditions. No recurved or other sensitive bow is the correct weapon for hunting purposes.

There are three distinct types of bows: The straight-end longbow, the short flat bow, and the composite or self-recurve bow. Besides these

main types there are many bastard designs that may have some feature of one or all of the other types. Of all the varying designs and combinations of features, there has been only one bow developed in modern times that makes a better hunting bow than the conventional English longbow, and that is the American semi-long bow.

This modern type is not quite so long as its English prototype, but is a little wider and considerably flatter. At that, the American semi-long is not so flat as the American Indian short bow, and many times bowyers make the semi-long with recurved ends. However, the recurved ends make it too sensitive for a good hunting weapon.

I know many hunters who swear by the recurved bow for hunting and once in a while these fellows kill a deer, a wild boar or maybe a bear, but for every deadly kill, they have a dozen misses. Any archer who does not make a clean kill once out of every four shots is not doing very good shooting. A good hunter, stalker and shot should do considerably better than that. I am speaking of shots at standing game, of course.

One of the fellows I met had been a state field archery champion for three years straight, and he told me he had made no less than ten shots at deer, none farther than twenty yards away. Three of them he said, had been nearer

"No matter what kind of bow you shoot, no matter whether you shoot freestyle or barebow, if you are shooting a bow and arrow I am with you."

Hill establishing new flight record in 1928.

than twenty-five feet. I could not for the life of me figure what was wrong with his shooting until a few days later, he showed up backstage where I was appearing, with all his hunting equipment.

He had one of the most beautiful, delicate bows, with almost if not quite the fastest cast of any it has ever been my pleasure to examine. It was a lovely recurved osage with a glass back and plastic belly, four feet ten long between the nocks and pulling sixty-nine pounds at a twenty-seven inch draw. The string was as thin and delicate as a flight bow string. His arrows were just as lovely and well made as his bow, but entirely too light, and the broadheads were too short, too wide and too thin for accurate shooting. They were 1¼ inches wide and less than two inches long, with three cutting edges.

I shot some of the broadheads out of his bow into several thicknesses of celotex which we found backstage in the theater. The wide, short, three-bladed head windplaned so badly and the bow was so tricky and sensitive that I had trouble keeping the arrows in a three-foot-square target at fifteen yards. Each arrow ducked and dodged like a frightened teal, even inside the building, where there was no wind, not even a breeze. Once or twice I failed to get a perfect loose or I flinched slightly with my left

The type of bow Hill preferred and which he discusses
here performs with efficiency of machine in his hands.

hand, then the bow started going places and the arrows got out of the bow so badly they barely caught the edge of the target, even at that close range.

Now I knew what was wrong with the chap's shooting. No wonder he had never killed a deer! No man alive could call his shots with that equipment, at any distance.

I asked this archer to shoot his equipment for me, so I could watch to see if I could detect anything wrong with his technique. His results were little better than mine, yet his technique was flawless, so far as I could see.

Then, in turn, we both shot my equipment at the same distance and were seldom off-center more than a few inches.

The last time I saw this archer before I left the city, he told me he was making another bow and was getting some properly made broadheads for the next hunting season.

Why archers will go out year after year, get close-range shots, continue to miss their deer, and still stay with short recurved bows and improperly constructed arrows is beyond my comprehension. Maybe the beauty of such bows and the music of the delicate strings is more pleasing to such hunters than delicious juicy steaks broiling over the campfire, but I prefer the steak.

I have been asked this one question thousands of times: "Why don't you use a recurved bow?" I can answer without hesitation: *I am not skilled enough to shoot a short recurved bow accurately.*

This simple statement is not meant as a jest: it is the straight truth, and I am not ashamed to admit it.

Doug Kittredge (left) and Howard Hill held mutual respect
for each other's knowledge and abilities, but did not
necessarily agree as to what is best in bow design today.

*(Although relatively young in years, Doug Kittredge
is rapidly becoming known as the Grand Old Man of
modern archery. He operates an archery tackle business
at Mammoth Lakes, California. He was highly respected
by the late Howard Hill, although they didn't agree on
tackle needs.)*

THERE is no doubt that the greatest name in modern
archery was Howard Hill. Here was a man who accomplished archery feats that well may never be equalled. A
man with a forceful, vibrant personality who it was impossible not to enjoy being around. A man who visited
every American household through countless movies,
books and articles. A man whose successes in the sport
of archery made him the recognized leader.

It is a human trait to follow the leader. To do, ourselves, exactly what the leader does. To use the same
equipment. To hope that by such mimicry we too will
achieve a similar success.

The controversy of Longbow versus Recurve has
come about because of the unusual case of a leader
acclaiming the value of a type of equipment which, in
actual practice by the majority, is found to be inferior
and has thus been rejected.

I personally don't believe this controversy ever will be
really settled as long as Howard Hill remains the

symbolic leader of archery prowess. There always will be
those archers who are not satisfied with their skill and
who, in their quest for better results, turn to the leader
for his recommendation.

The fact is that the average archer who has been in
the sport for more than two years has owned an average
of three different bows during his quest for superior
performance and increased archery skill. During this
beginning period, the archer very likely has owned or
seriously tried a longbow.

Yet the proof of which type of equipment actually
proves itself the better performer is the fact that better
than ninety-seven percent of the archers who have shot
two years or more use a bow of modern recurved design.
Ask yourself, "Would this archer have decided on a
recurved bow, had a straight end longbow given better
results?"

Furthermore, if a longbow design actually were
superior in performance, wouldn't at least some of the
bow manufacturers recognize this sales potential and
have at least one longbow in their line of bow models?

Let's take a look at the reasons why this amazing
rejection of the "master's" style of equipment occurs.

Howard Hill came from the old school. He was
weaned on archery in the days when to shoot a bow was
to show the world that you were some kind of a nut
who played around with kid's toys...or simply didn't

know any better. In that era, equipment as we know it today was non-existent. There were practically no manufacturers of archery tackle, so you made your own. Bows were made of wood and wood as a material demanded that it not be overstressed or fracture would occur. The age-old English longbow design had proved its worth, was reliable, easy to construct and did the job well.

However, compared with modern fiberglass materials, wood is a grossly inefficient spring material. In the old days, when a man wanted to hunt with a bow, he needed to use a bow weight of at least 65 or 70 pounds — and preferably more — to get the power needed for reasonable flatness of arrow trajectory and deep penetration.

To hold a bow of such high weight requires more than just a loose grip...the shooter holds on rather tightly. This bow grip pressure makes it difficult to shoot without twisting the bow limbs out of line slightly with the bowstring, and the bow design which is least sensitive to this bowstring mis-alignment gives the most accurate results.

Through the years, much experimentation was carried out. Short-length bows were found to be faster shooting. because the short limbs were bent into a tighter arc with the same draw length. But it also was found that the extra finger pinch formed by the narrower angle of the bowstring made shooting a short bow with dependable accuracy difficult; the extra speed normally was not worth the chance of missing the object being shot at.

Recurved bow designs were known to give great speed. The ancient Turkish bows had the greatest efficiency of any bows known to man and a search always for more speed and flatter shooting trajectory has been a compelling sales argument with archers as it has been with gun enthusiasts. Thus, recurved bows made of wood were developed. It was found, however, that with the heavy weights needed for hunting efficiency and the tight grip needed to shoot such equipment, the early recurved bows were lacking in maximum accuracy.

With the tremendous development of plastics and fiberglass during World War II, bows underwent rapid changes.

Fiberglass on bows was introduced by Frank Eicholtz. The technique of making a bow by gluing several laminations together enabled the bowmaker to make whatever shape of bow he wished. The as yet unattainable performance and speed of the old Turkish bows acted as a carrot in front of a rabbit's nose and all sorts of highly curved and stressed bow designs popped onto the scene. At first, results were poor, but as materials and construction technique advanced, results were astonishing.

Archery was a rapidly growing sport. Many new people were taking it up, but there was a serious lack of real engineering talent as the sport had not yet developed to a point that it would financially support such high-priced design assistance. Everything was developed by the "cut and try" method. As today, all bowmakers proclaimed their product to be the greatest. Recurved bows had great speed and flat trajectory, but they often lacked stability and accuracy when shot under hunting conditions. It is no wonder that Howard Hill remained wed to his firm belief in the dependable longbow.

But times have changed. Archery as a sport has become big business. Enough archers now buy equipment from large, well-financed firms that the latter can employ the best in engineers to design their products. It has become known what makes a bow stable and dependable, what makes a bow fast, or what makes a bow sensitive to shooting technique variations.

To remain in business, today's bow manufacturer must produce a saleable product. The most saleable bow is the one that looks the best...but even more important, performs the best.

All modern bows are a compromise of desirable features. If a bowmaker designs a bow to shoot as fast as possible, he sacrifices the service life, or he makes it difficult, if not impossible, to shoot with accuracy. If he designs only for maximum stability and accuracy, he loses speed and convenience of size.

Today's archer is invariably interested in different phases of the sport and in his equipment; he wants the features most important to success in the particular archery activity in which he is interested. As no one bow can do everything the best, we see a wide variety of bow designs offered the archery public, so the archer can select a bow with features designed specifically for his interests.

Some bows today are designed with the tournament shooter in mind entirely. Competitive shooting demands the utmost in accuracy and the ability to shoot exactly the same shot after shot. The tournament archer can take all the time in the world to make his shot, he can establish his stance, he can aim deliberately. Score is the thing and a few points at the end of a tournament can spell the difference between winning or losing.

His needs in equipment differ from those of the bowhunter, who asks for reasonable speed, but more important, a bow which will be ultra stable so it can be shot with dependable accuracy under the varied conditions found in the field. This shooter doesn't have a chance to warm up before the shot is made.

Archers today can choose between hundreds of different kinds of designs of bows. They can select a bow with any feature desired, or a bow with a blended combination for all-purpose use. There are long bows or short bows, fast bows, ultra-stable bows, bows physically heavy or light...but all of them are recurved!

It's the recurved bow that gives the results. This design feature makes the bow faster and smoother than it is possible to make any straight end longbow...yet depending upon the rest of the bow design, it also can be ultra stable and suitable for any bowhunting need.

Take a look at the Jack Howard Gamemaster, or the Smithwick Citation, both bows built for dependability in the hunting field. A fifty-pound bow in either of these makes gives the flatness of trajectory of an eighty-five-pound bow in the old wood style, yet both have a stable quality that makes it almost impossible to shoot erratically.

Compare these hunting bows with the smooth shooting, ultra-fast Hoyt or Wing tournament bows which are perhaps sensitive to shooting error, but give great speed and flatness of trajectory when used with lightweight aluminum tournament arrows.

Today, the archer buys a bow for the purpose he has in mind...he may want a hunting bow, he may want a tournament bow, he may want an all-purpose bow, but chances are better than nine out of ten that he will own a bow of recurved design.

The archer who switches to the old-fashioned longbow is a man who usually has not achieved the results he wants. He feels that the teachings of the recognized leader, Howard Hill, are worth a try. He soon finds out that the longbow does not have nearly the speed of his modern recurved bow, it is rough in the hand, it does not draw smoothly and his accuracy actually does not increase.

Kittredge got this world-record elk with a compound.

(Doug Kittredge, long an outspoken proponent of the recurve bow, was something of a holdout when it came to the introduction of the compound bow. However, he eventually tried one and we prevailed upon him to offer his thoughts on his initial experiences. It should be pointed out that he took a record elk with a compound bow in 1975.)

FOR YEARS I'VE been a firm believer in the use of a quiet, dependable, lightweight conventional bow. A compound bow was okay for a target shooter, but for a bow-hunter, no way. They were too heavy, too involved, too complicated, too noisy — they weren't bows, but contraptions!

Last Fall I hunted seriously with one and my ideas are rapidly changing; not that I think the present breed of compounds is the full answer for the serious bowhunter, but they show promise.

Some years back Tom Jennings was talking to me on the phone as excited as a new bride, sort of mumbling about a strange new bow design and a weird-looking prototype. Jennings asked if I'd be around so he could show it to me. We've been friends for many years and he thought this would simply blow my mind.

So there we were, standing seventy yards back from some old bales, this monstrosity in my hands. My disdainful comments just bubbled out until I was urged to just shut up and shoot an arrow.

I did and immediately underwent the compound syndrome of having my mouth drop open as the bow un-folded to its let-off weight. I almost dropped it in fright. Then my mouth fell open again as I saw my arrow pass more than two feet over the bales. That arrow never seemed to slow down! After another half-hour, I was convinced of the fantastic speed possible with this so-called bow, but equally convinced that all the cables, pulleys and gadgets that made up this nightmare never would make it in the hunting field. That prototype was as heavy as a pair of wet Levis. It clanked and rattled. It was like trying to shoot a mechanical bird cage.

As time passed, Jennings refined and developed this bow. Others saw the writing on the wall and they entered the field. Tournament archers began posting fantastic scores. It came to where no rightful target shooter would be seen on the line without a compound. The market for these bows boomed. Manufacturers were at each other's throats trying to be first in the development of a new idea, a new approach, a new look. Everyone wanted to make his bow faster, more closely tuned, then simpler and cheaper. Either performance on the tournament line or the cheapest possible price seemed the goal. Let-off weights were reduced to an extent that it was like falling into a swimming pool backwards when the weight rolled over. This was great, everyone said! And can you make it even lighter? People were beginning to shoot bows that held at only twenty pounds or even less. One could hold all day long, only releasing when the shooter's mental conditioning told him everything was perfect; physical strain no longer causing a hurried shot. Special release aids sprang up on the market to take advantage of the need for the better way to release these low bow weights consistently.

And in all this furor there began to emerge a new breed of bowhunter — the man who used the compound. Many old-time bowhunters who tried the contraption didn't like the mechanical concept, or didn't care for the way the bow handled; but others fooled around with it enough to develop means by which they could accept it in the field, usually going to heavy peak weights. I suspect this was because it was the only way they found they could get the bows to shoot well for them.

In these old-timers' footsteps followed the new bow-hunter, brought up with the desire to shoot a bow like the big boys they were reading about, yet unable to handle the heavy weights they used. They were led along by the manufacturers who were riding the tournament boom of producing bows designed specifically to give fabulous performance with ultra-light target arrows. This new bowhunter found himself with a hunting bow perhaps peaking at fifty pounds, but with holding weights at only twenty-five or

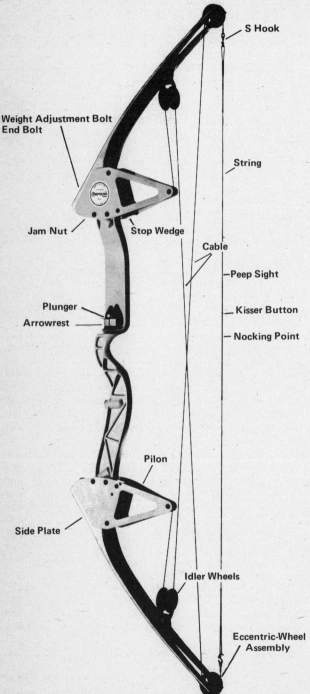

S Hook

Weight Adjustment Bolt
End Bolt

String

Jam Nut

Stop Wedge

Cable

Peep Sight

Plunger

Kisser Button

Arrowrest

Nocking Point

Pilon

Side Plate

Idler Wheels

Eccentric-Wheel
Assembly

thirty pounds, using hunting arrows which were selected by combining the peak and let-off weights, then dividing by two to arrive at a bow weight average to which he matched his arrows, winding up using hunting arrows as light as 375 grains; virtually a target shaft of a few years ago. Ultra speed became the driving force. Use of small vanes, small four-fletch, small broadheads, small shafts, small anything,

as long as it would shoot with the flattest possible trajectory, became popular.

The old-time hunters scoffed at this type of equipment; some because of the type of bow, others at the unnatural lightness of the equipment. But this new breed of bowhunter was at the mercy of the manufacturer, who was so consumed with his mania to be one step ahead in the designing field that, in my book, he overlooked the bowhunter's peculiar needs completely. Sure, he offered him equipment, but it was warmed-over versions of either his successful tournament stuff or cheapened equipment in which he had cut as many corners as he dared in his race to produce a bow at the lowest price.

I try all equipment I can lay my hands on. To my way of thinking our nation's bowhunters have been gravitating steadily to a form of bowhunting tackle better suited to the target range.

The compound design has permitted us to store a considerably greater amount of energy into a bow than we've ever been able to do before, in part through the drawing of a weight heavier than we would normally want to hold at our full draw, actually making us work more in drawing the bow, but allowing us to work less in holding it ready to release. Because of the relatively light weight that we hold at full draw, when we release the arrow it is not given the amount of thrust needed to cause it to bend and to perform as it usually would do when shot in a bow of conventional design having the same holding weight, or shot in a bow having the same peak weight. It was found that arrow matching needed to be a compromise between these two weights, thus reducing the spine and weight of the arrows which would be used normally by an archer, vastly picking up his arrow speed and affording a much flatter trajectory flight. The bowmakers emphasized the amazing arrow speed and flat trajectory by recommending as light an arrow as possible.

All of this is fine when we shoot at targets where maximum accuracy is the prime factor, but when hunting big game, not only must we concern ourselves with accuracy, but we must be even more concerned with the effect of the hunting arrow when it strikes home. How does it penetrate, what happens when it contacts bone, what about the poorly located hit? There is a tremendous amount of resistance to an arrow penetrating living flesh. The muscles grip the entire shaft area. They resist the cutting effort of the ferrule. This resistance to penetration exerts an opposing force to the entry of the arrow and rapidly slows it down. This opposition force is overcome only through the combination of how much the arrow weighs and how fast it is traveling, a force called inertia.

Experienced bowhunters know that the difference in arrow speeds at thirty to fifty yards, where most game is shot, hardly varies over fifteen percent even between different types of bows and different weights of draw. However, a person can vary his arrow weight by almost one hundred percent, depending on the type and weight of the bow and the particular arrows used with it. This ability to increase arrow weight greatly increases the ability to overcome penetration resistance. As a rule of thumb, he who uses heavy arrows has more formidable tackle than he who uses light arrows.

I believe this is what has happened with the compound bow in the hands of many of the new, less experienced bowhunters as they have followed their quest for a faster shooting arrow through the reducing of the arrow spine and weight to get it to shoot well from their basically tournament-designed so-called hunting compounds.

So what do we do? After shooting a compound for months now, I know the impossibility of my going back to the good old conventional bow. I tried mine today, just to see for sure, but it feels like drawing back a broom handle and the arrow travels towards the target like a stream of water from my garden hose. Going backwards is not the solution.

In the beginning, I could shoot them with my heavy hunting arrows pretty well. They flew straight and my accuracy seemed consistent. I just couldn't hack the cumbersome feel of the bows and they were far too heavy physically to carry around all day. These old bows averaged a let-off around twenty percent, making the peak and holding weights much closer together, so the averaging of these weights produced an arrow more in keeping with the peak weight selected; a weight usually somewhat greater than would be used with a conventional bow, meaning the hunter could use his normal-weight hunting arrows and get good flight.

But the fantastic first impression of a compound-type bow is the amazing let-off weight as you draw it. With a bow which only lets off twenty percent, this change in weight does not seem too great, but with a fifty percent let-off bow, the feeling the archer gets is fabulous! It also means the shooter can use a bow of considerable power built in through the high peak weight, yet he can hold the bow at full draw like it was made for a woman. The bow market has demanded more and more let-off accordingly and the bowmakers have gone along with these demands.

But tell me, can you consistently release a twenty-five or thirty-pound bow weight using your fingers, particularly when using a bow length under sixty inches and the string angle at full draw grips itself viselike around your fingers? I seriously doubt it. You will find that your releasing ability dramatically improves as you increase the force of the bow-string pressing on your fingers to a point where you'll find a weight which no longer just rolls the string off your fingers, but which literally snaps your fingers apart into an open position without any roll-off at all. It is at this point that you'll find your consistent accuracy immediately improves, for the bow weight that pops your fingers open also gives your arrow a straight forward push, not a sideways flip.

Most bowhunters use their fingers to draw. They don't use mechanical releases because fingers are easier and faster to use in the woods. I have to believe that the holding weight of a hunting compound is a vital thing to a serious bowhunter. Through working with other bowhunters, trying many types of bows myself, I've come to the conclusion that a holding weight of forty pounds is just about the bare minimum a man can expect to be able to shoot with dependable accuracy using his fingers and when under field conditions of cold and rain, as well as tiredness and unpreparedness, as experienced when hunting. With the modern fifty percent let-off type of compounds, this would require an eighty-pound weight. Who can pull that with ease? Even a forty percent let-off would require muscling back a sixty-seven-pound bow; this still with the bare minimum of forty pounds holding weight. And when you just go up to a forty-five or fifty-pound holding weight, it can make an even greater difference in your releasing ability, but such would require bows so heavy in peak weight that only Hercules could swing it. Perhaps even of more importance than the ability to release these light holding weights is, what happens to the hunting arrow?

Assuming you are selecting anywhere close to a heavy enough hunting arrow to insure adequate penetration on game, you will have far too stiff a shaft to match the initial powder puff thrust of the light holding weight. Again, were a hunter to have a forty percent let-off bow, with a minimum forty-pound holding weight, he would have a sixty-seven-pound peak and I would personally recommend to

him a hunting shaft size 2018, only compromising as far as a 2016. Both shafts are far more than a forty-pound bow can handle, with the result that the shafting barely bends as it first starts past the bow on release, moving outwards some twenty-five percent past the bow before the turnover of the eccentrics slams the arrow with the full force of the sixty-seven-pound weight. At this point the arrow has become a sort of pendulum with the heavy weight of the broadhead dangling out on the end. It is in this position that the arrow receives this great impact, and if in any manner the arrow is not passing the bow in perfect alignment, but is perhaps moved a little out of line due to the string having rolled off the finger tips, the pendulum action is greatly accentuated and the arrow gyrates wildly from the bow in an almost sideways position by the swinging force of the heavy broadhead pulling it far off course.

A hunting arrow is nowhere nearly as well balanced aerodynamically as a target arrow. As you further lighten the shafting, you put it even more out of balance. This condition makes a hunting arrow more susceptible to changes in its performance due to human technique errors as you lighten the holding weight; a vicious circle indeed!

In my opinion, a bowhunter holds a responsibility to hunt with equipment capable of dispatching the game he hunts. I believe that to do this job, a man needs to use a bow of sufficient weight, or power if you will, to move his arrow at a sufficient rate of speed to provide the necessary killing penetration through arrow inertia, which is only possible when he also couples his bow weight with a reasonably heavy arrow weight. I do not care to see bowhunters using bow weights of under fifty pounds, whether with a conventional or a compound bow, to hunt big game. Nor do I care to see bowhunters using arrow weights which fall much below 500 grains, for my personal experiences have shown these lighter weights not capable of doing the job when a poor hit is made.

Now then, where does all of this leave us if we want to take advantage of the fantastic potential of the modern compound as a hunting tool?

First of all, buy a bow with the least amount of let-off, not the most. Think of it as asking yourself, "Do I want high let-off or high performance?" The closer the peak and the holding weights, the easier it will be to correctly match your hunting arrow and have it fly well consistently. You will have a far better release and the dependable accuracy that goes with it. Select as heavy a peak weight as you can draw comfortably a half-dozen times. Many of the better bowhunters are selecting peak weights of sixty-five pounds and up, in order to give the highest possible holding weights and to permit handling of hunting weight arrows efficiently, particularly with the high let-off bows we see today. Joe Johnston of Easton Aluminum tells me he is getting his best flight using eighty and ninety-pound peak weights!

Certainly most men can draw through a sixty-pound peak normally and rarely should find it necessary to go below a fifty-five-pound peak in any compound hunting bow.

Fit your bow with an adjustable arrow rest that can be moved in or out from the side of the bow to permit adjustment for various arrow flight problems you might incur with your particular style of shooting or with the characteristics of the individual arrow you select to shoot; the Pacer Hunter II is an excellent example of this sort of rest, being flexible and usable with or without a cushion plunger. Buy hunting arrows that are matched as closely to the peak weight of your bow as possible, rather than to the holding weight or the average of the two; then make use of the adjustable rest feature, and possibly a cushion plunger, to adjust to your particular arrows. — *Doug Kittredge*

Chapter 3

BASICS OF ARCHERY

Equipment, As Well As Technique, Is Of Great Importance . . . And Expert Coaching Can Help !

IN the past, there seems to have been an aura of mystery surrounding every champion's shooting secrets. Actually, good shooting form — that which makes champions — is little different than just plain good posture.

In short, the so-called "secrets" of champions and certain coaches are nothing more than certain "feelings" of good form, which to them are something to be closely guarded and doled out in small doses so the uninitiated will not learn too much and present competition.

This article will deal with the shooting techniques that may be considered basic, but we will carry it beyond, so that all physical aspects are covered. Mental attitudes are important, but are so closely coupled to the confidence one may gain from correct form that form must be first and foremost for the serious archer.

We will attempt to show that, by concentrating upon good posture, and by taking logical steps, good shooting form — and good shooting — are attainable by anyone with normal facilities. I realize that I may be unleashing a tempest among some competitive shooters, but I firmly feel that there are no "secrets" to good shooting; only good, sound, logical form, and the confidence and mental outlook resulting from this.

Probably the greatest single drawback to the development of an up-and-coming archer is the inept advice always available from the well meaning but unqualified and self-styled coaches.

The first lesson for the individual who wants to learn to shoot correctly is to ignore all advice given by anyone other than the qualified coach involved. All of this may seem extremely basic, but I've seen hundreds of instances wherein mental confusion and lower scores have been derived from inept advice, thus discouraging a promising shooter to the point of giving up archery entirely. In short, there is no room in the learning schedule for the novice to include a lot of experimentation — only practice on the **proper** form. Leave the experimenting for the experts!

Let's break the elements of shooting form into two parts: First, we'll discuss the basics of such

form, step by step, as simply as possible. Then we will get into the various problems and their cures.

I agree that, on some points, there may be differences of opinion among the experts, but I have found the following method to work well and have learned that it is much the same as other professionally recommended shooting methods. It differs primarily in that this is a simple approach — with the so-called mystery taken out.

Correct shooting form may be broken down into a number of basic steps. We, however, will limit our study to four such steps, using the theory that the fewer steps, the less effort required by the neophyte to remember them in proper sequence. The steps are as follows: (1) Preparation for the Draw; (2) Draw and Anchor; (3) Hold and the Aim; (4) Release and Follow-Through.

But before we discuss each step, let us dwell briefly upon the difference between shooting with a sight and shooting without. The primary difference is the fact that, without a sight, the archer is visually shooting the arrow. He is dependent upon seeing the arrow for his alignment and elevation. Small variations in the cant of the bow and even in his anchor, usually are compensated for instinctively.

Exact placement of the feet for shooting will differ slightly from one archer to another, but this affords an idea of what is proper stance.

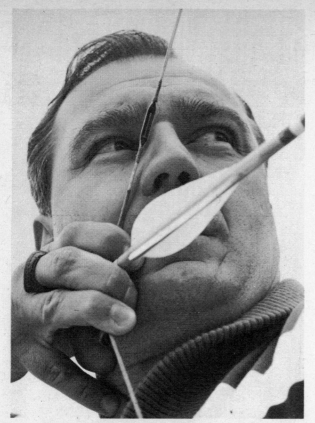

This archer apparently utilizes the corner of his mouth as anchor for a specific range. The expert has different anchors for varying ranges.

When shooting with a sight, the archer is dependent only upon the sight for his aim. so the anchor and bow position are more critical. The sight shooter also is more aware of variations in his aim. Consequently, he is under more mental stress in his form.

Usually, the sight shooter will anchor lower than the bare bow shooter, because he needs the lower anchor to obtain more distance from his sight, and because a multiple-point anchor is usually easier to obtain from a lower anchor. One more difference is that many bare bow shooters do not find it necessary to align the string (place it in the same relationship between eye and bow), whereas the sight shooter must align it. This, again. is due to the fact that the bare bow shooter gets his alignment from the arrow. itself.

With these thoughts in mind, here are listed the basics for proper form — and the ultimate scores:

PREPARATION FOR THE DRAW: The feet should be in line between 45 and 90 degrees to the target. but not over 90, with the shoulders in the same line as the feet. The head should be held erect and facing directly at the target. The chin should be parallel with the ground. not raised or lowered. And it should be kept in mind that the head should serve as an independent unit to which you draw. It should **not** be moved into the anchor; instead, the anchor should be brought to the head.

THE DRAW: Place the drawing fingers on the string so that the string is well into the first joint, then wrap the fingers well around the string so that the grip on the string is strong.

With the bow arm, elevate the bow until the sight

is on the target **without** elevating the bow shoulder. This will create the feeling that your head is well above the bow shoulder. Be certain that the bow is being held perpendicular.

Draw the string with the drawing arm, being certain you are doing three things: **(1)** Draw directly to the anchor, not coming in from the top, bottom or side. **(2)** As the draw is being made, try to feel that your back muscles are doing most of the drawing. It is important that all of the pulling and pushing feels as though it is directly in line with the target. **(3)** Be certain your bow shoulder moves only slightly from its original position at the start of the draw. It may move inward slightly, but definitely should not move up or down.

Three fingers are on the string, using flipper in this instance. Note how joints are hooked so that there is strength against the string.

THE HOLD AND THE AIM: This is probably the most complicated of the four basic steps under discussion, but don't let it throw you. Take it easy, and follow these instructions.

The line of tensions (pushing and pulling, if you want it simplified) again is directly toward the target. This can be seen by the tendency for the sight to settle easily.

Any undue movement of the bow shoulder during the draw will destroy this line. Also, any attempt to hold by **pulling** with the arm instead of **holding** with the back will destroy this line.

Undoubtedly the most difficult part of holding is the ability to hold with the muscles in the back of the drawing shoulder rather than the drawing arm. This is accomplished by a smooth, even transfer of the tension in the arm to the back, **during** and after the draw. The result is an almost relaxed feeling during the draw and hold. If too much tension is held in the upper arm for too long, this transfer

RELEASE AND FOLLOW THROUGH: If all of the previous steps have been carried out correctly, the release will follow easily. There are a few subtle points regarding good release, however, which might help in mental attitude.

First and foremost, keep in mind the earlier discussed matter of tension being held in the back. Good

to the back becomes almost impossible.

It is difficult, even for an expert, to tell the difference between faulty use of the bow shoulder and a fault in the drawing arm and shoulder. (We can speak of this fault as a broken line of tension; not enough, or even too much tension. This tension should be only enough to keep the arrow from creeping forward.)

A faulty bow shoulder generally will cause your arrows to scatter more wildly. Faulty tension in the drawing shoulder will cause a collapse; this may still group your arrows — but not in the center of the target.

A sight that stays in a particular spot outside of the target center usually indicates fault in use of

Instructor offers advice, as this beginner is commencing her draw. She has hold on the handle that may be too tight, wrist not straight.

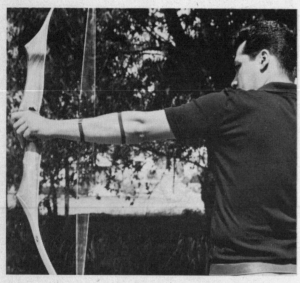

At full draw, it is important that the elbow is straight. It should not bend or start to buckle. Proper bow weight is important here.

the bow shoulder. A sight that centers but will not sit still usually is due to one holding with the arm rather than the back.

Sighting is so tied to proper tension that all that can be said is for the shooter to use mental as well as physical patience to wait until his sight has settled on the center.

A too common fault is to shoot too soon, when the sight first touches the target center, or when it is in the area but has not stopped moving.

All too often, a shooter says that he has a problem in freezing off the center, then finally finds that, due to improper tension or line of tension, he is torqueing the sight off center. Of course, psychological freezing does happen, but this, more often than not, is started by the incorrect line of tension; many times the mental attitude can be solved by correcting the physical problem.

sighting is a must as discussed. The sight must be steady in the center of the target. Flinched releases usually are caused by poor sighting.

In regard to mental attitude, it would appear from experience that one should concentrate upon tightening the back of the drawing shoulder rather than the actual opening of the fingers. Those who concentrate upon opening the fingers often cause a loss of this tension just prior to release.

The release hand should move to the rear easily. This must be a **result** of good tension and must not be forced. The effort to make the hand move to the rear without the proper tension will cause one to flinch.

The follow through, again, is a **result** rather than a true function in itself. Good tension, aiming and release will result in good follow through. The lack of a follow through will indicate poor form in one of the other facets.

That's the system. I'm certain there will be those in the top competitive ranks who will find fault with it, complain that I've neglected to offer the secrets of good shooting, but these are the secrets, if there really are any.

In working with thousands of beginning archers, I have found that I can have them shooting respectable scores in but a few hours if they will follow the basics outlined here.

So give it a try and don't worry about the secrets. You will find them for yourself.

Techniques
Of An Olympic
Gold Medalist

*This Olympic Champ reveals
the techniques that won an
Olympic Gold Medal.*

RATHER THAN DEAL strictly in textbook-type theories, let's take a look at techniques and thoughts of John Williams. Now associated with Wing Archery, he was a teen-ager when he won the gold medal for the United States in the 1972 Olympics. His success has led to a mammoth resurgence of archery as a high school and college sport. It is from these ranks that future Olympic hopefuls are certain to come.

"I started shooting at the age of 8 and received my first bow for my ninth birthday," he recalls. "My mother and father were the basic reason for my early interest in archery. My father started shooting for the sake of hunting, got involved in field archery and then target archery.

"He taught my mother how to shoot and later, when I received a bow for that birthday, he taught me. He has been and will probably remain my one and only true coach, although my wife is trying."

There has to be something said for the senior Williams' coaching abilities, for at 15 — in 1969 — John Williams was first in the world team tryouts and shot a FITA world record round of 1242 points. That same year, he was second in the World Championships at Valley Forge, Pennsylvania, and also placed third in the National Archery

Association championships in his introductory year.

At 17 years of age — in 1971 — he was first in the world team tryouts, representing the United States, then took first in the World Championships in York, England, upping his NAA status to top dog by winning first in the Nationals that year.

A year later, at 18, he was first in the Olympic tryouts in this country, then won the gold medal in the 1972 Olympic Games, putting the frosting on his cake of personal achievement by scoring first later that year in the World Field Championships at Udine, Italy.

Williams' archery career took something of a back seat when he entered the Army in October 1971, following his graduation from high school. However, the U.S. Army realized the potential of their new recruit and tended to encourage his shooting on his own time — since the Armed Services are fully aware of the propaganda values of having some of their own among Olympic contestants. It doesn't hurt the recruiting program either.

As a result, Williams was assigned to special services, which deals with athletics and sports, serving with the unit until his release from active duty in August 1973.

Since that time, he has graduated to the professional

ranks and, using a Wing Competition II bow, won the 1975 Professional Archers Association Outdoor Championships in Pinehurst, South Carolina. In that outing, Williams' score was only six points off of perfect and he was five points ahead of his nearest competitor, according to Jim Ploen, another noted archer who now is with Wing Archery. In the four days of shooting, Williams scored 299, 298, 299 and 298, out of each day's possible three hundred points.

For such competition, Williams shoots a thirty-eight-pound bow, but with his thirty-one-inch draw this brings the draw weight to about fifty-six pounds. For the PAA title, he shot Easton 2115 arrows equipped with plastic vanes.

Upon discharge from the Army, Williams accepted a post with Wing Archery, operating out of the firm's headquarters in Jacksonville, Texas. He also enrolled at Texas A&M, attending that institution for three semesters, then transferred to San Bernardino Valley College in California, a school that has one of the nation's outstanding archery programs.

As a professional, he continues to represent Wing in exhibition shooting and in advising on school programs around the nation. But perhaps his greatest contribution has been the advice he actually has been able to pass on to other up-and-coming shooters who have aspirations toward that Olympic medal of the future.

By John Williams' own admission, much of the advice he tends to pass on is basic, but as he puts it, "Accuracy is based on handling the basics correctly."

In the matter of stance, for example, he suggests the archer "stand with good, erect posture, feet comfortably spread. Don't permit the left hip to extend toward the target, as this forces you to lean away from the target and misalign the shoulders. There are variations that prove more successful for some than others, of course. In the open stance, one should place the left toe on a line to the target and the right toe slightly ahead of the line."

For what is termed the square stance, Williams advises one to "place both toes on line to the center of the target." This, incidentally, is the stance he prefers for his own shooting. If one favors the closed stance, he suggests placing the left toe on line to the target, with the right toe slightly behind the line.

His advice is aimed at the right-handed shooter, of course, but one has only to reverse the procedures he advises for left-handed shooting.

For correct bow-hand positioning, "Pick up the bow with the left hand. Keeping the wrist straight, let the bow settle comfortably in the V between the thumb and index finger, then close the fingers gently around the grip."

Nocking the arrow may seem something one simply does as a matter of course, but Williams became a champion by taking care in all phases of shooting. He even has some thoughts on use of the drawing-hand position and nocking the arrow:

"With the bow hand, hold the bow at a forty-five-degree angle to your body. Lay the arrow on the rest, holding and guiding it with the index finger of the bow hand. With the

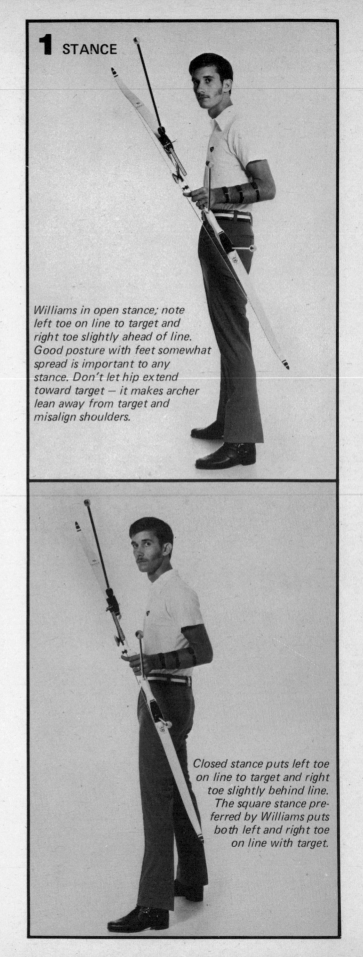

1 STANCE

Williams in open stance; note left toe on line to target and right toe slightly ahead of line. Good posture with feet somewhat spread is important to any stance. Don't let hip extend toward target — it makes archer lean away from target and misalign shoulders.

Closed stance puts left toe on line to target and right toe slightly behind line. The square stance preferred by Williams puts both left and right toe on line with target.

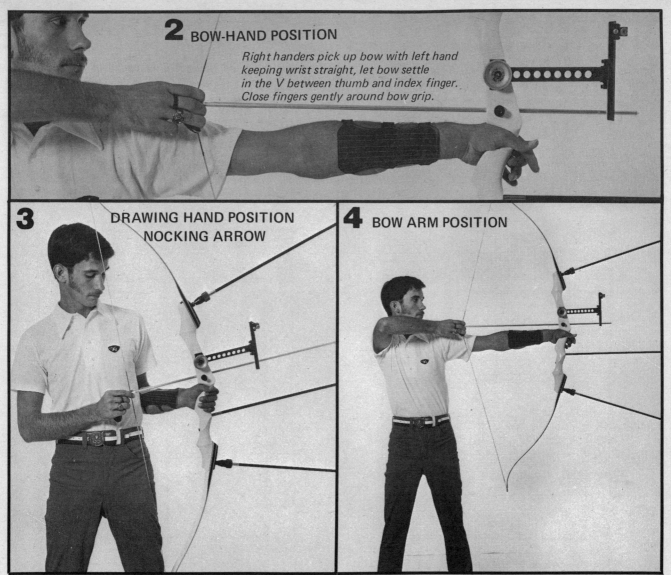

2 BOW-HAND POSITION

Right handers pick up bow with left hand keeping wrist straight, let bow settle in the V between thumb and index finger. Close fingers gently around bow grip.

3 DRAWING HAND POSITION NOCKING ARROW

4 BOW ARM POSITION

Above left: Correct nocking procedure — bow at 45-degree angle, arrow on rest first, then nocked; for drawing; index finger should be above nock, middle and ring finger below. Above right: Good bow arm position; extended straight toward target, wrist straight and elbow rotated down away from string path.

drawing hand, place the nock between the nocking points on the string. Position the index finger above the nock, with the middle and ring fingers below it. Then, with the fingertips, form a hook around the string with the string crossing at the line of the first joint of the fingers.

"With the arrow on the string, raise the bow, extending the bow arm straight toward the target. With the drawing hand, draw the bowstring back part way. Pause, check the bow-hand position, then, keeping the wrist straight, rotate the elbow down and away from the path of the bowstring. Check again for a straight wrist," he advises.

One should keep the bow shoulder down, drawing in a straight line to the anchor point, keeping the back of the drawing hand straight throughout. One should draw to the same anchor point each time, of course.

In his own successes, Williams has found that, if shooting instinctively, the best anchor is high, with the tip of the index or middle finger at the corner of the mouth, the thumb relaxed under the jaw. For freestyle shooting, he prefers a lower anchor point, the string at the center of his chin, the index finger under his chin. In this style, the string touches the tip of his nose. While this makes for success on his part, Williams does point out that there will be slight variations, depending upon the individual's build, facial characteristics and other physical variables.

"In my case, when the string is aligned properly, it is seen as a blur in line with the arrow or the edge of the bow window," he says. "This serves as a rear sight in aiming."

In instinctive shooting, Williams draws to his anchor, pauses and holds to aim. "At close distances, the arrow tip

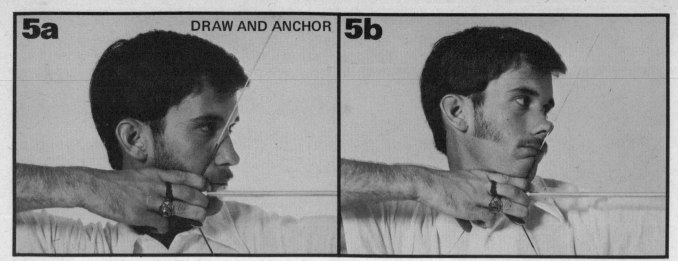

5a DRAW AND ANCHOR **5b**

Left: Instinctive high anchor with tip of index or middle finger at corner of mouth. Right: Freestyle low anchor string at center of chin, across tip of nose and index finger under chin.

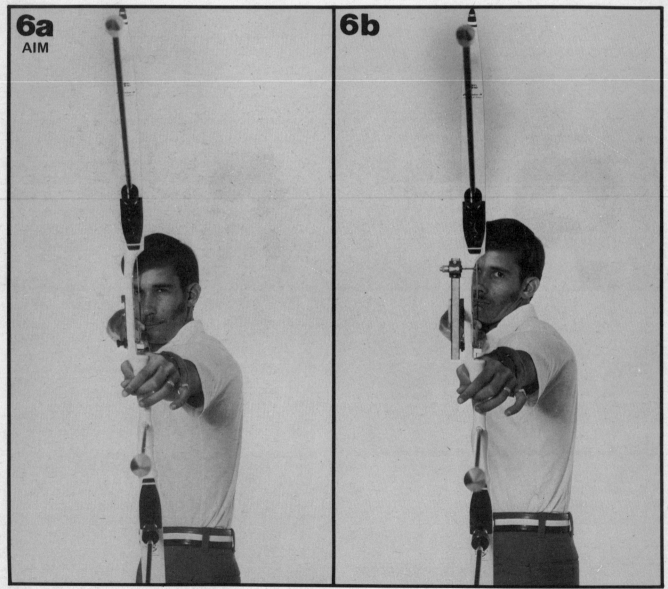

6a AIM **6b**

Left: When aiming instinctively draw to anchor, pause and hold to aim. At close distance, arrow tip is seen below target center; the greater the distance the higher the point of aim will become — sometimes above center or even target. Right: Use a sight as a reference for known distance. Hold sight pin on center of target. To correct sighting error always adjust pin in the same direction as the arrow misses; up for a high miss and down for a low miss. Always avoid snap shooting and relax.

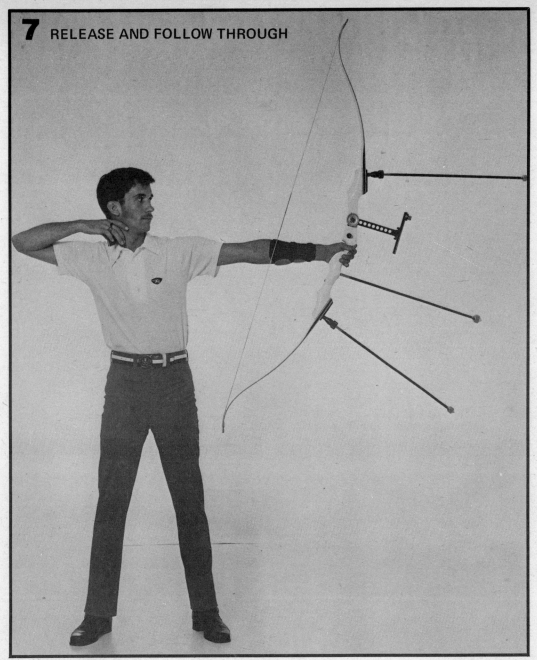

Release and follow-through are factors; relax drawing hand to let fingers open. Let drawing hand come back along face or neck in straight line. Keep concentration on target and hold head still until the arrow has reached the mark.

is seen below the center of the target," he says. "At greater ranges, I hold the tip closer to the center of the bull's-eye, and at still greater distances, above the center."

For freestyle shooting, Williams uses his sight as the reference for a known distance. "I hold the sight pin on the center of the target. To correct a sighting error, one always should adjust the pin in the same direction as the arrow misses."

Williams — and others — feels that many potential outstanding archers fail to achieve championship status in the end because of their inattention to release and, even more important, follow-through.

For the release of the arrow, Williams advises, "Relax the drawing-hand muscles to permit the string fingers to open. Let the drawing hand come back along the face or the neck in a straight line toward the shoulder."

For the follow-through, his own technique is to "hold concentration on the target. I hold my head still until the arrow actually hits its mark."

The individual is bound to find other techniques that fit his style of archery, but these are the basics, and if one can follow them to the letter as has John Williams, he'll be a long way along the trail to target success. — *Jack Lewis*

CHOOSING YOUR EQUIPMENT

Thoughts Have Changed Considerably In Recent Years, And Advances Still Are Being Made.

EACH YEAR, THOUSANDS of potential new archers go through the painful motions of buying a new bow and a batch of assorted tackle only to find they are not able to hit much more than the broad side of the proverbial barn at ten paces.

The basic problem is a lack of information before running down to the local sporting goods store or writing a mail order house and blowing $100 on the wrong equipment.

Who can be an archer? This takes in nearly everyone from six to one hundred, there are a few prerequisites however, which include, the archer having at least one eye and one hand. Other than that, there is little to stop anyone from a paraplegic to a perfect physical specimen from being a top archer. It's mainly a desire to shoot well and practice after selection of the proper equipment.

Selection of the proper equipment depends on whether you are going to become a bow hunter or a target archer. It also varies with the physical makeup of the potential archer. Most new enthusiasts to the sport have a tendency to overbow themselves, unless they get proper professional advice. Their first purchase many times will be a bow with a draw weight many pounds over that necessary to do the job. Also, the novice will have a multitude of problems in trying to draw a heavy bow with muscles that haven't been used before. The end result is poor shooting and a disappointed novice archer, who may chuck his tackle into the nearest trash barrel.

Selecting a first bow is pretty simple, when one follows a few basic rules. First, if at all possible, the novice should contact his local archery club, a certified instructor of the Professional Archers Association, or some archer who has been actively involved in the sport for a number of years. Your local archery store may be of assistance, however be sure that the store manage-

ment is completely familiar with archery and not just selling the goods.

You may not be in an area where professional or expert advice is available, so the next best thing is to write to a major bow manufacturer. Most will be glad to help you select a bow that will start you off on the archery trail.

The basic information necessary to select your bow is

Measuring one's draw length is one of prerequisites in the selection of a bow. Distance from the fingertip to fingertip is applied to the chart shown on page 40.

AMO Wood Arrow Spine Selection Charts

TARGET ARROWS

Bow Wt. at Draw Lth.	*Arrow Length								
	24	25	26	27	28	29	30	31	32
20 - 25	A	A	A	A	A	B	B	C	D
25 - 30	A	A	A	A	B	C	D	D	E
30 - 35	A	A	A	B	C	D	E	E	F
35 - 40	A	A	B	C	D	E	F	G	H
40 - 45	A	B	C	D	E	F	G	H	I
45 - 50	B	C	D	E	F	G	H	I	J
50 - 55	C	D	E	F	G	H	I	J	K
55 - 60	D	E	F	G	H	I	J	K	
60 - 65	D	E	G	H	I	J	K		
65 - 70	E	F	G	I	J	K			

FIELD & HUNTING ARROWS

Bow Wt. at Draw Lth.	*Arrow Length								
	24	25	26	27	28	29	30	31	32
20 - 25	A	A	A	A	B	B	C	D	E
25 - 30	A	A	A	B	C	D	D	E	F
30 - 35	A	A	B	C	D	E	E	F	G
35 - 40	A	B	C	D	E	F	G	H	I
40 - 45	B	C	D	E	F	G	H	I	J
45 - 50	C	D	E	F	G	H	I	J	K
50 - 55	D	E	F	G	H	I	J	K	
55 - 60	E	F	G	H	I	J	K		
60 - 65	E	G	H	I	J	K			
65 - 70	F	G	I	J	K				

* For all practical purposes arrow length and draw length may be considered the same.

AMO Bow String Tension Chart

Bow Length	String Length	+ (8) 20-30 lbs.	+ (10) 25-35 lbs.	+ (12) 35-45 lbs.	+ (14) 45-55 lbs.	+ (16) 55-75 lbs.	+ (18) 75-100 lbs.
72	69	80 lbs.	90 lbs.	110 lbs.	130 lbs.	150 lbs.	170 lbs.
71	68	"	"	"	"	145	165
70	67	75	85	105	125	"	"
69	66	"	"	"	"	"	"
68	65	"	"	"	"	140	160
67	64	70	80	100	120	"	"
66	63	"	"	"	"	"	"
65	62	"	"	"	"	135	"
64	61	65	75	95	115	"	155
63	60	"	"	"	"	"	"
62	59	60	70	90	110	130	"
61	58	"	"	"	"	"	150
60	57	"	"	"	"	"	"
59	56	55	65	85	105	125	"
58	55	"	"	"	"	"	145
57	54	"	"	"	"	"	"
56	53	50	60	80	100	120	"
55	52	"	"	"	"	"	"
54	51	"	"	"	"	"	140
53	50	45	55	75	95	115	"
52	49	"	"	"	"	"	"
51	48	40	50	70	90	"	135
50	47	"	"	"	"	110	"
49	46	"	"	"	"	"	"
48	45	35	45	65	85	"	130

* Bow weight categories are based upon bow weight at 28" draw length.
+ Number in parenthesis is suggested number of strands in type B or V207 dacron or equivalent.

your weight, height, age and physical condition; also purpose for which you plan to use the bow. From this information, whether you are writing a manufacturer or selecting a bow from the shelf of your local dealer, it can be determined what will suit your need.

For the novice, it may be best to purchase one of the inexpensive bow and arrow kits marketed by most of the leading manufacturers. These bow kits come with all the necessary equipment to start one in target practice. This allows the new archer to try the sport and become familiar with the tackle at a minimum of expense. After a period of familiarization and practice one can move on to heavier bows and more expensive equipment for use in field, target or hunting archery.

Nearly every bow manufactured today is called a recurve, the upper and lower limbs of the bow curving away from the shooter. The older and now less popular bow that has been used for several centuries is called a long or straight bow. The recurve has been internationally accepted and is preferred by the vast majority of all archers, because it gives the arrow greater speed with less draw pressures and is superior in all-around performance.

AMO Wood Arrow Spine Deflection Values

+ DEFLECTION	
1.20 to 1.00	A
1.00 to .85	B
.85 to .75	C
.75 to .65	D
.65 to .58	E
.58 to .52	F
.52 to .47	G
.47 to .43	H
.43 to .40	I
.40 to .37	J
.37 to .35	K

+ *Deflection is measured in inches with shaft supported on 26" centers and depressed with a two pound weight.*

* *AMO spine symbol designation.*

Bows vary in length from about four to six feet, for the most part, the shorter bows will produce greater arrow speed and are lighter and easier to handle. The shorter bows, fifty to sixty inches, are used mostly for hunting. The longer bows used in target and field archery are easier to draw, more stable and have a smoother release. The longer bows will shoot more accurately than the short bow. They measure from sixty-four to seventy inches in length. Therefore, when selecting a bow, one's height and the use of the bow must be considered.

Next in the selection of the bow is the draw weight. This does not involve the actual number of pounds an individual bow weighs on a scale, but the number of pounds of force required to draw the bowstring. This is the area where most beginning archers make their errors in selection. For your first bow, its best to purchase one that is light enough in draw weight to allow you to shoot accurately, while building your muscle tone and your confidence. After you have mastered the lighter weight bow, it is time to move into a bow weight that will suit your shooting requirements.

The bow weight for the beginner should be light enough for the novice to become proficient in the sport. For most women and children, twenty-five pounds is a good start. Then, depending on how much the individual shoots and practices, he can work his way up to a thirty or thirty-five-pound bow. In the case of the average man with a good draw length, a thirty-pound bow is good for the beginner.

The light bow allows the new shooter to draw the bow easily and not put a great strain on unused muscles. This allows the novice to give more concentration to developing good shooting habits, such as aiming, anchor points and holding. If a heavy bow was used initially, most new shooters would be shaking hard enough to put the arrow off the target and as a result may well become disenchanted with archery and may give it up entirely.

The next prerequisite in the selection of the bow is to determine how many pounds of weight the shooter is pulling at a full draw. Each person's arm length varies, so two people of different size drawing the same bow will be pulling more or less pounds of draw weight, depending on the length of the arms and chest. The person with the shorter arm span will be pulling less draw weight than the longer armed archer, when both use the same bow.

To simplify and standardize the selection of equipment in the sport of archery the Archery Manufacturers Organization, which is made up of all the major American Archery equipment manufacturers, came up with bow, string length and wood arrow standards.

Manufacturers who converted their products have

The arm guard is a major consideration for all archers. Shooting without one can lead to a painful arm bruises.

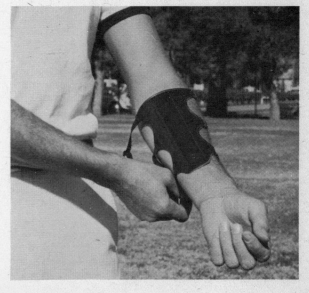

identified their products with the AMO symbol. The AMO prefix to bow lengths in inches mean that the bow has been manufactured to a length that properly uses a bowstring designed with the identical bowstring marking. An example of this is: A bow marked AMO 60" 50 pounds will brace to the proper string height with a string marked AMO 60" 45 pounds to 55 pounds.

What does this mean to the beginner when selecting his first set of archery tackle? The draw weight of nearly all bows is measured with the bow drawn at twenty-eight inches. This is the average draw length of all archers; if your draw length is shorter you will draw less weight than the AMO marking. Conversely, if one's draw length is longer than the twenty-eight-inch average, the pounds of pull will be greater than the AMO weight marking. The draw weight of a bow will vary with the length of the draw approximately two pounds per inch. Using a forty-pound bow, if a person's draw was twenty-seven-inches, the bow weight would be thirty-eight pounds or, if another archer using the same bow had a draw length of thirty inches, the draw weight of the bow would increase to forty-four pounds for that archer.

To select the proper bow weight, one first must have his own draw length measured. Perhaps the simplest way to accomplish this is to have another person assist you. Take a lightweight bow — around twenty pounds — then select a long arrow, thirty inches or more; next draw the bow to full length, anchoring the string on your chin at the corner of the lip. Do this several times, taking the most comfortable anchor point each time. After two or three draws of the bow, draw it again to the same anchor point on the face and have your coach or helper mark the arrow with a pencil on the face of the bow where it sits in the arrow rest. This should be done three or four times, each time having the person draw the bowstring to the maximum length and anchoring his hand on the face. The pencil marks will be within a fraction of each other and your draw length will be the distance from the pencil mark to the bottom of the slot.

Another easy way to determine one's draw length, especially if you don't have access to professional help or a bow, is by the use of a yard stick. This is the chest-to-fingertip method.

Place one end of the yardstick against the center of the upper chest at the approximate base of the neck. Then reach out on the stick with both your arms extended straight out in front of you. The distance from you to where the end of your fingertips measures on the yardstick is the correct arrow length for you. If fractions occur, choose the next highest whole number.

The third accepted way to measure your draw length is to have someone measure your outspread arms from fingertip to fingertip then use this table to determine your proper arrow length.

Arm measurement	Arrow length
57-59"	22-23"
60-62"	23-24"
63-65"	24-25"
66-68"	25-26"
69-71"	26-27"
72-74"	27-28"
75-77"	28-29"
over 77"	30-32"

The proper length of arrows is most important for if one purchases a shaft that is too short, he can overdraw the arrow beyond the arrow rest on the bow and injure the shooter or someone else. For the beginner, it's best

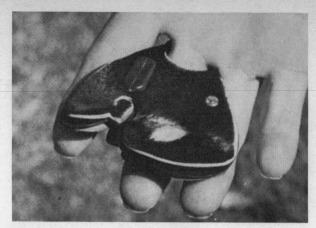

Finger tabs are recommended for beginning archers, as they keep the fingers from being scored by the string.

to shoot arrows that are a little longer than the draw length. As the novice archer progresses, he can shorten the shaft to the proper length.

The following is a series of excerpts from the American Manufacturers Association standards of most modern bows and arrows:

"AMO bow length standard is designed to be three inches longer than AMO bowstring master that braces bow at proper string or brace height. Bowstring master will carry only the bow length designation. Example: A bowstring master designated as AMO 66 inches (bow length) will have an actual length of 63 inches.

"Cable length is determined by placing loops over one-quarter-inch diameter steel pins and stretching under one hundred-pound load and measuring from outside of pin to outside of pin. Tolerance is plus or minus one-sixteenth-inch. End loops of cable will be 1¼ inches long and plastic coated.

"Bow weight is the force required to draw the bowstring twenty-eight inches from the back of the bow at the arrow rest.

"Draw length is the distance, at archer's full draw, from the nocking point on the string to the back of bow at the arrow rest.

"Arrow length is the distance from the bottom of the neck slot to the back of the arrow head. This standard applies to all types of arrow heads: target, field, hunting, et cetera."

For the arrow to hit the point of aim at which the archer is shooting, the arrow must be matched in spine to the weight of the individual bow. Spine, explained more fully elsewhere, means the stiffness of the shaft. As an arrow is released from the bow, it will bend slightly as it clears the handle, then will straighten out in full flight before hitting the target. An arrow that is not matched in spine to a bow will bend too much or not enough and be thrown off course while in flight to the target. AMO has set up standards for the selection of spine for wooden arrows:

"Draw length is the distance, at archer's full draw, from nocking point on string to back of bow. For standardization purposes, all bows are weighed and marked at twenty-eight inches draw length. To determine bow weight at draw length longer or shorter than twenty-eight inches, use the draw weight correction factor of twenty in the following formula: Bow weight at twenty-eight inches divided by twenty and multiplied by the

number of inches draw length differs from twenty-eight inches subtract or add this amount to the bow weight at twenty-eight inches, depending on whether or not draw length is shorter or longer than twenty-eight inches."
Examples:
1) Bow Weight = 42 lbs. Draw Length = 25½".
42 lbs. ÷ 20 = 2.1 lbs. X 2.5" = 5.25 lbs.
42 lbs. − 5.25 lbs. = 36.75 lbs. at 25½" draw length.
2) Bow Weight = 38 lbs. Draw length = 30".
38 lbs. ÷ 20 = 1.9 lbs. X 2 = 3.8 lbs. + 38 lbs. = 41.8 lbs. at 30" draw length.

NOTE: The spine recommendations shown here serve as a basic guide for wood arrow spine determination. The best spine for a particular need may not always correspond with the charts.

The bowstring also must be selected properly. When the bow is braced, strung, there should be a specific amount of tension on the limbs to obtain the proper draw weight. As a general rule, a bowstring is three inches shorter than the length of the bow. For proper fistmele or brace height, the measurement is done by using a bow square that attaches to the string at the nocking point and extends to the deepest cut in the handle of the bow. There is no set measurement for a given bow and the manufacturer's directions for brace height should be checked before making any changes in the string length.

Here again AMO has set up standards for bow strings and height:

"String height is the perpendicular distance from the bowstring to the pivot point of the bow handle, when bow is in strung condition.

"Bowstring length is three inches less than bow length designation (example: seventy-two-inch bow length requires sixty-nine inch string length) when loaded as per bowstring tension chart and stretched by placing string loops over one-fourth-inch diameter steel pins. Measurement is taken from outside of pin to outside of pin. Tolerance is plus or minus one-eighth-inch after twenty seconds under tension load of chart.

"Bowstring will carry only bow length designation and bow weight category. Example: AMO sixty-six inches 35-45 pounds."

The other tackle available to the archer comes in a wide variety and price range. For the beginner, there are several must items that come in the bow kits or can be purchased separately. Most important are the arm guards, finger tabs and quiver.

Arm guards are made of either plastic or leather; the plastic is a little cheaper in price, but all cost under $5. Finger tabs protect your three drawing fingers and come in a variety of forms, from a type of half glove to a small tab that just covers the string fingers. The glove may be a little more expensive but for the novice archer it should prove easier to control.

Quivers come in most every shape and size and can be hung from the hip, side or the back. This is mostly a matter of personal choice and whether you plan to shoot targets or hunt.

The bow stringer is considered by many instructors to be necessary equipment. There are several types on the market from an inexpensive cord type to a wooden bow stringer. The bow stringer will prevent you from twisting a bow limb, while stringing your bow and make stringing safe.

Other accessories include bow case, string keeper, nocking points, string wax, extra strings, storage rack, et al. The list of tackle is almost endless and, as you become more familiar with archery and the wide range of equipment available, you can select the proper tackle to fit your own needs.

No story about archery for the beginner would be complete without a mention of safety. Here are a few basic rules for adults and children. Before shooting any bow, check your equipment over to insure that there are no splits or cracks in the bow. Then carefully string the bow; most bow damage is caused by improper stringing or handling. Give a final check after the bow is strung to insure there are no twists in the limbs and the loops are seated in the bow nocks. Check the bowstring for worn or frayed spots and be sure the nocking points are in the proper position.

Arrows should be checked to insure that the fletching is secure and there are no cracks in wood or fiberglass shafts.

The golden rule of archery might be to never draw and release a bow without an arrow. Shooting a bow without an arrow can result in breaking the bow and injury to the shooter.

Along the same lines, don't try someone else's equipment unless you are invited.

Never shoot an arrow straight up into the air. This is extremely dangerous, as the arrow is difficult to track, when it is coming straight down on you and it can easily hit you or someone close by.

Use a target or backstop that will stop your arrows; bailed straw, cork or sandbags. Be sure that you are backed up by a hillside or suitable stop.

Check your shooting range to insure that there is nothing in the flight path of the arrow that will deflect it and cause injury to someone or loss of your shaft.

Wear an arm guard. If you don't, you will find out why this is a most important item of tackle, as you doctor your bruised arm.

When shooting on the range with other shooters, keep the nocked arrow and bow pointed down range and don't practice behind the shooting line.

After shooting your arrows, wait until the range is clear and move on command or with all shooters to remove your arrows from the target. When removing the shaft from the target, pull them straight out at the same angle they entered the target. Keep both hands close to the target as you pull.

Never shoot or point at anything you don't intend to hit. Use common sense and this will make archery safe for you and the sport.

Extreme heat or dampness may affect the bow, so do not leave your bow stored in the camper, car or attic where it will be exposed to heat. If the bow becomes wet, dry it off before putting it away. A coat of wax will protect your bow from the elements. To store a bow, it should be unstrung and hung vertically by the string or laid horizontally across two pegs.

The better care you take of your archery tackle the better it will perform. Be careful in the selection, then follow through with proper care. – *Chuck Tyler*

Is The Compound Bow For You?

WHEN COMPOUND BOWS came out several years ago they were regarded as "just another gimmick" by many hunting archers. There are few bowhunters today, however, who don't have a healthy respect for compound bows. The compounds are proving to be deadly hunting tools in the hands of competent bowmen.

I'm not a habitual experimenter myself, but I finally got around to trying a compound. It was an interesting experience and maybe, if you're one of the many undecided archers, I could share my compound bow experience with you and help you make up your mind.

As a bowhunter, I've always been pretty conservative with regard to equipment. But about a year ago, Tom Jennings, president of Jennings Compound Bow, Incorporated, agreed to loan me one of his bows for the forthcoming hunting season. I told Tom I would evaluate it strictly from a bowhunting point of view and that I was primarily interested in what it was like to hunt with a compound as compared with a regular bow.

The Jennings bow arrived in the Spring, giving me plenty

of time to get used to it before hunting season. The first thing I did was lose the set of wrenches that were included for adjusting and tuning the bow. But they had set it for sixty pounds at the factory, which was fine with me, and evidently they had tuned it well for me so I just started practicing with it.

I practiced a lot during the Summer, but never could get the hang of the bow. Along toward the end of the Summer, I was totally discouraged and nearly ready to send the bow back with apologies.

Somebody told me that I was having trouble because the release on a compound is far more critical than with a recurve bow. So I dug down in my gear box in the garage and found a Wilson Strap Tab release I'd experimented with a few years back. I took the release and the compound bow out to the dirt bank where I usually practice and was surprised to see that the little gadget did the trick. After shooting only a few arrows, I decided that the Wilson Strap Tab and the compound bow were made for each other.

Based on this early experience, I think I can say that

More and more compounds are seen at archery tournaments. The let-off provides for easier holding — important for a target archer who may shoot dozens of arrows in the course of a couple of hours.

anyone who is seriously thinking of getting a compound bow for hunting had better plan to try an artificial release if they have any trouble in adapting to the shooting peculiarities of the compound.

My first hunting experience with the compound bow was in August when I went up to Colorado for the archery deer hunt. I saw a lot of elk, but didn't get any action on deer. I did, however, get to do a heck of a lot of stump shooting with the compound bow. There's nothing like field practice to get you acquainted with a new bow. By the time I came back from the Colorado hunt, I was convinced I could kill any stump, dirt bank or weed patch that came within sixty yards of me and my Jennings bow.

While waiting for bow season to open back in New Mexico, I did some arrow experimenting. In Albuquerque, where I live, few people had compound bows at the time, so I had trouble getting advice on what size arrows to use. I'd been using sixty-pound wooden shafts and 2020 aluminums up to then, but needed to go to something much lighter to get the full speed out of my bow. That's one of the nicest things about a compound bow — the fact that you can use a substantially lighter arrow than with a recurve bow of equivalent draw weight. Jennings advertises his compound as being "up to fifty percent faster than any recurve bow." I don't have access to a chronograph, but I've been shooting hunting bows for a long time and my good, old twenty-twenty eyeballs are convinced that the compound puts out a horrendously fast arrow.

The arrow that I finally settled on was a 2016 aluminum, fletched straight. With the compound set on sixty pounds, the 2016s flew like miniature lightning bolts. The trajectory was so much flatter that for the first few practice sessions with these shafts I couldn't keep from shooting over the mark.

As opening day drew closer, I practiced more intensively with the Jennings, especially at longer ranges. The Sandia Mountains, where I do much of my bowhunting, offer the archer a lot of tempting shots at longer ranges. Fifty and sixty yards are not uncommon, and I knew that the compound, with its zippy arrow flight and its flat trajectory, could handle these shots.

On opening weekend, I had my first shot at a deer with the compound bow. I was easing around a bend in a trail that went alongside a meadow when a two-by-two buck appeared in the early morning mist across the meadow. He was about fifty or maybe fifty-five yards away, standing broadside, and looking like he was about to leave at any moment. I drew back, let fly, and missed. The arrow was too high. If he'd been a large camel, I might have grazed the top of the hump.

I was disappointed about missing him, but what the heck, I thought, his antlers needed to grow another year anyway. The interesting thing about missing that buck was that he had stayed perfectly still and not run away until the arrow had passed over him.

This told me that the compound was shooting quietly. The compound bows are advertised as quiet shooters, but I'd heard some that sounded downright noisy. I was worried about mine until after this incident. Actually, it's all in the tuning, as I learned later.

I had no more shooting action during opening weekend.

Bob Lambert prepares to try the Jennings compound for the first time. Compounds require much familiarization at first.

Later, about the middle of that week, I was prowling along down an abandoned Jeep trail toward sundown and came upon a bedded doe. She was about fifteen yards away and there was considerable foliage between myself and the doe. She had seen me, but I was wearing quiet tennis shoes and was fully camouflaged, so she didn't seem too spooky, just a little nervous. The problem was that I didn't have an arrow on the bowstring and my strap tab release was in my pocket. I'd packed away the arrow because I was on a steep downhill gradient and didn't want anything sharp poking on me if I should slip and fall.

Turning slowly, I faced away from the doe and quietly sneaked an arrow out of the quiver, attached it to the bowstring, then fished the strap tab out of my pocket and hooked it up.

I half expected the doe to be gone by the time I turned

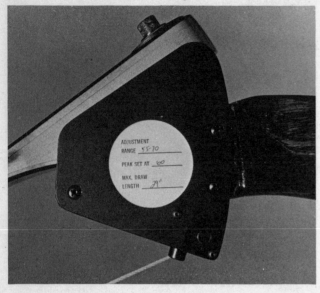

Tag on Jennings gives range of pull adjustment, peak set and draw length.

to face her, but she had stayed in place. Drawing back the arrow, I leveled the shaft at the base of her neck, aiming meticulously through an awkward tunnel in the foliage, and let go. The arrow went through the foliage and through the doe almost simultaneously. It came out the other side and disappeared in the bushes somewhere and I never saw it again. The deer dashed a short distance and went down dead.

As I walked over to the deer, I thought of how odd it was to have practiced all that long-range shooting and to get my deer at such a close distance as fifteen yards.

I think any bow would have done the job at that short distance, and I doubt if it would be realistic to say the compound bow was the deciding factor. The flatter trajectory of the compound bow may have been an aid, because the arrow had to get through a rather tiny opening in the foliage to get to the deer, but I'd hate to put any money on it.

If you're undecided about whether to switch to a compound bow, this matter of the compound's extra speed may have a bearing on your decision. The odds are really against you in bowhunting and anything you can do to tip the balance in your favor is worth considering.

Let's say that doe of mine had been a huge trophy buck

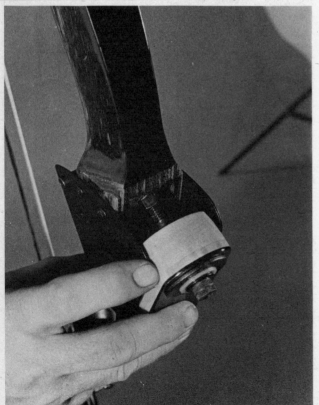

A closer look at the method by which the limb is adjusted on the Jennings. Note sturdy design.

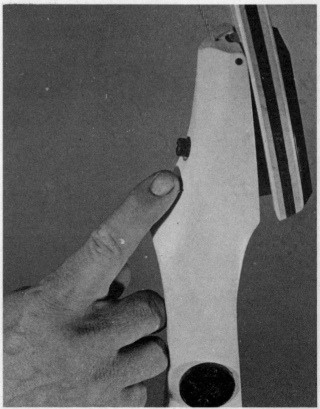

Limbs on the Wing compound are adjusted by this hex-head bolt.

instead, and let's say he was standing tense and ready to bolt instead of bedded down. A compound bow might very well have made the difference between a trophy of a lifetime and a thin air shot. I've seen a tensed-up deer whirl and get away from a recurve bow's arrow at a distance of eighteen yards, and I'm inclined to think a compound would have made the difference in that encounter.

I have no illusions that the compound-propelled arrow is inescapable, though. That dream was shattered the first time I took a thirty-five-yard shot at a spooky deer, which was about a week after I bagged the doe. The area where I do my bowhunting allows two deer, and I spent the rest of the season hunting with the compound, but didn't get a second deer.

This proves something. The compound bow, though definitely superior to any recurve bow, is not a cure-all. It does not add to the skill or luck of the hunter. The man behind the bow is the final deciding factor in whether or not game will be taken. There are plenty of guys walking around in the woods with fancy, expensive bows, both compounds and recurves, who have never killed a deer with an arrow and never will — mainly because they don't know how to hunt and aren't willing to learn.

But I think I can definitely say that anyone who is al-

The Precision compound has a turnbuckle for adjusting tension.

ready a hunter will be a better hunter with a compound bow in his hands. And probably anyone who is a serious-minded beginner will find his road to success a lot shorter if he starts out with a compound bow.

One really big advantage of the compound bow is that it's adjustable in draw weight. When you feel your strength gaining with practice, you may want to go to a heavier draw weight. With a recurve, you have to trade in your bow to do this, but with a compound you just get out your wrenches and dial it up.

When I used the Jennings bow, I got accustomed to the sixty-pound draw weight early in the season, so I located someone with a set of wrenches and we set mine up to seventy pounds. I worked with it this way for a few days, but didn't like it, so we cranked it down to sixty-five and I was satisfied with that draw weight for the rest of the season.

Another bonus you get with a compound bow is the substantial let-off in draw weight once you get past mid-draw. This allows you to have a rock-steady hold at full draw, even with a hunting-weight bow. Whether you're perched in a tree stand waiting for a whitetail to turn his body sideways or crouched on the ground waiting for a muley to meander out from behind a bush, you're unquestionably going to be better off with a compound than an ordinary bow.

On the disadvantage side, there are some things that might make you think twice before investing in a pulley bow. First of all, they seem to be in a state of evolution, as manufacturers continue to make changes in the original compound bow's design. Don't let yourself be a part of anybody's research program. Bowmakers have a responsibility to give their new products a full and thorough testing both in the factory and in the field before putting them on the market, and most do. But it's something to watch out for.

Another thing about the compound is that it's got so many moving parts, you need a dealer in your community to service it. If you happen to live in a remote area, you could have a whole hunting season ruined if your compound went haywire and you couldn't get to a dealer.

The sheer physical weight of the average compound is a matter to consider. The Jennings model I used weighed six pounds including bow quiver and arrows, a heavy burden to make matters worse, when I was stalking a deer, it became very cumbersome to maintain the compound bow in a semi-ready shooting position. The only answer to this problem is that manufacturers need to devise lighter materials for compounds without compromising on durability.

I see that several of the compounds now on the market do offer lighter weights, and that's encouraging. While the weight is going down on compounds, the price is not. They are just plain expensive.

The price may be what is keeping many archers from buying compound bows. Most of them cost around two hundred dollars and a lot of guys are reluctant to put out this kind of money.

I like the compound bows myself but haven't bought one yet. I think I'll watch them evolve a while longer and hope they get lighter. — *Ray Nelson*

TUNING TACKLE FOR ACCURACY

These Tricks Of The Sport Should Improve Your Scores

SUCCESS for the racing driver is based fundamentally on a superior car coupled with his superior skill. These two basics must be enhanced to the optimum level by fine tuning of the equipment and application of the driver's expert knowledge of the capabilities and performance limits of every vital part of the car.

Similarly, an archer must have good equipment and good technique as basics for competition. Performance will be enhanced by general as well as custom-fine tuning of the bow to the archer, and by application of the archer's technique with an eye for the effect of variables in equipment setup and use.

To illustrate a point, a friend of mine was having trouble with an occasional high arrow. The condition worsened until a little analytical thinking and checking revealed the nocking point on the string had moved a bit low, and the arrows were glancing ever so slightly upward from the arrow rest.

The equipment, in the first place, should be of good quality and closely matched to allow for proper tuning. Undoubtedly the arrows are the most important item of equipment for accurate shooting. Any old stick and string will do a fair job of grouping well matched arrows, but mismatched or random arrows will not group well even when shot from the most expensive bow.

The draw weight of the bow should be as heavy as one can draw repetitively and comfortably hold for aiming without quivering. The bow should be one of efficient design and materials, fast but without stack, narrow tipped but not to the point of sacrificing stability. Composite wood and glass recurved limbs designed to be fast, stable, and forgiving are a good choice for the serious archer. For those who wish to stray from the conventional, the compound bow has proven its worth in competition as well as hunting.

In field archery the shooter must draw and hold for steady aiming at least 112 arrows. The bow should be light enough that the archer may shoot the last few as effectively as he did the first few arrows. The hunter, on the other hand, uses a heavier bow as his shots are infrequent and penetration is of major importance.

Determine your arrow length by drawing a long arrow or a yardstick to a comfortable full draw. After a few practice draws to limber up, have a friend mark the arrow about one-half inch ahead of the arrow rest.

Selection of arrows to match the bow can be done quite accurately using the manufacturer's charts. Cast and design of a bow have much to do with selection of spine, but as these factors are not easily measurable, the charts are based on draw weight. Shooting technique and personal preferences will also enter into the experienced archer's choice of spine and, especially in aluminum, of shaft weight and point weight. Some professionals even shoot unpainted aluminums as they feel unequal paint thicknesses adversely affect uniformity.

Bow accessories affect performance and make the equipment either more or less tunable. Type and location of arrow rest, arrow plate, bow sight and nocking point all do something for tunability and accuracy.

The arrow rest should be located vertically over the pivot point of the grip so that torquing or heeling will not change relationship of the arrow to line of sight. It should be located only high enough on the window to allow positive clearance of the arrow over the shelf, yet provide some vision below the arrow as needed on long targets by the barebow archer. A small amount of upturn to cradle the arrow is permissible as long as it does not interfere with lateral movement (paradox) of the arrow as it leaves the bow.

There are many types of arrow rests. Some are rigid, some are flexible, and some get themselves out of the way as the arrow passes either by pivotal action or by flexing. With proper tuning the arrow need not touch the rest after the instant of release as the rest serves only to support the tip of the arrow before launching. A somewhat flexible rest is preferable to the rigid type, especially with a finely tuned bow where a poor release might result in the arrow glancing off the rest.

The arrow plate has been given greater consideration of late. There was a time when this item consisted only of a softer material than the wood of the bow, such as a piece of leather glued to the wood. Under some circumstances this is adequate, but for fine tuning something more sophisticated is needed.

As the amount of center-shot has a great effect on paradox, or the amount of horizontal wiggle the arrow goes through as it leaves the bow, a means of adjusting or building out the pad from the side of the sight window is desirable. It is possible to shim out the pad as needed, but this is quite inconvenient, and you are apt to do a minimum tuning job to avoid making many adjustments. An adjustable pad which screws in or out is much more convenient to use.

With the conventional release, there is some lateral bounce from the arrow pad at the instant of release, and the arrow should pass by the bow without touching. The amount of give inherent in the arrow pad or pressure point has a bearing on the amount of bounce. Under most circumstances the bounce from a rigid pad is too harsh. Something a bit softer is better, and the degree of give needed varies with the archer's shooting style.

This cushion effect is provided on some products by softness of the material used, or by spring action of a more rigid but thin material such as steel or plastic. Some manufacturers provide a means of varying the degree of resiliency by a pressure point which is backed by an adjustable spring or screw.

Stabilizers are desirable in target shooting. Some hunters like a modified type of stabilizer, but the advantage of this is questionable when weighed against the fact that a bow so equipped will be more tiresome to carry and somewhat slower to use when a quick shot is required. Stabilizers are made in many types depending upon the manufacturers' beliefs and the archers' desires. There are varied ideas as to what a stabilizer should do.

One school of thought feels that the stabilizer should prevent torque. The idea is to prevent the bow from moving until the arrow is well on its way, should the archer be inadvertently applying a twisting or heeling force. For this application the stabilizer generally consists of a weight held away from the bow on a rod. The longer the rod, the greater the amount of stabilization.

Sometimes a shock-absorbing coupler is used at the point of attachment to the bow to let the bow move slightly as the arrow passes and to make smoother shooting. This does have a cushioning effect, but whether such a flexible connector tends to defeat the purpose of the stabilizer in the torque department is a point of conjecture.

Another school of thought is that the purpose of adding weight is to absorb recoil, and for this purpose the stabilizer is short, or even integral with the bow handle. It may be of solid steel, or it may be of a flexible or shock-absorbing material. It may be single, or it may be distributed and strategically located in a plural form. This version of the stabilizer does help to minimize jar and makes a more pleasant shooting bow, but there is some sacrifice to torque prevention.

Stabilizers generally are placed forward of the bow on the back (the far side) for more than one reason. We already mentioned the torque prevention factor. Another reason is to cause the bow to tilt forward after release. This definitely is preferable to placing it on the string side which cause backward tilt and interferes with the string. The forward location helps to make the tail of the arrow clear the rest.

The exact setup or combination you will use for stabilizers should be in position on the bow when you tune and sight it in, as the stabilizer does affect arrow flight.

There are many requirements if one is to be successful in national tournament competition, but equipment that is right and is properly tuned is of major importance.

As a final check on the nocking height and its effect, stand twenty to thirty yards from the target. Using your regular fletched arrows, concentrate on the arrow's flight with both eyes open and watch for vertical wiggling or porpoising. When satisfied, install a nock locator permanently on the string. Check the nocking height with a bow square and note the reading for future reference.

Check for horizontal wiggle, or fishtailing, using the bare shaft method while standing five yards from the bale, noting the angle of entry in relation to the line of flight. If the nock end is to the left or right of sight line, adjust the arrow pad in or out for a greater or lesser degree of center-shot until the position of the arrow in the bale matches line. Also assure yourself that the arrow is not slapping the sight window as it leaves the bow.

Now that you have permanently established the nocking point, this is the time to finally position and install the peep sight or kisser, since the location of these accessories is related to the position of the nocking point. They should be of a height which feels natural and comfortable at full draw, with no undue cramping or straining of the anchor hand or tilting of the head.

When the distance of these items has been established from the nocking point, record them on your bow square, if it has provisions for these settings.

The last adjustment to make has to do with the vertical line of the front sight. When the sight is perfectly vertical, all shots near or far will be in perfect line. The trick is to assure that the sight bar is plumb on every shot. Instructions on mounting a sight generally advise mounting the sight parallel with the string. This is usually a good idea but not an absolute necessity. If you feel more comfortable with a canted bow, go ahead and set the sight bar on a slight angle. The only real limit is that the sight pin may disappear behind the bow when set low for long shots, but this can be remedied by using an offset string peep. It is important that the level and sight bar be exactly at right angles to each other.

The target archer uses a front sight on the bow. This can be an extensive subject, and we shall only touch on it here. The main points of consideration are type and location of the sight.

The most popular type consists of a vertical slide bar on which the sight carriage moves. The mechanism may or may not have convenient provisions or adjustments for windage, elevation, tilt, or movement of the sight bar itself. It may be calibrated numerically, in which case the archer uses his own table of sight settings derived from sighting in at the various distances. Or the sight may provide a blank tape upon which the archer will make his own height marks for the distances without need for a numbers chart.

Another style of sight is the quadrant type with a pivoted arm movable in elevation protruding at the back of the bow. The end of the arm carries a laterally adjustable sight pin. The quadrant is marked in degrees and increments of a degree for setting to predetermined elevation angles. The pin on this sight can even be set below the arrow for long targets.

Location possible with most sights may be on the face of the bow, on and close to the back of the bow, or extended from the back of the bow. It is generally conceded that accuracy is increased as distance of the sight from the eye increases. A limiting factor is that the forward set sight may require either use of a prism or positioning of the reticle below the arrow on the long targets. This is true especially in the case of light equipment and a short draw.

There are many other exotic and complicated types of sights intended to perform additional functions such as checking draw length and preventing torque. The archer must weigh the shooting correction value of these devices against the added costs and encumbrances and make his own determinations as to desirability.

The barebow archer uses no mechanical means of positioning the tail end of the arrow outside of pulling to a uniform anchor point. The sight archer is allowed aids for a more positive rear sighting action. In its simplest form the rear sight may be a mark on the string, or a bump of serving thread or tape at eye level. Perhaps the best, for those who do not find the limited peripheral vision too annoying, is a string peep.

An archer who anchors beside the jaw has a greater field of view through the peep than the shooter who anchors below the point of his chin since the peep hole is closer to his eye. The usual type is installed in the string itself, with half the number of strands passing on either side of the peep sight. A few turns of serving above and below hold it in place. There are also offset peeps which allow laterally parallel sighting in cases where the front sight is obliterated by a part of the bow or its attachments.

Some target archers use a kisser on the string, a wafer type of attachment which is positioned after the draw between the archer's lips, providing a more positive height for the anchor. In this case the vertical line is generally established by sighting beside the string. There are those who use both a peep and a kisser. This seems

Krista Kaiser, nationally recognized as a top college archer, understands the importance of stabilizer rod. Its purpose is described fully in this segment's text.

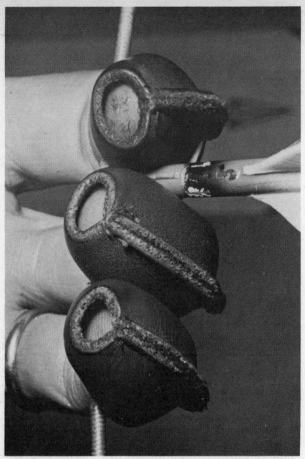

The nock should pinch the string just enough to be snug. Finger stalls should fit properly to protect against cut of the bowstring. Note the two-fingers-under hold.

like too much, as the peep alone will establish both line and elevation, but these shooters must have their reasons.

Some form of nock locator for uniformly positioning the arrow nock on the string is necessary. This may be a mark, but a bump for the nock to stop against is better. This bump may be built up of serving or tape, or it may be an item made especially for the purpose. It may be of a type made to slip on, shrink on, or clamp on to the string.

Use of a clicker or draw check has become very common. An important intent is that it alerts the archer audibly or visually when he has reached the exact draw length needed for uniformity of technique and height of impact. Some archers use the signal as a triggering aid — something that tells them when to let go — and feel this to be the main reason for using a clicker. The signalling instrument may be a simple stick-on device or it may be a sophisticated mechanical or electronic unit. A clicker for the barebow class must be designed for installation below the arrow.

Another item used in shooting a bow is the release aid. This may be a shooting glove or a simple tab for the conventional release. Tabs are available with various features. There may be one or two finger holes, or the tab may be held on the middle finger with a leather thong. Some have a leather surface while others feature a hair surface for greater slipperiness. There are tabs without the usual arrow slot for shooting with three fingers under and tabs with a lug to avoid finger pinch.

Lately fantastic scores are being shot with artificial release devices made generally of plastic in the form of

hooks and rings. A bowlock is one hook device which has been with us a long time.

A revolution seems to be taking place in archery equipment, with new items and new designs for existing items coming out in a steady stream. This is a good sign, as it indicates a rapidly growing sport with great interest and enthusiasm, and expanding technology.

The best bow in the world will not group the arrows well if the equipment has not been tuned to the particular archer using it. Merely installing the accessories of your choice on the bow will not guarantee accurate shooting. It is now necessary to do a step by step tune-up to get all these attachments performing at peak efficiency.

It is good to have the nock of the arrow pinch the string slightly. A good degree of pinch is indicated when the nock, while the arrow is hanging from the string, will support just slightly more than the arrow's own weight. Mid-Nox and Bjorn nocks are made to pinch the string gently. With monofilament serving, you can slightly sand the area of nocking for a good fit, if the nocks are too tight. If the fit is too loose, the string should be built-up with another layer of fine serving thread or tape. The archer who shoots with three fingers under will want the nocks to grip a little more, as the arrow must hold itself on the string during the draw.

Proper string (brace) height is a compromise between reduction of jarring noise and good cast. A low string height or fistmele makes noise and vibration upon release, moves the arrow faster. A high string height will provide smoother shooting with a sacrifice in cast. It is wise to sacrifice a little speed in order to have a smooth shooting bow. The greater string height should make the bow less sensitive and reduce the tendency of the string to strike the bow arm.

Try shooting at the bales using a long string for low string height and a short string for greater fistmele, twisting or untwisting (clockwise to shorten) the string for length variations. After arriving at a conclusion, use a string which will give you the length desired with only a few turns.

The nocking point of the arrow on the string should generally be slightly above the point where the arrow makes a ninety-degree angle with the string. The main object is to have the fletching pass the bow without bouncing off the arrow rest with a small angle so that the arrow planes downward. An amount of one-eighth-inch above square is often recommended.

This is not a hard and fast rule, as several conditions can affect nocking height. A bow with a more limber upper limb will require less (or no) additional height above square. Use of a stabilizer will lessen the amount required. Type of grip is another factor. A low wrist or heeling will require a higher nocking point than the high wrist position. The low wrist archer may need to position his nock locator as much as five-eighth-inch above square.

To check how the arrow leaves the bow will involve some prerequisites. You will need a butt or arrow stopper of a type which has little or no grain so that the position of the arrow in the butt will give a true indication of its angle of entry. A pile of sawdust or fine sand is probably the best material for this purpose. Also you will need some bare shafts or at least one arrow with the fletching stripped off.

To determine optimum nocking height, make a mark on the string using the bow square at a point one-eighth-inch above ninety-degrees. Standing five yards from the butt, take a few shots using the bare shafts or the arrow sans fletching. Note the average angle of entry. If the nock end of the arrow in the butt points downward from the line of sight, the nocking point is too low, indicating the arrow may be glancing off the rest. If the nock end points upward too much, the nocking point is too high. A slightly high condition is the better of the two. — *Emery J. Loiselle*

Compound Tuning Made Easy — Or, At Least, Easier!

COMPARED TO A recurve bow, the compound can look like a confusing piece of machinery, so it's only normal that a archer new to this piece of equipment wants to know what he has to do to keep it tuned for top shooting.

All of the compounds are pretty much the same in design, but we selected a Jennings model for use in investigating the requirements for tuning. So here are the step-by-step results of our investigations.

How To Change A String On Your Compound Bow

Step No. 1: Loosen jam nuts on weight bolts. Most archers keep jam nut only finger tight so it may be loosened in the field without a wrench. Apply counterclockwise force on the nut with fingers of left hand and simultaneously turn the weight adjustment bolt — using allen wrench supplied with your bow — counterclockwise and jam nut will loosen. Do not, at this point, loosen or turn tuning keys.

Equally as important, if not more so, is an easy way to replace a worn or frayed bowstring when the archer is alone in the woods or on the tournament field.

About five years ago, I was competing in San Diego King Arthur tournament. The bowstring on my compound bow suddenly resembled a feather duster, with most of the strands broken. The strain of one more shot no doubt would put my bow out of business.

At that moment, to my knowledge, there was no device which would hold the "S" hooks in position while a new string replaced the frayed one. At least, no one in my group had anything of that nature.

The archers in nearby foursomes probably figured the members of my group had lost their minds. Not so. We were combining our resources to replace the old string. Our ingenuity came up with a method something like this:

Ken Ostling, a tall and strong Las Vegas indoor champion, grasped the eccentric cams, one in each hand. He then sat down and placed his foot into a hand grip. He requested Calvin Ridenour to hook on the new string while he, with exertion of considerable strength, relaxed the cables enough to allow Ridenour to hook on a new string. My assignment was to keep quiet and stay out of the way.

While the procedure accomplished the task of changing a compound bowstring, each of us figured there had to be a better way. As of this writing, there are several devices manufactured especially to hold the bowstring loops in their respective positions and tension. The one, in my estimation, which is the easiest to use and most efficient for a lone archer in the woods or on the tournament field, is shown and described in the photos here and on page 67.

The device is the product of Pat Norris, owner of Bonnie Bowman Archery in Oakland, California. A local dealer should be able to supply what I have described.

Since cramming the bowstringer into a hip pocket would prove an undesirable method of transporting the item, what's the best way? My suggestion is to tape the device to your bow quiver, into the middle of your spare arrws. I don't believe the deletion of one arrow will be noticed. Of course, if the archer uses an over-the-shoulder quiver, transportation would present no problem.

Step No. 2: Before you go hunting or attend a tournament, you should mark the limbs along the sideplates at your favorite draw weight. This is in case you lose count of the end-bolt turns, or the end bolts come all the way out. Loosen end bolts approximately eight turns — will vary some depending on the draw weight of your bow — by turning end bolts counterclockwise. Cables and string should be loose, but not out of the tracks in the end wheels.

Step No. 3: Lay the bow on its side with string facing you and sight window up. Turn right eccentric end wheel clockwise until it snugs the cables, then drop your allen wrench in the lighting hole in the wheel that is closest to the back side of the limb. Turn left eccentric counterclockwise and drop a pen, pencil, small stick, nail, etc., in the lighting hole nearest the back of the limb. This will keep the eccentric wheels from turning and letting the cables tangle on the tuning keys or come off the idlers. The string should be loose at this point and come unhooked easily. Unhook the string, noting double-loop hookup on S hook. Replace new string in the same manner on the S hooks.

Step 4: Remove allen wrench and other pin from the eccentrics. Make sure cables are in the tracks. Take up end-adjustment bolts approximately half the number of turns you let off. Examine end wheels to make sure cables are in the tracks. Examine cables at the idler wheels. Examine cable at the tuning keys to make sure the cable is not crossed. Cable must be laying even and no overlapping at any place on the tuning key. Cables should be easy to move into correct position; however, if they are too tight, loosen

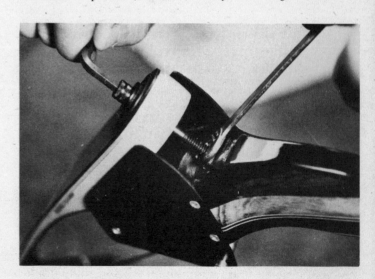

Step one involves loosening of the jam nuts on the weight bolts. Usually, these are kept finger-tight when in the field.

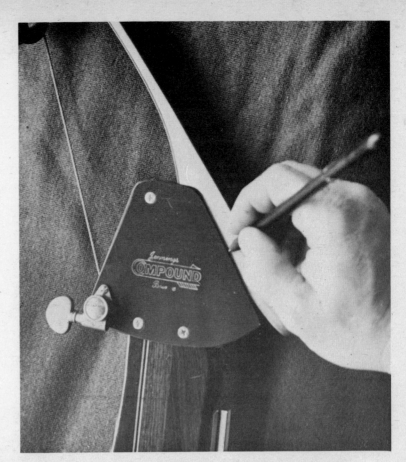

Step two: Mark the limbs along the side-plates at your draw weight. This is to prevent your losing count of the turns.

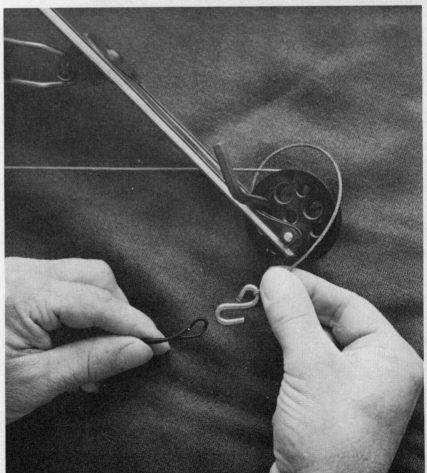

Step three: Lock eccentric in place so that string can be unhooked without snarling.

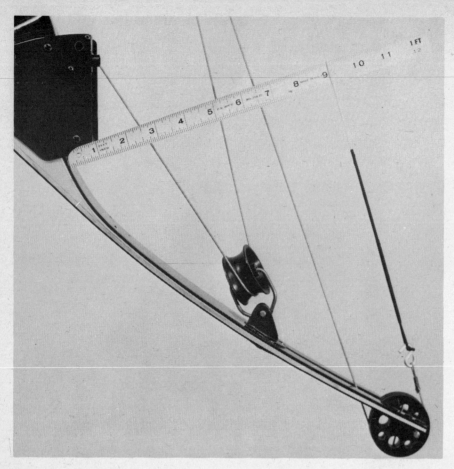

In changing the cable, measure the tiller height for both of the limbs and record the distances, marking the sideplates.

end bolts enough to take off tension. When cables are right, take up end bolts to line on limb or the correct number of turns.

Step No. 5: Replace nocking point, kisser button, peep sight, etc. A bow square is necessary for this job if you want to do it right. Hunters should have a prepared string

Typical tuning keys, as discussed.

complete with nocking point, with them in the field at all times.

How To Change A Cable

Step No. 1: Lay bow down with sight window up and string facing you. Measure tiller height. Measure both limbs. Record. If you have a favorite draw weight and have your limbs marked along the side plates, you will not have to measure tiller. Loosen jam nuts and let off both limbs approximately eight turns, as in changing a string.

Step No. 2: Start at fray or break in cable to be changed and follow to tuning key which controls this cable. Loosen lock screws in tuning key of cable to be changed. Turn Grover-type key counterclockwise to loosen and cap screw-type of key clockwise to loosen. Loosen key until all wraps are off the reel.

Step No. 3: Grasp cable one-half inch from hole in reel and push cable into hole and keep pushing until stop swage comes out the end of the reel. At times, it is necessary to probe with a thin instrument — ice pick, scribe, etc. — into end of the reel to dislodge stop swage. Snip stop swage off cable with sharp cutting pliers. Pull cable out of reel. Unthread cable off idler and out through the slot in the limb. Turn eccentric wheel until setscrew in center of the wheel is opposite end of limb. Remove this set screw completely. Use small, round pad to protect cable from being cut by set screw. Save this pad.

Step No. 4: Unhook string from S hook. Remove cable from eccentric. You might have to out-shrink tubing from cable to pass through hole in eccentric. Your replacement cable will come with S hook installed, new shrink tube and new stop swage. Drive a finishing nail into a board. Hook the old cable and the new cable on the nail by the S hooks. Make ninety-degree bend in the new cable exactly the same

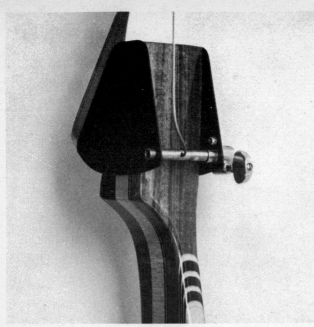

Turn Grover-type key counterclockwise
to loosen and cap screw-type clockwise.

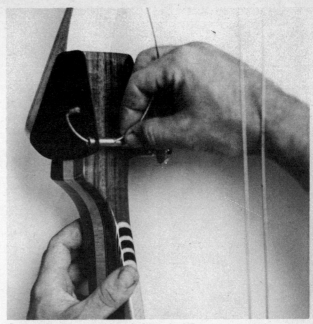

Grasp cable one-half inch from hole
in reel and push cable into hole to stop.

Author discusses hand position and technique for final tuning by means of
shooting arrow into the backstop and making adjustments as indicated.

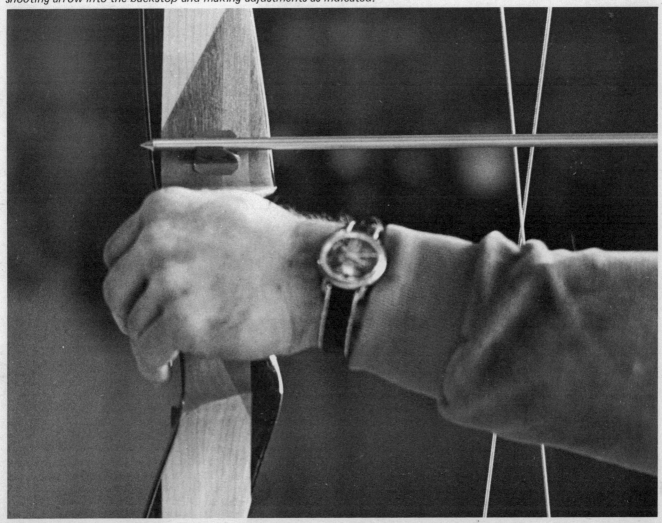

Sandy Hildreth, of Potsdam, New York, used her compound to bag a buck at John Lamico's Colorado camp.

as the old one. The factory does not pre-bend the cables, because this varies with the size of wheel, draw length, etc., of your bow. Feed new cable into eccentric wheel in the same direction you removed the broken cable. Replace round pad in setscrew hole. Screw setscrew in until it makes contact with cable. Make one-quarter turn more

Step No. 5: Slip on shrink tube and feed cable back through idler in the same direction as you removed broken cable and into the hole in the reel of the tuning key. Pull cable out of end of reel and pull until eccentric stops turning. Measure four inches from the end of the reel and cut cable with sharp cutting pliers. Slip on copper stop swage and swage with tool supplied. Pull swage back into reel as far as it will go and bend cable slightly to hold. Turn the Grover tuning key clockwise until you have two turns on the reel. Cap screw tuning-key counterclockwise Re-hook string, making sure cable with S hook, extending out of eccentric, is wrapped around eccentric through slot in limb before you hook up string. Take up several turns on end-bolt adjustment screws to take slack out of cables and string. Note: If your limbs are not marked, be sure and keep track of turns so you can return to your favorite draw weight.

Step No. 6: Take up on new cable tuning key until eccentrics balance with each other. Do this by observing the distance between the cable near the S hook in relation to where the cable goes into the eccentric. Take up only the tuning key where you replaced the cable. Do not turn the other key, as it should stay in original position for a single-cable change. Fine tuning is done by feel. Shrink the shrink tube with a match, torch or any other movable source of heat.

Fine Tuning Your Tournament Compound Bow

1. Check the tiller heights. To refresh your memory, the lower-limb tiller should be one-eighth inch less than the upper.

2. Test draw your bow to check roll-over of the eccentric cams. If they don't roll together, adjust by means of the turning keys mounted on the sideplates.

3. Install a handle center-reference point. To do this, place a two-inch piece of masking tape between the upper sideplates on the inside of the handle so you can see it when bow is held at arm's length. Mark an accurate center line between the two sideplates that can be seen from five or six feet. This will be used as a visual center reference.

4. Install a squeeze-on nocking point — do this gently, as you might be moving it later. Locate it five-eighths of an inch above ninety degrees from the arrow rest. This set-up is for nocking point over the arrow, one-fourth inch Bjorn nocks and ledge-type release aid. Finger shooters, using a leather tab, usually prefer to nock slightly lower by approximately one-sixteenth of an inch. Nocking points, of course, are personal and require slight adjustment by the individual archer.

5. Clamp bow in vertical position in a padded vise. Nock arrow and place on arrow rest.

6. Adjust your cushion plunger or adjustable rest in or out until the bowstring bisects the arrow from point to nock when the string is aligned with the center-line mark on the masking tape — pasted between the two upper side-plates. Stand back several feet to do this aligning. Double check nocking point height and that your cushion plunger — if used — strikes center of the arrows.

7. Stand at shooting mark, approximately six feet from a unidirectional backstop — excelsior bale is good — placed at shoulder height. Shoot with your best technique. Should arrow enter nock right — right-hand shooter — increase poundage. Work one pound at a time — one-fourth turn. Remember, both limbs exactly the same. If arrow enters nock high, lower nocking point. If it enters nock low, raise

nocking point. Finger shooters may require a cushion plunger or adjustable arrow rest set slightly outside of center.

8. When you have acquired good arrow entry at six feet, try several at twenty to thirty feet. If you get extreme deflection, either you are too center-shot or you are striking your fletching. Adjust center-shot out just a little. If you think you are striking the lower hen-feather fletching rotate nock on the arrow.

9. The best hand position is a straight wrist with the back of the hand flat, bow handle load carried on the base of the thumb — not the thumb. The less thumb contact with the handle, the better. If you shoot with a low wrist, turn your hand so the knuckle line is diagonal to the vertical line of your bow.

10. With a release aid, you can shoot bow weight — holding weight — down to fifteen pounds or less with good arrow flight. Some finger shooters find it difficult to get good arrow flight under thirty pounds — holding weight. Since you are always holding and releasing a lighter weight with a compound bow, a good, relaxed release will have to be developed. The more you shoot your compound the better your release will become. You will learn to relax your fingers after the peak load, which occurs at mid-draw. — *Roy Hoff.*

Several companies make restringing aids. This one is from Bonnie Bowman Archery, Oakland, California.

Chapter 4

Servicing Your Compound

REPAIRING YOUR OWN compound bow seems to be taboo to manufacturers and compound owners alike. Manufacturers usually provide instructional literature with new bows, but much of it is devoted to what not to do, along with warnings that tampering may result in nullifying the guarantee. You are advised to run to your dealer when any little thing goes wrong. This is understandable, since the compound is a sophisticated piece of equipment, easily damaged by a tinkerer who hasn't proper knowledge and understanding of the mechanisms. Most compound bow owners go along with this advice.

What if you live fifty or one hundred miles from a dealer? Can you afford the time and expense of waiting for your bow to be returned from the dealer or manufacturer? With proper know-how, you can do a better job of adjusting and repairing your compound, because you will put more time and tender loving care into it than the dealer.

If your bow is still under guarantee, reread the manufacturer's warranty and warnings, and do nothing to void the guarantee. Next, check over your specification sheet to make sure it is current and accurate. Check the limb size, eccentric size, bow weight range, draw length range, draw weight setting, draw length setting, upper and lower limb tiller measurements, and nocking height. Make reference marks on the bow for checking the settings in the ball park. Mark the limb centers between the side plates; scribe a line on the side of the base of each limb along the edge of the side plates, and mark the sides of the eccentric wheels along the back of the limb tips.

Become familiar with your compound. This text relates to a right-hand bow of the early conventional Allen and Jennings version. Consult your manufacturer's literature for more pertinent illustrations and information. Most compounds are manufactured under the Allen patent, and the workings are similar, although the means and mechanisms may differ.

Close visual inspection of all the parts and workings of the bow will do wonders to help you understand and remember the intertwinement of parts and adjustments. Look at the limbs and notice how they are attached to the bow.

The compound is a sophisticated piece of equipment, but with proper know-how you can do a good job of adjusting and repairing.

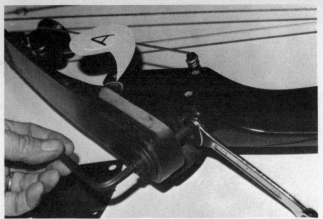

Left sideplate is removed to show half-round phenolic block on which limb pivots when limb bolt is turned in or out.

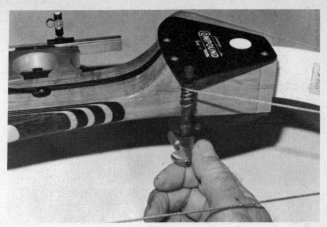

Cranking in the cable at the adjusters will increase the draw length, but draw weight also will be increased.

See what the weight adjustment mechanism, perhaps a limb bolt, looks like. From the side, notice how much the limbs are angled from the riser. Study the amount of bend of the limbs in the strung position, and refer to your specifications to see if your bow is set in the upper or lower end of the bow weight range.

From the back of the bow starting at the S-hooks, follow the cable to the eccentric. Notice that it almost encircles the left-hand groove before entering a hole drilled at an angle through the diameter of the wheel. The cable exits in the right-hand groove, following that groove for just a short distance before going to the idler pulley and cable adjusters at the opposite limb.

Note that in the strung position, an imaginary line drawn through the axle and the center of the wheel is quite parallel with the limb. The main portion of the wheel is forward of the axle, and the long cable going to the opposite idler is

farther from the axle than is the pigtail (S-hook portion) of the cable. Leverage is negative in nature in this position, making the draw heavy near the start.

Draw the bow slowly while watching the upper eccentric. Note how the forward portion of the wheel rises out of the limb. As the wheel peaks over, the front and rear cable sections become more equidistant from the axle. At full draw the leverage situation has reversed, so that the forward cable section is closer to the axle than is the pigtail section. Leverage is now working for you in bending those heavy limbs. In effect, the 180-degree turnover of the eccentric has lengthened the limb, making it easier to bend. This is what provides that wonderful let-off or decrease in draw weight at full draw. The more the axle hole is offset from center, the more let-off is provided.

Note that, as you draw the bow, the long forward end of the cable winds up in the empty right-hand groove, while

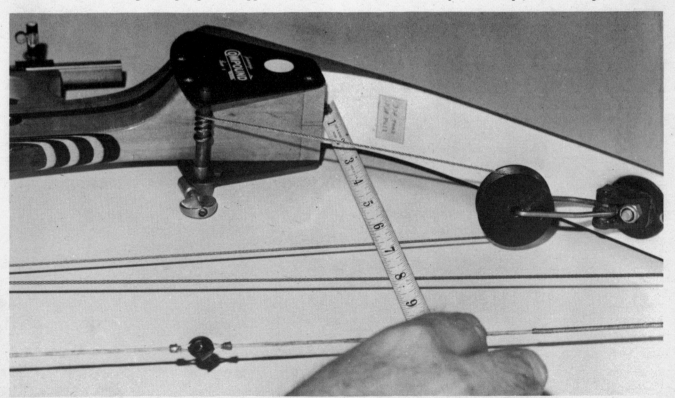

Tiller is difference of upper and lower measurements taken perpendicularly from string to deepest part of limb base.

Above: At rest, eccentric wheel is pulled forward and down into limb slot. Diameter through axle is almost parallel with limb. Below: At full draw, diameter through axle is still almost parallel with limb, but eccentric has rotated 180 degrees, giving longer limb leverage and let-off in draw weight.

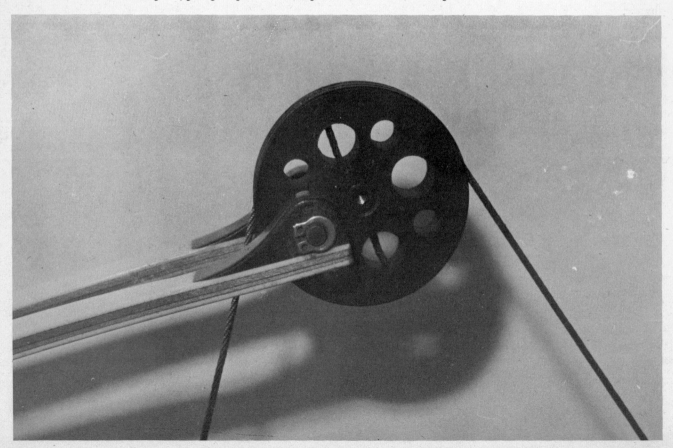

the long pigtail wrapping in the left groove plays out. With the bow at rest, inspect the empty space in the left groove where the cable enters the hole to where the pigtail leaves the groove. If the wheels are the right size for your draw length, there should be just a little empty space, but the cables should not touch each other.

A small amount of space here indicates the draw length is set to maximum in the draw length range, giving the most let-off. A large empty space in the groove, say one inch or so, indicates the wheels are a bit large for you. You can increase the draw length by cranking in the cable at the adjusters. With this condition, you have less let-off but a faster bow.

At the opposite limb, the same cable riding over the idler pulley helps bend the lower limb, and this is why all adjustments interact with each other. Tightening limb bolts to increase draw weight humps up the limbs, pulls the idler pulleys farther apart and pulls the eccentrics deeper into the limbs and increases draw length. So, when you heavy up the bow, you must also shorten the draw length by letting out cable at the adjusters.

Tiller can be measured with a tape measure or roughly checked with an arrow by placing the point against the deepest point at the base of the upper limb. Hold the arrow perpendicular to the string; place your thumb nail on the arrow at the point where it crosses the string. A similar check at the lower limb without moving your thumb on the arrow should normally show a slightly shorter measurement by one-eighth to one-quarter-inch This difference is not always proper, depending on your push point with the bow hand, height of the arrow rest or limb strength.

The eccentric wheels are in good balance when, by visual inspection or by feel with the bow hand as you draw, both wheels peak over and reach their stops at the same time.

Adjusting features on the conventional compound consist of a pair of limb-adjusting bolts for changing draw weight and a pair of cable-adjusting mechanisms for adjusting draw length. Making these adjustments is not that simple, as movement of any single or any pair of the mechanisms will interact with and change any or all of the other adjustments. These instructions are brief, so consult your manufacturer's instructions also.

DRAW WEIGHT — Decreasing draw weight by turning out the limb bolts also lets the wheels rise up out of the limb slots a bit, decreasing draw length as well as draw weight, so now you must adjust the draw length by taking in cable. Work back and forth between limb bolts and cable adjusters until both draw weight and length are correct. Count turns and do the same to each mechanism of a pair in order not to disturb wheel balance. In doing the reverse to increase draw weight, make sure you do not exceed the weight range of your bow.

DRAW LENGTH — Cranking in the cable at the adjusters will pull the wheels deeper into the limbs thereby increasing draw length. This interacts also to hump up the limbs and heavy up the bow, and there is a danger that you might exceed the top-rated weight for your bow. Therefore, when increasing draw length, let out the limb bolts a couple of

turns first, then touch up back and forth between pairs of adjusters, doing the same thing to each of the pair to avoid upsetting eccentric balance. Draw length is shortened by letting out the cable, then cranking in the limbs a bit to bring the draw weight back up to normal.

ADJUSTING TILLER — Chances are the bow was tillered correctly when you purchased it. If your tendency is to stress the upper limb more than ordinary (high wrist or high-set rest), you may need to adjust for less than the one-quarter-inch variation or minus tiller at the upper limb. To do this, turn in the upper and turn out the lower limb bolts the same amount. This will not change draw weight or length, but it will upset wheel balance. You will have to bring the eccentrics back into balance with the cable adjusters, and a slight relocation of the nock locator may also be in order. The inverse is true — if you heel the bow or walk the string below the arrow, thus stressing the lower limb more, you may need more tiller, perhaps over one-quarter inch more at the upper limb.

ADJUSTING ECCENTRIC WHEEL BALANCE — Perhaps the most disturbing and baffling condition is when the eccentric wheels get out of balance. This occurs when something slips, the bow has been serviced or a curious person turns one of the adjustment mechanisms. There should be no need for fear, once you understand what happens and how to correct it.

Try this little experiment just to see what happens and to learn by feel that the wheels are out of balance: Let out the cable at the upper key about four complete turns. This adjuster controls the eccentric on the lower limb. This will put the eccentric wheels out of balance, and you can now learn to see and get the feel of this condition. The immediate effect of that simple maneuver is that the eccentric balance is adversely affected. Also, the lower wheel turns over first and reaches full turnover first. Draw weight is reduced as well as draw length. The riser is unstable, since the lower end will move forward and then back during draw. Tiller of the limbs is changed, and the nocking point is raised.

You can see as you draw the bow that the lower wheel starts turning first, stops at full draw before the other, the lower end of the riser moves forward at mid-draw and the long stabilizer jumps upwards. At rest, you can see that the upper eccentric is now pulled deeper into the limb, and that the empty space in the left groove is now less than at the lower wheel.

By feel, you will note that the draw is not stable and smooth. The riser rocks in your hand as you draw. The bottom end moves forward, while the top end moves backward. You can feel the uneven rotation of the eccentrics in your drawing hand as an up-and-down movement. With a little experience, you can feel this phenomenon more accurately than you can see it.

To bring the bow back into balance, crank in the cable at the upper key the four complete turns you previously let out. If the lower end of the riser moves forward first as you draw, crank in cable at the upper adjuster and out at the lower. Do the opposite for an inverse condition.

The amount of empty space in pigtail groove indicated by the pencil is a key to whether eccentrics are of the proper size for a particular archer's draw length.

Repair work should be accomplished with the bow lying on a tabletop or flat work surface padded with corrugated board or a piece of old carpeting. The bow should be positioned window-side-up, string nearest you, and upper limb to the right. All instructions apply to a right-handed bow — reverse for left-hand.

Before doing anything to your bow, study the working mechanisms and cable routing, and form a mental picture of them. Be sure present specs are recorded and reference marks are established on your bow. Bear in mind the limits of draw weight and draw length for your particular bow, and be certain you don't exceed them. Always turn the upper and lower adjusters the same amount to keep the bow in balance. Use these instructions in conjunction with the manufacturer's literature.

RELIEVING TENSION — For lengthy storage, it is wise to relieve tension on all parts of the bow, including the string, by loosening the jam nuts and turning out the limb bolts four full counterclockwise turns.

CHANGING A CABLE — Proceed, as in changing a string without a bowstringer, to loosen limb bolts eight full turns, and place the bow on a padded work surface with window up and top limb to the right. Tension the bowstring a bit to pull the wheels up in the limb slots, and place a tool like an ice pick into the lightening hole nearest the backing of the limb in the eccentric having the cable which will not be changed.

This is to avoid disturbing the cable which is to be retained, especially the coil of cable at the tuning key drum. Even if both cables are to be changed, proceed in this manner and work on only one cable at a time, so the undisturbed cable can be used as a sample and for reference in routing, installing and adjusting the new cable.

Follow the frayed cable to the tuning key which controls it. Refer to the manufacturer's instructions for your particular model. In the case of a Jennings bow, snip the cable close to the adjusting key, unravel the short end from the mandrel and push the cable into the little hole in the drum until the end with the stop swedge protrudes. It may be necessary to poke from the opposite end of the mandrel with a long thin punch or an ice pick to dislodge the swage. Snip off the swage, then grasp the cable near the small hole in the mandrel with pliers and pull the end through.

Loosen the setscrew holding the cable in the eccentric

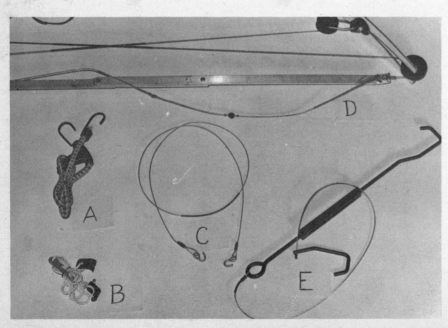

Various types of compound stringers: (A) Rubber shock cord; (B) tent stake cord; (C) cable with S-hook terminals; (D) folding slotted claw flatbar; and (E) turnbuckle for two-wheeler T model.

wheel and, grasping the S-hook pigtail, pull the cable from the eccentric. If the cable has shrink tubing at its center, slit the tubing for removal, or cut the cable above the tubing, if you have no use for the old cable. The old cable could be used in making a bowstringing tool.

Prepare the new cable by making the ninety-degree pigtail bend at exactly the same location as in the old cable. If you have a pigtail-bending template, this is the time to check to see that the bend is in the exact location for your wheel size and draw length. Push the free end of the new cable through the diameter hole in the eccentric, making sure the cable enters the hole end which is in the upper groove.

Pull the cable through until the pigtail bend bottoms in the groove, then lock the cable in the eccentric by turning in the setscrew until it bottoms on the cable, then give it a quarter to half-turn more. Route the cable through the idler pulley at the opposite limb, making sure that where the cables cross at bow center, the cable from the lower wheel crosses over and not under the cable from the upper wheel.

If the new cable is not plastic-coated, slip a length of heat shrink tubing onto the cable at this time. Push the cable end into the small hole in the tuning mandrel after

bending the end up slightly with pliers, so the cable will come out the upper end of the hollow mandrel. Pull the cable until the eccentric is down in the limb slot; measure and cut the cable to leave four inches protruding from the end of the mandrel. Remove one-half inch of the coating if the new cable is plastic-coated, and install a stop swage on the end of the cable. Grasp the cable at the small entrance hole in the drum and pull the stop swage into the mandrel as far as it will go.

Loop the pigtail end with the S-hook through the limb slot and around the upper groove in the eccentric, then hook on the bowstring, looping it around the S-hook in the same manner as at the opposite limb. Check the cable routing against the undisturbed cable, making sure it is properly seated in the grooves at the eccentric and the idler pulley.

Turn the adjuster in the proper direction to wind on the cable. Keep some tension and guide the cable onto the mandrel in neat coils with the other hand. Tighten until the eccentric is pulled into the limb slot the same amount as the opposite eccentric. Tighten the limb bolts the eight full turns you had loosened them. Check during tightening to be sure the cables are seated properly at the wheels and the

Idler assemblies with removable axles can be installed without detaching cables at the adjusters.

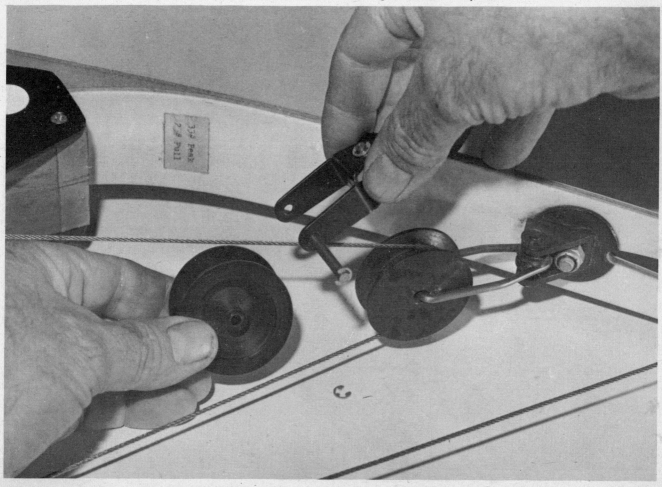

coils are close and neat on the tuning mandrel.

Also check after four turns to see if the eccentrics are still synchronized. Compare the empty space in the pigtail grooves and readjust the tuning key for only the new cable, if necessary. Shrink the tubing on the cable at mid-bow, if the cables are not plastic-coated, with a match or a candle. Check out the draw weight and tiller measurements, and make final adjustments by feel as described in the section on adjusting eccentric wheel balance.

If the intent is to change both cables, now is the time to start on the second one, repeating the same procedure described for the single cable change.

CHANGING ECCENTRICS — If you are changing only one eccentric due to a damaged wheel, it will not be necessary to disturb the good wheel or its tuning key. Proceed as for a single cable change with the addition that you will replace an eccentric wheel as described later.

If both eccentrics are to be replaced with wheels of a different size, remove both cables completely following the procedure in the section on changing a cable.

Prepare the new wheel, or wheels, and cables prior to removing the old wheels. Place the new eccentrics on the work table in their relative positions, Number 1 to the right upper limb and Number 2 to the left with stamped numbers up, with axle holes away from you. If changing only one eccentric. make the pigtail bend in the new cable at exactly the same location as the old. If replacing with different size eccentrics, you will need a cable-bending template or jig, or

a table of pigtail lengths for the various wheel size and draw length combinations to determine the exact pigtail length for your situation.

Make the right-angle bend in the cables. Insert the loose end of one cable into the diameter hole from the right side of wheel Number 1. This end of the hole should be in the upper or left-hand groove of the eccentric. Pull the cable through with S-hooks pointing toward you, until the pigtail bend bottoms in the groove. Lock the cable by turning in the setscrew at the center of the wheel.

Remove the old eccentrics, noting the position of parts on the axle. Remove the upper retainer ring, then with the axle overhanging the edge of the workbench slightly, drive the axle down with a long slender punch just enough to remove the upper spacer and the eccentric. Leave the lower, or longer, spacer in position on the axle. Move the new wheel with cable into position over the axle in the limb slot. Keep the stamped side up, and place the spacer on top of the wheel. Insert the punch through the limb bearing from the top into the spacer and the wheel to keep everything aligned. Tap the axle up from the bottom, while moving the punch about to center the parts over the axle. When the axle protrudes at the top, reinstall the upper retainer ring. Repeat the same procedure at the left or lower limb.

Route the cables, and install the ends in the cable adjusters. Install the string, then wind in cable and tighten limb bolts all as described in the section on changing cables. The cable should coil upward on the reel as you wind. Limb

The end of the new cable is pushed into the small hole and out the upper end of the hollow reel and snipped off, leaving four inches for coiling. Note the swaging tool on the sideplate.

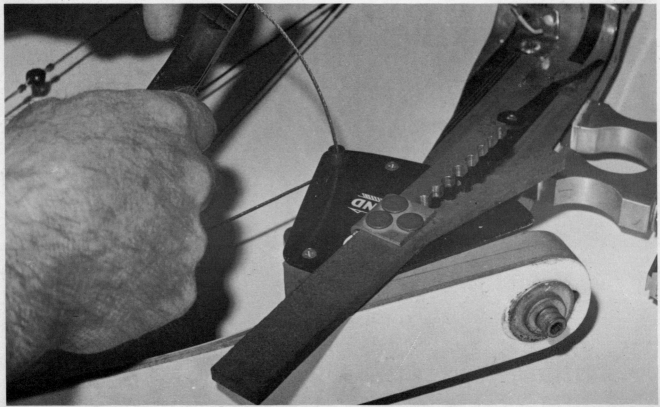

butts may have become dislocated, so check the seating of the half-round pivot blocks before fully tightening limb bolts.

Refer to previous sections on adjusting and setting tiller, and adjusting draw length, draw weight and wheel balance. Adjust roughly at first, then alternate between pairs of mechanisms for final touch-up.

If both eccentrics were changed for a different size, the bow setup is essentially from scratch. The draw length is easily checked and adjusted, but you will need a method for setting the bow at the draw weight you desire. Speaking of draw weight, different-size eccentrics will change the weight range of your bow, so be sure to keep within the new peak weight allowable. If you don't have a bow weighing jig, here is a way to check bow weight. Place a bathroom scale on the floor of your garage or basement. Hang the bow at its deep handle center from a large peg in an overhead joist above the scale. Tie it on, if you wish, to make sure it won't slip off and bean you. Pull the bowstring down while standing on the scale. Read the lowest figure the scale drops to at about mid-draw and again at full draw. Subtracting these figures from your true physical weight will give you the peak and relaxed draw weights.

CHANGING IDLER PULLEYS — In changing idlers, if the mechanisms are different from the original, and the wheels are nonremovable from the brackets, you will need to break down the bow as you would in changing cables, including snipping off the stop swage to remove the cable end for threading through the new wheels. The new wheel brackets attach to the limbs with one bolt each.

If the change involves replacement of only one bracket similar to the old, proceed as in a single cable change, retaining undisturbed adjustments at the cable going through the idler, which will not be replaced for reference in setting up and balancing after installation of the replacement bracket. This will also require snipping of the stop swage to thread the cable through the new bracket.

If you are replacing only a wheel or wheels, and the existing brackets have removable axles, you will not need to snip the stop swage or remove the cable from the tuning adjuster. Also, you will not need to unbolt the wheel bracket from the limb. Simply relieve tension by turning out the limb bolts eight turns. Remove the retainer rings to remove axles at the idler wheels, install the new wheels on the axles with cables in place over the pulley wheels, snap on the retainer rings, then crank in the limb bolts eight turns.

CHANGING LIMBS — Replacing limbs on a compound involves complete breakdown, reassembly and adjusting of the bow. This is not as difficult as it sounds, since it is merely a combination of the procedures for changing eccentric wheels, idler pulleys and cables, if they are also to be replaced. Setup and tuning of the bow will be from scratch, using adjustment instructions previously covered and reference measurements from your personal specifications sheet. — *Emery J. Loiselle*

The new cable and replacement eccentric are in relative position for installation. Note proper manner of wrapping pigtail after installation.

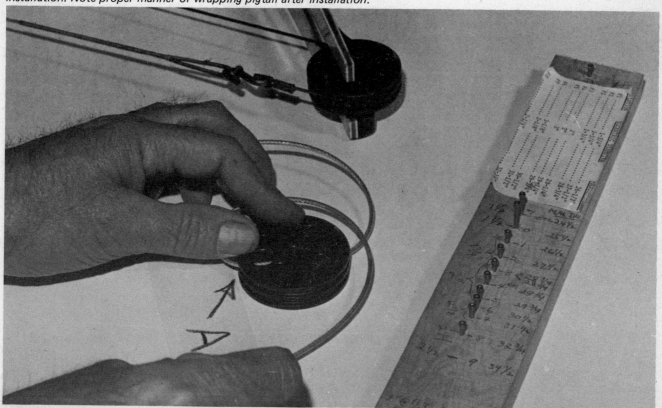

Chapter 5

GETTING THE SHAFT

Arrows Have Been Fashioned Of Many Materials, But Here Is A Rundown On What's Happening Today — Starting With Aluminum

Jim Easton practices what he preaches. Long an avid competitor, he uses shafts of his own manufacture on range and in the field.

WHAT BEGAN AS a boyhood intrigue with the bow and arrow developed, over the years, into a full-time, highly complicated business that found James D. (Doug) Easton dubbed "Mister Arrow" by archers around the world.

Easton died in 1973, but by that time, his son, James Easton, had become an executive in the operation. The younger Easton has taken over and continues to offer the quality and know-how that were his father's trademarks.

The late Doug Easton was a soft-spoken man whose quiet manner was hardly indicative of his knowledge and background in the field. At the time of his death, he had more than forty years' experience in all facets of tackle making, but he became best known for the aluminum arrow shafts, which he perfected. Today, the Easton shaft is sold in virtually every free country around the globe.

The fact that a major aluminum company attempted to build a similar arrow and failed is evidence of the thought and professional know-how that has gone into the development of the Easton line, which today encompasses thirty different sizes. Included are arrows for every weight of bow and of every accepted arrow length.

As a youth, Easton was shooting in a field near Watsonville, California, his home, when an elderly gentleman also armed with bow and quiver happened along,

The two exchanged thoughts and ideas, the elder offering some expert advice and finally pausing to inspect the youthful neophyte's home-built bow.

"Where did you learn to make this kind of bow?" the older man asked.

"I read Doctor Pope's book," Easton replied.

"I am Doctor Pope," was the simple reply.

Easton was somewhat awed by this chance meeting with the fabulous Saxton Pope, one of the all-time great shots and a pioneer in the development of modern day archery equipment. The doctor was, at that time, conducting his medical practice in the vicinity.

Precisely what direct effect this chance meeting had upon Easton's future is impossible to chart, but in 1922, he began the manufacture of archery tackle. Today, the Easton plant occupies some 75,000 square feet of floor space in Van Nuys.

Each run of shaft is controlled in weight to better than 1/500th of an ounce from the master samples, and spine — or stiffness — is controlled to better than .001 inche of deflection. These two close controls are what make the finished arrow accurate.

However, there was a time when Doug Easton momentarily felt that the complete laws of physics had gone awry, and that his empire was about to crumple about him.

One of his customers returned a dozen arrows, complaining that they were not uniform. When placed upon the scales, Easton found this to be true. In fact, the needle virtually went crazy; it was impossible for an aluminum arrow to weigh that much.

Eventually he removed the points and found that some of the shafts were empty, some were full of water, and others were partially full.

To the day of his death, Easton didn't know how this came about, although he suspected it was the purchaser's idea of a practical joke.

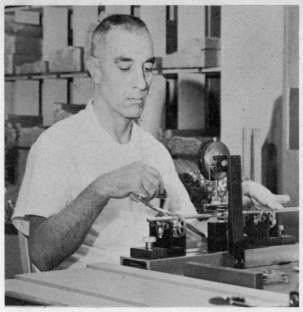

Although the Easton plant has an especially designed shaft straightening machine, it has been necessary to straighten some of the shafts by handwork.

To install point on aluminum shaft, the nickel-plated steel point is crimped into short length of a high-strength aluminum tube. Assembly then is glued with hot ferrule cement into shaft. Cutaway shows the fit.

Although we were given the complete Cook's tour of the plant, and a minute explanation as to how the arrows were manufactured, much of this information regretfully cannot appear in this story. Some of these trade secrets, derived from long years of experimenting and the development of expensive machinery, are only slightly less classified than the missile program.

There also are machines that make the variety of target points designed by Easton, and to swage the finished arrow shafts to the nock.

Each of the arrows turned out in this California plant has the identifying number sandblasted into the surface of the metal, and each of the shaft sizes and alloys is marked differently by machine.

Before the days of high development among alloys brought about by World War II, Doug Easton experimented with cedar arrows and was recognized for his

Spine is the measured deflection of a shaft depressed at center by 870 gram weight. Tolerance of the spine is maintained by the exacting diameter and weight controls.

Nock has been ground away to show conical taper in the aluminum shafts, protecting against damage to the end of arrow. The plastic nock may be shot away by another arrow, but taper is designed to divert the points.

work in this field. In fact, such champions of the era as Ruth Hodgert, Larry Hughes, Ralph Miller and others set records with these shafts.

But Easton realized that no two pieces of wood, no matter how perfectly matched, have exactly the same characteristics of weight and density. Further, these properties can change with variations in humidity, and other factors.

Doug Easton always was inclined to marvel at the patience necessary to produce near-matching arrows. To make arrows of championship quality, it was necessary to take selected cedar in a large-enough single billet to produce 250 shafts.

The wood was split, sawed, milled for the beefwood footings which strengthened the point of the arrow, then glued, trimmed and rounded by turning.

The extremely high strength of today's Easton aluminum shafts is checked constantly on this tensile tester by actually pulling segments of the shafts until they break. Continuing checks are made of each lot of shafts turned out to insure that the strength is maintained.

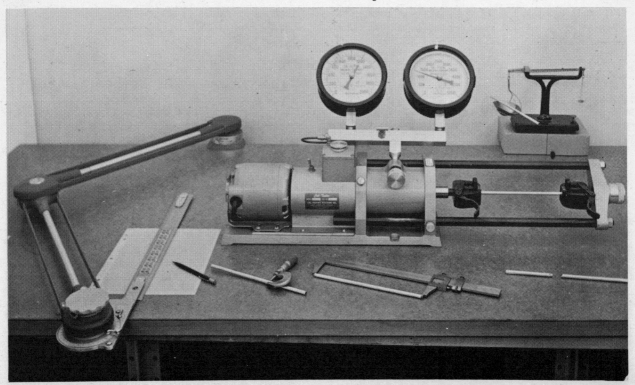

But this was only the beginning. It then was necessary to segregate these shafts by weight, then by spine and balance, which could be regulated by fine tapering. Out of this, there might be a few dozen tournament arrows that were matched properly. And it was through these labors that Easton came to realize the need for standardization.

During the war years from 1941 to 1945, when most aluminum was being absorbed in aircraft, Easton was

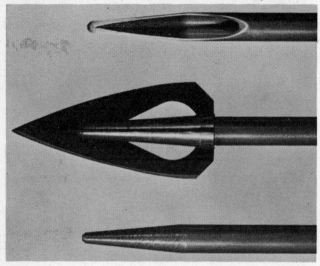

Cutaway shows how the aluminum shaft is tapered in its forming to carry the broadhead. At bottom is the shaft as it is seen upon delivery and before it becomes an arrow. This is done today only on custom-order shafts by Easton.

Various heat-treating phases follow the drawing of the shafts from alloy stock of larger diameter. The final stage is the immersion of the shaft in a molten salt bath, followed by a quick quench in cold water to give it the proper temper.

only able to procure enough for experimental purposes.

But before the war put a clamp on strategic materials, Doug Easton had perfected an aluminum arrow of tubing that measured 9/32 inches in diameter with a wall thickness of .020. It required a point with enough weight to balance the finished arrow two inches in front of center, and weighed 400 grains — or sixty grains less than a similar arrow of cedar. It was with a set of these arrows that Larry Hughes took the 1941 National archery crown at Portland, Oregon.

This particular arrow, incidentally, is still a member of the Easton line and is listed as the No. 1820 shaft.

During the war years, like many another manufacturer on the verge of success, Easton found the moratorium on aluminum a frustrating experience, but continued to experiment with an eye toward the day that hostilities would be ended. In 1946, he set up the machines of his own design for drawing the one-inch aluminum tubing down to the size of the shafts he wanted. And it was during this era that the alloy now called 24SRT-X(R) was developed. This particular compound boasted a high tensile strength which has been steadily increased by new developments in the field of metallurgy. Today it tensile tests at well over 90,000 pounds per square inch!

Today, in addition to the arrows bearing the 24SRT-X trademark familiar to serious archers, Easton is producing shafts in other alloys, which contains zinc as well as the earlier alloy's manganese, magnesium and copper. These shafts bear Easton's designators of XX75(R) and X7(R)

The Easton firm hasn't turned out finished arrows for approximately twenty-five years; their crew is kept busy simply keeping up with orders for shafts.

In addition, the defense industry has found Easton's tolerances so rigid that the plant is making some aircraft and electronics components from finished shaft material. In fact, watching hundreds of arrow shafts being chopped into lengths of less than an inch is enough to make an avid archer weep!

In 1948, the firm was producing sixteen stock sizes of aluminum arrows and an order for a hundred shafts was considered big business. With the new international interest in archery and its renewed place in Olympic competition, the name that the Easton shaft has developed for itself has come to mean quality and accuracy; a single order may run as high as 120,000 shafts.

In keeping with the idea that to stand still is to move backwards, the Easton firm is making aluminum products for other sports that have found an instant market.

Easton also makes ski pole shafts for such companies as Scott USA, K2 Corporation, Allsop, Hope and others for use in their highest quality ski poles.

The first successful aluminum bat for college play was developed and produced by Easton in 1972. Although aluminum bats for Little League and softball have been around for several years, Easton was the first to solve the technical problems required to make a bat of usable weight and still maintain the strength and dent resistance required for college-level play. This bat was the first aluminum bat to be made with the same weight and balance characteristics of the best wooden bats.

Other Easton products are lightweight tent tubing, backpack frames, deep-sea trolling rod butts and ultra-precision industrial aluminum and stainless-steel tubing for the aircraft and aerospace business.

There have been many success stories based upon blood, sweat and toil; the late Doug Easton's is one of these stories and that success is being added to by his son. It simply proves that, if you want the world to beat a path to your door, don't worry about mousetraps. Build a better arrow! – *Jack Lewis*

FORGING AHEAD

Wooden Shafts Have Taken On A New And Accurate Look Through Scientific Matching!

ONE of the first materials used for arrows was probably a reed. These usually grow straight and have few if any kinks, but they certainly aren't strong. Next came the small shoots of willows or some other straight wood and today we can pick from the best dowelled woods and the synthetics such as fiberglass and aluminum.

The first arrows usually purchased by a novice archer are Port Orford cedar. This is the cheapest and most available material for making arrow shafts. But when the hunter tries to get a cedar shaft with the proper spine for his new hunting bow with a sixty-pound draw, it is next to impossible to find a cedar material that will give the proper spine.

Each archer has his own requirements that a shaft must meet and these usually are most exacting. One other factor is cost. When a hunting shaft is shot at game it often isn't recovered. Not many of us can afford to throw three dollar aluminum shafts into the woods and forget them.

There is a shaft material that has greater strength than Port Orford cedar, the weight of glass or aluminum, and the proper spine to meet the exacting requirements of the tournament archer or the most critical hunter. These shafts are Forgewoods.

There has been a great deal said about this material the years I have been in archery, but I had never seen any. When a product sounds as good as the Forgewoods, there is no better way to find out than first hand.

A letter to Bill Sweetland, operator of the Forgewood plant in Eugene, Oregon, brought a dozen Forgewoods in a variety of grain weight but with the spine to match my fifty-one-pound Drake Hunter. I had asked for a variety since I wanted to determine which would fly best from my bow.

In the same carefully wrapped box were two Forgewoods spined at 20-30 pounds and two spined at 70-80 pounds. This, of course, was less and more spine than I required but it had interesting results.

The nine shafts spined for the Hunter had a low grain weight of 360 and a high of 415 grains. This, as mentioned, was intentional. The little shafts weighed in at 260 and 280 grains respectively. These were in a diameter of one-quarter-inch and looked like knitting needles compared to 11/32s I have been shooting. The fifty-pound spiners were of 18/64, and 19/64 registered as 18 and 19 in the catalog. There were the #20 or 20/64 shafts in the 70-80 spine and they weighed in at 520 and 580 grains.

These weights were on the cards wrapped around each group of shafts, but being the doubtful type, I put them on my balance to see how they trued out. Right on the button for all shafts. This card business was a new one to me also. I have gone through a few hundred Port Orford cedars, breaking them and losing

them in the field. Over a period of time, I have learned a bit about shaft materials. In the usual order of one hundred there might be a few extra heavies that will weigh in at 350-400 grains or more. This is still the raw shaft, no fletch or dip added.

The card that comes with the Forgewood is what might be called its pedigree. When I found the shaft I liked, all I had to do was check back to identify each shaft and send either that code number or the card itself to the Forgewood plant and I could be guaranteed of receiving a set of duplicate shafts.

These shafts had some unusual characteristics. They were without doubt the smoothest I ever had received. The diameters are smaller than the 11/32 and this made me wonder how they would perform in comparison. Included with the regular group of Supreme Forgewoods were two Battleshafts that were footed. The method of manufacture on these footed Battleshafts and the regular unfooted Forgewood is unique.

Bill Sweetland started making Forgewoods in 1949 and still is experimenting to make a better product. He had the idea for Forgewoods for years but felt he didn't have enough knowledge to do the job as he thought it should be done. What better way to learn

Forgewood, a compressed cedar, has been developed to the point that shafts are matched and react the same on bow.

about timber than going to college and majoring in forestry? This is exactly what Sweetland did and was graduated from the University of California. He tried his hand at that field but kept coming back to his original ideas regarding the manufacture of Forgewood arrows.

The first steps in the manufacture of these shafts parallels the regular Port Orford cedar shaft in that the best possible aged cedar is found and cut in the forest. These bolts measuring about thirty-six inches in length then are brought to the factory and stored in a cool warehouse to prevent end-checking or cracking. From this point on they lose any resemblance to the regular cedar process.

The bolts are brought into the shop, run through a

saw to get one flat surface, then the entire bolt is cut into flat-grained boards about seven-eighths-inch thick and uniformly trimmed to thirty-four inches long. Some batches of cedar are cut slightly thinner or thicker to adjust the final density, since all boards will be compressed to the same final thickness of seven-sixteenths-inch.

They again are stored under controlled conditions and after proper time and humidity factors have been met, are brought in for compressing. The secret of the Forgewood process is kept in the hands and books of Sweetland and he won't allow anyone in the press room, but he explains the process in this manner: the boards are stacked into a great hydraulic press. The press is set to stop at seven-sixteenths-inch so any boards cut to seven-eighths-inch thick will be pressed to twice their original density, or two hundred percent. Other boards will be pressed to 170, 190 percent, et cetera to get the various spine and weights desired. The pressure is applied by the hydraulic press together with the proper temperature for a specified length of time. They use no plastics resins or fillers in the process but merely compress the natural cedar to their specifications, before it once again is stacked in a warehouse to regain equilibrium with the atmosphere. Another two inches of length will be trimmed off so the thirty-two-inch pressed boards may be cut into squares. These squares are put into a dowelling machine and the finished Forgewood emerges from the end of the doweller. Sweetland wasn't satisfied with the usual dowelling process so he modified his machines.

This might be the end of the process for most shaft materials but is merely the beginning for the Supremes. The shaft material is sanded to give it a high gloss and uniformity, then it is passed onto a machine that will grade each according to quality. This quality test includes straightness, uniformity and a check for possible knots or other imperfections. After grading by machine, all shafts again are checked visually by women trained to spot imperfections. The shafts then pass onto an electronic spine testing device where they are spined. They are weighed on a Shadowgraph and sorted.

The Forgewood Practice grade, the lower priced line, is made with the same exacting care as the Forgewood Supreme, the only difference being that Practice shafts didn't measure up to the rigid requirements to obtain the Supreme label. The shafts that don't meet the Supreme label will be sorted into descending quality grades named Battleshaft, Hunter and Practice grades which are matched according to standards set by the company. These are offered to the archer at a reduced rate and even the Practice grade will give him excellent rabbit or squirrel shaft material.

As the Supremes are weighed and spined those that fall into the heavier spine and grain weight also are separated to give the hunter the heavier spine required for his bow and a variety of grain weights.

Another process gives the archer what is called a "footed" shaft. In past days they used cedar for the main part and on the tip they would splice in a heavy, strong wood such as purpleheart to give the shaft a stronger spine toward the end, where it normally breaks. Sweetland devised a system to give the archer a footed shaft without the problems of splicing.

For footed shafts in Supreme, Battleshaft or Hunter grades, the blank is cut with greater thickness on one end, the thicker section to become the footed end, the thinner to be the nock end. This material is put into the hydraulic press the same as the regular shafts but when compressed, it comes out with a higher density on the foot or tip of the shaft. This also gives the footed Forgewoods greater weight if someone desires an extra heavy shaft.

The shafts are coded by having the nock ends marked with a red dye to show the nock end of unfooted shafts. For footed shafts, the nock end is color coded with a black dye. These footed shafts have the tip of the shaft compressed 2.1 times the density of regular cedar and it wouldn't do to get the wrong end at the nock, hence the color coding system. The

Bill Sweetland, developer of Forgewood, checks a bolt of cedar in storage at Oregon plant awaiting big squeeze.

unfooted shafts are compressed uniformly throughout except for the nock end, which is somewhat softer. This gives the arrow the quick recovery action of a tapered shaft, but again it is important to put the nocks on the dyed end.

The first Forgewoods were sold to dealers and to archers and not many finished arrows were made at the plant. In recent years, Sweetland has added a fletching and dipping section as well as cresting so he can now ship completed arrows coded to an archer's needs with a pedigree card attached. They still sell the raw materials for those who prefer to make their own shafts.

Sweetland started archery at an early age and his inventive bent comes from his father, who was an

To illustrate the toughness of Forgewood after it has been compressed, Bill Sweetland drives a dowel from an arrow shaft through plywood of an inch in thickness.

inventor. Sweetland found he loved archery and when he graduated from the University of California in 1938, he accompanied his parents on a trip to England and while there competed in the FITA tournament as a United States representative. He bowhunts every year and has many deer to his credit. This, of course, helps him in his work and research since he has first hand knowledge of the problems and requirements of the archer, both in the hunting and target phases.

He combines his other hobbies of canoeing and raising racing pigeons with his hunting trips. The canoe was one of the first methods of transport in the early west and can be used in any water area to great advantage when hunting. On his hunting trips he quite often takes along a racing pigeon and upon arrival at his hunting area, releases the bird to fly home with a message to the family that all is well.

He designs a great deal of the machinery used in his plant. He is continually experimenting and recently took a piece of red cedar 2 x 4 and compressed it to total density. This gives it about the same characteristics as lignum vitae in regard to weight and density.

When I received my Forgewoods, the first step was to mark the tip end with the diameter size, the weight in grains and the spine. I planned to dip them in clear lacquer rather than a color so I could watch the wood and see what, if anything, happened. I took two of

the shafts while dipping and put them through my favorite Chinese red dip to give them the usual treatment of my other shafts but reserved the rest for the clear dip.

After marking the tip with the code I devised I cut to my twenty-eight-inch length from the nock end to retain as much of the density on the tip as possible. The footed Battleshafts didn't cut any different than the usual cedar.

I smoothed the cut, then filled my dip tube with one part clear lacquer and two parts thinner ratio. When I dip my cedars, I usually let the arrow drop down with its own weight, then push it to the bottom slowly pulling it out of the tube to get the best coating I can. I cheat a little and use a silicone additive for better coating and smoothness.

When I dropped the Battleshaft, as I usually do, it plopped straight to the bottom of the tube! I had forgotten the simple fact that these shafts had the air squeezed out of them and no longer were buoyant like normal wood. There was no way to retrieve the shaft other than pouring out the dip, shaft and all, to get it back. From this point on I held onto all shafts while dipping. I dipped them twice to get a good even coat.

I took half of the shafts and ground the nock end and the taper for the field tips and broadheads on a standard grinder. I prefer this method and had no trouble with the Forgewoods. The other half I cut with the Blackhawk taper tools.

Included with these shafts were several nocks for the 16, 18, and 19 diameter shafts. For the big 20s I used some five-sixteenth I had in the drawer. All these nocks were two colors for each size. For my Battleshafts, for example, I put on black nocks and a three-fletch spiral green-dyed gray bar hunting fletch. All fletch used was five inches in length and one-half-inch high with a parabolic cut. I made them as I normally would except for each different weight or type I used a different color nock and fletch color. On the little 20-30 pound 16s I put a three-inch target fletch, using Dupont Duco cement.

For the first shooting I decided to use the taper hole field tips included in the set with four headshrinkers and some taper hole blunts. These field tips and blunts are made by Sweetland to match his quality shafts. The Match-All points have the tapered nonskid tip that I prefer, but the best part of these heads is that they fit flush with the finished shaft. On the five-six-teenth shafts—the 20s—I used some regular field tips and the difference is worth mentioning.

The standard field tip leaves a high ridge around the back of the head where the tip is supposed to be flush with the shaft. I believe the taper hole field tip is stronger than the parallel type. I seem to have less breakage with the taper, at any rate. One great advantage of the flush fit of the match-All is that it makes it easier to pull from bales.

With the fletching done, tips added and all codes recorded I started shooting the Forgewoods. I compared them with the regular Port Orford cedar I had on hand and with some fiberglass shafts. I had designated that these Forgewoods would be used for field tips and broadheads so they were a bit stiffer in spine than regular target shafts would be.

All shafts flew true and the only difference I found was the difference in weight of the shafts. After several sessions with the Forgewoods I could take a shaft and place it where I wanted, then take a lighter or heavier shaft and put them in a good group. Of course this was an experiment and any regular set of Forgewoods all would weigh the same, within the tolerances shown in the Forgewood catalog.

I also included the 500-plus grains of the 70-80 pound spined shafts and found that, even though they were about twenty pounds over my spine, they flew straight but I did have to allow for that extra weight. You take a raw shaft of 580 grain, add a 125-grain field tip plus about 40-50 grain of fletch and dip and the

Peg driven through board with hammer shows little damage, although it did round off in forcing way through wood.

Left half of this length of Port Orford cedar has been compressed to fifty percent density for hunting shaft.

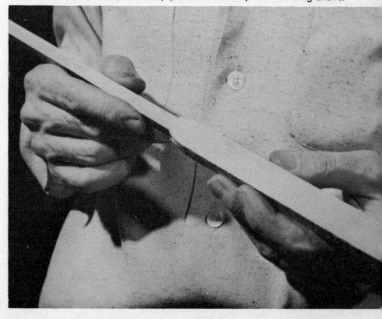

Forgewood arrows, shot through this three-quarter-inch pine plank, showed good penetration and proper toughness.

nock and you are getting up there in the weight factor, but these heavy shafts were designed for a bow 20-30 pounds heavier than mine. For penetration they would be terrific.

Then I became curious about the little knitting needle 16s. I had shot them from my wife's target bow that draws only twenty-two pounds and they had shot true. I hunted through the closet for my old horsehide jacket, put it on along with a good heavy glove on the bow arm, added shooting glasses to protect the eyes, then took the 16s out for a thirty-yards shot at the bale with my fifty-one pounder. I expected the shaft to explode in the bow on release; that is the reason for the protection. This type of shooting isn't recommended, but it was in the interest of science.

I came to a half-hearted full draw, then pulled the final kinks out of the arm and let fly. The arrow didn't explode, it went so fast I had trouble following it to the target. It was dead center, no right or left movement, but right where I had been holding. Since this experiment I have shot this shaft many times to show others how it will move out.

This brought up the age-old question of spine. Here I was shooting a mixed bag of shafts, some at 20-30 spine, most at 50-55 and two at 70-80 spine and there was no apparent right or left deviation. Whether I unconsciously allowed for this I don't know. All I know is that all shafts flew straight and the only problem I seemed to have was vertical, due to weight variance.

During this testing I intentionally shot a footed Battleshaft into a cement block wall at a distance of about twenty yards. I expected the shaft to break and it did. It left the field tip imbedded in the cement and the shaft broke cleanly about three inches from the

tip. Cedars, when they break, will splinter up the shaft and make slivers. Glass will more or less explode, the walls of the shaft collapsing. The Forgewood seemed to break like the fiberglass in that it didn't splinter. I bent, twisted and tortured the shaft to see if it had splintered up the shaft. This same thing happened to one of the little 16s when it went through the bale and broke on the wall. My bales get badly shot up by using broadheads in them so I also dropped another Supreme through the bales to make three broken on the block wall and all the same characteristics.

The next thing I wanted to know was how the Forgewoods performed with broadheads on their ends. This is where the ingenious headshrinker comes in. None of the shafts would take the 11/32 broadheads I had. The headshrinker is made of aluminum by Sweetland to remedy this situation. The inside diameter of the head shrinker is designed to fit the different Forgewood shafts and the outside diameter will fit the 5/16 or 11/32 broadheads. How else could you properly mount an 11/32 broadhead on a 18/64 shaft? I took the torch and *Ferr-L-Tite*. I attached the headshrinkers to the three different broadheads with the hot stick-type cement, then the entire assembly to the shafts with the cement. I used the Black Diamond Eskimo, the Ace HiSpeed and the Black Copperhead Magnum, all at 125 grains. The first two are two-blade heads and the Magnum is a four-blade type, but all blades are the same length, no bleeders added.

For me the best way to tell whether the shaft is flying true is to back off at least fifty yards and let the broadhead fly. Closer, the wind doesn't enter into the problem. I held all in a good group.

I took the Forgewoods on a hunting trip last fall. They were in a quiver with bits and pieces of camping gear stacked in, around and on them for about 2,000 miles. We had rain—not in the wagon, of course—but they did get damp and when I got back and tried spinning them, they spun as true as when I left.

After trying all the shafts, I think for my own personal needs and desires I would prefer the footed Battleshaft. This affords the added strength that I like in the tip of the arrow and I can get just about any spine and grain weight I need. Although the Supreme is a little closer in spine and weight tolerances, I can match my shafts with my equipment and I can use the economy of Battleshafts. I like the smaller diameter of the Forgewood shafts and they stay in my Bear bow quiver with no problem.

Bill Sweetland, who created the Forgewood concept, has sold the name and techniques. For further information, contact Phillip Lieske at Forgewood Products Company, P.O. Box 172, Centralia, Washington 98531.

Harry Drake, who has broken and holds more flight archery records than any other in that field of archery, states in letters to Sweetland: "The shaftings arrived, I don't know of anything that gives me more pleasure than opening those Forgewood parcels and examining the contents. In flight the arrow is of importance equal to the bow, and I simply don't know what we would do without Forgewoods. It's an awful thought." – *Bob Learn*

Getting The Shaft

SHOOTING GLASS

Modern Technology Has Brought About This Tough But Accurate Fiberglass Arrow.

You COULD LAY the blame on the Egyptians or the Phoenicians — they both have been credited with the discovery of glass and its early use in containers and ornaments.

Glass has been replaced to some extent by modern plastic, but the glass we use today is in a far different form than the hard, crystalline product to which we have been accustomed. We wear glass, woven into fabrics the drapes in the home are now fireproof, since they are made of woven fiberglass, and one of the major breakthroughs in the field of archery came when fiberglass and resins were put into use in the back and facing of modern laminated bows.

One of the leaders in the field of fiberglass products for the archers is Gordon Plastics, Incorporated, located in San Diego, California. They are perhaps best known as the manufacturers of Bo-Tuff, a leader in the backing and fiberglass facing materials for laminated bows. With a product like this you might think they would sit back and let it do the job and bring in the weekly paycheck; not the Gordons.

There are three Gordon brothers: George, the eldest and president of the firm; Dave, the production manager responsible for research and development, as George refines the new processes in the lab to the production and final shipment, and Don, in charge of public relations and marketing.

George Gordon founded the company in 1952; Dave brought his talents and knowledge in 1953 and Don came in to handle the sales and public relations in 1955.

In 1960, they started experimenting with a new type of fiberglass arrow. The usual method of making fiberglass arrows is to take a sheet of woven fiberglass, impregnate it with resins, roll it and cure it. This process didn't appeal to the Gordons, so they experimented and perfected a parallel fiber instead of the cloth material and started production in 1964 on their Glashaft.

After four years of research they came out with a shaft that had two stages of longitudinal fibers and four stages of fibers wrapped around a Swedish steel mandril to give them the quality product they wanted to market.

This also gave them the finished product from raw materials.

The production starts with the Swedish steel mandrils in a hopper that automatically feeds them onto an endless belt and into a roving machine. This machine takes fiberglass in strands and not only spins them around the mandril, but also has them laid out along the

As the raw shaft material comes from the curing oven, the first cut is made on this complicated mechanism.

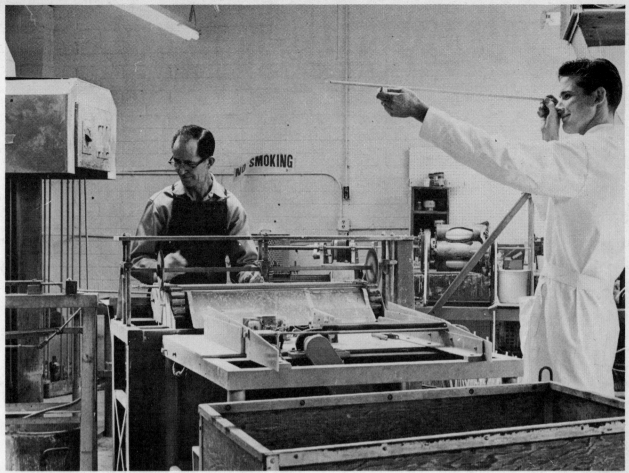

The shop foreman, Wayne Dent, spot checks straightness of Glashaft, as it moves off the cutter. The shaft must be ground, spined, graded and marked before shipment.

A centerless grinding machine gives constant quality, spine to shafts, regulated by degree of grinding.

length of the mandril to give a double strength to the shaft. The winding and horizontal fibers are fed onto the mandril, and as they emerge from the first whirling drum, are impregnated with an epoxy resin. At this point the color of the fiberglass is introduced and almost any color desired can be achieved by adding the coloring to the resins.

There are four stages wherein the fibers are wound onto the mandril and the color is held throughout these stages. The basic colors and the color of the Glashaft arrows are white, brown or tan. In quantity order of 1000 or more, they can give a distributor almost any color desired. They had some experimental colors in the shop, including green, light red and one that affords a beautiful camouflaged shaft that they had dubbed the Meadowlark Egg color. It was a mottled brown and off-shade white. One problem would be finding these arrows after they had been shot, but conversely they would be hard for game to spot, too.

When the mandril reaches the fourth and final spinning drum, the shafting is one continuous tube. The mandrils are a specific length and an automatic cutter cuts through the sticky fiberglass-resin material, then the attendant moves them onto an endless chain that moves slowly through the electric oven, curing the shafts. They emerge at the other end of the oven and the mandril is removed before the rough tubing is placed onto an automatic cutter that cuts the shafting to specified lengths. Then they move to a sanding station.

Jack Pennington cuts a steel mandrel that carries the epoxy-impregnated fiberglass filaments before curing.

For years, the father of the Gordon brothers, Dr. James A. Gordon, ran the sanding machine until he passed away in 1965. A retired Presbyterian minister, he was just filling in to keep busy in his retirement at the age of ninety-three. The shaftings are placed in a hopper and the rough edges are sanded glass-smooth by a centerless sander to a controlled diameter for the required spine and weight.

From the sander, the shaft pass to a straightness tester that automatically rejects the crooked or slightly out of line shafts and passes the top quality shafts over the rail and to the finish box. From the machine they go to the hand stages of spining and sorting.

They are spined on a production model spine tester and placed in their proper category. After they have been spined and sorted they move to the printer where the trade name, Glashaft, is printed on the side of the now completed shaft.

This method of making the Glashaft is better in the weight-to-strength ratio then some other styles and they can get greater stiffness or spine for the same weight. The finished shafts are boxed and shipped to dealers and distributors.

Although they have perfected a good fiberglass arrow material, the Gordons are experimenting continually, not only with the colors to make the shafts, but in more ways to improve their present product. Dave Gordon showed me a shaft that looked a bit large to go out of my fifty-pound bow. I was right; they were making a run of shafts with a ninety-pound spine!

When the shafts are shipped, the nock inserts and the

From left: George, Dave and Don Gordon check Nocksert with a micrometer before going into the production run.

target tips are weighed and shipped with them. Broadhead inserts are included, if ordered. The nock inserts and broadhead inserts on the market until now have been made of aluminum.

Gordon Plastics has perfected a molded nylon Nocksert that is designed to fit into the fiberglass shaft to give true alignment with the shaft and offer, at the same time, an almost indestructible nock. It is all one piece and slips into the tube with a little pressure. You can glue it with epoxy or other cements, but just twist it in and it will stay with no play.

They now are finishing a broadhead insert of the same molded nylon material meant to replace the

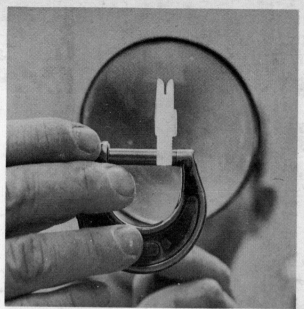

Gordon's Nocksert is of nylon and is made in different sizes to fit varying inside diameters of glass shafts.

Mandrels of steel are fed into the machine at right and, as they reach first divider, they are encircled with the epoxy-impregnated fiberglass filament used in shafts.

A section of fiberglass shaft is placed in the furnace for a burn-out test to determine the glass/epoxy ratio.

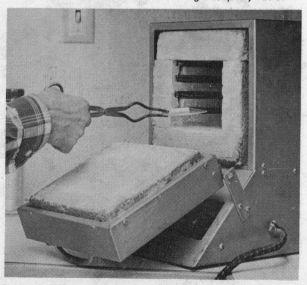

standard aluminum insert as we know it. Nylon has tremendous wearing qualities and, after many rounds of shooting with the Nockserts, I have only once had one come out. The shaft ricocheted off a rock and broke the nylon insert out as the tip broke. No material will hold up well under such conditions. I built up the string in the serving area to make the nock insert fit tightly, then shot the shaft from the bow, thinking I might pull the Nocksert from the shaft. It didn't and it wasn't glued in.

Of nylon broadhead insert, I have one of the early test models and wondered how to put on the broadhead with the nylon insert. As a trial, I took the nylon insert, pressed it into the fiberglass shaft and then heated some Ferr-L-Tite stick cement and smeared a bit on the insert. Next I heated the broadhead in the normal manner and placed it on the insert. What I wasn't sure of was the reaction of the nylon to heat. The broadhead went on with no problems and, after cooling, it spun true.

The next test was to remove tip and broadhead, depending on the shooting to be done. The broadhead warmed up and slipped off with no problems and the nylon insert was where I had put it on the shaft. I had marked the spot.

Many hunters say they have tried fiberglass with the broadhead and found it was low in spine; that it went wobbling off toward the target. Gordon recommends moving to a higher spine for broadhead shooting. If you would shoot a G spine for target, then switch to an H shaft and you should get excellent results, using the same bow with broadheads.

The Gordon brothers spend hunting seasons in the field armed with bows and their arrows. Dave has been continually successful in bagging his deer in the Elko, Nevada area. George and Don have hunted Kaibab several times and last year went to Colorado for elk. They have firsthand knowledge of the archer's problems, then do their best to help the archer in the field with that knowledge. – *Bob Learn*

Getting The Shaft

STEEL YOURSELF

Comes The Stainless Steel Arrow For Shooting Bricks And Other Tough Game!

AMERICAN INGENUITY HAS come through again. Archers now have a successful stainless steel alloy arrow. Tried in the past, drawing and working the steel into relatively light straight shafts was a problem, but the Hunters International Corporation of Warren, Michigan, solved the riddles with the Fur-Long SS (stainless steel) alloy arrow. The interesting newcomers are sold ready-made — and made they are, beautifully appointed in the natural steel hue for most of the shaft distance and painted white on the aftershaft portion with meticulous pinstriping of alternating gold and silver rings. At least this is the way my set looks.

The arrow is a four-fletch pitched right a few degrees, using four-inch-long contrasting white and gold plastic vanes. Due to the stiffness of the arrow combined with the 75x105-degree fletch, there was no cable clearance problem whatever on the four different bows I ran them through. The size I selected for testing was the 3147, comparable, the manufacturer says, to a 2219 aluminum, which happens to be the arrow that works best through my Jennings seventy-pound Expert Hunter two-wheeler that I selected as my test bow.

Since the Fur-Long SS is normally measured against the aluminum arrow, I chose to run my tests using the 2219 XX75 by Easton. My particular XX75s were in the silver offering rather than the popular Autumn Orange. Normally, I would fletch these with five-inch turkey feathers, but in trying to maintain at least a closeness in arrow types I used five-inch plastic vanes, not having any four-inchers on hand and being too darn anxious to test to wait for an order or to try to find them in town.

Of course, the arrows were the same length — thirty-one inches for my draw. Here is what they weighed fitted with the same type points averaging 124.5 grains each: the SS weighed in at 699.0 grains ready to go. The 2219 weighed 634.0 grains. If this seems heavy, it must be remembered that we are talking about arrows actually a bit over thirty-one inches long, as well as stiffly spined for my seventy-pound Jennings. The Fur-Long comes in other sizes, naturally, from my heavy 3147 to a light 6432 designed to shoot along with an aluminum 1816 size. I had no opportunity to shoot a lighter SS, such as the 3645, which is like an aluminum 2020, in my Jennings seventy-pounder. Whether or not it would have stabilized, I don't know. Still, I think the comparison a fair one.

Mainly, it would be interesting to test several areas:

The Fur-Long stainless steel alloy arrows were tested with this seventy-pound Jennings Expert Hunter compound.

speed — how fast would these arrows fly out of the compound test bow as compared with the 2219?; retention of initial velocity — would the SS lose less of its original speed in comparison with the 2219?; trajectory — how much would the SS drop over normal archery ranges?; flight distance — how far would the SS shoot out of the test bow?; and toughness — just how tough would the new SS prove to be?

Also, the idea of applying certain ballistic conceptions to the new SS arrows had to be entertained, at least a little, because Hunters International has selected the term Sectional Density in explaining the ballistic benefits of their new SS arrow.

First, speed. As might well be expected the heavier SS arrow did not leave the bow with as much initial velocity as the 2219. In fact, my first speed tests with the SS told me something was wrong with either my chronograph or another variable in the test. It turned out to be the nock, and this is important for future owners of SS arrows so they won't make the same mistake I did. My nock channel was simply too small for the big string on the seventy-pound bow, so I wrongly, but very carefully, filed them larger. I don't think I destroyed the accuracy of the arrows because they all went right on the money in testing, but filing was no way to open up my small nocks and they were still too small and were hanging onto the string, causing a distinct velocity loss. I learned later how to properly fix the nock size situation.

The nocks are an interesting new insert type made of aluminum, integral with the shaft. In fact, they almost appear as if a notch were cut into the very end of the shaft itself. But style alone is not the only difference. These special nocks are designed metallurgically to be quite malleable; they will bend in and out a good number of times before they crack. Therefore, carefully squeezing the nock shut if it is too large, or prying it open, is the way to custom-fit it to the bowstring.

After my nocks were properly sized, velocity went up, all the way from a meager 160 foot-seconds out of the fast bow, to 182 foot-seconds — that with an arrow weighing almost 700.0 grains, and of smaller diameter than an aluminum of the same spine. Of course, the sleek 2219 XX75 Silver was no slouch out of the two-wheeler. It crossed my Skyscreens at an average of 205 foot-seconds. Supposedly, and according to the advertised ballistic advantages, the SS was to retain more of its initial speed than the aluminum. I wanted to find out if it really would.

As stated, the SS left the bow at 182; the 2219 was making an even 190 foot-seconds. At thirty yards the SS was doing 169 and the 2219 was flying at 178 foot-seconds. Simple subtraction shows that the SS was slower by twenty-three foot-seconds to start with; slower by fifteen foot-seconds at twenty yards; and slower by nine foot-seconds at thirty yards. Why didn't I test out to forty and fifty yards? I would have liked to, but nailing the light-sensitive areas means hitting a target two inches wide, maybe six inches high, and on top of that having to nail not only one of these, but two — the start and the stop circuits — these ten feet apart, and not just once, but at least five times to get an average. So, I settled for the twenty and thirty-yard readings and I think they told a lot.

So, it is easy to see that the SS did hold more of its initial velocity, though it was slower in speed from zero to thirty yards than the 2219 is over the same range. The aluminum lost 7.5 percent of its velocity at twenty yards; 13.5 percent by the time the arrow reached the thirty-yard

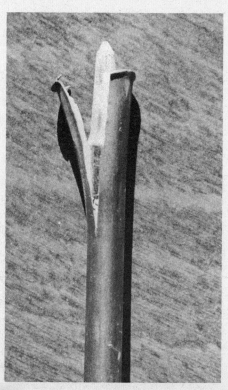

Left: In field testing the stainless steel shafts, Sam Fadala found they retained a high percentage of the initial velocity. (Below) The steel shaft was split about an inch after being shot against a brick at a range of twenty yards from the compound.

mark. The SS lost only four percent at the twenty mark and seven percent at the thirty-yard measurement. Roughly, we can say that the SS, over that particular range and for that particular test with that bow on that day, lost about half the speed that the aluminum lost. Of course, this is not an entire ballistic story in itself, but it was interesting to see the advertised claims basically held up.

We have to dive into the concept of Sectional Density sometime, because Fur-Longs are advertised as having a lot of this property. But what is it? In a sense, it is the key to the high retention of velocity. Sectional Density, or SD, is a number we come up with when we divide a projectile's weight in pounds by the square of the diameter of that projectile in inches. Mainly, I am familiar with this term in connection with firearms ballistics and many other readers will be, too. In fact, we get a pretty good idea of SD looking at two different calibers. For example, a 200-grain bullet in caliber .45 has an SD of .139. Taking another 200-grain bullet — remember, the same exact 200-grain weight — but in caliber .30 we go up to an SD of .301, which is ballistically better.

My 3147 shaft would have an SD of about .763, while the 2219 would go something like .579, according to the Hunters International figures. The gain is almost thirty-two percent in this one category, then. Going back to the 200-grain .45 caliber bullet versus the 200-grain .30 caliber is going to retain more of its initial velocity than the .45.

They go faster, but do they shoot flatter? No. I sighted the bow in carefully with the 2219 for twenty, thirty, forty and fifty yards with my four-pin bowsight. This, of course, meant that the 2219 would be at zero at each of these four ranges. Where would the SS hit on the target by using the same pins at the same distances? Here is what happened. At twenty yards the SS was four inches lower. At thirty yards the SS was six inches lower, eight inches at forty and 11½ inches at fifty yards. Of course, had I sighted the bow in with the SS it could have handled the zero-to-fifty-yard range of shooting without too much problem. But the 2219 was flatter shooting and no doubt of it.

How come, if the SS arrows are so streamlined that they win hands down in the SD criterion for ballistic excellence, they don't actually shoot flatter than the aluminum over normal archery ranges? Robbing another idea from firearms ballistics may answer the question, at least in part. Looking at the very familiar .30/06, for example, we see that a 110-grain handload takes off at a ripping 3400 foot-seconds from the muzzle of the rifle. The same figures show a 150-grain .30/06 bullet going off at 3100, a full three hundred foot-seconds slower. But the SD of the 150.0 is better — .226 against .166 for the 110.0. So the 150.0 will shoot flatter over normal .30/06 ranges, right? Wrong! Sighted in for one hundred yards, the 110.0 bullet hits 9.9 inches low at three hundred yards, 48 inches low at a full five hundred. The superior 150.0 hits 11.2 inches low at three hundred and 49.4 inches low at five hundred. Way out there someplace, the ballistically superior 150.0 will catch the 110.0, but not over normal ranges. How come?

Part of the answer is time of flight — how long that projectile is in the air before it reaches its destination. The longer it soars up there above the ground the longer gravity gets to put its forces to work on it pulling it down. Interestingly, the 150.0 actually arrives at five hundred yards going faster than the 110.0 because its better ballistics have helped it retain velocity. It looks like this: 150-grain, 2319 foot-seconds at three hundred; 1880 at five hundred. The 110.0 is going along at only 2279 at three hundred and 1690 at five hundred, quite a bit slower — but still flatter shooting.

Okay, then how about flight shooting? Maintaining as close to a forty-five-degree angle as possible, I shot both the SS and the 2219 in the open sand dunes where it would be safe to fly them as far as the seventy-pounder could launch the arrows. I fired them in groups, first an SS, then a 2219, and so forth discounting any arrows that were not in a

To conduct tests on the new shaft material, Fadala used only the size 3147 SS type.

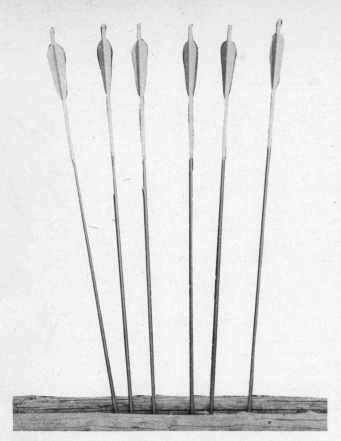

The SS arrows tested were four-fletch pitched right a few degrees with plastic vanes four inches in length.

group away out in the sands where they came to rest, the points of all arrows buried deeply in the sands. The maximum range for the 2219 was 292 yards. The maximum for the SS arrows was 284 yards. Under different conditions, we have to remember, either arrow may have shot farther, or not so far. This isn't important to our test. Only the comparative values are important, and the reader can draw his own conclusions from them as he sees fit to do.

Toughness testing brought a few laughs. I decided to head for an archery field range that happened to be near a dump to fire a few of them off at some really formidable targets, such as defunct car bodies, planks and bricks. The latter proved the most interesting, but as I was blazing away with these beautiful arrows a couple archers had arrived at the field range. Feeling eyes on me, I looked up. Standing about fifty yards from me were two fellows, an amazed look on their faces.

"If you don't like those arrows," one of them said, "I sure will be glad to take them off your hands." I told them I never went into the field without first giving my arrows the acid test. If they could survive contact with a car body at twenty yards, they would do just fine on big game. I don't think that response satisfied the archers.

From about twenty yards out the SS shafts out of the seventy-pound bow stung a red brick with quite a blow. Red dust puffed off the brick and pieces adhered permanently to the point of the arrow. I am afraid a direct blow did not do the SS any particular good. It caused the tip to jam back so hard that it split the first half-inch of the shaft. However, the arrow remained almost straight. I say almost because there was a slight bend, but I did get it straight again and the arrow was fitted with a new insert

and was in use once more, though a half-inch too short for me. In all fairness, the 2219s proved very tough, too. The bricks split them back a bit farther, but again, they could be and were made straight and put back into service, though not out of my bow with my long draw length.

So what? The new SSs are interesting, but do they fill any gaps in the needs of archers? I think so, and at the same time I don't see them as a replacement arrow for other types because they are unique and useful in their own right. I am not a target man, but these are stable arrows indeed and I would be much interested in seeing a target shooter seek gold with a set. I think he would find the SS shaft a good one.

And there isn't a doubt in my mind that the narrow, tough, heavy, yet ballistically excellent SS arrows will

Fadala felt the nocks on the new SS arrows should be opened carefully with a wedge so they hold on the string but do not pinch down on it.

penetrate a good deal of big-game hide. The answer lies in one word — appropriateness. I have been hunting pine hens recently. My arrow loss is about fifty percent. I doubt that I would care to toss SS arrows costing several bucks each into the trees to be lost forever. The good old expendable and biologically degradable cedar is right in that case. My recently tested tapered graphites shot at about 230 foot-seconds out of my heavy bows. I think I would elect for them on an antelope hunt. A fiberglass can be useful under a lot of conditions and recently I nabbed a good bunch of rabbits shooting some Browning 11s. The great aluminum arrow matches up with compound bows like peanut butter goes with jelly. They all have their places.

The archer's choice has been widened again, this time with the stainless steel alloy arrow. Highly durable, deeply penetrating, accurate and far-flying, they are a super addition to the already great lineup the manufacturers have given us. An archer can be proud to add a set to his tackle box. — *Sam Fadala.*

TESTING THE NEW GRAPHITE SHAFTS

These Innovative Shafts Are Far-Flying And Strong — A Great Addition To The Fine Array Of Projectiles Already Available!

Sam Fadala uses a staff to steady his aim in testing the new graphite shafts in the snowy Idaho wilds.

SOMETHING NEW IS nothing new to archers. Each month we are happily pelted with the latest designs and innovations from the manufacturers, from bows to brush buttons. Usually, the change is a face-lift or a little new makeup for an old familiar item. Sometimes, the new is revolutionary. The graphite shaft is more in the latter category — a new concept, an addition to the many fine shaft styles and materials already available to bow shooters.

The moment I got my hands on a set of graphites I was burning to test them, to see what they could really do. My models were produced by the Lamiglas Company of Kent, Washington. At this point they are designed with the hunter in mind, not the target shooter, although a target graphite will be in the works later. Shafts should be in the stores for sale by March of 1977. Made of material akin to that used in the very fine graphite rods of the fisherman, the shafts also differ in form. They taper. The nock end accepts the nine-thirty-seconds of an inch fitting, while the tip is sized more toward the dimensions of the eleven-thirty-seconds of an inch shaft. Aerodynamically, one might expect the opposite. However, it depends upon whose theory is being applied. Drag and penetration of a shaft tapered from nock to point can be superior under certain conditions.

It should be noted, of course, that Lamiglas is not the only maker of graphite shafts at this point. Other makers include Hercules, Incorporated, of Magna, Utah, and Gordon Plastics of Vista, California. The Lamiglas shafts were selected for our investigation simply because they were the first to come into our hands.

I did not have to weigh my graphites to know that they were lighter than any other shaft I had tried in similar spine. The scale, though, proved what I had guessed at: They were lighter. Other overt physical properties, aside from lightness and tapered quality, were less obvious. The color seemed darker than similar shafts in fiberglass in the raw state; but color can be changed in the manufacturing process from natural to any hue. The graphites had a lead pencil look in color. The texture was much like that of fiberglass.

Testing has to have the ground rules spelled out before

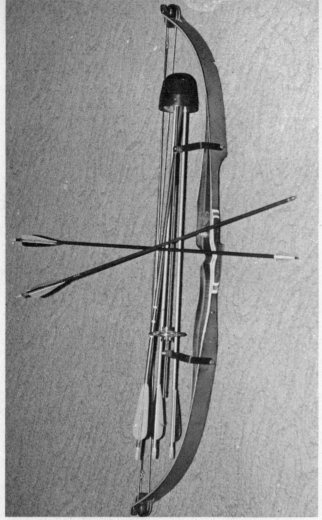

Test bow was 61-pound Wing Impact I compound. Arrow with covered head is Razorback with its protective plastic case. Other is field point used in testing.

launching into the actual field work. How an item is tested can make all the difference. Unfortunately, bias can be entered at the outset. In order to minimize any such bias, I decided to set things up in what I would call a semiscientific test manner. I wanted to get rid of, or at least avoid, the tester's plague — the extraneous variable. All that fancy term means is that the cause of a certain result is not what it appeared to be and the wrong data is presented to the reader.

Getting rid of the extraneous variables, then, to the best of the tester's ability, is paramount in importance. Phony outcomes result when these little gremlins are allowed to exist. A good example can be taken from tests applied to children and learning. Let's say we want to find out if Johnny can read better under Program A or Program B. So, we give a pretest to see how well Johnny can read before he starts the programs, and a post-test to determine his improvement after the programs. Johnny's teacher under Program A is a little doll recently out of college, cute as a pointer pup. Miss Cordelia E. Bludgeon, child hater, runs Program B. Johnny does a damn sight better under A than B. Is A a better program than B? Who knows? The real factor was teacher, not method. So it goes with other types of testing as well.

One way to avoid some of these factors is to keep things fair by trying to maintain consistency. So it was that all of the test arrows were fired from the same bow and fletched the same way with the same vanes, using the same nocks —

except that the graphites took the nine-thirty-seconds. All shafts were cut the same length, of course, 31¾ inches to match my draw.

The only bow used to cast the arrows was a Wing Impact I in the sixty-one-pound draw weight. I chose this model because of its long relaxed valley, which allows it to be less sensitive to arrow change in spine than some other types I've tried. Also, the fifty percent relaxation was nice for long spells of repeated shooting.

I did not have test machinery, so in order to reduce the variation in my own form I did two things. First, I shot many times and took the overall average performance, cutting out any obviously ridiculous data, such as that one arrow that perhaps catches the wind and sails twenty-five yards farther than its mates. Also, I used a Moses Stick for my shooting. What's a Moses Stick? Actually, it is a walking staff made for hiking and support. It served here to support my bow arm, thus keeping my aim much more standard than it would have been without the aid of the stick.

I wanted to see how the graphites would do in comparison to other shafts of man-made materials. I selected a fiberglass arrow that suited my bow. This turned out to be a No. 9. The most stable arrow out of the Wing to date had been the Easton Autumn Orange shaft in 2117. However, the Wing also shot the Autumn Orange 2114 well, so that aluminum arrow was included in the test.

First, the bow was sighted carefully for the 2117, the workhorse shaft that had been used most often in the past. A four-pin sight was used, set for twenty, thirty, forty and fifty yards. With a Flipper rest, this shaft was on the vertical and the horizontal at all of the sight ranges. The idea was to see where the other three types of shafts would land in comparison to the 2117 as the standard for the bow.

Total weights of the shafts went like this: the No. 9 weighed in at 571 grains; the 2117 at 585 grains; the 2114 at 515.6 grains; and the graphite 27-96, which was the spine for my bow with its fifty percent relaxation, weighed in at 434.2 grains. The points were field type and selected because they only varied in weight by 0.5 grain among each other. The average weight of the points was 124.5 grains. The average nock weight was 15.5 grains for the Bjorn eleven-thirty-seconds and 7.5 for the Bjorn five-sixteenths. Total average vane weight was 40.5 for all shafts.

I weighed different types of vanes and ended up using the S&K transparent type of standard five-inch hunting pattern. These, of course, weighed out at an average of 13.5 grains each. The contoured S&K was lighter, 10.9 grains, but I did not have enough on hand to use them. The Pro-Fletch five-inch weighed 14.2 on the average for comparison. All of the vanes were mounted the same way, slight cast right in pitch; straight clamp on a Miller Master jig. The idea was to produce as similar a drag on all shafts as possible. Nock inserts were aluminum on the two glass shafts, and, of course, tapered integral types on the Eastons. The switch-a-point system was used for points.

Although I used the five-inch plastic vane in my tests, I discovered later that the stiff graphite would stabilize well with a four-inch vane, placed straight on the shaft, no twist. For hunting I still like feathers, forgiving of release and brushes with branches, so I used a five-inch feather on graphites that went into the field after game. The tapered graphite has two interesting properties that have to be mentioned: first, it is probably the stiffest shaft per weight that we have, second, it has a huge spread in the area of spine. The graphites flew well from bows ranging in the thirties to the seventies in draw weight. The archer need not buy according to spine, then, as one does it all.

Mainly, I wanted to test for four major criteria: accuracy, trajectory over normal ranges, flight distance and strength. I found, first of all, that the four kinds of shafts were proper in the Wing bow. None veered left or right over the normal ranges. I wondered how much variation the bow would handle, so I tried a set of No. 6s in fiberglass. They flew off the line. A set of 2216s did not work either. Without machinery, accuracy testing becomes pretty hit and miss, but let it suffice to say that none of the arrows performed poorly under the conditions I had to work with. All of them were accurate.

Trajectory over the twenty to fifty-yard range separated the arrows from each other, however. Naturally, the 2117 was right on because the bow was so sighted for it, since it was the test shaft. Although the 2117 was heaviest in weight of the arrows, it did shoot flatter than the No. 9. The trajectory results can be seen in the Trajectory Test Chart.

Although I had no sophisticated testing devices, Lami-glass did and they agreed to test trajectory using their fancy shooting machine, thus taking much of the human factor out of the testing. Here is what they did using a Jennings four-wheel compound in thirty-inch draw, seventy-pound weight. They sighted a 2213 shaft to be dead on at fifty yards. Then, leaving the bow in the shooting machine in the exact aiming position, fired a 2020 shaft and the graphite. The 2020 hit fourteen inches below bull's-eye and the graphite struck seventeen inches higher than the bull's-eye.

TRAJECTORY TEST CHART
Rise (+) Drop (-)

YARDS	No. 9	2117	2114	Graphite
20	-3 in.	0 in.	+1 in.	+2 in.
30	0 in.	0 in.	+7 in.	+8 in.
40	-1 in.	0 in.	+6½ in.	+9½ in.
50	-9 in.	0 in.	+5 in.	+8 in.

It does not take a scientific genius to figure out that the results of the trajectory test over standard ranges are inconclusive. First, if placed on a graph, it would seem that the No. 9 did a little dance en route. Low at twenty, it joined the 2117 at thirty and then dipped again below the line of sight for forty and fifty yards. The 2114 had a sense of humor, too. But the data is presented the way it happened. And it is possible to make a "gut reaction" conclusion that is no surprise. The graphite shoots pretty darn flat. It ought to. It's light. This sort of conclusion resembles smacking your fingers with a hammer to prove what you already knew — it's going to hurt. But we also can see that trajectory is not a function of weight alone. If it were, the 2117 would lose to the No. 9, but it doesn't.

As an aside in the testing, I wanted to find out which sight pin I would have to use to hit right on the money with the new graphites at fifty yards. Would the thirty do it? I was curious. It turned out that the forty-yard pin set for the 2117 shaft was right on target at fifty with the graphites. I held the forty pin on the gold and produced hit after hit. That does not translate that the graphite is ten yards flatter than the 2117, but it is another indication of how these new darts do fly.

The flight test was fun. I couldn't find a real flat spot in the badlands where I tested, but I did locate a lonesome stretch of sandy hills where I could safely fly my arrows upward. I used a homemade device to keep me honest in my arc of hold. This was simply a board cut to forty-five degrees with a bubble level strung below it. My wife Nancy stood beside me and moved my bow arm until the arc between bowstring and the horizontal was close to the forty-five-degree mark. I know it worked fairly well because the arrows grouped remarkably close to each other in a string pattern, rather than being scattered about. They flew far, but not as far as possible because my ground was flat where I stood, but turned into a rise in the distance. So, this was not a test to see how far any of the arrows could go. It was a test of a comparison of the distances only.

Again, providing that weight alone is not the sole determining factor in flight of the arrow, the 2117 whipped the lighter No. 9. The No. 9 flew an average distance of 240 yards. The 2117 flew 254 yards. The 2114 landed 261 yards away and the graphite went 277 yards.

As for toughness, I performed a simple test. Of course, it

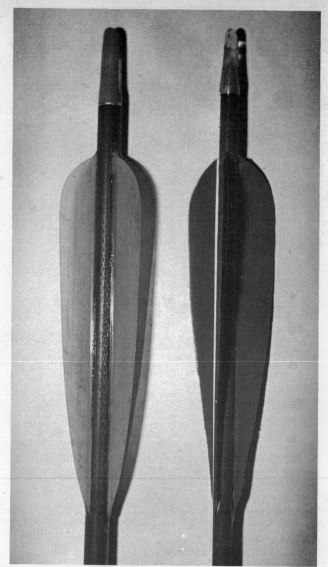

Shaft on right is the graphite shaft, compared with a No. 10 fiberglass shaft on left. Fadala found that feather fletching was forgiving of a bad release.

all depends upon the medium used in such a test and shooting into a big plank the way I did does not prove that the graphite will resist snapping if it strikes a green tree limb sideways. But the test was valuable because it did give an idea of just how strong the new graphites are — and they are.

All of the arrows took terrific abuse. I stepped off fifty yards and whacked the shafts directly into a dry 8x10 pine board. At fifty they all survived. So I moved up. The thinner-walled 2114 bent first, then the 2117. However, both were straightened on a Groves and were none the worse for wear after the test. The No. 9 was totally destroyed at thirty yards. The shaft took on a compression fracture near the tip. Neat plugs of arrow diameter were blasted through the other side of the wood on each shot, but in reality the hole made was a bit smaller than the shaft size. So, there was a terrific pressure coming in from the side of the shaft bearing down on the walls. The graphite took this pressure apparently better than the No. 9. However, the graphite is tapered. Theoretically, it could well be assumed that the easing of pressure due to the decrease of contact saved the graphite and not its construction. No matter the reason, the graphites proved very tough.

I did experience some unfortunate breakage in sandy country. For some reason, the physical construction of the shaft allows for breakage just behind the point insert — apparently when the line of force departs from straight to another line. Why the arrows took such punishment from direct hits on pine but broke in sandy mediums is a question for the experts to resolve. I am sure they will be working on an answer. One distinct aid in decreasing sand breakage was the addition of the Bear Tufftip, the small metal band designed to protect the very forward portion of the shaft. Also, it should be pointed out that under field conditions no unusual breakage occurred, not even when a graphite zipped through a tough javelina at twenty yards and struck the rock wall of a cliff.

What about penetration? Again, time will be a better tester because many different conditions can then be placed upon the new shafts. Penetration is much a matter of the medium being struck. For example, the granular nature of sand slows a rifle bullet badly and a fifty-pound bow usually will drive an arrow farther in sand than a .30/06 rifle will shoot a standard hunting bullet. On straw targets and on

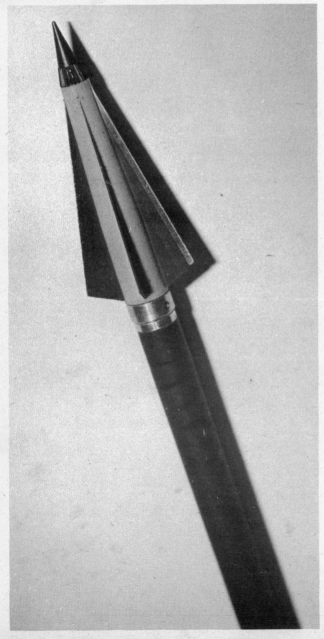

Used in his two kills with graphite shafts, Fadala tends to favor the NAP Razorback Five broadhead. The shaft was equipped with interchangeable insert.

sheets of cardboard, all of the arrows penetrated well and no real conclusion could be drawn as to which was best. Asking a physicist friend of mine at the University of Calgary in Alberta, Canada, about penetration, his explanation was quite complicated and not as straightforward as I thought the subject to be. Yes, penetration would go with velocity and mass, all right, but shape of the projectile was important, too, along with several other criteria that helped to muddy the waters of explanation. My suspicion, and it is not much more than that right now, is that the tapered quality will enhance penetration as well as arrow extraction since it would seem that the pressure bearing on the walls of the shafts would decrease as the shaft continued into the target. Again using the shooting machine, the graphite went up against other arrows in a penetration test on what I believe was HHI524D Class A foam. Again, the Jennings four-wheeler was used and it sent its thirty-inch 2020 out at 208 and the graphite out at 243. At fifty yards the chronograph read 193 for the 2020 and 219 for the graphite. The 2020 went 12¼ inches into the foam; the graphite went 11-5/8ths inches into the foam.

Game departments, at least some of them, have concluded that arrow weight is the most valuable asset in penetration and reliability. If so, the new graphite is going to be in trouble with some of these state departments' laws. For example, Wyoming demands that elk, grizzly bear or moose bowhunters arm themselves with arrows weighing at least 500 grains fired from bows capable of launching these missiles at least 160 yards. My finished graphite in 31¼-inch length, even with a heavy broadhead, simply won't make the grade for weight. After all, with a 124.5-grain head and full-size vanes it weighed only 434.2 grains — way short of Wyoming's wishes. Yes, super light darts the size of toothpicks sure won't penetrate well, I know. But velocity cannot be totally discounted. I will bet that there is a ratio where optimum penetration will result, but that is fodder for yet another test.

My field testing of the shafts turned out to be a deer/javelina hunt in Arizona and I was lucky enough to get one of each, an old doe mule deer and a boar javelina. Using a seventy-pound Jennings Expert Hunter two-wheeler I hit the deer at thirty yards and she went straight down and remained down. The javelina was twenty yards and he flopped off a little ledge and fell a short distance to another ledge, where he did not move after hitting the ground. In both cases the new NAP Razorback Five head was used and the combination was very impressive — fast graphite and well-designed broadhead. Two harvests do not constitute a thorough test, but my initial reaction, especially when the graphite zipped through branched bushes and still made it to and through the hog, was positive.

Now we know that the new graphites are super. Toss away your other arrows and turn solely to the new shafts, right? I say wrong. The new arrows are super and archers are going to love them. But they are best thought of as a great addition to an already fine array of good projectiles for our bows. When I got serious about the bow fifteen years ago, I was using cedar shafts. I still use them today because they have a definite place in the scheme of things. So do other types.

I see the graphites especially well adapted to the hunting field where added range is desired and where the "depth of kill" is to be increased. Another archer, independent of me or Lamiglass, did some testing of the graphites and found that he gained about four feet in his gap at eighty-five yards, graphites over 2020s, using a seventy-pound bow. On an antelope hunt that sort of gain might make the difference between a trophy or a miss.

The graphite is one more choice for the already pampered archer. Strong and far flying, the arrow will be at home in the game fields, and I'll bet a lot of serious archers are robbing the piggy bank right now for a set that will be in the quiver by next open season. Initially, the cost is going to be on the high side and exact prices are not yet decided on. Cost to the archer will go down, however, as the new graphites catch on. I think they are going to be worth the investment. — *Sam Fadala.*

SHORTCUT TO VELOCITY

If You Wonder How Fast That Arrow Really Flies, Here Is How To Find Out!

If comparing various types of arrow shafts, fletchings, a shooting machine such as this can help to standardize the tests, as each draw remains the same throughout.

THERE HAVE BEEN articles on methods for determining the velocity of an arrow. Some of these articles have offered relatively simple methods, while others have proven highly complicated and require expensive equipment.

However, engineering techniques provide an exceedingly simple and relatively foolproof method for accomplishing this type of test and offering desired information regarding arrow speed in flight.

AN ARROW'S VELOCITY can easily be determined by calculation, if several things are known:
1) the air drag on the arrow
2) the arrow's weight
3) its initial angle of elevation

Some years ago, an enterprising gentleman determined by test the drag force of an arrow in an air flow. This force varies with the diameter, length and, of course, fletching size of the arrow. As long as we restrict ourselves to remain within certain limits, we also may say the force is proportional to arrow's velocity squared. In so doing we must restrict the ranges we may be interested in computing to one hundred yards or less. Beyond that range, the error increases rapidly.

THE DRAG COEFFICIENT — a characteristic of a particular arrow — when multiplied by the arrow's velocity squared will yield the value of the force slowing up the arrow at that moment. An interesting relationship can be gotten when this drag coefficient is divided by the arrow weight. We have then what may be called the drag/weight ratio. Analogous to this are two autos of exactly the same shape, except one is 1000 pounds heavier than the other. Which do you believe will be straining more against a sixty mile-per-hour air flow? If you thought the lighter auto, you are right. The lighter car has a higher drag/weight ratio, consequently will tend to slow up faster. An arrow, then, behaves exactly the same way.

Ninety-five percent of target arrows will fall twenty

Velocity has close connection with accuracy on target range. Matched arrows allow one to maintain much the same velocity, when the other variables remain equal.

While velocity has a good deal to do with penetration, the results of this test show that design of the head is even more important, particularly with broadheads.

Chapter 6

percent above or below an average drag/weight ratio. These upper and lower limits are shown on the accompanying chart as dashed curves. Thin-wall aluminum shafts and arrows with large fletching will have high drag/weight ratios, requiring more initial velocity than lower ratio arrows to reach the same target. Thick walled aluminum shafts and arrows with small fletching or plastic vanes will have lower ratios. All other aluminum shafts, along with glass and wood arrows, fall into the average drag/weight ratio category.

The last consideration for computing the velocity is the arrow's initial angle of elevation; i.e., the angle of the arrow leaves the bow. Here one may think a sensitive instrument is required. Not so, for the archer uses a trigonometric relationship between his eye, anchor and arrow which can be used as an effective measuring instrument, accurate to less than one-tenth of a degree.

It can be said, then, the angle of elevation is equal to the angle between the arrow and the archer's line of vision of the target (see sketch); a relationship that asks us only to seek out the necessary distance from the target to have our arrows drop into the bullseye. In other words, with the top of the arrow point sitting in the bullseye, find the range from target where the arrows will drop right in. Most archers have learned this range from experience.

Thus, to use the chart to determine the arrow's speed all that is required is to know the above range and measure the length of the arrow used and the anchor distance (vertical measurement from eye to top of shaft as close to nock as possible).

ONE WORD OF CAUTION: the anchor dimension should be measured as accurately as possible for good results. It should be checked just before each shot is released by someone standing along-side the archer. The eye, top of scale, arrow point and target all should lie in a straight line. The scale should be held vertically, as close to the archer's eye as possible and as close to the nock as is possible. Scale readings should be from eye to top of arrow shaft.

THE SIGHT SHOOTER can use his pin to determine his arrow speed. All he need do is measure the distance the pin is above the arrow shaft, add to this the distance his nocking point is off-set from the perpendicular and subtract the total from the distance his eye is from his

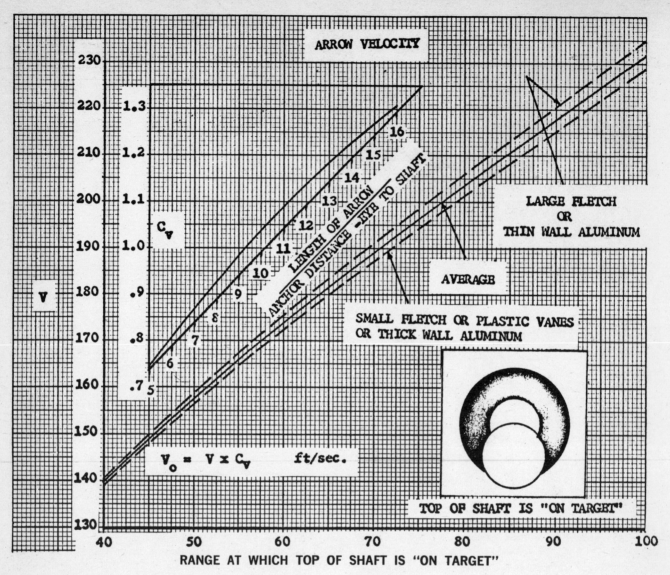

ARROW VELOCITY

LENGTH OF ARROW

ANCHOR DISTANCE = EYE TO SHAFT

LARGE FLETCH OR THIN WALL ALUMINUM

AVERAGE

SMALL FLETCH OR PLASTIC VANES OR THICK WALL ALUMINUM

$V_0 = V \times C_v$ ft/sec.

TOP OF SHAFT IS "ON TARGET"

RANGE AT WHICH TOP OF SHAFT IS "ON TARGET"

EXAMPLE: An archer draws a 29" arrow which is considered neither too heavy nor too light in weight and has normal size fletching. This can be called an average shaft. Someone measured the distance from his eye to the top of the shaft when he was at full draw, and it was found to be 2.75". (A field anchor).

The archer knows from experience that he holds his shaft point on target at 60 yards. The arrow's exit velocity can be found with this information using the above chart.

Entering the chart at 60 yards and going up to the curve labeled AVERAGE, then moving to the left, a value of 173.5 is read. This is the speed the archer's arrow

would have had if he were to have a 3.0" anchor and 28" long arrow.

The value 173.5 must be corrected by finding the proper multiplication factor (Cv). Divide the arrow's length by the measured anchor distance; i.e., 29"/2.75" = 10.54 and entering curve at that value read off Cv = 1.063.

The archer's arrow speed is 173.5 multiplied by 1.063, or 184.4 ft./sec.

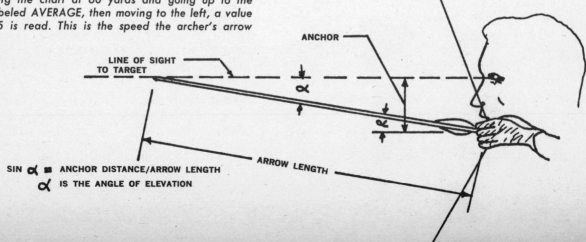

ANCHOR

LINE OF SIGHT TO TARGET

ARROW LENGTH

SIN α = ANCHOR DISTANCE/ARROW LENGTH

α IS THE ANGLE OF ELEVATION

There seems no practical reason for determining velocity of a given arrow, but natural curiosity can lead to complicated experiments; system outlined remains simple.

anchoring point. This would then be his "anchor distance." Using the range at which the sight was set, then measuring the distance from pin to nocking point, which will then be his "arrow length," the sight shooter can readily get his arrow speed from the chart.

Why should an archer be interested in knowing his arrow's speed? He does not need to know this in order to be an effective shooter. Yet he must evidence some interest, because he makes reference to the same phenomenon when using terms such as "good cast" or "fast arrow."

However, the more technical-minded student of archery can find many reasons for knowing arrow speed in terms of numbers. He can then do performance analysis on his bow, checking arrow stiffness, mass and speed for compatability. Once any one arrow speed is found, the door is open for mathematical treatment for any arrow's performance in the bow. Performance also

includes finding the arrow which will shoot flattest and, in addition, meet certain requirements as far as spine and weight are concerned. The faster arrow may not necessarily be the flatter shooting, since drag must be taken into consideration. A thorough analysis of this can be made. It is evident that a big advantage is found here, in that the optimum arrow can be selected for a bow without expensive and painstaking trial and error.

An archer employing the gap or point of aim system can easily compute where to place his arrow point for any range or any arrow by using a simple formula.

Similarly, a sight shooter can calibrate his sight for any weight shaft mathematically. Changes in velocity (and settings) due to light, heavy, wet and new bow strings can also be investigated more thoroughly.

Finally, an evaluation of the bow itself in terms of efficiency, reflecting the manner in which the overall bow performs, is feasible. – *Lawrence Luterman*

Chapter 7

THE FINE LINE

The Bowstring Is One Of The Least Understood Facets Of Archery

IT always has been a source of amazement to me of the lack of knowledge shared by the average, as well as the more experienced archers, about bow strings. Possibly this situation stems from the fact that so few archers actually make their own strings. Those who do not have to rely on suppliers to lead them in the right direction concerning their own particular needs.

At one time or another, the question will arise as to whether these suppliers in their own right are qualified to levy this information upon the archery public. If there are no doubts about a supplier's eligibility to convey this knowledge to his clients, then all well and good. But what if the scales balance in the other direction? This then is a case of the blind leading the blind, and it is the archer who suffers in the long run.

If a supplier cannot answer pertinent questions concerning the bow string, and ease any doubts an archer may have about these questions, then he should turn towards other sources that can be more informative. Without a doubt there are exceptions to every rule and these exceptions apply to bow strings, but an archer will be further ahead if he sticks to the hard and fast rules adopted by the leaders in both tournament shooting and hunting or their suppliers. These rules are flexible to a certain extent, but they serve as a sound basis from which an archer can start. Then as he progresses in his chosen field, he can experiment with them, until they fall into place for his own particular situation.

When purchasing a bow string an archer always should take his bow along and fit the string right there. To me this is a necessity, as many things govern the correct string length.

Most bow manufacturers mark the length on their bows, but contributing factors lead to variables in bow lengths. While one manufacturer may measure his bow for length around the back side, another one may measure his along the belly side. This different procedure in measuring, can mean sometimes one-half inch difference in the finished bows. Also limb and bow design contribute to this situation, as do heavily reflexed and deflexed bows. Some bows such as the short reflexed bows put more tension on the bow

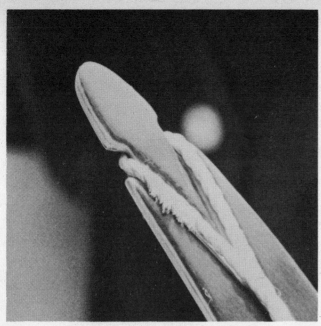

A bowstring often will become frayed at the loop. If it breaks, this often can do damage to an expensive bow.

With the nocking point located and marked by this knot of string, the arrow is placed beneath the marker.

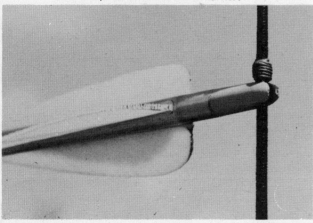

The manner in which a bow is strung can have much to do with how long a bowstring will serve its proper function.

When the nocking point on the bowstring has been properly determined, a knot is tied to mark the spot, then drop of glue is put on the knot to hold it in place on string.

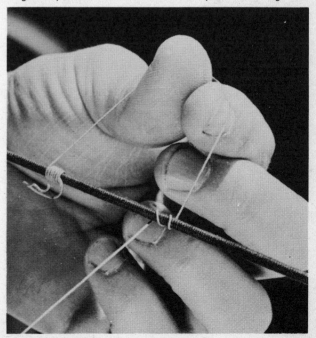

string at strung position than do deflexed types. Therefore the bow string should be slightly shorter to begin with so as to compensate for this increased stretching of the bow string. Also, some bow string materials stretch more than others, and different construction of bow strings may lead to more or less let down on the finished bow string.

The endless string stretches very little after completion, whereas the Flemish, or Laid string sometimes stretches as much as an inch. This is largely due to the differences in construction of the strings. The endless string is usually made with little or no beeswax, and only requires a few twists to keep the continuous strands together. Whereas the Laid string is heavily waxed to keep the individual strands together while under construction, and on completion the Laid string is twisted quite a few times so as to keep the string from parting in the loops when first strung on the bow. The major stretching factors in the Laid

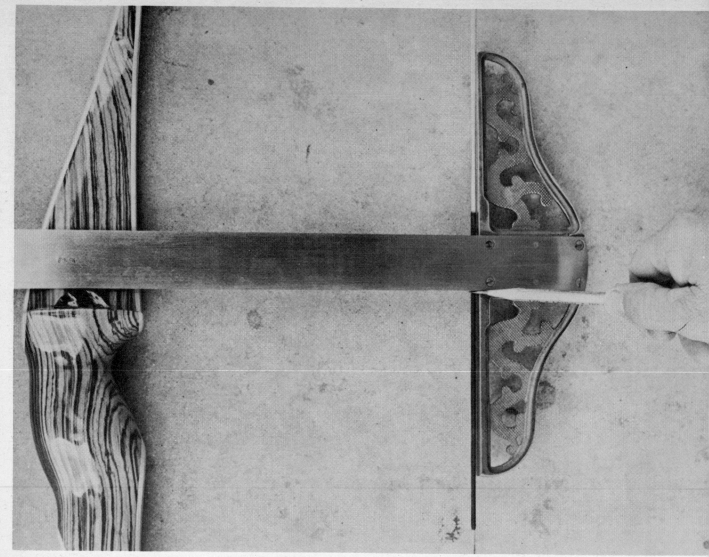

To determine proper nocking point on bowstring, one uses a T-square, marking string perpendicular to the arrow rest. This position then may be moved upward about one-eighth inch to allow for tillering of limb.

string is that the use of so much beeswax holds the individual strands apart, and when the bow is strung the strands tighten, and come together forcing the beeswax out. The Laid string requires more shooting in than does the endless string, as it will continue to stretch for some time. The endless string is preferred by most archers, as once the initial stretch is gone, it will remain almost constant as far as height goes.

String height should stay within a small degree to insure consistent shooting. Many archers fail to shoot a string in properly before a tournament, and wonder just what is going on when their sight settings are off, in the case of the sight shooter, and the bare bowmen will wonder why his picture has changed so drastically.

As a string lets down in height, the bow picks up cast. This increase of cast is not too noticeable at the shorter distances, but out around forty yards it begins to come into focus rather quickly, and at sixty yards you may pick up as much as half a target with one-quarter inch decrease in string height. The reason for the increase in cast is that the arrow is receiving more power from the limbs by staying in contact with

the string longer. This point is argued rather strongly at times, but it still remains a fact that a high string loses cast, and a lower one gains cast.

If an archer buys a commercial string that already has been served in the middle he is taking a chance that the serving will pull apart as the string takes its initial stretch. Most bow string manufacturers serve their bow strings under the same tension that will be applied to the string for the given weight bow for which it is designed. But if the bow string has been served under little or no tension, then this situation can occur.

Another prime reason for the serving to pull apart is the twisting of the bow string to gain or decrease height. If the twist is made in the same direction as when the serving thread was put on, all well and good, but if the twist goes against the direction used in serving, then it will tend to loosen it.

The correct nocking point of the arrow on the string is of great importance. If any one point about bow strings is exacting to a point of perfection, then it has to be the nocking point. This one phase of archery

The string at top is commercially made, while the other is a handmade Flemish splice type. However, the lower string has seen much use and has stretched to thinness.

This greatly enlarged photo of the serving on bowstring shows how vulnerable it is to fraying. This usually is caused by fingers or the string hitting the arm guard.

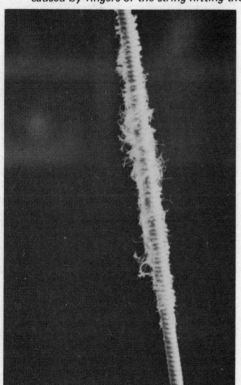

is so individual, that if two archers shoot the same bow with the same arrows, chances are they would have to use different nocking points for perfect flight of their arrows. The reasons for this are varied and many, although they deal with bow construction, and bow tillering plus the fact that almost every archer holds a bow slightly different, and the pressure of his release fingers on the string are different.

A nocking point should never be determined until the string has been shot in, and lost all of its stretch. Then a mark should be made on the string at right angles to the arrow rest. This can be done with a square, or one of the nocking jigs on the open market.

Place the bottom of your nock on this mark and shoot a few arrows. If the arrows oscillate up and down then move your arrow up the string until you get perfect flight. If you carry extra strings, then you should be sure that all of the nocking points are the same on each and every one of them. Varied nocking points can mean the difference of coming home with a trophy — or just coming home.

The number of strands per string usually is determined by the weight of the bow. And if there are manufacturer recommendations available, they should be followed rather closely. The least number of strands you can get by with is preferred, as the lighter string improves cast, and smooths out the bow. It is not the physical weight of the string that brings about the added cast, but the fact that the lighter string will stretch more when it reaches strung position after being released. This allows the limbs further action forward. This results in the arrow staying on the string longer as with your lower string height. The heavier string is much stronger, so will not stretch as far, and does stop the limb action much quicker than the lighter string. This sudden stop with the heavier string will produce a noticeable jar in some instances.

Keeping your strings at perfection levels is much easier to do than keeping your emotions and shooting abilities above par. – C. Johnson

RIG A JIG

This Do-It-Yourself Project Can Save Frustrations In String Twisting

Craftsman assembles the string jig after all parts have been made and assembled. Materials cost only a few dollars, but can provide one bowstrings he requires.

THE IRISH are famous for their jigs and archers who desire to make their own bowstrings need one. String jigs are made easily and most of the materials can be found in your culch pile.

The list of materials includes a 2 x 4 at least fifty-six inches long for the baseboard and three pieces of 2 x 4, each two inches wide, for legs for the baseboard; a piece of three-quarter-inch plywood that will cut two arms twenty inches long and five inches wide at the center; two ½ x 3-inch machine bolts with wing nuts and washers; four unfinished furniture legs nine inches long; four 5/16-inch nuts and four small screws with washers or something similar; a piece of quarter-inch or smaller rod material and the tools found in most home workshops. These materials, if purchased, would run about $2.50. Not counting the wood, you can make a string jig that will allow you to make strings for the longest or the shortest bow on your rack.

Cut the 2 x 4 to a length of fifty-six inches. Cut three pieces of 2 x 4 into two-inch blocks to use as legs for the baseboard. The 2 x 4 can be hardwood, but construction pine or similar smooth wood will do nicely. Mark out on the plywood a tapered arm that will be 4½ inches across at the center and will have a distance across of two inches just before the ends are rounded. A straight cut will do as well but the tapered cut gives more body to the arms and makes them stronger. These arms will be mounted on the 2 x 4 baseboard and will support the table legs. Drill a half-inch hole in the center of the two arms to fit the half-inch machine bolt.

Set the arms aside for the time being, and put the two-inch block legs on the 2 x 4. The legs go at the center and one on each end. Drill a half-inch hole three inches from the right end of the 2 x 4 for the machine bolt.

On the other end measure in three inches, then mark a center line down the 2 x 4. This later will be the adjustable part of your jig. Continue the line for nineteen or twenty inches. Mark the ends of this line, then drill a half-inch hole on each end. The center of the 2 x 4 will be cut out to one-half-inch width following the center line to the two half-inch holes that overlap, cut with a power jig saw or a hand jig saw. After the slot has been cut, rasp the sides smooth.

At this point there will be one hole in each of the two

The hole in the plywood arm is countersunk with larger drill so that the nut holding the leg will be beneath the surface of the wood. This avoids string hangups.

The arms for the jig are fashioned from plywood. They are traced on wood, then cut out with the saber saw.

These legs usually come with a metal cap on the end, merely a large metal cover which is held with a small nail. To remove this, just take a screwdriver and insert under the end cap and it will lift off easily. There is also a brass band about two inches down the sides of the legs. This will be retained since it will give strength to the leg and for the rods to be inserted. After the cap is removed, drill a hole the size of your metal rod about one and one half inches into the top of the leg. Drill through the metal cap and on into the top of the leg. The easiest way to do this is with a drill press, holding the leg in a

arms and one hole on the right end of the baseboard and a twenty by one-half-inch slot on the left end. The half-inch bolt will fit into this slot and the end hole. Attach the arm through the center hole with the wing nut. If assembled at this point, there will be a frame for the jig and the crossarms for the legs.

The nine-inch legs have several advantages. They are long enough so that when serving with a rapid server there is enough height from the arms to allow it to swing freely. They are solid and will not give, as the string is wound onto the arm. They are inexpensive, costing about forty cents each for the cypress wood variety. These legs are to be mounted on the crossarms and must swing freely so that the arms may swivel from a right angle to parallel the baseboard.

The mounted bolts attached to the legs aren't long enough to go through the three-quarter-inch plywood, so they must be cut. Mark a line around the base of the leg about three-eighths-inch from the bolt end, then saw the three-eighths-inch from the bolt end of the leg with a coping saw or some such easily controlled cutter. Be careful if using power equipment that you don't cut the bolt, too.

When the wood has been cut to the bolt, the small piece will come off easily. Use the cut off piece from the leg to mark the center hole on the end of the arm. Mark it so that it is flush with the end of the arm and drill a five-sixteenths-inch hole at the center mark on both ends of both arms.

With the wood cut off, the leg will now fit into the arms and just about be flush with the bottom. Use a larger drill and countersink the depth of the five-sixteenths nut. Tap the nut lightly into the countersunk hole and the leg will screw into it leaving the bottom of the arm flush, allowing it to swing freely around the baseboard.

Holes are drilled into the bottoms of the table legs, as explained in the text, then metal pegs inserted in each.

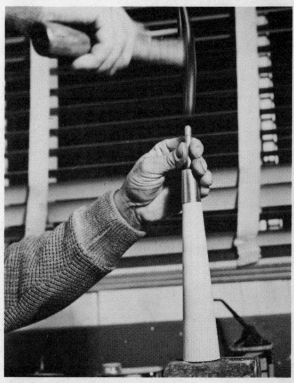

vertical position with a vise. If you don't have a drill press in your shop, it can be done by placing the leg in a vise, then carefully drilling the hole with a hand drill.

Cut four lengths of metal rod strong enough not to bend when the string is being wound on, in this case one-quarter was used, but it doesn't have to be this heavy. Cut them long enough, about 2½ to three inches, to fit into the drilled holes in the legs and leave about an inch to an inch and a half above the leg. Grind the ends of the rod to take off the burr, and if you like, you can taper the end to make it fit easier into the hole. The hole shouldn't be too big since the rod should fit snugly. If

Minimum expense is involved in fashioning this jig to make strings in less time than is required otherwise.

the hole is drilled too small, the wooden leg will split when the rod is driven into it. Tap the rods into the end of the leg and then screw the leg into the hole and the countersunk nut in the bottom of the arm.

This gives you a roughed out jig. The arms are attached to the baseboard with the half-inch bolts, then the washers and wing nuts to allow the arms to be tightened firmly. As it sits now the jig will give years of string making service. It may be painted but since the arms swivel on the board, the paint may peel. A stain will make the jig look better and also help preserve the wood. A light sanding on the wood and the stain gives it a professional look.

This then is the jig for the archer to make any size string from the shortest to the longest. If you have a ultra short bow and find you can't get your string made on this jig, cut the slot more toward the center of the baseboard and you can make strings as short as you like. You also can make strings for the popular sixty-nine-inch bows.

Turn the arms so the ends are the farthest distance apart, they will be parallel with the baseboard. Measure with a tape the distance from the outside of one rod to the outside of the other rod at the extremes. To make it simple, set it at sixty inches. Now turn the arm carefully in the slotted end of the board and, when it is at right angles to the baseboard, tighten it firmly with the wing nut. Now if you place a section of tape measure at the exact edge of the arm, the inside edge should have the sixty-inch distance placed there. The string is measured with the arms turned parallel with the baseboard, but the string is started with the arms at right angles to the board. By placing your section of tape — a metal refill works nicely — you can set your adjustable arm for the desired length of the string you are planning to make.

This last bit isn't necessary, but will help you to make the strings the same each time. To check your mark and the tape placement, release the adjustable arm, move it to another measurement, note it and then turn it parallel with the baseboard, take your other tape and check the outside measurement. A few checks will give you the proper placement, then the section of tape may be tacked or glued to the baseboard.

This is just one variety of the many types of jigs that can be made. The legs may be substituted with metal rods the entire length, the arms may be made of pieces of pine or hardwood; the plywood was selected for its strength and resistance to warping. The baseboard may be made of hardwood; not necessary but if you have a chunk in your scrap pile it is stronger and smoother than pine; the legs of the bottom of the baseboard may be eliminated if you plan to clamp the jig in a large vise, it will serve just as well. The nine-inch legs may be shorter or longer as you desire and they may be of hardwood also. If hardwood were used throughout, you could take your jig and put it in the living room as a conversation piece if the little woman will let you.

The idea on this string jig is to give you the basic idea of how to build one; it may be modified as you see fit or as your wood pile warrants. The materials for this one were all purchased except for the wood, for less than $2.50.

The tools needed would be a power drill, assorted drill bits, a hacksaw, nails, a jig saw for cutting the slot or, if you have a bench saw, the slot is a simple cut, or if you don't have the jig saw but just have the half inch drill it may be drilled and then smoothed with a wood rasp. The wing nuts are easy to tighten and give a solid hold on the arms.

One more finishing touch might be the addition of a small screw with a washer under it on each of the legs on the outside. This will serve as a holding point for the beginning and ending of the endless string. — *Bob Learn*

A Little Time And Dacron Can Make You An Expert Bowstring Builder!

THE STRING'S THE THING

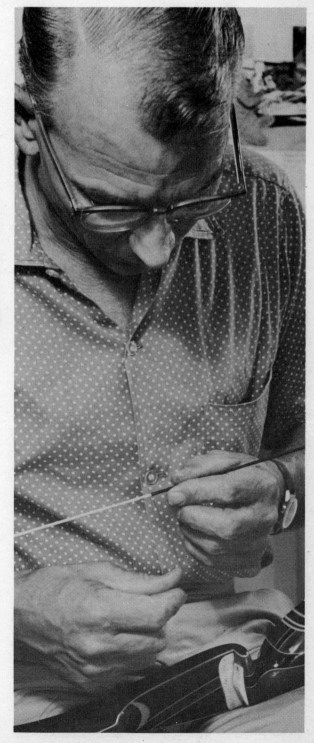

THE FIRST THING many archers learn to make is the bowstring. This may seem complicated to the beginner, but after making one or two it becomes easier. The string jig is, of course, one item you need to make or buy before making the string.

There are two basic types of string material offered to the archer today, the regular unstressed dacron string material and the newer pre-stressed and waxed dacron B. Years ago the main source of string material was flax, but this has been replaced with this newer synthetic material. Dacron is purchased from the local archery shop or from a mail order house. The type isn't important, but if you are just getting started, it is best to use the pre-stressed, waxed variety. This is the latest on the market and gives excellent results.

The first thing you need is the length of string to make. This usually is taken care of quite simply, since you no doubt will make a string for your own bow and know its length.

To find the length of your string, place the string from your bow on the jig, stretch tightly and this should give you the desired length for the new string. However, this may not always be true, if your present string is not correct for your bow. If you have no string but just the bow and desire, this presents a different problem. Take a tape measure the length of the bow, following the

When the proper length is determined, the dacron line is wound on string jig with continued steady pressure.

Beeswax is applied after the neck ends have been marked. This is explained more fully in the accompanying text.

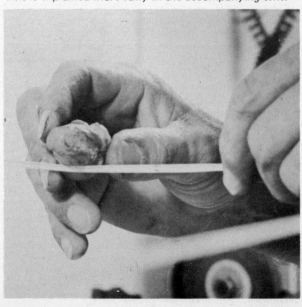

recurve on the inside as you would hold the bow for shooting, from tip to tip. From this total measurement subtract 3½ inches, and this should give you the length to make the new string. Bows may be of many lengths, from forty-eight to seventy inches, so there is really no standard. In my collection I have 54, 63 and several 66 inchers, and each requires a little different string to perform properly. Once you have determined the proper length to make your strings, you can mark your jig; from then on, it is merely a matter of how many you want to make.

Let's make a string using the string from your bow or take one of the spares from your tackle box. Turn the arms of the jig so they are parallel to the base and place the loop of the string on one end, then place the other loop on the opposite arm. This now is pulled tight and should give you the new string of the same measurement. Sometimes the first string for a new bow or from a new string jig will be either too long or too short but it will give you something from which to work. You have to make one to find out where to go: either longer or shorter.

Loosen the arms of the jig and turn them at right

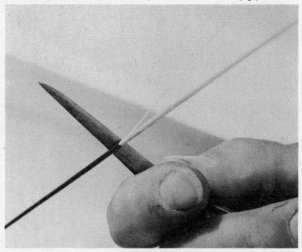

After the serving is tied off, cut the end of the strand of dacron secured previously to the screw on jig post.

angles to the base. Be careful on the moveable arm that it doesn't slip. On my jig, I drilled a hole on the lower arm and placed a pin in it so that this arm always will be at the proper angle and give the same results each time. On the moveable arm, I make a string or two for a bow and, when I find I have the proper distance in the jig, I drill a shallow hole for this arm and pin it. Then the next time I want a string for my bow, I run the moveable arm to the pin setting for that bow, drop the pin in, tighten the wing nut and string away, knowing it will be of the proper length.

Let us assume you have the jig set for the first string to be made. The arms are at right angles to the base and you are ready to wrap on the dacron. The number of strands used for the string will depend upon the weight of your bow and the type dacron you are using.

The chart illustrates the number of strands that should be used:

Old type dacron			New waxed dacron		
20-30	lb.	10	to 35	lb.	8
30-40	lb.	12	35-45	lb.	10
40-50	lb.	14	45-55	lb.	12
50-60	lb.	16	55-65	lb.	14
60-70	lb.	18	65-70	lb.	16

There are other factors that enter into this strand business. If you are using a tournament bow and wish the finest tuning, you may want to use the minimum number of strands to give your bow the best performance. The fewer the strands, the more singing or twang the string will give. The hunter will be using a bow upwards of forty pounds, so he will be using fourteen or more strands. The more strands you use, with common sense, of course, the less noise the string will give. Some archers solve this problem by making all their strings of a certain number such as sixteen or eighteen and they have

the necessary strength and they are getting the smallest amount of noise. If you make the string too thick, it will not allow the nock to seat properly and will not give the bow a chance to give the performance for which it is designed.

We will make a sixteen-strand string for a fifty-four-inch bow. First we set the arms with the string from the bow for length, turn the arms at right angles and pull tight with the wing nuts so they won't turn. The stationary arm is pinned so it can't turn, but the moveable arm isn't. We don't know if the string will be right, so we will check it after it is completed. If it is what we want, pin the moveable arm for this length.

Using about five pounds pressure, this amount will burn the fingers as the dacron is turned around the jig but not enough to cut or hurt the hand. Wrap on sixteen strands counting each side, or if you prefer, eight times around one corner; it all comes out the same. As a final check if you count the number of strands between the arms in front of you there should be eight; likewise, there will be eight on the opposite side. The small screws in the arm of the jig will serve as a holding point for starting the string and as a holding point when you have the number of strands you desire. Wrap the dacron around the holding screw and cut it off.

The next piece of equipment can be made from a piece of wood, a piece of arrow shaft, or as I did, from a piece of plexiglass. This is marked off to serve as a guide for the distance between the ends that the string is served on the upper and lower loops. For the first string you may not worry about the different loops, but later you will want to make the upper loop a little bigger. This allows the string to move down the upper limb

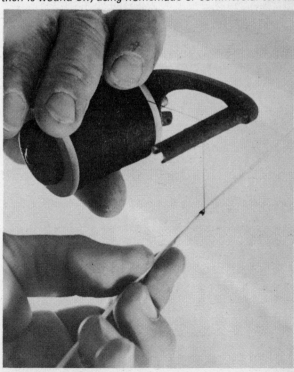

This serving is started by hand for a couple of turns, then is wound on, using homemade or commercial server.

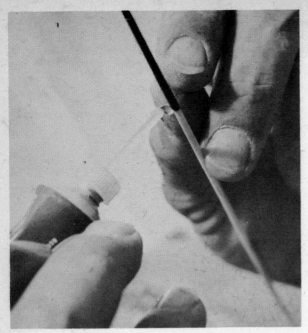

If the serving is done correctly, it will hold, but a drop of quick-drying glue at ends is a precaution.

serving and start hand serving the string to finish off the serving.

You will notice, as you serve the string onto the dacron, the six wraps you have made beyond the serving now are coming off as you serve on. If the serving and wraps are not diminishing evenly, you have the loop going the wrong way.

Remove the wraps, reverse the loop and wrapping and start over. When you finish, if you have the wraps placed properly, the wraps will run out and you will have six or seven tight serves around the end of the serving and a loop of thread left over. Take the loose end of the serving thread and pull it slowly. The loop will pull into the serving and you will have a tight finish on your serving. Cut the loose end off and you are ready to serve the other loop after putting a dab of glue on the tied-off serving.

Go to the other end of the jig and serve the other loop in the same manner. It makes no difference which you do first.

When both loops are served, pull the pin on the base arm and loosen both wing nuts. Now turn both arms at the same time so the string and arms are parallel with the

when it is strung and unstrung. If the loop isn't big enough, it won't move far enough to allow these operations. The lower loop is smaller since it is left in place on the bow.

I have a piece of plexiglass marked so that I can make the upper loop four inches long and the lower loop three inches. This guide also is designed to be on the center of the string when the tip is over the wing nut bolt. This gives me the same results every time.

Wax the string heavily with beeswax and mark with the guide a line to start and to finish. Start your server by laying the string along the dacron and wrap it by hand for several turns, turning away from you, until you can use the server. Servers can be made or purchased from your local shop. It keeps the tension on the serving thread — usually nylon now but cotton will work as well — constant and gives a fine, even serving to the finished product. If you have no serving thread, you might rummage through the little woman's sewing box and find some type E nylon or some cotton thread. If neither are available, spin off some dacron onto a spool and use this. It is heavier but will work.

Serve down the string to the end mark, pull out about a foot of extra string, cut and place the server to one side. Retain tension on the loose end or the serving will unwrap and you will have to serve by hand. Now tie off the end. This seems complicated to many, but it is the same thing you do when you wrap the eyes on a fishing pole.

Take the loose end of the string and make a loop beyond the serving. You normally will serve away from you, so take the string and bring it through the loop in the opposite direction to the serving. Run the string around the dacron loosely for about six or seven turns. Now lay the loose end of the string along the completed

Operation of the jig is a simple matter, once one has become familiar with the sequence of production events.

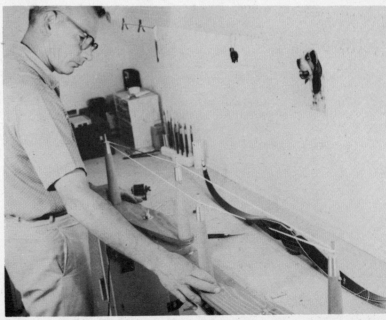

baseboard. Keep tension on the string and tighten the wing nuts. Now slide the string around the posts until the loops are around the end rod on the arm. They probably won't be even, but that is better, since when you serve the ends they will taper a bit instead of jumping from the strands of the string to the loop serving. By having them staggered in length, they will serve a neater end, but if they are even it makes no difference. Now take your server once more and start serving at the end of the served loop and serve toward the post about a half inch or so; the distance is determined by the size of the loop you want when you are finished. After you have served toward the post, reverse and serve back over the already served section and on down the string toward the center for about six inches.

The reason for the double serving on the loops is to give them the added strength, since they will be under more stress when stringing and unstringing than the rest of the serving.

When you have the desired distance down the string,

By turning arms of the jig, the string is rotated into position for the next step, the serving of the ends.

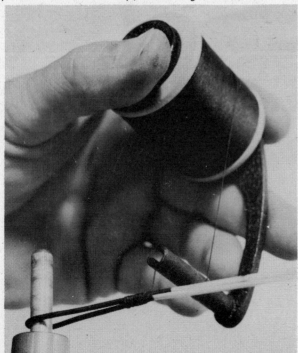

pull out about a foot or more of thread and cut, retaining tension on the serving. This time when you make your loop and prepare to tie off the ends, make about twelve wraps since this part of the string will receive more whipping than the loop section did. Tie off and cut the loose end, put a dab of glue on the end where you have finished the serving, then move to the other end and repeat the same process, double serving toward the post and then reverse and serve down the string about six inches, tie off and glue.

You now have a nearly finished string. The center serving remains. If you are sure of your jig and the settings, you can serve the center section on the jig. If not, take the string off the jig and put it onto your bow. This also gives you a chance to check the string to see if it has the proper fistmele. Since we are using the old style dacron which hasn't been stretched, the string probably will be a little too high. Take a piece of beeswax and wax the string heavily. Now take a piece of leather and place it around the string and move up and down the string rather rapidly, at the same time apply pressure. This serves two purposes: it impregnates the string with beeswax and stretches it at the same time. Check the fistmele now to see if it has changed. It should have dropped a bit. If it has dropped too much, remove the end of the string from the bow and put a few twists into it. You should allow about one full twist in three inches. If you need more twists than seem reasonable, you made your string too long. Reset your jig and make another shorter string. If the string still is too high after rubbing it with the leather, you have your jig set too short.

When you have the fistmele to your approval, take a square and mark the right angle from the arrow rest. Allow either more distance below this ninety-degree mark or make your center serving in even inches above and below for a balanced string. Most center servings are about eight to ten inches long. Start the serving with the string on the bow and serve from the bottom up for a right-hand bow since this will put the center serving in a tightening twist when you nock your arrow and brace the bow. Serve to the end mark, giving at least ten or twelve wraps to tie off, since this part of the string will receive the most whipping. Add a drop of glue and your string is finished. Before you shoot it, you will have to add your nocking point.

There are many types of nylon that can be used for serving. While browsing in a fishing tackle store I saw some beautiful multi-striped nylon, type E; just what I wanted for serving. I purchased two or three spools and made some of the wildest bowstrings you ever saw. When I showed my strings around, I was informed these weren't new and were outlawed in instinctive competition shooting. This was a shocker, but it seems some instinctive types had been using the multi-striped strings and using the different colors as range markers when shooting in competition.

It's fun to experiment, as with the multi-colored serving. Try different lengths, different number of strands and different servings, until you find the combination that works best for you. You may make all strings with eighteen or twenty strands and serve with black cotton, or you may make your hunter strings with the fewer strands, then camouflage them afterwards.

Regardless of the final decision, there is nothing like having the first string fit right for the desired performance. – *Bob Learn*

Most People Can Make A Bowstring, But Tying It Off Becomes A Problem.

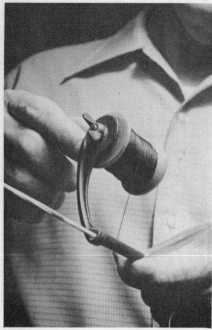

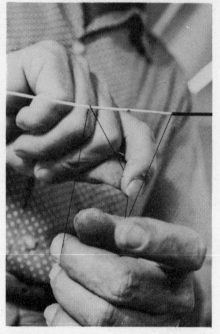

1. Most people can make a bowstring, but tying it off is the problem. Serve to the end of your mark, pull about two feet of extra thread out and hold it, cutting off the remainder.

2. If you served with the server moving away from you, make a large loop at the bottom of the string on same side from which string came off.

3. Bend thread around string, bring end through loop and back to you. Hold tension on string at all times to keep it from unraveling on you.

4. On the center serving, make at least ten loops around the string, keeping the thread moving in the opposite direction to the serving.

5. After ten or so wraps of thread, bring the end of it along the serving, moving back toward the section that already has been served as described.

6. Hold tension on the string as you had serve loose end back from section you stopped serving. If proper loops are made, thread will unwrap where you made serving loops.

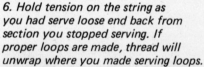

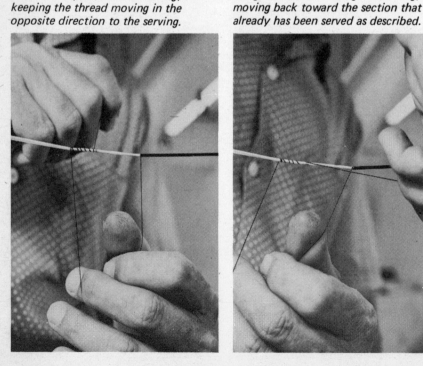

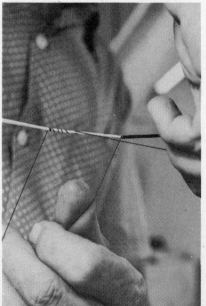

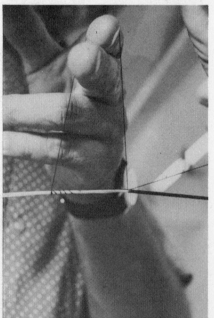

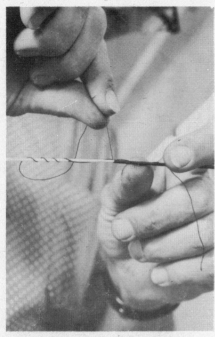

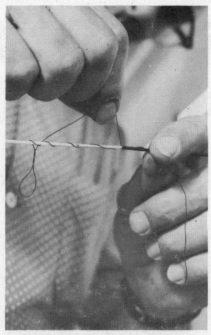

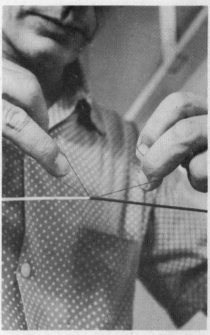

7. Continue serving the thread by hand and your loop will move off the string as you serve on. (Remember that all photos appear opposite from the way in which you will be serving.)

8. One can see the wraps moving off the left end, onto right in photo. Hold constant tension on string for tight serve; also hold loose end.

9. When you come to the end of the hand serving, you should end up with single loop on left and loose end on right. Note the tight wrapping made.

10. Pull the loop into the serving by pulling on the loose end of the tread. Pull tightly into serving, so loose wraps tighten, won't unravel.

11. Pull the little loop tightly into the serving. When done, one should have a continous serving, which has no breaks, no loose ends showing.

12. Cut the loose thread from the serving after you are certain of the proper tension. To assure that it doesn't unravel, use drop of cement.

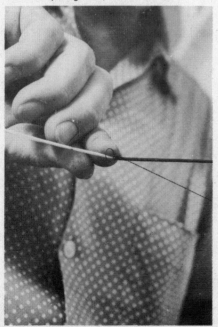

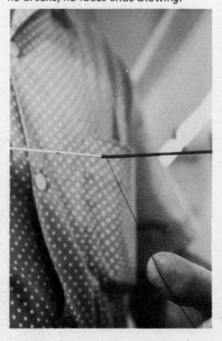

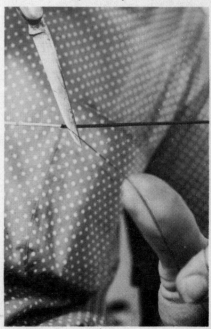

Chapter 8

FATHER OF THE LAMINATED BOW

The Secret Of This Type Of Bow Was Lost In History; It Had To Be Rediscovered To Enter Modern Archery

spot to fifty pounds, and with this bow, Lowell Drake shot an official distance of 491 yards. With the sixty-two-pound bow Drake shot a practice distance of 555 yards and an official distance at the same meet of 567 yards in the sixty-five pound class.

Eicholtz made these bows using a glass back on the tension side, a yew core and a plastic Lamicoid face on the compression side. The bow had to be thinner due to the strength of the plastics. He made two bows of the same style, one thinner than the other, but they shot the same in performance tests.

In early 1949, Eicholtz started working with George Gordon to develop a uni-directional fiberglass that would have proper recovery properties and durability to

Frank Eicholtz, who is credited with the design of the modern laminated recurve bow, inspects current types.

T HERE is an old saw that grinds out a tune: nothing is new; only different in style or design. This is true of the modern laminated bow. If you walk into a sporting goods store to inspect different bows on the rack, you may see a few hickory self bows — they still make them, you know — and alongside may be a solid glass bow, still a self bow in its own style. Next to these may be one of the modern laminated glass and hardwood bows.

The laminated bow dates back centuries. The Turks made a laminated bow of hardwoods, horn, sinew and held it together with wrappings of leather or sinew and glue. They shot a wicked arrow, but when subjected to heat, would stretch and the poundage and cast would vary. When cold, they might break. The modern laminate of fiberglass and hardwood has resiliency and is virtually immune to temperature changes.

Some Orientals still make laminated bows of bamboo that measure seven feet in length. These are used mostly for ceremonial shooting with the thumb release and the long draw characteristic of the Japanese style of archery.

Many people have experimented with different types and styles of bows, but one man had an idea, proved it successful and made bows of laminates for years.

Frank Eicholtz read about the Oriental bows, and their laminated construction, then tried making them of bamboo, horn and most other plausible combinations — and some that weren't. During WW II he tried making bows from Lamicoid, a plastic material that he had used in making illuminated signs. He tried this material on the face of the bow. It worked and started his idea of applying plastics to the bow laminations. Fiberglass was a critical material during the Forties, but in 1944 he talked with Dr. Glenn Havens of Narmco, a fiberglass company, and had the doctor make a bit of fiberglass for an experimental bow. Eicholtz tested different forms and resins and had trouble finding the right combination. Some bonding agents wouldn't hold, but finally he got a bow to stay together.

He made two of these with a plastic Lamicoid face and hickory backing with weights of fifty-five and sixty-two pounds, using the long Oriental recurve. Harry and Lowell Drake wanted to try flight with these bows. They took the two to the 1946 Southern California Archery Association flight shoot and Harry Drake shot the fifty-five pound bow on a practice round for a distance of 533 yards. He wanted to compete in the fifty-pound class, so took a scraper and reduced the poundage on the

*Eicholtz inspects a seven-foot Japanese bow of bamboo.
This is one of many specimens he studied over the years.*

withstand the constant compression and tension. Gordon took strands of fiberglass and laid them out in a straight even form, impregnated them with resin and held them in that pattern until cured.

"This early work with Frank Eicholtz on uni-directional fiberglass started us on the manufacture of fiberglass facing and backing that is used today on our modern laminated bows," George Gordon, now president of the Gordon Plastics, Incorporated, says.

As a test on the new material, Eicholtz made and strung a fifty-two-pound, sixty-six-inch bow and hung it on the wall for two years. Periodically he checked the weight; it always came to the same fifty-two pounds. However, the string had to be replaced several times.

Further experiments showed the yew core didn't have the necessary strength, so Eicholtz began testing other woods for the core of the laminates. The tests on maple proved excellent in shear strength, it was easily available, had good grain and offered excellent gluing properties. Maple still is the most popular wood core for the modern laminated bows.

When Eicholtz first started cutting the sight window into the handle riser, other archers said they were doing fine with the conventional type of bow, sans window. The early risers were of Osage orange which is strong, has good weight and color, but hard to find. He used

maple on the lower priced bows, and walnut on production models.

During his tests he found that laminated risers offered better appearance than with the relatively small handles then used. He extended the length of the handle riser to increase the recovery rate. By shortening the working limb, it will vibrate faster and recover more rapidly, giving the arrow greater speed.

The idea that the shorter bows are faster was true of the old self bows, Eicholtz claims, but this isn't true of the laminates. If you take a fifty-four-inch laminate and compare the working limb length with the sixty-six-inch bow, you find they are almost the same length. The difference is in the riser length. A short bow shot at a short range usually will shoot high, giving the illusion of being faster than the long bow, but at sixty yards, the longer bow will be much faster. Eicholtz has tested this theory on velocity machines.

The idea of the center-shot bow isn't new either, and Eicholtz tried this in his experiments. Center-shot, when incorporated in a bow, helps to eliminate the bending of the arrow around the bow on release. He found that in going to the center-shot style the riser wood had to be hard enough and strong enough to withstand the pressures, so he beefed up the opposite side of the bow.

The ancients used meticulously compounded animal

and fish glues on their laminated bows. Eicholtz tried several bonding agents before finding one that proved satisfactory. First he tried casein glue, since it is less susceptible to moisture, but found it didn't have the high strength and durability required. He finally hit on the epoxy resins that were new at the time. These bonding agents cured rapidly and had the desired strength and durability. The only times that the new composites would break was when improperly heat treated or when uncemented areas are left in spreading the epoxy. The epoxy was dependable and colorless, and the more rapid curing time made a high rate of production possible. He used forms fitted with electric heat controls for proper curing.

During his tests, Eicholtz found the cross section in the limb construction worked better with a narrow, thick limb since it had more rigidity. For example, if you take a piece of hardwood one-eighth by eight inches, you can twist it in your hand. Now take a piece of the same kind of wood in a one-inch square and try to twist it. Apply this principle to limb construction with common sense and a narrow but thick recurve limb will

These three Eicholtz models show some of experimentation done in center-shot angle of handle. Bow in background had raised handle with arrow rests on both sides. Center bow illustrates buildup of the arrow rest, while the third bow is an early model of center-shot hunter bow. Below, the same bows, showing their overall conformation.

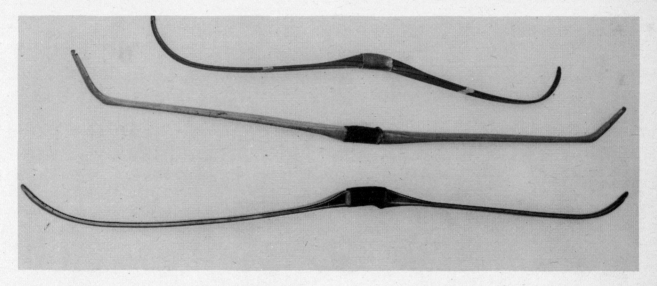

be less liable to twisting and becoming badly aligned. However, most bow manufacturers keep them wider to maintain the strength in the nock end, which receives the most punishment.

When Eicholtz began experimenting with laminates, he also went to the recurve bow design. With the added strength of the laminates and the ease of forming them into the desired shape, it made the recurve practical.

A recurve is a lever working to your advantage. More reflex gives you more pounds per inch working for you. A straight shank, or handle-high reflex bow will shoot very fast, but there also will be a great deal of shock in the handle and bow arm plus instability and a tendency to squirm. By adding deflex, you arrive at a compromise between the recurve and the pound per inch drawn, reducing the shock and stabilizing the bow, but slowing down the shaft.

The tendency is to have more recurve to offset more deflex. The recurve must reach the right point at full draw to have top efficiency. Too sharp a recurve and it is inefficient and the same is true of not enough recurve. Deflex is needed so the arc of the limb comes away at the tangent to the root of the handle riser at full draw.

Too much deflex takes away from the thrust which can only be offset by longer recurves and you are back at the same problem. By trial and error over a period of time Eicholtz arrived at a happy medium in the reflex/deflex ratio for his bows.

Gene Sissler and I were rambling around the hills, popping squirrels, keeping careful score and an eagle eye on each other. Nothing whets the shooting eye better than friendly competition. I was shooting a brand new forty-nine-pound model from a major manufacturer, one of the company's newest. Sissler had an old stick that he shoots with deadly precision. Curious, I glanced at the style and manufacturer. It was one of Eicholtz' early models in forty-five pounds and Sissler claims it is the only bow he owns and the only one he wants.

Though the two bows were made years apart in time and the manufacture and style were radically different, the basic components and construction were the same: a fiberglass face, laminated maple core, hardwood riser, center-shot window and fiberglass back. The bowyers and the styles were different, but this is true of a degree, if you compare the modern laminate with the early Turkish or Persian bows or the Japanese laminated bows.

Chapter 9

THAT STABILIZING INFLUENCE

There Are Several Kinds Of Fletches And Determining The Proper Type Depends Upon Use!

CUTTING a feather on a shaft used to be a matter of finding a goose, turkey, heron or other long feathered bird, plucking a feather, tying it to a selected shaft and letting the arrow fly. A bit crude, but that is the way it was done.

Today the tyro or experienced archer has a wide selection of materials and equipment from which to pick. You still could pluck bird feathers, as they used to, but it isn't recommended for accuracy and dependability.

As archery became more popular and the science of shooting became just that, a few changes were needed.

The most popular fletch is from the turkey. According to turkey pluckers, there are only four or five good feathers on each wing. The long pointer feathers have a high oil line, good quill and the best are from tom turkeys; sorry girls. There are two sides to each bird; a right and a left and feathers are used from both wings. The left wing is the more popular as the right wing is trimmed, usually, to prevent the bird from flying the coop.

The turkey fletch is divided into two categories: barred gray and white, and the solid white fletch from the cultured birds raised for Thanksgiving dinner. These two are subdivided into dyed and natural styles.

The graybar is the stronger of the two. Most dealers will state this and follow up with the fact that white feathers come from smaller birds, hence a lighter quill and oil line. The feathers are selected from the thousands that fall from the harvested birds and the best are taken for the archer. These are machine stripped, then the quill base is ground uniformly and packaged. You can purchase one or several thousand, depending upon your needs.

Did you ever look closely at that feather you put so carefully on your arrow? It is a work of art. Separate the vanes, the feather section and look with a magnifier at the little hooks and grooves. They might be called the first zipper, since that is what they resemble. You can separate them, run them back together and they will hook again to give the appearance of never having been touched.

The oil line referred to in many fletching articles and catalogs may be seen by placing the feather at an angle against the light. This will show the high glossy appearance against the quill line. If your feathers have no oil line or are low against the quill, they are not top grade feathers.

A good fletching feather will have a high oil line, over one-half-inch high, which will run the full length of the feather. This is true of both the barred and white fletch. Colors are obtained by dyeing the feathers.

Many archers shoot nothing but the gray-barred fletch, an economical buy as they are the cheaper. Others will shoot nothing but the solid white fletch, since it provides a guide for following the arrow to the target. Follow a graybar down the range, then try a solid white and see the difference.

The target archers use a white or dyed white fletch about three inches long. The hunter may use a graybar or white, depending upon his reasoning, but they are usually five inches long to help hold the weight and to stabilize the planing tendency of the hunting broadhead.

In the not too distant past you bought your feathers full length and cut your own. Now you may order full length or die-cut feathers, already pre-cut to your specified length and shape white, dyed white, graybar and dyed graybar.

For a long time the turkey feather was it. More is available today. For the highly tuned target archer, who wants top speed and constant flight, Max Hamilton designed **Plastifletch.** These are small pre-cut vanes of plastic. They come in sizes ranging from 1-5/8 inches to the big vanes that are 3-2/8. Plastifletch offers one thing the turkey feather doesn't: consistency.

The turkey feather is good, but the cuts made on the feather are never the same. No two feathers will

These are various type of fletching materials available. At bottom is Fletch-Ette; on left is gray bar with its Fur Fly tip; at top is white turkey feather fletch with spiral; upper right is oft-favored helical shield cut.

have the same characteristics. Plastifletch has been used by many champions and non-champions successfully. Some archers have a problem hitting the bow when shooting the Plastifletch, but this can be overcome by fine tuning the bow.

Along the same line is Fletch-ette made by Action Archery Products in Oregon. These are made from a soft plastic material, with all three fletches on a tube. The tube fits around the shaft of the arrow and, whammy, instant fletch ready to shoot. The size varies from two and one half inches to four inches for the target and hunting archer.

Also on the market is the **Deer Flite** plastic vane. This is mounted on the shaft singly, but in a runner or trough that is first mounted on the shaft. The vane is slid into this trough and again, instant fletch. The newer style of Deer Flite mounts directly to the shaft and doesn't use the trough system. The runner or vane is cemented to the shaft with a fletching jig.

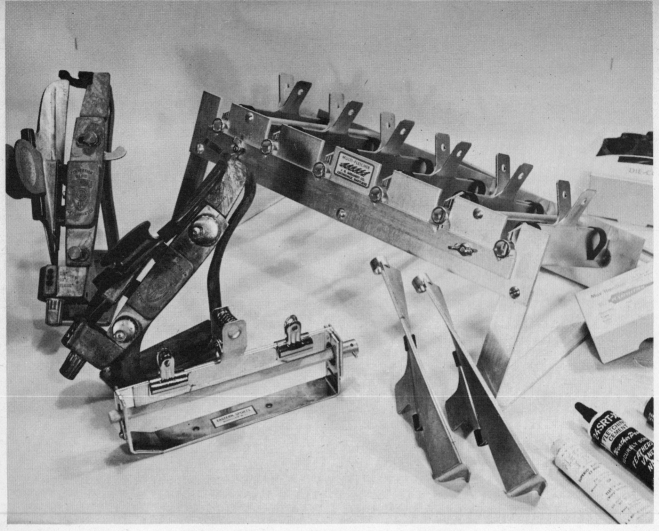

There are numerous fletching jigs now being sold. Those shown here constitute a cross-section of various types.

Sweetland's Fur Fletch is brand new. This is made from rabbit skins and has some advantages. It comes packaged in any color you like. Each strip of bunny fur is one-quarter-inch wide, with a piece of paper on the back that is pre-glued underneath. Pull the paper off, take the shaft and wind the fur around it clockwise or counterclockwise and once again, instant fletch.

Fur fletches are successful in indoor archery where the grouping is very close. You certainly can't break the bunny fur by hitting it with another shaft. Several schools are trying this fletch with success, as the archery director or student can easily rewrap a damaged shaft. They will take a lot of abuse before needing replacement. When they fly to the target and hit, they give a cotton ball effect, so you have no trouble following the arrow or finding it in the target to determine your hit from a distance. They don't work too well in a good wind, but Sweetland is working on this and hopes to be able to offer the hunter a similar fletch for the field to stabilize the broadhead and make a silent fletch for the hunter.

Now that you have been exposed to many of the fletches on the market, you must choose a method of attaching the fletch to the shaft. The tool used for conventional fletching is called a jig. It consists of a clamping device to hold the feather or vane, a rack to hold the arrow and clamp and adjustments on the rack to offer the archer a variety of styles for making his fletch.

Perhaps the oldest name in fletching jigs is Bitzen-burger. This jig does everything except shoot the arrow. It will make a fletch right or left, straight or helical, in the three-fletch in 120-degree gradations, and four-fletch in both the ninety-degree and seventy-five by 105 increments. This is all done with one jig and an instruction book. It isn't difficult to operate and offers the ultimate in fletching for the serious archer.

If you desire to buy, they also make a template. You could make your own, to assure that each time you change the jig from one style to another you obtain constant results. A magnet holds the clamp to the side of the frame and gives consistent fletch, depending upon the operator. It has a self-centering nock receiver that assures the fletch will be mounted properly.

It would be cumbersome to describe all the jigs being sold today on the market. The reason for mentioning the above two is to indicate the wide range in prices and variations offered by professional jigs. Arrow manufacturers take the best jigs, put as many as fifty on a round table, and fletch each jig as it comes around. That is too professional for some of us, but there is a happy medium.

The Multifletcher, made and sold by J. G. Geghardt Company, is a very satisfactory solution. It is an aluminum rack made to hold six clamps. It is versatile. It has two sets of nock indexes, both self-centering. With one model you can fletch your shaft in 120-degree increments or turn the nock receiver over and four-fletch in 75 x 105. You can purchase the straight clamp or the helical. For the helical you must specify right or left wing.

With the straight clamp you may adjust all six jigs simultaneously by loosening the clamps in the back, making your setting, then doing the same in front. This insures the six fletches will be identical. You may fletch either right or left wing feathers with the straight clamp by making the proper adjustment.

The clamps will hold a long fletch for the hunter or a small one for the target archer. You have the advantage of fletching six shafts at one time all the same. A solution I have used for years.

Now we need shafts. It used to be a straight willow wand or bamboo stave. Now there are three basic materials for arrow shafts: Port Orford cedar; fiberglass, and aluminum.

Port Orford cedar is the oldest. A light, straight-grained wood found in Washington and Oregon, it is popular and inexpensive. Most archers start shooting with cedar shafts. Many hunters use nothing else. Cedar shafts are becoming harder to get, and may come a day when there will be no more Port Orford cedar.

Shaft material made from Port Orford cedar, refined and compressed, is called **Forgewood.** It is made by Bill Sweetland in Eugene, Oregon. He takes the regular cedar material, compresses it, produces a strong stiffer spined shaft that gives great penetration. It is still cedar and is handled as regular cedar where fletching is concerned.

Fiberglass arrows are made by several manufacturers. A few include: Gordon Glashaft; Micro-flite; and Ace glass. The methods used in making fiberglass arrows differ with the maker.

Some take woven fiberglass materials and wind them on a mandrel of their specifications, impregnate them with a resin solution and dry. Others, like Gordon Glashaft, take the fiberglass filaments, which resemble fine white threads, wind them around a mandrel as they lay them along the mandrel and add the resin. The end product, no matter what process is used, is a shaft that is tough and light in weight.

It is hard to get them out of line. They are more rugged than cedar, more expensive, but will last longer. They make excellent hunting shafts, and they are impervious to weather.

Even well dipped and treated cedar shafts may warp, but fiberglass will withstand both high and low temperatures. If it gets too hot, there is a possibility that the resins might warm enough to move and flow a bit, but I have never seen it that hot. The fiberglass shafts are used successfully by many target archers and have been a big boon to the schools, since their equipment takes a terrific beating.

The ultimate in arrow material, for uniformity, weight and performance is the Easton aluminum shaft. They are the undisputed leaders in this field, and have spent time and money researching and perfecting their product. When you finally decide to go for broke, whether for hunting or target, you will go aluminum. The Easton Company is still using the standards developed by Doug Easton in the late 1940s.

They now offer at least three grades of shaft materials: the 24SRT-X; the XX75s, and the newer X7s. These shafts are always being improved, if you can improve on the best, and they now make the new X7 and the XX75 with a higher bend resistance.

This gives us the materials needed for making and fletching arrows, the fletch, jig and shaft.

OUR first fletch will be with a graybar feather and for the hunter. We will use a left wing feather and have three choices of mounting it on the shaft. We can make it a straight fletch down the middle of the shaft with no angle of any kind or a spiral, which still uses

Although the feather may be precut, there still is some need for removing excess material with pair of scissors.

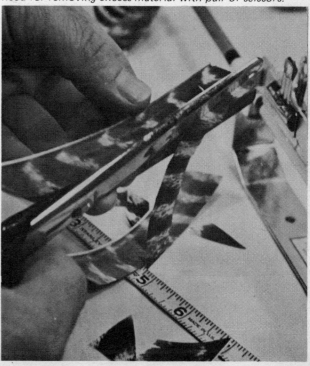

In front is a regular Port Orford cedar shaft, while a fiberglass type is behind it, followed by Micro-Flite, also of fiberglass, Easton X7 and 24SRT-X aluminums.

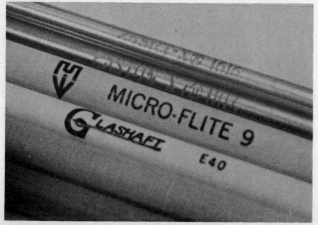

Precut feather, which is cut to proper length, trimmed, now is ready to go into the clamps of fletching jig.

the straight clamp. We angle the clamp holding the fletch to the left a little bit.

Using the Simplex fletcher made by Eastern Sports, we can move the nock end to the right and lock it in position with the set screw. We now move the front end adjustment to the left and check to see where the clamp will be on the shaft. If we go too far, the fletch will not have any shaft to adhere to and will dangle over the edge, making a sloppy finished fletch. About one degree will give a good angle to the fletch with the appearance, when finished, that it moves around the shaft, but it doesn't. This will give more stability to the arrow especially when using broadheads which may have a tendency to plane if there isn't enough feather in back to hold it.

Our other choice is to make a helical fletch. The Simplex does have a helical clamp either right or left wing. The helical actually curls the fletch around the shaft and really puts a twist in the arrow when you send it down the line. Some hunters use the spiral fletch, while others prefer the helical type. You can experiment yourself or check your local shop as to which you should buy or better yet, buy one or two finished arrows in each style and shoot them before buying your fletching jig. Most jigs on the market are available in the straight or helical clamp and one can buy either or both for the same jig. It is important, however, to de-

termine whether you desire right or left wing in the helical clamp, since it can't be adjusted.

Which is the best, right or left fletch? Most archers agree there is no appreciable difference between the two types. One thing to make sure, however, is not to mix a right and left wing shaft in the same quiver. I have always shot left wing and I'm right-handed. Some archers say a right-handed archer should shoot right wing feathers, left-handed archers shoot left wing, but this is a matter for personal experimentation.

To fletch the cedar shaft material it first must be dipped in lacquer. After the lacquer has dried and the nock has been placed on the shaft in the proper position, the shaft is placed in the jig.

Placement of the nock on a cedar shaft is important. It you look closely at an undipped shaft, you will see how the grain of the wood is close in two places on opposite sides and wide in the other two. Place the nock of the arrow so the narrow bands of the grain will bear against the side of the bow. This gives the stiffest section of the arrow against the bow and will give you the best flight for your arrow.

If you place the nock on the shaft with no attention to this little detail, no two shafts will fly the same, since they will bend in a different manner when shot. If you are using speed nocks, place the index on the narrow grained section.

Turn the nock index on the jig to the first position. This usually is indicated by a dot, a flat section or may be determined by the pin in some jigs being aligned so the index on the nock points up. Place the shaft in the nock receiver and lay the rest of the shaft in the follower of the jig. Take a clamp and make a mark on the side to tell where you should put the back of the fletch. The Bitzenburger jig is graduated at the back of the clamp in one-eighth-inch increments to help in this procedure.

The back of the fletch is placed so that the finished fletch will be at least one inch from the string when the shaft is placed in the string to shoot. This allows the fingers to close on the shaft without having the fletch in the way. If you get them too far forward they will be in the way of the bow on a five-inch hunting fletch. Make a mark on the clamp and check before you set the fletch to the shaft.

After the proper distance has been determined, take a full length feather for a five-inch hunting fletch. Remember there is only **one** good cut to each feather. If you are making rabbit arrows or ones that don't have to be exact, you can move toward the bottom of the feather and cut from there. Using this method you can get one five-inch cut and perhaps one four-inch cut from each feather for plinking arrows but when you are out for the best, make only one cut from each feather, regardless of how long, it may be and how much the temptation may be to try for two.

With a pair of scissors clip off the heavy base of the feather about one or two inches back from the end, depending upon the quality of the feather. Use a ruler or make a simple template to mark the distance on the feather to make your other cut. Make it five inches from the cut end. Now you will have a feather cut from the heart of the long pointer about two inches high and with an angle on the top. For ease in fletching I cut the top of the feather square with the top of the quill. To make it easier for the feather to go into the clamp and to prevent the feather from becoming curled in the clamp, I cut the side of the feather along the outside about three-quarters to one inch from the quill. This gives a neat looking feather to go into the jig and it handles nicely.

Place the trimmed fletch in the clamp and have the base of the quill or the heavy end facing toward the point of the shaft. The back of the quill or the top part of the fletch will be toward the nock. Slide the fletch downward and forward into the jig to insure that the fletch will go in smoothly and hold the clamp wide to prevent the feather from getting jammed in the clamp. When the top part of the quill reaches the mark made on your clamp, close the clamp on the feather. Leave about one-eighth-inch of the feather away from the clamp. You may vary this, but you should leave a small distance between the clamp edge and the quill of the fletch.

Take your cement and run a small amount down the ground base of the feather. If your ground base is wide, it is best to trim it with a pair of scissors before applying the cement, but most feathers won't require this extra step. As you squeeze the cement from the tube, move the tube down the ground base slowly, leaving a long, even flow of cement on the quill. The long applicator such as that on the Fletch-tite tube is a great aid in applying cement.

When you have the long, even line of cement on the quill base, place the clamp containing the fletch in the jig. Start from the back and lower the feather and clamp slowly onto the shaft. Make sure the base of the clamp is in its proper slot or position so you won't have to make an adjustment and end up with a sloppy finish on your shaft. Most cements are lacquer solvents and they will make the lacquer soften. Then, when they do dry, they bond with it with added strength.

After the clamp is in place with the fletch on the shaft, you can take a needle or similar small, pointed object and run this down the quill base to make sure the feather seats properly on the shaft. Then gently apply downward pressure on the clamp and let it come to rest on the shaft with the fletch held firmly on the shaft with no gaps. It takes a minimum of twenty minutes for the cement to set. Make sure the cement has set and dried before removing the clamp. If the clamp is removed before the cement has dried, the feather will have a tendency to curl on the shaft both at the top and bottom. This gives an odd looking and poorly performing arrow. Make sure it is dry.

While you are waiting for the fletch to set you can cut the other feathers in preparation to fletching. From now on it is merely a repetition of the first step to finish each arrow. When the second fletch is ready to be placed, the nock receiver will be rotated one turn for the 120-degree fletch and the second fletch applied in the same manner. Likewise, with the third. When the final fletch has dried and you remove the finished job, it will look rather crude compared to the finished product. It will resemble a flu-flu arrow in some respects, but you have more work to do.

Since we have used a full length feather and only made the length cut for the fletch we still must cut the

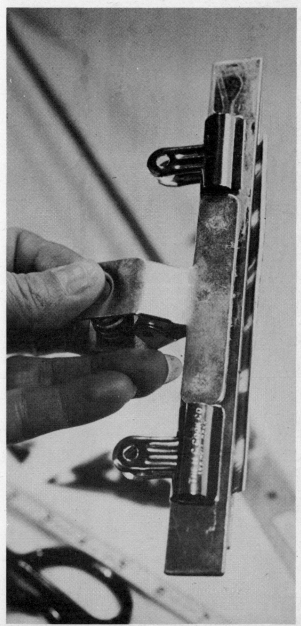

A fletch that has been trimmed with a pair of scissors is placed in clamp of Simplex jig and now is ready for application of the cement that goes on the ground base.

A Variety of Equipment Makes Fletching Arrows More Simple Than In Days Of Yore

shape we want on the feather itself. This may be the shield cut that many prefer or the parabolic. Some hunters prefer the parabolic, since it makes a neat finished arrow and they say the shield cut has a tendency to whistle a bit as it wears down.

You need a feather burner now to make the finish cut on the feather. These range from a few dollars in kit form to the Young Feather Trimmer. The principle is to use a nichrome wire, bent to the desired shape. Rotate the shaft in a block to allow the hot wire to burn the feathers to shape. You may have a little trouble bending the first wire or two, but it is easy once you practice a few times. The wires last a long time and you can make any style or shape with them. You can make one for your target fletch and another for you hunting fletch. They are easy to change and adjust.

The height to burn your fletch will depend on your shooting. If you have trouble getting a clean release and want a forgiving arrow cut your fletch about five-eighths of an inch high and it will hold a bad release. If you shoot a big broadhead it might pay to test the high fletch to see if it will hold it better. The average height for a hunting fletch is about one-half inch.

If you like, you could make a high fletch, then shoot it, burning it down as you test to determine the proper height for your style and type of equipment. It is easy to do by just moving the burning wire in a bit at a time and you can really fine-tune your equipment this way.

After the fletch has been burned to shape and the burn sanded, the forward point is cut on a slant to make it pass the sight window without deflecting interruptions

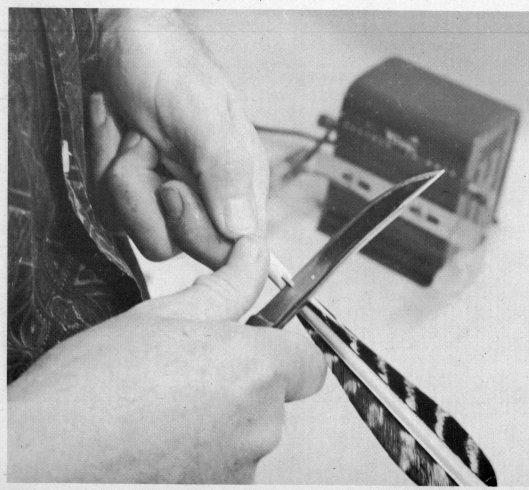

One can determine when aluminum shaft has been cleaned properly, as water will move down it evenly and not in the droplet form shown that indicates shaft is not clean.

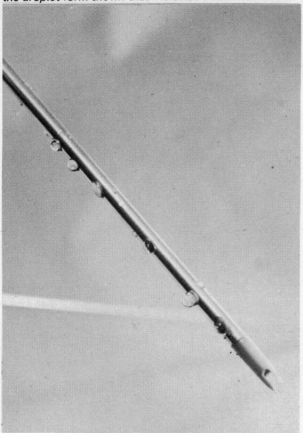

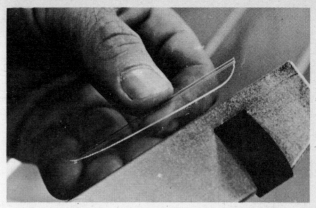

To fletch with plastic vanes, precut plastic material is placed in the clamp, then positioned properly for alignment, thus keeping fletches even around the shaft.

Turn the burner on or plug it in and, when the wire is glowing, place the shaft in the guides, being careful not to jam the feather into the wire. Then slowly rotate the shaft, burning the feathers to the desired shape. It is a neat cut and fast after you have done it a few times.

You now have the finished shaft with the burned fletch, but we're not through yet. Take an emery board and use this to remove the charred edge on the feather. A piece of sandpaper will work just as well.

You will notice that the front edge of the fletch is a bit high, and when you run your hand over this edge, it grabs. This can cut your hand when shooting or even pull the fletch off the shaft if this rough area catches on the bow or rest.

There are two ways of removing this edge: with a sharp knife or a rotating sander. A sharp knife is perhaps the easiest and it merely requires making a slanting cut forward down the edge of the quill cutting the edge to a taper where it meets the shaft. Do it carefully or you may peel some of the dip off the shaft, if you slip.

The grinder method is great and it is equally simple. If you have a small craftsman's sander wheel, use this to taper the quill base to the sanding disc. It removes the edge and tapers the cut at the same time, giving it a professional finish.

We sand the fletch to remove the charred burn, grind or cut to remove the roughness so all that remains is a little dab of cement on the forward end of the fletch where it joins the shaft at the taper and another drop at the top of the fletch. This is to prevent the feather from lifting up. When it dries it gives the leading edge a smooth finish.

THERE is a shortcut when fletching with turkey fletch. There are pre-cut or die-cut feathers on the market that will allow you to fletch your shafts, not burn them. They usually come in packages of one hundred or by the dozen. You merely place the fletch in the jig and apply the cement as in the regular procedure. They save the time of burning, give a satisfactory fletch and come in various sizes to accommodate the hunter and target archers.

If you still prefer the full length fletch and object to burning, there is another method, using the **Little Chopper** sold by Waterloo Archery in Waterloo, Iowa. I have choppers in two different sizes and they really pop out the feathers. They are made with a cutter blade shaped in either the shield or parabolic cut from two and one half to five inches. There are three sizes in each and you can get two different lengths from each size. They vary about one-half inch on each form.

You place the full length tom feather in the base, lower the blade onto the feather and whap the top of the cutter head with a hammer. The blade cuts the fletch

The cement tube is squeezed to removed bubbles in the applicator tube. When cement begins to flow smoothly, apply thin coat along grooved base of plastic fletch.

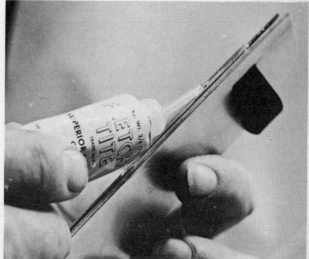

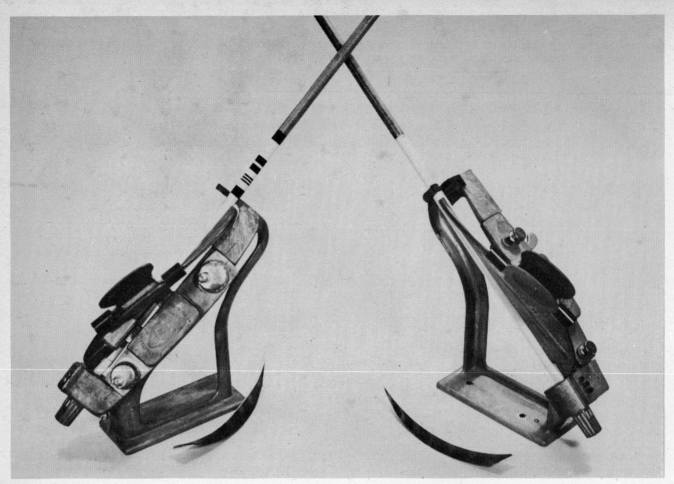

*Bitzenburger jig at left fletches right helical feather,
while one on right is holding the left helical fletch.*

and out pops a perfect die cut feather. I ordered two
sizes, the P5 to cut from 4-1/2 to five inches for the
hunting fletch in the parabolic cut, and the S3 which
cuts a 2-1/2 to three-inch shield cut for the target arrows. My first attempt was a success. Out came a beautiful shield-cut fletch three inches long with the end of
the quill already tapered. All that is necessary is to place
the die-cut in the clamp and fletch the shaft.

When I tried the long five-inch model, I had trouble
at first with the heavy base quill and had to make a
second tap on the base end. You can make the feathers
fly with the Little Chopper. In less than an hour I had
over one hundred of each size boxed and ready to fletch.
These sell for about $15.

Regardless of the method used for cutting — burner,
purchased die-cut or your own die-cut with the Little
Chopper — you have a good fletch. You seldom see
anything but feather fletch on a wood shaft, but you
can experiment with other types.

One that caught my eye was the Fletch-ette. These
are three pre-formed plastic fletch on a tube base with
the three fletch mounted on the tube. They can be
mounted quickly by placing them in warm water and
slipping them over the end of the shaft. You can give
them a bit of a spiral by holding one end and twisting
the tube a bit. I placed three on three different shafts
— two on woods, one tipped with a standard field tip
and one with a Black Diamond broadhead. The third
shaft was aluminum. I placed a lower parabolic fletch
on it. These shafts are spined for a fifty-pound hunting

bow, so I took them out to see how they would perform.

I usually mount my arrow rest on the shelf of my
hunting bows and I was curious to see if the large vanes
would clear the shelf. They didn't! I had arrows all over
the bale and on two occasions the broadhead went into
the ground about ten yards in front of the bale. I was
shooting from a distance of thirty yards.

I wondered if it could be the rest on the shelf causing
my problem. I took another fifty-pounder that had a
Herter's brush rest mounted about one half inch up the
sight window from the shelf and all three shafts flew
straight and centered in the target. The plastic vanes
hadn't cleared and were kicking up off the shelf,
giving me an erratic flight. Once I changed the arrow
rest position they flew well.

The Fletch-ettes would be a good back-up kit to
carry on a long trip. If you get into rain or snow conditions, merely slip these over a few unfletched shafts.
They would do well at a camp or school, as they will
take a lot of abuse and are easily changed if damaged.
Further tests would be necessary to see how they would
hold for serious target work, but that would be for
the individual to determine. Some people can't shoot a
stiff fletch like this. They range in size from 2-1/2
inches for target to four inches for hunting or field
work. They will fit shafts from one quarter to eleven
thirty-seconds of an inch. There are comparable sizes
for glass and aluminum.

For Forgewood compressed cedar shafts you follow
the same procedure as for a regular cedar shaft. First

dip in lacquer, then fletch. They have a smaller diameter than the regular cedar materials but fletch the same.

The fiberglass shafts offer the archer a middle choice between the cedar and aluminum. They are rugged, not quite as finely tuned as the aluminum and better than the wood. There are archers who will take exception to anyone who doesn't tout their favorite. They all have their place and all are good in their own way. You are the final judge and must decide what you prefer.

When you obtain the raw shaft in fiberglass, the length will vary. Some manufacturers and dealers will cut them to your specification, others sell the raw shaft. An unfinished fiberglass shaft is about thirty-two inches long. Both ends may be rough.

When you cut these materials to your length, it requires cutting from both ends to remove the rough edges. Make a ninety-degree cut for the nock and adapter or target point to meet. Cut about two inches from one end, turn it around and cut your desired length. A hacksaw works well on fiberglass, but be careful you don't get filament threads. I use a small miter box that allows me to hold the shaft firmly against one side for a ninety-degree cut. As I make the first cuts, I rotate the shaft slowly to make a circling cut around the outside of the shaft. By the time you have done this there is little left to hold the shaft together, so it takes a slight cut to go through.

Lightly sand the ends to remove any rough edges. Place the nock insert, or if you have a Gordon shaft, the combination Nocksert. If you prefer, you can purchase the aluminum or magnesium nock inserts for the fiberglass shafts. The cutting should be slow and careful to prevent a filament from pulling off the ends.

Your shaft is cut to length. Now you can take a two-solution epoxy from the dime or hardware store, mix and apply a reasonable amount to the insert and

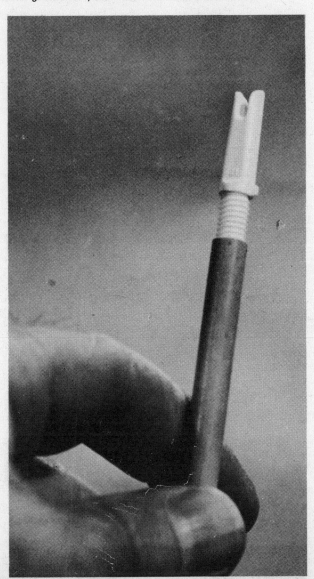

The nylon Nocksert is placed in the tube of fiberglass forming the shaft, then the nock is screwed into it.

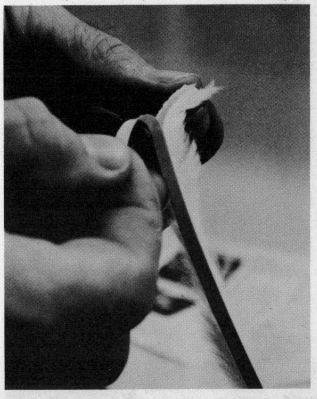

If you prefer Sweetland Fur Fletch for flu-flu arrows, peel the backing off the rabbit fur and place it in your hand to wrap shaft, starting about 1½ inches below nock.

adapter or target point. I prefer to make one epoxy mix and do both ends at the same time.

Set the shafts aside and allow the epoxy to harden. If you are in a hurry, place them near a light bulb and cover them with a small box or lid.

When the epoxy is set and the insert won't turn, you are ready to continue. If you prefer to dip the shaftment of your fiberglass in a lacquer dip, do so now, using the same procedure as for wood shafts. After the lacquer I use the **Fletch-tite** or Easton cement. They work on all types of shafts, while Duco is used only on the lacquered shafts.

Now for the undipped fiberglass shaft. Take your nocks, put a dab of cement on the insert, then place the nock on the insert and twist it around. This gets the cement flowing around and into the grooves on the insert and coats the inside of the nock.

When you first start making shafts into finished arrows you may regard the nock as just a piece of plastic to guide the shaft on the string. You're right, it does. However, a crooked nock sends off an erratic arrow. Put your nocks on as straight as possible. Place them on your cresting lathe and rotate them slowly. If the nock is out of line or off center it will wobble. If you work with it as it dries, you can get your nock on very true. This helps eliminate one more problem in the finished arrow.

With Fur Fletch, a recently introduced material, lay it on shaft by hand. It won't stick where it shouldn't.

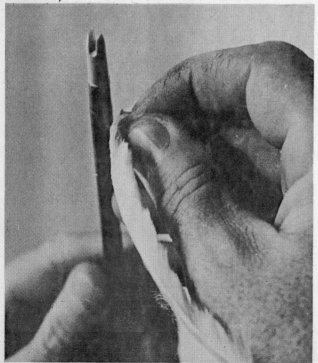

When fletching fiberglass and aluminum, the relation of the nock to the shaft is unimportant. Let the nock cement dry and you are ready to start fletching.

The cements don't adhere well to fiberglass material. In some cases the shaft may be covered with a very fine powder from the factory. Wipe the shaft, take a portion of Fletch-Tite, squeeze some in a lid or small jar, add an equal amount of lacquer thinner. Take your cresting lathe and a large half-inch brush, dip it into the solution and, as the shaft rotates, brush it onto the glass shaft from the nock far enough down the shaft to cover the length of fletch you intend to use. If you have no lathe you can make a small dip tube and use the same mixture. It will require more for the tube than the brushing technique. You could brush it on freehand, but the lathe makes a neat, fast job.

The sizing you have just placed on the shaft makes a good bonding base for the cement on the fletch. This coating is light and dries rapidly. You can now take your shafts and place them in the jig, put your fletch in the clamp and proceed as before. The Fletch-Tite may take longer drying on the glass, so allow at least twenty minutes. Rotate and continue until you have the shaft fletched.

Aluminum shaft materials are relatively new to the archer. Easton made his first aluminum shafts in the middle thirties and went into production in the late forties. The Easton shafts are considered leaders in the field. People have found problems in fletching the aluminum shafts directly on the metal and bypass this by dipping the shaftment in lacquer, then proceeding

The nock end of the Easton shaft is swaged at the factory, so there is no nock insert. The shafts will come to you cut and tipped if you so order. A small fine-toothed saw is a must if you do your own cutting. A small rotating blade works well on glass and aluminum. Most dealers have a cut-off saw designed for cutting the aluminum and glass shafts square on the end with no ragged edges. The only end you need to cut with the Easton is the point end.

For fletching your shaft without dipping in lacquer, here is a method prescribed by James Easton:

Take a cleaning powder like Ajax and scour the nock end of the shaft, then rinse until the water flows off leaving no droplets behind. Wipe the shaft with a clean paper towel, or dry it by the heater or a portable hair dryer. Don't touch the cleaned area as the oil in your hands will form a surface and the cement won't adhere.

Position your nock then place the shaft in a jig. Put your fletch in the clamp, apply a thin coat of one of the special fletching cements for shaft material, then lower the clamp onto the shaft. Rotate and finish fletching.

Aluminum will pick up moisture rapidly. This factor plus the moisture on the cement may cause the fletch to fall off later. Fletching aluminum shafts in hot, moist weather can be a problem. Most arrow manufacturers will fletch only in an air-conditioned room where the humidity and temperature can be controlled.

Easton is experimenting with a new anodized coating which will improve the bonding surface for the fletch. The anodizing process will add a brilliant or muted color, leave a thin, hard surface on the shaft and be more porous than regular shaft material. You fletch directly to the shaft without dipping.

Plastifletch adheres to all the above shafts but is

used usually on aluminum by serious archers. They can be fletched in the same jig with the same cements. Plastifletch can be mounted with a small spiral or straight down the shaft. Max Hamilton says some archers have tried a helical fletch with the plastic vanes and had trouble clearing the bow.

When using Fur Fletch by Sweetland, make sure you have a clean shaft and apply the fur as directed. To be double safe you can place a drop of cement on the front of the fur, hold it down until the cement dries and do the same at the back of the fletch. This gives added strength and makes a smooth surface to pass over the bow.

One other use for the little bunny strip is to wrap one around the shaft just behind the feather fletch. This provides a dab of white to aid in following the shaft to the target or game. It has little drag effect used in this manner.

The question of whether to go straight, spiral and helical becomes a matter of individual choice as does the selection of right and left wing feathers and fletching. Test and see what you prefer. There is something to be said for all of them.

I recently obtained a Drake Keyhole target bow with

Cement is run along the side of the jig face and onto the shaft. The correct cement must be used for proper shaft, whether wood, aluminum or glass material. The jig already holds fletch; template is held by the pin.

Fur Fletch is being made in a variety of colors and the maker claims that it will not tear under normal use.

an open center section. You shoot straight through the middle of the bow. There is no archer's paradox to contend with, and I have been experimenting with fletch and shafts. I took some light fiberglass shafts and fletched them with a Plastifletch with a one-degree spiral.

I took the bow out to the bale and those arrows started going all over. I could hold them on but couldn't get a group to suit me. I knew it wasn't the bow. The release was clean, so it had to be the spine of the shaft or the fletch. I took another group of the same shafts and put a straight fletch on them, right down the middle. This is just the way those shafts flew right to the gold as if they were magnetized.

The flight archer will use nothing but a straight fletch, one of the smallest used. They provide a bit of guidance on the back of the light missile and a minimum of mass.

The spiral fletch is found on most arrows today. It is easy to apply, and even the inexpensive arrows are using a spiral and some helical. The little arrows you find for the kids usually have a high, short fletch right down the middle, since it is the fastest way to get the job done.

The longer the fletch, the more stability it gives to the shaft. The higher it is the more forgiving it is, if you have a bad release or have a heavy broadhead on the tip of the shaft.

I have seen archers shooting target with a six-inch triple fletch about three-eighths inches high. I have heard of a successful hunter who shoots short balloon shaped five fletch.

The style of the cut, the number of fletch and the type is up to you. Experiment and find one that fits you best. There is nothing more pleasing than walking into the field or range with a set of shafts you have made yourself. That is one of the satisfactions of archery.

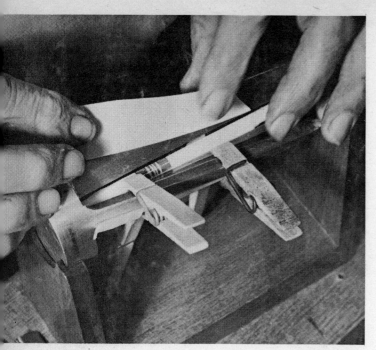

After cement is on the shaft, the fletch is placed along the side of the jig and pushed down onto the shaft. In doing this, one always must follow the curve of the jig.

One Step More: The Correct Fletching Jig Has Much To Do With The Finished Job!

WHEN YOU bought your first bow, you weren't sure of the poundage, style or make to buy. You checked around and bought the one you liked best. Your first arrows were probably fiberglass or perhaps cedar shafts, but once again you weren't sure of what was best.

Several months and many hours of practice later, probably with several meets under your belt to back up your decision, you purchased a set of spine and weight-matched aluminum arrows with your selection of colored shaftment and fletch. Perhaps you even went to mid-nocks instead of the hunter style indexed nock. When you bought those new shafts and tried them out, you knew you had the ultimate. There was nothing else to be done but to improve your style and get more practice to overcome your shooting problems.

We all think that there is just one point and that you can't go beyond this in tackle. There is one step beyond, however. There is the fine tuning that is done by the marksmen who are continually out in front. Much of this leadership is due to natural ability, practice and more practice, but there are the little things that these people know about from years of shooting.

When you ordered your "ultimate" arrows, what fletch did you have put on them? How long was it? Was it a spiral, helical or straight fletch? These questions can bring about discussions and, in some cases, heated argument among the archer groups, but they are all part of the game and sport of winning.

What do the champions use in the way of fletch? I asked Rube Powell of Chula Vista, California, five times national field champion, what kind of fletch he uses in competition.

"What do you want to know for?" Rube countered.

"There are many archers who are in the top brackets in shooting and it isn't only a matter of practice that puts them there, They have more finely tuned equipment than I would have and I'm sure there are other people who would like to know the finer points of the game," I explained.

Powell reached back into a box under his workbench and brought out a metal device that looked like a cylinder with the center cut out. This was his answer to the type of fletch he used in his shooting. He has sold shafts fletched with this jig to many archers and there are now a total of six national winners, including free-style and barebow, using his arrows.

The unit is actually a finely machined, true helical fletching jig made of aluminum. It looked different, but was it different?

The jig gives about the truest helical fletch that can be made. This is done with the use of the machined metal centering device that will fit all size shafts and metal templates that are used to help attach the fletch to the shaft. Clamps are used to hold the templates in place while the cement dries. The end product is a fletch of almost unvarying consistency, and this eliminates one more small difference between the champion and the runner-up.

What advantage is there to a helical fletch? This question can be argued in hunter and target camps for many hours, but perhaps the best solution is to try them yourself.

One thing the helical will do is to straighten out a shaft more rapidly in flight than a spiral or straight fletch. This can help if you have a problem of a bad release — if anything will help a bad release.

Few if any arrows are straight-fletched now. Perhaps there are some that are purchased by mail or in the cheaper price range, but nearly all shafts have a fletch that is set off to give it a spiral on the shaft or a helical fletch.

Perhaps the greatest difference in the jig that Powell

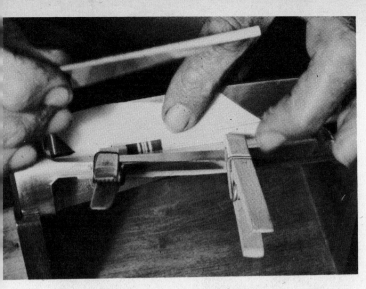

With the fletch in place and held tightly against the shaft, metal template now is ready to be put in place.

might be a possibility of the nock taper being cut wrong. This, of course, would cause bad alignment, but the other types of shafts don't have this problem.

The shaft is centered, the plastic sectioned upper guide is pressed firmly into the top of the jig and you are ready to go to work. The cement is placed on the shaft

Shaft with plastic spacer is fitted into the jig. Tip of shaft at bottom is without nock. If wooden shafts are fletched on jig, the nock taper should be accurate.

uses is that the shaft is placed into the jig without the nock. Most jigs require that the nock be mounted first, then the shaft placed into the jig and the fletching done as usual.

The shaft first is fitted with the centering device, which has several plastic V-shaped guides, held by a wire which will center the shaft into the top of the jig. The device is placed over the end of the shaft and the shaft lowered — sans nock — into the jig. The nock then is inserted on the aluminum or fiberglass shaft centered in the bottom of the jig. These nock inserts are true in alignment. If wooden shafts are used in the jig, there

Template is placed on the fletch, pushed about an eighth-inch from edge of fletch, then is clamped into place. Other types of clamps may be used instead of clothespins.

133

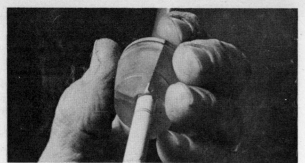

The plastic tip of the jig is made in three pieces to fit around the shaft and to close down evenly upon it.

The helical jig will fletch all three feathers at same time. After fletch has dried and has had time to set, the shaft then is removed by pulling out of top of jig.

itself, instead of on the fletch as when using the other types which hold the fletch in a clamp. This cement is run along the shaft, following the contour of the jig, and the fletch is placed gently on the side of the jig, then eased down onto the cemented shaft. The metal template is placed on the jig about one-eighth-inch above the quill. The template is held in place with clothespins or paper clamps and the jig is rotated to accept the second fletch on the shaft. The same procedure is used on each of the three fletches which are spaced equally around the shaft in arcs of 120 degrees.

The fletch curls around the side of the shaft, giving an even, exactly matched fletch each time. The jig fletches all three feathers upon the shaft merely by rotating the jig, placing the fletch on and clamping. When all three are mounted, the jig is set aside to allow the cement to set. The shaft then is taken out and the fletch burned to the shape and cut desired by the buyer.

This gives a beautiful fletch, but we still have no nock. This is remedied by placing the shaft, after the fletch is burned, on a level surface and determining a parallel with that level surface. The nock then is mounted with the string groove of the nock running parallel with the level surface and cemented into position. Since all three fletches are spaced evenly, any of them can be the cock feather. This can be marked by a different color fletch, or all may be the same color. This gives an almost perfect fletch, backed up by a constant nocking system which will give better results on the range.

To be sure that the nock is properly mounted, Powell

Fletch is burned and nock put on the shaft in the final operation. This should give shooter true helical fletch.

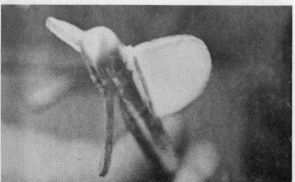

places the shaft between two devices that have rotating wheels, and the shaft turns freely with the tip on one set of wheels, the opposite end of the shaft rolling on the other set just below the fletch. The small motor is turned on and the shaft rotates slowly, while the nock alignment is checked to see that it is perfect. If the nock is mounted a little off-center, the wobble of the nock will show quite clearly with this machine. It also will show whether the shaft is crooked at any point, since the irregularity will show clearly.

This type of fletching jig can be used for shafts other than just target types, since it will accept a fletch up to 5¼ inches in length. This length is not really necessary even with broadheads for the hunter.

I saw a hunter who was experimenting with helical fletch, shooting in his backyard. He had Black Diamond broadheads mounted on three shafts; all three were of the same weight and spine and shot from the same bow. He had his bales behind the house and situated so the shaft started from the bow, but as it passed the house, encountered a strong crosswind. The long spiral fletch wobbled a bit as it passed behind the house, the long helical would hold true with little perceivable wobble and to top it off, he had one of the shafts mounted with a short 3½-inch helical. He showed this to me and I shrugged: it wouldn't make it past the crosswind. He nocked the shaft, loosed it and it never hesitated, but flew straight all the way. – *Bob Learn*

Cresting Is Just The Touch For Your Freshly Fletched Arrows To Give Them That Personal Look!

THE crest goes back many years. European knights had individual crests that flew from their helmets to identify them in combat and jousting. This crest later carried over to the shield and to the coat of arms that still is used today.

The basic idea of the crest was for identification. The American Indian used a crest or marking on his arrows so the owner could identify his kill or count coup on the enemy. The Orientals used crests on their shafts much the same way for identification, and even in the modern age, we still use the basic idea of the crest to identify our shafts on the archery range, and hunters use identifying crests on their hunting shafts.

The first item needed for cresting is a lathe. If you are brave and the little woman is out of the house for several hours you can adapt her mixer, one of the variable speed models, into a cresting lathe. The small portable mixers work very well for this if the marital consequences are worth it. Cresting lathes also may be purchased from most local archery shops or ordered through the mail. They range in price from about $11 for a kit to as high as you want to pay.

Base for motor is large piece of wood to give stability. Base and arm of lathe can be joined. Foot control is modified by attaching bent piece of copper to control.

Using paint properly mixed with thinner, the pin stripes are added to the dry crest. Some prefer gold or silver to make shaft stand out as a professional cresting job.

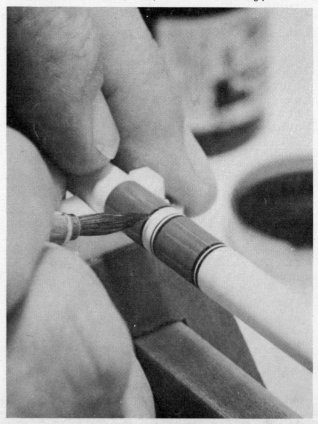

I built my own lathe. The materials used are simple and can be found almost anywhere. The wood I used was rather on the exotic side: Brazilian rosewood, a white walnut rider and lignum vitae runner, this topped with a teflon notch to hold the shaft. But the design will work just as well if it is made from a pine two-by-four and other scrap you may have in the wood pile.

In addition to the wood for the basic assembly you need a motor to turn the arrow shaft. This motor doesn't have to be large or powerful, but it must have a speed control to give you a slow but constant speed. The kitchen mixer works great if you have an old one, or a small motor with a variac control for varying the voltage will do the trick well, but there is still another solution.

I priced motors in an electrical shop and the cheapest I could find was about $6.00. The variac control ran about twelve bucks more, so this made the cost of the project more than it would cost to buy one already made. That is no advantage unless you like to tinker. What I wanted was a lathe that would be cheaper than I could buy and equally as good. If you already have the variac control, the biggest expense is gone, so the motor would cost little. But I had nothing but the desire.

There is a sewing machine repair shop in practically every town; mine is no exception. I went to the local shop and picked up a sewing machine motor from the repair section and the foot control used for running the motor, both for only $4.00. The sewing machine wide and 1½ inches high with a center cut made to fit the width of the rail. On top of the lignum vitae rider I cut and placed a small piece of teflon for the arrow to ride in; nothing more than a V notch.

The materials and dimensions can be varied as the builder sees fit. The rosewood finished beautifully and a coat of epoxy was applied to bring out the grain. If you can't find a motor assembly like the sewing machine motor, you can purchase one from your archery dealer or mail order.

After you have your lathe completed, the next item is brushes. I went to an Oriental import store and bought some of their artist brushes, worked the loose hairs from them and they work fine. If you like, you can buy red sable brushes used by artists, but they can cost up to $5.00 apiece. I paid an average of thirty cents for mine. You may purchase your cresting lacquers and brushes in a kit from the dealer or use the *Pactra* lacquers found in most art and paint stores. To see how they would work, I also tried the *Zynolyte Speed-E-Lac* brushing lacquers. They worked fine.

But before you can crest, you need a means of holding the arrow in the lathe motor. There is a variety of commercially made cresting chucks for this purpose but I took a piece of half-inch surgical tubing and put this over the motor drive shaft. Tests showed I could crest a shaft with no point, a field or target point and even a broadhead. The shaft, of course, usually is crested before being fletched and without points of any kind.

The technique I used departs from that used by many archers in one respect. The nock end of the shaft is placed in the chuck on most lathes and the other end rests on an arm about six to twelve inches away. If the shaft is crooked or the nock not mounted correctly it will wobble and you end up with a crooked or wobbly crest. In my own technique, the tip end of the shaft is inserted into the rubber tubing and the sliding V-notched rider is moved to keep the area being

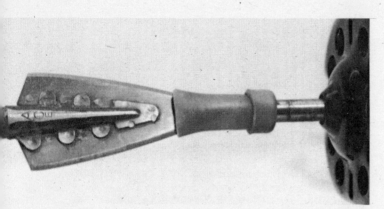

Sharpened broadhead is inserted in rubber tube adaptor makes it possible to crest finished arrows. This will allow shooter to bring some of his old shafts up to par.

motor is made to work at various speeds and the control, with modifications, can serve as the variac. I hooked up the motor and the control, then found that I had to devise a method for getting a constant speed from the motor without using my foot on the control. I tried a C-clamp but this didn't work. I finally used a piece of copper strip material, drilled and tapped to fit a wing-type threaded bolt like you have on barbecue attachments, then drilled and tapped another hole into the bakelite top of the control. This gives me a wing nut to cinch down the motor control for any speed desired.

The components ready, I set about assembling them. The rosewood proved difficult to work but the finished product was worth it. The long section for the base measures twenty inches long and 2½ inches wide. This was cut at a forty-five-degree angle on top to give the block some shape. This is not necessary but it looks better than a right angle. The motor base was made in two separate units for easier storing.

One was a wider piece, five inches wide and five inches long. This, too, was cut with angles. The motor was mounted to the base block with a screw, using the motor mount that came with it from the repair shop, merely a right angle piece of metal. The foot control, modified for table use, sits alongside the motor.

On top of the longer base section I put a runner of white walnut, seventeen inches long, one-half inch wide and one inch high. For a rider to run on this rail I used a piece of lignum vitae. This rider is 1¼ inches

Plastic vee forms saddle for the shaft in which it can turn evenly, as the painted crest is being applied.

*These are raw materials for a cresting lathe: wood, a
sewing machine motor, foot control to regulate speed;
a light piece of wood for rail and another for rider.*

crested continually under steady support. With this method it makes no difference if the shaft is crooked or straight since the area being crested always will have a steady, firm support for the arrow to ride on.

The shaft is already dipped and the nock is in place when the cresting is done. The first touch you may want to add will be to put a fine line around the area below the nock to cover the bare wood left by cutting the nock taper. This dresses the shaft and makes it look better. The same will apply to glass when the nock insert may be seen below the nock.

The pattern and design for cresting are purely personal choice. Many archers sit down with a lathe, shaft and several colors in front of them. They start cresting with the wide brush, applying the main area or base color of the crest. They follow this with a pin stripe to cover the ends of the base color and may add a further fine hair line of gold or silver lacquer. If this shaft turns out to their liking, the archers often mark the different colors and stripings on the card, then place the card in front of them so they can then crest all the shafts in the same manner.

One of the first problems I encountered was my lacquer. I tried to use it straight from the bottle and it was too thick. A good method for thinning is to take a few brushfuls and carry them to the lid of the bottle you are using, add a few drops of thinner until the lacquer will spread evenly on the shaft and flow smoothly in application. Too thin, it will run and too thick, the lacquer won't flow and the crest will come out as a bunch of globs. You may have to add more thinner from time to time if you are cresting many shafts, since it

*There are many types of adaptors to fit on the lathe
and allow the shaft to turn properly. Some are magnetic,
but rubber tubing over end of drive shaft works as well.*

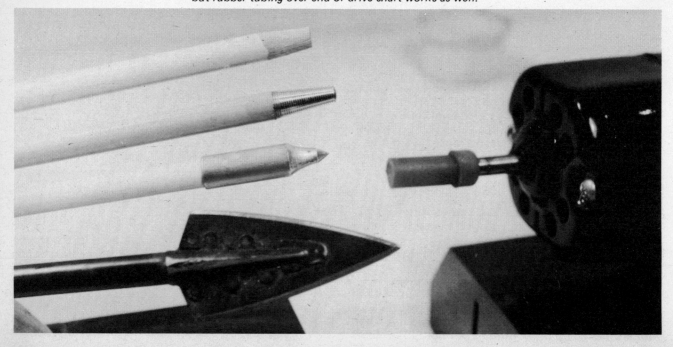

*A proper fletching and cresting job often allows one to
tell difference between novice and outstanding archer.
Pride in equipment has psychological effect on scores.*

evaporates rapidly.

The base color is applied with the large brush. One should have a finer brush to add the hair and fine lines to the crest. Two brushes will do but you may want to use one heavy, one fine and one extra fine, this last for the hairline work.

When dipping the lacquer with the brush, I took the little drop off the bottom of the brush by wiping it on the side of the lid. I couldn't get a good crest no matter what I did. By experimenting, I found that by leaving that little drop and merely taking the brush with a full load of paint to the shaft it made a smooth, even crest. The same applies to the fine line work.

If the motor proves hard to regulate for a constant speed let it turn a little faster than necessary, then use the left hand to press the shaft gently in the V notch. This will slow down the revolutions per minute and you have more positive control. The rider is moved back and forth on the shaft to make the shaft turn smoothly at all times. Of course, one must wait for the lacquer to dry before moving the rider to a painted area. If this rider is even a few inches from the shaft where it is being crested, it will work well.

The shaft can be crested with the fletch on with no problem. If you have some shafts already made up with fletches and broadheads attached, it still will work

in this lathe. I tried it to find out.

There are several things about cresting that not only can dress up the shaft but prove helpful in the field. For the hunter round, where one needs to identify his first, second and third arrows, if he needs that many, a single, double, and triple band around the individual shafts designates these special arrows.

One archer runs this coding system on the shaft where the fletch will be, puts his fletch on as usual, then when he goes up to the bale to pull his shafts, he has immediate identification as to which shaft made the hit for proper scoring.

You also can run your crest far enough down the shaft so that you have a constant brace height check on the string. If you find the brace height that gives you the best results, measure it, then place your shaft in the bow, nock it and mark the arrow at the point you want as your constant. If this should be too far for the crest to run you can make a small band to mark this brace height. When in the field or on the range, it gives a constant check on this important item.

Variations are fun and you can experiment on old shafts or as I do, pieces of broken shafts I have thrown into a box. This will give you material for practice and, when you feel that you are ready, crest your favorites.

Chapter 10

A LOUSY IMAGE

Making Yourself Difficult To Find In The Bush Is The Name Of The Bowhunting Game!

HE MUST have been at least a twelve-pointer by western count and huge. He appeared to be wearing a rocking chair for a rack. When he lowered his head, I moved into position. Everything was right, the wind to my face, full camo on face and hands as well as the suit. I slowly moved the bow into line. He raised that head, snorted and took off into the timber. I hadn't even drawn the bow.

Perhaps this has happened to you. How many hunters have you seen taking to the field with full camouflage suits, including the blackened hands and face or even the full treatment with the camo stick on face and hands? Some even use a bit of shrubbery to blend more, and in hand is that shiny new hunting bow, tuned in and ready for the trophy buck. This isn't new in hunting camps. Many hunters go the full route with camouflage and somehow neglect the bow.

That piece of shiny new glass on the back of the bow that faces the game when you draw acts as a mirror and can spook any game before you can draw. Walk in front of a glass-backed bow and see how it reflects the light. Some bowmakers put a camouflaged glass pattern on the bow with the backing mottled in greens, browns and blacks but there is still the reflection of the glass.

If you have a favorite on the rack that is a work of art with colored inlays and multi-colored hardwoods in the riser, you hestitate to smear it with camouflage to prevent the glare.

There are many ways to camouflage your bow that won't cover the art work, but will take away some of the glare.

Perhaps the simplest method is the bow sleeve or bow sock. These are merely tubes of camouflage material made to slip over the limbs of the bow and eliminate the reflections. They may be purchased from dealers or shops or you can make them yourself. One way is to lay out the material, allow enough to make the seam and stitch that seam on one side, making a long, tapered tube. Place it on the bow all the way to the arrow rest on the upper limb, then make another to fit on the

lower limb to the handle. They won't allow good purchase if they are brought all the way over the handle. A piece of plastic tape around the sleeve at the stopping points covers it.

The limbs are covered, but the handle and window of the bow still are uncovered and will bounce a bit of light; you have removed about ninety percent of the reflection with the bow sock.

Want a simpler method? Go to the drug store and buy some surgical gauze tubing. It can be slipped over the

From left: standard bow; one with commercial bow sleeve; bow wearing homemade sleeve; bow painted for camouflage; one covered with Saunders camo tape; camouflaged quiver.

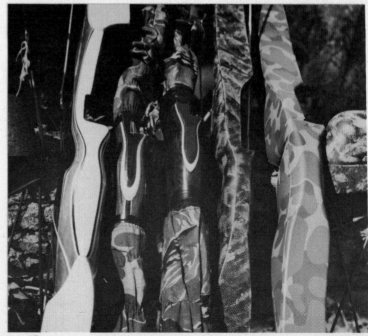

*When hidden in underbrush of the normal hunting lands,
the camouflaged hunter's figure merges with shadows.*

limbs nicely. You will have to paint it or dye it, however, to get rid of the white color.

The theory is that deer are color blind. They see everything in shades and tones of gray. A big solid blob like a bright red shirt or any solid color will spook them; hence the camouflage. There is a suit of camouflage on the market that is a red basic color with blotches of lighter red, green and brown on it. This is designed to protect the rifle hunter from other hunters, yet break the pattern of the solid color and theoretically camouflage the hunter from deer.

When you make your sleeve or bow sock, you may want to stitch some elastic material into the inside before putting a seam in it. This will make the sleeve pucker and grab the limbs along the bow's length and also prevent it from flopping. If you don't want to go to the trouble and still want to make a sleeve, take some small rubber bands and place them along the limbs of the bow to give the same effect on the sleeve. This is the simplest and fastest. The bands will break in time, but usually will last through the hunting season.

One problem with the sleeve is that it does leave the handle and part of the window open, and when carrying the bow, you may get a bounce of light from these areas.

Another method recently introduced by Saunders Archery is Camo Tape. This is a self-adhesive that will stick to the bow, diminish the reflection and may be removed with little problem at the end of the season. In the package, you receive two pieces long enough to cover one upper limb and one lower limb on the backing. If you want to cover an entire bow, buy more tape. I took two packages and covered a sixty-three-inch bow with just a bit of uncovered area on the base of the handle where the hand will cover it when shooting.

The tape goes on smoothly. Just follow directions and work the air bubbles out as you move down the limbs with the tape. It has a paper backing and you peel this off as you move the tape along the limbs. Saving all pieces, I used small scraps to cover the riser section and had just enough. If you own one of the new style hunters such as a Groves, Browning or one of the other makes that features the protruding riser in the handle, you can't put a sleeve on these very easily. With about three packs of the Camo Tape you could cover one of these bows for full camouflage and still be able to remove it when you finish hunting and want to show the workmanship of the woods and construction. The tape is flat in finish and won't reflect light even in direct sun.

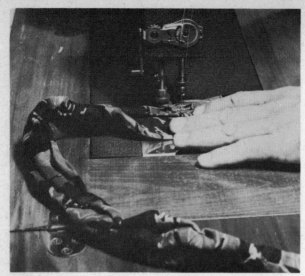

A few minutes with the wife's sewing machine, if she will show you how to operate it, should be enough time in which to fashion a camouflage sleeve, as described.

When you reach a certain point in bowhunting, you become more interested in hunting and less interested in the bow as a show piece. At this point, some get a can of flat black enamel spray paint and cover the entire bow with a removable paint base. This will give you a semi-permanent camouflage, but may be removed with paint solvent. Many hunters prefer this system and you will see many different patterns and colors.

Take your favorite hunting bow that you want camoed, remove the string and arrow rest and any other devices you don't want painted, then hang the bow by a string. First cover the entire bow with the black base coat.

The method of applying the camouflage varies, but I chose a flat interior-exterior vinyl paint and had one quart of flat white for a base color. Buy some tubes of color pigment that will mix with your paint and use this to get your camo color. I used burnt umber and chrome green oxide, as both can be varied from a light color to dark by the amount of pigment from the tube. Take a lid from a coffee can and put a spatula of white base paint on this. Mix the color from the tube till you have the tone and shade desired. If the paint is too thick, add thinner or, as most vinyl paints are water soluble, add water for the proper consistency.

Take a piece of fine pinwale corduroy material, which can be purchased in a dry goods shop, and fold it to make a pad with the ridges of the corduroy in one direction. Rub this in the paint, then spread it on a board or paper to get the right amount. Test this by dabbing the pad until it leaves color on the board, but not in big splotches. With the pad, dab the color — brown or green — onto the limbs, handle riser and edges with the stripes of the corduroy pattern all going in a diagonal direction.

This small amount of paint dries fast, so you can take another piece of the same material, make some other pads and use them to dab other colors onto the bow, using the opposite direction for the original pattern.

When you finish you will have a cross-checked pattern with no large areas of one solid color — and a

sneaky camoed bow. You can vary the size of the lines on the bow by getting a wider pinwale corduroy material. Too wide will give you a big blotchy effect, so test it on paper or a board before dabbing the bow.

Another system using the same black base coat utilizes the same colors but now we use a sea sponge — one of the those old-style ocean sponges that has the large open pores in it. The new synthetic sponges with the fine composition are inadequate for this type of painting. Use the same technique, dab the sponge into the mixed colored paint and in turn dab the sponge onto the bow in a random pattern. Change color and repeat, filling in some of the gaps left from the other colors. Remember, when you paint the bow with the flat black, to paint it solid.

When you dab the camo colors on the bow, whether you use one, two or three colors, leave some room around these colors so you don't end up with a solid mass of blotchy paint and ruin the effect you are after. Allow some of the flat black to show through and this will give you a well camouflaged bow that will last for years. Rain won't hurt it or wash it off the paint, the finish of the bow is covered and, if you decide to remove the color to get back the wood pattern of your bow or to change the camo colors, take the base paint off with paint thinner or by sanding. This is an operation you usually won't perform, since when you paint a bow, it stays that way for hunting. There is no problem with the paint chipping or peeling unless you painted over a waxed finish and there is a reaction with the paint. Clean the wax off and this won't occur.

A few of the problems that the other camo methods may present can be a bow that is slippery with the bow

Although a pair of scissors is used here, razor blade or a knife will do to trim tape to contour of the bow.

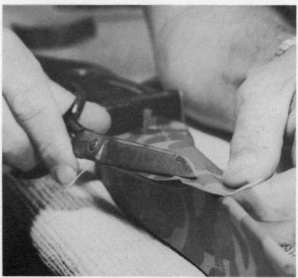

sleeve on it. While unstringing a hunting bow with a camo sock on it, I moved a bit fast, and my left hand slipped on the waxed surface of the bow. This caused the bow sock to slide under my hand and I got a good bang on the side of the head. The stringing and unstringing with the tape may cause it to peel from the sides a bit, but Saunders provides two strips of tape to attach to the sides of the bow for ease in stringing. The tape is great, fast to apply, full covering and easy to take off with no damage to the bow. Sleeves work well and remove even faster and easier, whether homemade or purchased, but painting gives an almost permanent camouflage covering for your hunting bow.

If you have artistic talent you can paint leaf patterns in different colors on the limbs and handle for the camo effect.

When you have the newly camouflaged bow in hand and head out to the hunting area, what about your arrows and quiver? If you use a covered back quiver, this is no problem, since these usually are camouflaged already.

A few years ago, I finally decided to try the bow quiver, and although I was hard to convince, I am lost without one now. The Bear quick detachable is the one I own, but there is one problem with it. It is painted green but still shiny and a further situation that may develop is that the broadheads on the market now are long and some will extend below the protective cover of the bow quiver. With razor sharp broadheads, you want these heads covered to prevent cutting yourself.

I took a piece of scrap leather and cut this 1¼ inches wide to go around the bottom of the bow quiver hood. A bit of contact cement and the base of the hood now is

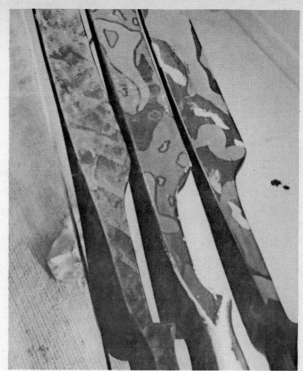

These three bows show the extremes that can be utilized when it comes to creating painted camouflage patterns.

After the flat black shade of paint has been applied, dried, use corduroy to dab on other shades of paint in a criss-cross pattern that breaks up outline of bow.

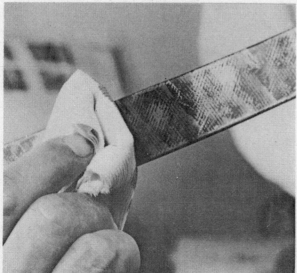

extended an inch to give me a protection I want.

With the leather in place and the cement dry, I took the same flat black spray enamel and sprayed the entire bow quiver, getting into the fine cracks and the inside of the hood to cover the lighter colored leather there. One can use the same colors used to paint the camouflage on his bow; the same procedure with the corduroy or sponge and dab the colors in a similar pattern onto the bow quiver. This removes another possible reflective source and now you are almost ready to go into the field with full camo suit, bow and bow quiver.

Not too many people camouflage an arrow. To paint them takes a while and, if you do too good a job, you never will find them! Gordon Glashaft offers several colors of camouflaged arrows. One is meadowlark egg which is an off-white or gray base color with splotches of brown in the resins, applied as the arrow is made. This makes a light camo color for the shaft and still diminishes the reflection and solid color. Another they make has rosewood coloring, which is a reddish-brown shaft streaked with black. It almost looks like a wood shaft.

With bow, quiver and shafts muted in color and reflections, adding a simple graybar fletch to your arrow will reduce further your image in the hunting grounds. I used the gray bar fletch on the rosewood and meadowlark egg shafts to give me the complete camouflage.

The white nock on the Glashaft will give me a guide to my shooting, while the full white fletch from eight arrows hanging on my bow would reduce the camouflage effect of the rest.

You might have a problem a few hunters have encountered with a well camouflaged bow. They lay the bow down to eat lunch or to check an area and have to hunt to find it. – *Bob Learn*

Chapter 11

BASICS OF BOWHUNTING

There Is More Than Simply The Sharpness Of A Broadhead To Be Considered In Taking The Big — Or Even The Little Ones!

All types of trophies are available to bowhunters in this age, as a great deal of political lobbying has been done on their behalf, bringing about special seasons.

Noise can help you get more game! The right sound, made at the right time, can be pure magic for the skillful bowhunter. The trick is knowing what sound to make and when to make it.

Sound plays a most important part in the life of wary wild animals. Much of what action they take is based on the sounds heard...or not heard. Some sounds can be instantly frightening, while others get a reaction of alert attention, but do not frighten. Sound can arouse curiosity or soothe an alerted animal. Some can attract and bring the critter to within petting distance of the hunter making them.

Anyone can learn to make a number of useful sounds, using your natural voice, materials at hand, or a commercial game call. The knowing bowhunter can use sound to bring the animal to him, to stop him, or to move him into a better shooting position. Often times, sounds occur from other sources than the hunter, himself, and knowing how the game will react gives the hunter opportunity to put himself in an advantageous position for a shot.

Outdoor sounds fall roughly into four general categories: (1) Those that alarm and frighten into instant flight. (2) Those that alert and get attention, but do not cause flight. (3) Those that attract the game to come into the sound. (4) Those that calm, soothe and reassure. Sounds from all of these categories can be of valuable use to the bowhunter.

Sounds which alarm and frighten game are sometimes used to flush game from dense brush. In India, loud noise plays an important part in moving game to the hunter during organized hunts. How often have you passed a dense clump of brush or aspen patch and thrown a rock into the center of it to flush out game on the other side?

The popular Herter's Rabbit Flusher call is designed to make a high pitched scream such as a hunting hawk might make, a noise calculated to cause rabbits to move so the hunter can see them and get a shot.

Sound that alerts game but does not cause flight can be of use when a couple of hunters are working together. A couple of years ago I was working down a steep canyon

Many gun hunters have given up firearms, feeling there is more challenge in bringing home the buck with a bow. Bowhunting also gives gun hunters an additional season.

into a feed ground where several nice bucks were browsing. My hunting partner, Jack Howard, remained high on the opposite canyon wall so he could direct me through the maze of brush. All of a sudden from his violent motions I realized I must be very close to my quarry. After freezing for a few moments I cautiously started around a clump of scrub oak and found myself eye-ball to eye-ball with a beautiful old four pointer not fifteen feet away. He had me riveted with his eyes and I didn't dare bat an eyelash, let alone start to draw. Jack's application of an attention getting sound saved the day...he started whistling softly and waving his arms. The buck immediately turned his head to look up the canyon at Jack and I was left with the most perfect shot a bowhunter could want — a buck but feet away, with his full attention elsewhere. For the record, I missed...but that's another story!

Very often, though, hunting partners can make use of a whistle, a grunt or other sound to get the attention of an animal away from their partner...or the use of an alarm noise to move the animal towards the other hunter. All sounds mean something to a wild animal. He pays strict attention to every sound he hears. If the sound is recognized as dangerous and close to hand, he bolts; if farther away, he moves off more slowly. If the sound is known to be normal to the area and time of day, such as the squeak of a mouse, movement of other deer, call of a

bird, etc. he pays no attention. When the sound isn't recognized, he comes to full attention and remains motionless until he determines whether it is friend or foe.

A sound which the animal immediately associates with a human is frightening and will cause him to move away from the sound...a cough, voices, ticking of a watch. A sound he doesn't understand, like the soft twang of a bowstring, will bring him to full attention until he determines what the sound was.

Animals can be brought towards a sound through its arousing their curiosity. Soft sounds which the animal does not know the source of and can't explain, often can cause him to investigate through natural curiosity. An old timer I once met in the back country told me that he could sit down patiently in rabbit country and by packing and scratching the ground gently with a stick, very often he would have a rabbit or other small animal slowly sneak up on him to see what was going on. The ticking of a clock left under a pile of pine needles will cause deer to closely investigate during the night as evidenced by the number of hoof prints found the next day. The use of a high pitched varmint call as a wavering bleat can call up all sorts of animals through curiosity...animals which are not predators, such as deer, antelope or pigs.

Bowhunters learn patience early in their experience and to look over an area, locating game, before open season.

The advantages of tree stands should be obvious, when it comes to outsmarting game; another chapter tells why.

Most commercial game calls normally work by imitating the actual sounds of the animal being hunted. By talking his language, you can tell him to come in and see what's going on. You appeal either to his hunger for food, sex, or other animals of his type. There are game calls on the market for just about every species of game. The best way to learn to use one is to buy a record of the actual animal sound. Listening first to the record and then trying to imitate the sound with the call.

A sound which creates a situation of interest in the mind of the hunted animal will also bring him in. Rubbing and knocking together of antlers during the rutting season can be like a magnet to a pugnacious deer or elk who thinks the sound comes from a couple of his fellows butting heads.

The growing sport of calling predatory animals such as bobcat, coyote or fox is based upon making the sound of a seriously injured and frightened small animal which the predator could easily capture as a free meal. Here you make no attempt to sound like the animal you are after; instead you try to sound like the animal he wants to eat. Just the squeaking sound of a defenseless field mouse as though caught in the crotch of a sage bush can call up a hungry hawk or bobcat.

Often the sound of an animal natural to the area can act as a calming agent to game the hunter has accidentally alarmed. During a stalk, a deerhunter might unexpectedly pop a small branch just as he is getting close to his quarry. The soft bleat on a rubber band deer call can sound like a small deer to the herd ahead and reassure them that there is no danger.

There are noises a careful bowhunter should guard against making. The wearing of hard surfaced clothing invites a loud scratching noise when the hunter moves through brush...a noise game immediately associates with humans. Better to wear soft woolens with a nap which deadens a scratching branch and makes it sound more like brush against animal hair.

A twig rubbing along your bowstring can make a very alarming sound which carries quite a way during a still morning. The sound of the arrow being drawn is a real attention getter, just at the wrong time. Every hunting bow should have a soft arrow rest and arrow plate. A piece of buckskin, bobcat hide, or simply a piece of mole-skin corn plaster will deaden all arrow noise, both of drawing and shooting.

Some years ago, I read Francis Sell's great hunting book, Advanced Hunting. A statement was made in the discussion on sounds to the effect that one of the most frightening to wild game was "no sound." There always is sound in the woods during any normal safe time. The only animals who move without making sound are those who are hunting such as a predatory lion or man, or those who are frightened and are quietly moving out of the area. When a deer feels something is about, yet there is no sound to identify it by, he immediately becomes frightened.

Sound can be associated with an activity and the animal pays little attention when it occurs. Fishermen working along a stream, or hikers on a trail can be talking to each other and making all sorts of noise yet run onto deer who pay little or no attention to them. I've seen one instance and heard of others where deer are intentionally walked right up to just by appearing to pay no attention to them and talking in a normal manner or making some other sound normal to the situation. A nice buck used to frequent the side of a fenced yard where a fellow would mow the lawn two times a week. A local hunter heard of this and tried several unsuccessful times to stalk the deer. Finally he tried pushing a lawn mower in front of him as he moved up on the deer...result: Venison in the locker. The minute the hunter did something that fitted into the pattern the deer was used to, the deer paid no attention.

One time, I was working my way along a deer trail into a lush feed area during the late afternoon and was not paying too much attention to what I was doing. All of a sudden, I became aware of a number of deer browsing the brush ahead of me still too far to get a shot. The brush was thick, I couldn't move without making some noise. I was right out in the open where my movement would be spotted the minute I got close.

Remembering Mr. Sell's advice about no noise being frightening and noise which is familiar to the area being okay, I decided I'd become simply another deer and see how this idea worked out. Getting down on hands and knees so my human outline didn't show, I slowly moved along the deer trail toward the deer. Every so often I'd pull at the browse as though I were nibbling at it. I allowed my wool shirt to brush the branches a bit. Like a feeding deer, I'd move a little way, then stop and browse. Gradually I gained on the deer. They would look down my way every so often, but paid little attention and certainly were not alarmed at all. In time I approached within good shooting range and got a nice shot. Noise can be a bowhunter's friend or enemy...it all depends on how it's used.

Under some circumstances, driving game through an area so that other hunters can wait for shots, works well.

I recently was asked — "What's the most important single thing in successful bowhunting?" Trying to answer this question required breaking down the art of hunting with bow and arrow into four groups of technique or understanding! 1. Equipment 2. Shooting Skill 3. Hunting Skill 4. Mental Control.

Mastery of each of these segments should be the goal of each serious bowhunter, whether hunting large or small game and it is difficult to measure success in terms of only one of these points; however, it is interesting that the novice bowhunter generally works hardest with his equipment and shooting skill, yet the Indian of years ago still is acclaimed the "king" of all bowhunters and he had equipment the likes of which no modern archer would be caught dead with and accuracy, due to this equipment which limited his accuracy, was but a dozen or so yards. His secret was his mastery of hunting skill and mental control which let him get so close to the animal being hunted that his limited accuracy wasn't a handicap and he could calmly make his shot count.

But let's assume we combine the hunting skill of the Indian with the shooting skill and equipment of the modern bowhunter and we have the "super" bowhunter as a goal to strive towards. Here's a hunter who finds and outsmarts game under all types of conditions; who gets shots up close; yet can hit consistently at seventy or eighty yards; a hunter who is not rattled by the unexpected, or the close proximity of a much sought after trophy...in short, the Super Bowhunter!

Basic equipment needed is: Bow, arrows, arm guard, shooting glove, quiver and accessories such as binoculars, camouflage clothing, bowstring silencers, etc. Of all the most important are the arrows...the bow is but the spring that launches the arrow and once the arrow passes the bow, it is up to its trueness of flight and killing ability to determine whether the shot is successful.

The head used on the hunting arrow is more important than the arrow, itself! This is what does the actual killing, whether by shock, using a blunt on small game, or hemorrhage from the cutting of a broadhead on big game. No matter how accurate the arrows, if the heads won't do the job when they connect with the game, all the effort has gone in vain.

With the exception of the flat-pointed blunt used on small game only, an arrow does not induce "shock" and kills only through rapid bleeding or damage to a vital internal organ. With a broadhead, sharpness is the prime consideration; not only sharpness of the very point, but most important, sharpness of the cutting edges. Regardless of the make or design of head, if you can't sharpen it easily to a better edge than your finest hunting knife, don't use it. Don't buy broadheads so much by looks or reputation as by how well you can put a sharp edge on them.

Next in importance comes arrow accuracy. Arrows which are not of the same stiffness and physical weight will not shoot from the bow in the same way...anymore than using ammunition in a gun which is not the same

Howard Hill (center) is the individual who did most to promote bowhunting. He shot this bear 30-odd years ago.

Fleet-footed game such as antelope are difficult targets and rarely are taken by bowhunters, because they feed in the open and there rarely is cover for making stalk.

load or bullet weight. Matched arrows are sold in sets of one-half dozen and up and must be insisted upon for any degree of shooting accuracy. Wood shafting continues to be the most popular due to relatively low cost, but more and more bowhunters are turning to the greater dependability and ruggedness of fiberglass or aluminum hunting arrows. After spending the considerable effort to get a good shot, it only makes good sense to use equipment with the greatest chance for success. And loss of arrows when big game hunting is not great...three, four or half-dozen arrows lost during the entire season is about average; a small cost for the return of absolutely dependable accuracy.

Fiberglass arrows offer fine accuracy and almost unbreakable ruggedness. But aluminum holds its own due to its even greater accuracy and flatter shooting trajectory.

Hunting arrows should have sufficient feather size to completely stabilize the flight of the arrow, even when a sloppy shot has been made — which often happens under hunting conditions when a shot has to be made hurriedly and without warming up. Fletching of five to 5½ inches in length by nine-sixteenths to five-eighths inches high in most popular. It always is better to have too large a feather than too small.

The kind of bow to hunt with is mostly personal preference, though the specifications selected by the average bowhunters are interesting. It is agreed normally that the longer length bows offer greater stability and accuracy, while the shorter bows tend to be more convenient to carry in the woods. The interesting thing is that most novice bowhunters tend to buy a short bow, but as they become more experienced, they start using longer lengths of around sixty-six inches.

Average bow weight is fifty pounds. A number of bowhunters who also use their bows on the ranges select an all-purpose weight of forty-five pounds, while a few who use their equipment only for hunting go up to fifty-five or sixty pounds. The greatest mistake made is to buy a bow with too heavy a draw weight. A weight you can't easily control causes poor shooting habits to form. It is far better to start out too light in weight and learn to shoot it well, going to a heavier bow later on.

Almost without exception, the most successful bowhunters use a recurved bow with a center-shot sighting window and of modern laminated fiberglass design.

The hunting quiver has developed into a specialty in itself the past few years. Really sharp broadheads will not remain sharp for long when the cutting edges touch each other, rattling around in a shoulder quiver or rubbing the leather as they are put in or drawn out. All of the better quivers hold each arrow individually, eliminating noise and dulling of the cutting edges.

Whether to use a bow quiver, back quiver, or one on the belt is a personal problem and often reflects the type of country being hunted. The bow-quiver is by far the most popular in brushy areas, but the belt and side quivers which hold more arrows take the field in more average hunting areas.

The balance of the archer hunter's equipment is much like that of the fisherman or rifleman...there is an almost infinite variety, with everyone choosing for himself and little of it having a direct bearing upon the hunter's ability to get game.

Many hunters ask: "How can I cut down the noise of my bowstring when I shoot? Twice last year I frightened deer with the noise before the arrow even got there."

Due to the slowness of an arrow this is a common bowhunting problem. The alert reaction of a wild game animal makes it easy for him to get out of the way of the arrow at even close range. Noise and movement are the two game frightening factors the bowhunter must guard against.

A variety of bowstring silencers is on the market, costing but a few cents. These fasten to the bowstring to dampen its vibration, much like touching a guitar string as it is plucked eliminates most of the sound. You can make a string silencer yourself by simply tying a two-inch piece of thick rubber band tightly to the bowstring about eighteen inches from each bow tip. Some adjustment of location is necessary for maximum results. Take care not to use a bowstring of too great a physical weight. Any weight on the bowstring requires a part of the bow energy to move it, energy which could help to propel the arrow.

How important is shooting skill to the bowhunter? There is no disputing the fact that anyone who can draw a bow and shoot an arrow would be a highly successful bowhunter, if his shots always were made at a close enough distance. Assuming that you could repeatedly get within ten or fifteen yards of a deer or four or five feet of a rabbit, no matter how poor your shooting, you would hit a good share of the shots.

But dependable accuracy with your bow can act as a substitute for the high degree of hunting skill needed to get in that close, or it can effectively lengthen out your hunting area, giving a chance to shoot at more game under more varied conditions.

The repeatedly successful bowhunter knows his own limitations of accuracy and styles his hunting technique to give shooting within this range. Few hunters are content with being "short range" shooters...they see too much game within bow range, but not within their own accuracy range.

Just a few weekends ago, a group of us were hunting Spanish goats on Santa Catalina Island and one of the bowhunters remarked about the great number of shots he had taken and missed. He made a statement heard quite often in bowhunting camps: "If I'd had someone with me who could really shoot, we sure could have knocked over the trophies."

Yes, shooting skill can play a most important part of your bowhunting success. It should be worked on and developed to a fine point. Most important, it is not really difficult to become a skillful shooting bowhunter!

Assuming you own suitable, accurate equipment, the problem is entirely one of knowing what to do,

practicing it until it becomes habit, then sustaining the skill during the actual hunt. There are so many good articles and books on the basic details of drawing and shooting a bow that it hardly needs repeating here. The mechanics of shooting are the same with all forms of archery, but the final method of application can vary — depending upon how you hunt and your temperament.

You must decide whether you want to be a deliberate hunter or a random hunter. A deliberate hunter has a temperament which organizes and plans his actions. He does not like random, haphazard situations. This type of person enjoys careful, slow stalking. He often seeks a particular head of game or looks for a shot under particular conditions. He's the type to patiently wait in a blind to learn just how the game works in the area he is hunting, then hunt with a preconceived, planned campaign. He picks his shots, usually shooting at standing game which is unaware of his presence, often passing up even close running shots. To this type of bowhunter, hunting technique is almost an art or science; when he takes a shot, it is a climax to an overall plan and he takes the utmost care in making the shot count. Quite often this type of bowhunter uses a hunting bowsight.

A random hunter enjoys just roaming around looking for something to shoot. He shoots often and under any condition, whether the game is running or flying or standing still, uphill or downhill, at great distance or not.

Bowmaker Jack Howard (left) and Doug Kittredge, both notable bowhunters, have learned the means of taking bucks the hard way. Kittredge authored this chapter.

There was a time, not many years ago, when the bow was considered inadequate for such large game as moose by fish and game officials, but this thinking has changed.

He often is not a good shot as we know in terms of target shooting standards and usually couldn't care less. He would like to improve his shooting, but standing in front of a target hour after hour leaves him cold. He works on the assumption that you can't hit anything unless you shoot at it and if enough shots are made, one is bound to hit. A bowsight is sometimes tried, but normally discarded as a hindrance in getting off a quick shot. He regularly fills his game bag.

The majority of bowhunters tend toward the "random" hunter type. If you are interested in being successful during group drives, when roaming the woods with a partner or two, when hunting rabbits or squirrels, etc; in short, skillful when the game is moving, you'll do best developing a style of shooting to allow you to simply point your bow like shooting with a shotgun without lost motion.

However, if you are the kind of hunter who wants to pussyfoot up to game, to outwit them from a concealed blind, to hunt specific trophies you'll be most successful with developing a deliberate shooting technique suitable for long distance accuracy similar to that used by the successful tournament archer. The use of a hunting bowsight can be a big help to this type of bowhunter.

Once you decide how you want to hunt and whether you are going to use a bowsight, the first step is developing your shooting form into a habit so deeply set that you automatically shoot without having to think about the mechanics of shooting.

This can only be developed by target shooting at fixed distances. An ideal place is your own backyard with no one else present to distract your attention. Habits are formed by doing the same thing over and over. The distance you shoot is not important, nor is what you shoot at. What is important is that each shot is made as perfect as possible...always go through the same motions, take more time than you would normally in the field; shoot each arrow as though it were the last you would ever shoot and consider it the one that's got to count.

It's important first to develop a habitual shooting technique before actually shooting in the field. By yourself in your backyard, you concentrate entirely on how to shoot, but in the field you concentrate on where you shoot and it is easy to form bad shooting technique habits.

Next is the problem of being able to shoot at unknown distances without previous warming up, and under any condition of terrain or shooting stance.

No field archery range will develop this ability once the course has been shot. The only practice for this development is stump shooting or plinking. Here a man

Daylight calling for foxes and coyotes usually is less successful than nocturnal efforts, but isn't impossible.

goes into the field and shoots at whatever he sees whether it be a pine cone, a clump of grass or a small bush. Vary the distances up to eighty yards or even more, but don't forget the close shots. Shoot only one arrow that counts, as normally this is all you'll get at game. Spend an hour or two stump shooting a couple of times a month, particularly in the few weeks before hunting season.

Most bowhunters tune their shooting to a fine point just before the hunt, but during the hunt the only arrows shot are at game or a little plunking as they walk back to camp. It doesn't take long to get rusty, as you'll find the first time you lay off a week or two. To put the odds of hitting in your favor when that shot at game presents itself, make it a point to devote at least half an hour a day to serious shooting practice whenever you are on a hunting trip. As when practicing in the backyard, try to make each shot count. One of the inexpensive sixteen-inch grass target matts is an ideal camp target and can make the big difference in success or failure.

To know where the deer are is knowledge many archers leave to luck. It's surprising, but at least half of the less experienced bowhunters hunt areas where there

are no deer. They choose their hunting area, because it appeals to them, rather than because it appeals to deer. Naturally, the more deer that inhabit the area you hunt, the better are the chances of success.

The knowing bowhunter keeps his ears open whenever he happens upon a conversation about good deer hunting. He is not afraid to ask "where," anytime a speaker mentions quantities of deer, especially big bucks, or particularly easy hunting. Whenever a speaker seems cooperative, follow through and find out exactly where he is talking about. Ask if he would pin-point the area on a map and carry an assortment of maps in your car so you can take advantage of such willingness to help. Be sure to get detailed information as to the best way to get there, where to camp, and what specific little canyons seem to be the best to hunt.

Keep a file of all such hunting area information you obtain. Learn when the informant was there last and show the date you obtained the information. Hunting areas have a habit of changing year after year and you will want to be sure to check out any old information before planning a definite trip.

Gun hunters are one of the best sources of hunting area information for the archer. Normally hunting during a different season, the knowing gun hunter often will pass on good hunting spots to an archer, where he wouldn't breathe a word of them to his fellow gun hunters. Areas that are good during the gun season can prove to be truly a hunter's paradise during the archery season, when the deer are not yet alarmed, and the bowhunter may find other archers don't yet know of the spot.

Take time before the hunting season to scout the potential areas you consider hunting. Do this reasonably close to the season; some deer herds move into or out of an area during the early fall and you will want to see the area as it will be during the actual hunt. If you plan to hunt with a buddy or two, each person can take a different area over a weekend and, by comparing notes, decide just where to go during the hunting season.

A rifleman's spotting scope of twenty-power or so will be worth its weight in footsteps during a scouting trip. It enables you to scan vast areas of hillside and valleys without walking through them. Look over the hunting country during the early morning and late evening hours when the deer normally move about, feeding. Pay particular attention to feeding areas, brushy hillside slopes, oak and aspen patches and the edges of meadows. Try to get an idea of the overall concentration of deer and how they are working in that area.

Take a walk into the hunting area looking for deer trails and other sign. Fresh tracks on well worn trails are a good guide to deer hunting area. Where trails are little used and you see but few deer during the feeding hours, the hunting will be sparse. A few such scouting trips made before the season will insure you of a choice of areas with the odds strongly in your favor for success.

Arrange to get into hunting camp a few days before the season opens. This gives time to set up camp, to become acclimated to a change in altitude, and most important, to scout the hunting area in detail. Time

By observing game trails and buck rubs in trees, one often can situate himself for a shot such as this one.

spent before the opening is worth more than the hunting season itself. It is better to sacrifice a few days of hunting to be in the "right" place on opening day.

Beware of making too much noise around camp. In some manner, deer apparently can transmit a feeling of fear and unrest for the entire herd, making all of the animals in the area jumpy. In hunting areas where vast numbers of hunters congregate, just the preliminary driving on local roads, voices, and noise of establishing camps can alarm the local deer to the point where they are difficult to approach, even on opening morning. It is best to try to pick hunting areas where there will be few other hunters.

There are three major methods of deer hunting with bow and arrow: Stalking on foot, hunting from a blind or stand and organized drives.

By far, the most popular is stalking. The ability to pussy-foot up on a wary wild animal without his being aware of your presence is a woodsman feat to be proud of! This is the hunting style of most beginning bowhunters, and ironically, it is the most difficult to master. To have repeated success, the stalker must have a thorough knowledge of deer, their habits and how they can be expected to react under various situations. The stalker must know where the deer are to be found; he must be skilled in moving slowly and quietly at the right time, with a knowledge of wind and a trained ability to see game in the field.

The Indian said — "Move a little, see a lot," and this is stalking in a nut shell. The key is to stalk in an area where you know there are deer. During a morning or evening hunt you are not going to cover a great deal of ground when you move as slowly as you should. Your previous scouting of the area will pay off real dividends when stalking.

The best time to sneak up on deer is the time of day when they normally are moving about. After they have bedded down, all of their senses are tuned to hear, see, or smell an intruder. With such hunting, the archer sees only the north end of deer going south...affording running shots of the worst possible type. With deer moving about feeding or to and from bedding grounds, chances are good that an animal will move towards the hunter.

Game usually moves early morning and late evening. The first three or four hours of morning and last hour or two before pitch dark are the best times to find game afoot. The stalker should be into the hunting area just as the sky begins to gray during the morning hunt. This often means leaving camp a half hour before daylight, using a flashlight to see with. Move quietly into the area and then wait for the hunting hour to approach. Take along a candy bar or sandwich to stave off hunger later on in the morning. Hunt until you find the deer have stopped moving around. This will usually be 9 to 10:30, depending on weather, moon phase and how much the deer have been hunted.

When deer stop moving, odds are against the hunter obtaining a good shot. As a certain amount of time has to be spent daily in camp, this is the best time of day to spend it. Go back to camp, eat a good meal, take a short

This bowhunter has thought of everything in regard to proper camouflage except his bow, which resembles beacon.

nap if needed...and practice shooting.

Here can be the most important activity of your bow-hunting trip! The average archer-hunter spends a good part of the year developing his shooting to a fine edge. Just before hunting season he practices continually. Then, what with getting everything ready for the trip, setting up camp, etc., the bowhunter hardly shoots an arrow until his first shot at game. Without a warm-up, he is rusty and with the excitement of the chance to fill the bag, often as not the shot is a miss.

Most archers start the afternoon hunt too early — and end it too early. Deer do not start moving well until just before dark. Get into the area you want to stalk late in the afternoon when the sun starts casting long shadows. Keep hunting until the last minute of legal shooting time. The later you hunt in the evening, the more deer you will see. Just for fun, some evening pick a feeding ground you can watch from a distance and stay there until it is too dark to see with your binoculars. . .you'll be surprised at how many deer seem to pop out of the brush just as the first stars begin to faintly show.

Take a flashlight with you on all evening hunts. If you are at all far from camp when you stop hunting, you'll need it to come in with, and if you get a deer down, you'll need it to track him.

The actual technique of stalking consists of carefully moving as quietly and slowly as possible through the hunting area. Keep concealed as much as possible, without exposing your outline to the open sky. Wear clothing that blends well with the surroundings. Camouflage can be of great help, providing it is soft enough not to make noise when a branch scratches it; washing a new camo suit several times before hunting is a great help. A camouflage bow-sock over your bow will conceal the glint of light reflecting on the finish. Stay on deer trails, rather than cutting across country. You'll make less noise and deer expect movement on a trail, but not off of one.

Moving slowly cannot be over-emphasized. Deer may be color blind and they may not be able to determine individual stationary shapes, but they have fantastic vision when it comes to detecting movement. The mere flick of your head when you turn at a sound, or the quick raising of a leg can be seen by deer a good quarter-mile away. It works well to move only ten to thirty paces, and then stop along side a bush or tree while you look carefully around a few moments before moving farther. By so doing, you may see a deer move into view that was concealed but a moment ago and which you would have spooked away had you continued a steady movement.

Be careful when approaching open areas, meadows and the tops of ridges. One of the most successful ways to stalk is along a ridge, keeping back from the edge when you move and sneaking carefully up to the edge every so often. This method keeps your movement, human scent, and noise concealed, allowing you to approach above the deer where he least expects it.

Soft-soled shoes are a must for quiet movement. Use foam rubber or crepe on boots or hunt in tennis shoes. I've known some bowhunters who slip out of their shoes and travel in stocking feet whenever they have to approach a deer to close range. Take care that your equipment does not rattle or squeak when you move. Remove all coins and keys from your pocket.

Human scent can be a great problem to the hunter. Hunting into the wind will help keep the scent from the game. A six-foot piece of fine thread fastened to the tip of your bow will act as a wind indicator. The smell of cigarette smoke is particularly offensive to game. If you don't smoke, you have quite an advantage, but take care not to wear your hunting clothing in a tent or car with smokers, as it will take on the odor in a short while. Campfire smoke is another bad one, as is the smell of automobiles. A good precaution is to have a set of camp clothes to slip into after hunting. Take several changes of clothing and change every few days. Take a sponge bath regularly. Don't overlook washing your hair and the use of a deodorant.

Pine or sage oil, used in moderation on the hunting clothes, can be a big help in masking human odor. Or try rubbing handfuls of pine or sage needles into your hunting clothes.

Hunting from a blind or a stand can be one of the most effective methods of bowhunting when done right. It eliminates the chance of your movement being seen and it gives you a chance to shoot at game under ideal conditions...when the game is unaware of your presence, is at close range and not moving. The trick is in selecting the location for your blind and in having the patience to remain in it during the hunting hour.

Scouting the area where you want a blind is a must! If you can determine how the deer move, where they move and when they move, you can pretty well work out a pattern to establish a blind in the best location. It is necessary that deer in the area be in reasonable concentration and that they are habitually doing the same things each day. Blinds located on a small saddle, separating one area from another, is often a good bet. The saddle should be such that there is only a narrow place for deer to cross, so they have to follow the same route each time.

Unusually lush, green feeding grounds are another ideal place for a blind. This is particularly true on a hillside where the feeding ground forms a sort of bowl and the hunter can stake out above the deer, waiting for the one he wants to feed within range.

In heavily hunted areas, where deer have been spook-

The bobcat is another predator that is found in almost all states and is considered legal game for bowhunters.

ed up a bit, the observing hunter can find little pockets of deer deep down in tight canyons or high up in a pocket on the side of a hill. Regular use of binoculars when in the field often will find deer locations others have missed. Whatever areas appear good for regular deer habits should be watched with binoculars to determine how the deer act, where they move from and to, and what time they normally start moving. Whenever you are hunting, scan the opposite hillsides and canyons to see what game is there...even if you don't intend hunting there that day, you might find the area alive with game for hunting later on, or for establishing a blind.

The blind should be built during the middle of the day, when game is bedded down and will not easily be alarmed into flight. Clear enough ground that you can move around in the blind without making noise. Get into shooting position in all directions where you might expect to take a shot. Clear out such branches as needed. Actually shooting a few arrows where you expect the deer to be, so you know the range when the time comes. The blind should be located twenty-five or more yards from where the deer will come. Closer shots are nice, but chances are the deer will hear you draw your bow.

A drop or two of deer lure or skunk oil along side the deer trail where you would like the deer to stop and lower his head while you shoot, will many times give you a shot like shooting fish in a barrel.

Get into your blind at least a half hour before you expect the deer in the area to start moving. This will usually be well before daylight or early in the afternoon. Be quiet sneaking into your blind area. Take enough warm clothing so you don't get fidgety. Do not smoke, or go to the "john" anywhere near your blind. If your blind is located in a tree, be sure you can shoot from it without falling out. Lie down and be comfortable until deer begin approaching. Carefully get into shooting position while the deer's attention is elsewhere than looking in your direction. Shoot when you can't stand the suspense any longer.

Grit your teeth and don't leave a well located blind until you are sure deer have quit moving or it is past legal shooting hour.

Organized drives are somewhat like locating a blind, as much as the deer habits in the area should be known. If you know which way the deer run out of a thicket or out of a canyon, you can station the shooters in the right spot for the best shooting. Drives normally result in running shots at close range. They are very exciting and can be productive for the archer skilled in moving shots. The drivers should work the area slowly with not too much space between archers. Quite often the drivers can get good shooting at game which is stationary or moving slow ahead of the drive line.

It is important that the stationed shooters remain on their stand location until the drive line reaches them. See there are enough archers participating, the drive line can be formed of two lines, one working about one hundred yards ahead of the other. This second line will get a chance at some of the smart ol' moss backs who sneak through the first line, think they have it made, then while they watch the first line of hunters, the second line does 'em in. The hunting principles of blending clothing, scent, wind, apply to driving as well as other forms of bowhunting.

Do not attempt to drive too large an area which cannot be completely covered. If the drive is made quietly, the next drive can be made right next to it. Drives work best when the game has bedded down during the middle of the day. – *Doug Kittredge*

The How Of Bowhunting With The Compound

BOWHUNTING FOR DEER in the semiarid hills of Southern California is considered one of the bowhunter's toughest challenges. Deer are affected by forage conditions and positions of heavenly bodies in their movement patterns.

Since hunting from a stand is virtually out of the question, the wary Pacific Coast blacktails must be stalked through the hostile terrain. It's hot, dry, the hills are steep with little cover and there's virtually no wind. Getting within shooting range of any game animal is a real challenge.

Bob Jensen of Orange, California, has been one of the more successful bowhunters in the Southwest. He has bowhunted for more than three decades and has entered more than thirty animals in state and national record books.

Jensen began bowhunting on Long Island, New York, at the age of 12. His first bows, the straight bows crafted by L.E. Stemler at his shop on Long Island, were of lemonwood, osage and orangewood. His first targets were the rabbits and squirrels still plentiful at the time.

He had a five-year break from hunting while in the U.S. Air Force. During that period, his parents moved from the Empire State to Santa Ana, California, where Jensen landed after finishing his service tour. It was 1952 and bowhunting interest was on the upswing in Southern California. Jensen and a few other avid archers founded and became charter members of the ORANCO Bowmen of Orange County, one of the state's first bowhunting clubs. He and his family still are active in the club today.

It didn't take Bob Jensen long to score on his first buck, a forked horn, in the Southwest. In 1953, he shot his first blacktail near his home in Orange County. He hunted each year in Los Angeles County and local foothills, but bagged his first trophy buck during a 1959 hunt in the Kaibab Forest, near the North Rim of Arizona's Grand Canyon. This buck had a 12x7 rack, with a thirty-three-inch span.

Since 1953, Bob Jensen has been putting one or two animals into the California or Pope and Young Club record books each year. What are some of this successful archer's bowhunting secrets?

For starters, Jensen travels light when hunting in California. "I carry a light, one-day backpack filled with my

This 550-pound boar was taken by Jensen with 60-pound compound at 40 yards. Kill was made at Paso Robles, Calif.

Taking a black bear without dogs is a challenge for a bowhunter, but Jensen has done it two times, using a compound hunting bow.

hunting essentials," he says. "Included in the pack are a canteen, laundry bag, saw, straight butcher knife, binoculars, bowstring, foil survival blanket, flashlight and a snack. The whole thing weighs about twelve pounds."

Jensen feels the one-day backpack is superior to the belt or waist pack. "It's my contention that a waist pack cuts off circulation to the lower limbs," comments the bowhunter. "Also, it gives the hunter a sore back from the pack and canteen bouncing near the kidney."

The laundry bag that Jensen includes in his backpack is used in packing out edible meat from a field-dressed and boned deer. "I think it's better to field-butcher a deer, especially if taken in rough terrain," Jensen advises. "This is much easier than attempting to carry out the whole carcass."

Using the straight butcher knife, he field dresses and bones the animal, taking all usable venison and dividing it equally into two sides of the laundry bag. This then is slung over his shoulder, with half the weight in front, half behind. "Using this system, it's easy to walk out of the hunting area. Field butchering will reduce the weight of a deer from approximately 150-175 pounds, down to about ninety."

Since bowhunters don't use stands in Southern California, Bob Jensen doesn't use camouflaged hunting clothes. Instead, he relies on a dark, pullover sweatshirt in brown or green with matching trousers. Because of his blond hair, he wears a dark-brown or green golfing hat and coats his exposed skin with camo grease paint.

"Because I'm on the move when hunting in California, I feel this attire is sufficient," says the bowhunter. "I just don't think camouflage clothing is an advantage when stalking. However, for tree stand or stationary hunting that's done in many parts of the country, camouflage clothing is a must, so the hunter can blend with the terrain."

Because the sun glistening on a bow is no asset to the hunter, Jensen paints his with a dull-brown Rustoleum. His shafts are dipped in an olive-drab, dark-green paint marketed by Fletch-Tight.

Since his California hunting is done primarily on the move, Jensen has adapted his hunting sweatshirt into a binocular holder. "I have a pouch sewn to the chest of the

This deer, considered mammoth by Southern California standards, was taken during a special Los Angeles Co. hunt. Jensen used XX75 Easton aluminum arrows to score.

sweatshirt that holds and keeps my Bushnell 6X25 field glasses from bouncing while moving in the field," he states. "They are readily accessible when I stop to glass a prospective area."

What type of bow does this hunter favor? He has hunted with everything from the aforementioned lemonwood bows to longbows, recurves, take-downs and, for the past several years, with a compound. His first compound was made by Tom Jennings, the man who's had a lot to do with the promotion and acceptance of the many compounds currently on the market. For some time, the Precision Compound has been Jensen's choice of compound bow. He's a member of the Precision Compound Bow advisory staff and has been instrumental in many modifications of Precision's compounds and plastic fletchings.

"I like a compound, because of the dropping off of the draw weight when the archer comes to full draw," he explains. "The compound will peak at approximately twenty-three inches of draw. From there, the draw weight will drop off sharply so the archer at a full twenty-nine-inch draw will be holding much less draw weight on the fingers, arms and back muscles."

As an extension of this, Jensen explains that if a compound peaks at fifty pounds at a twenty-three-inch draw, when a full draw of twenty-nine inches is reached the archer actually will be holding only thirty-eight pounds. "You have the thrust of fifty pounds behind the shaft and the comfort of holding only thirty-eight pounds of draw.

"I believe that a fifty-pound compound is equivalent in cast and speed to a sixty-five-pound conventional bow," he comments. "It gives the bowhunter who's small in build the opportunity to shoot a heavy bow without straining,

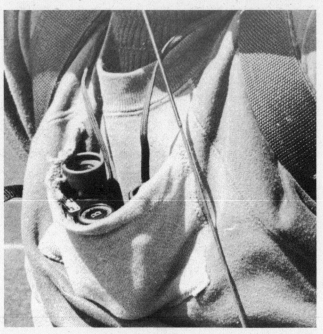

Right: Jensen carries Bushnell 6X25 binoculars in this homemade chest pouch sewn to front of his sweatshirt. (Below) This trophy elk was taken in Colorado in 1974. Jensen shot the bull from a tree stand after calling it in with a high-pitched elk call. He used a compound.

because of the drop-off capability of the compound. With the present compounds, the arrow trajectory is much flatter and the range for the hunter has been extended from a maximum of thirty yards out to fifty, sixty or even farther."

Compounds are not without problems, a fact with which Jensen readily agrees. Tuning, which in the compound's infancy was a major problem, has pretty well been taken care of by the refinements made by various manufacturers. Manuals accompanying sold bows give tuning information. Also, there are enough people experienced with tuning and

more problems with the compound hanging up in brush than the conventional bow."

Getting one's fingers off the string of any bow long has been a problem, and one a great many compound shooters experience. "The proper arrow nock, use of a finger tab or glove, and lots of practice with finger pressure alleviates this syndrome," advises Jensen. "Many target archers using the compound have turned to a release aid and there are some hunters who are using a release on their compounds. Most hunters feel the use of an aid when hunting is clumsy and will slow down the archer, perhaps costing him a shot. This is a matter of personal preference."

Jensen's Precision Compound has a draw weight of fifty-three pounds when anchored at 29½ inches. "It's a bow that's fast, easy to keep in tune and a top-quality product," he says. "I shoot with a glove, alternating with finger tabs."

Like most archers who've been shooting for thirty years, his first arrows were made from wood, mostly Port Orford cedar from Oregon. "As time passed and I became more serious about archery, I switched to fiberglass and used them for several years," he continues. "I currently use Easton aluminum arrows and think the absolute top-of-the-line hunting arrows are Easton's XX75. My hunting arrows are light 2213s, 29½ inches long. I like this light arrow, because I feel it gives me more speed and better penetration." Some hunters will disagree with this, but Jensen's record speaks for itself.

Of the hundreds of broadheads on the market, Jensen prefers the two-bladed heads. "I think they aid in getting

Jensen and son, David, compare old lemonwood longbow with the Precision compound former now uses to hunt.

shooting compounds around these days to help an archer with tuning problems.

"Maneuvering the compound through brush was at one time thought to be a major hang-up for the hunter," adds Bob Jensen. "But several thousand bows back, the various manufacturers decided this wasn't a deterrent as far as the consumer was concerned. Consider it another way: The conventional bow I used prior to obtaining a compound measured sixty-six inches overall, while my compound is but fifty-four. It stands to reason that I should have no

As a change of pace, Bob Jensen and his son have gone shark shooting with compound bows off Catalina Island.

Bowhunters tend to be meat hunters this is made evident by the spikes on this buck taken in Los Angeles County.

good penetration and they're certainly easier to sharpen," he notes. "I've used Bear broadheads among many others, but currently I'm using a Zwicki Black Diamond that weighs 125 grains and measures 1-1/8 inches across the cutting edges. I feel this head stands up much better in the rocky terrain of Southern California."

The split-finger anchor is Jensen's preference for bow-hunting tournaments: two fingers below and one above the nock. He anchors right at the corner of the mouth. There is no string walking or anchor changing allowed in the bow-hunting rounds of the NFAA or Orange County Bowmen.

"Although I've tried bowsights from time to time, I now shoot only instinctively," Jensen adds. "Sights might be the definite answer for many shooters, and each bowman must make the decision himself whether he's better able to hit the target with or without the aid of a bowsight."

Jensen is a definite advocate of the long shot when hunting, out to sixty yards and even farther. "The flight of the arrow has stabilized, the trajectory is flat and the speed will give greater penetration than a twenty or twenty-five-yard shot, when the arrow still is trying to stabilize," explains the bowhunter. "This is part of my reason for using lighter shafts and the two-bladed broadhead. While the majority of my shots come at distances between forty-five and fifty yards, I have made killing shots of ninety yards and even farther. Naturally, these long ranges are not recommended for novice bowhunters, but I submit that today's sophisticated bows, tackle and techniques make these long shots possible. The distance is determined by the archer's own limitations and such factors as weather, wind, the terrain and the like."

The bow quiver is regarded by many as simply an arrow-storage compartment clamped to the bow. Jensen believes it also acts as a stabilizer and takes some of the vibration out of the limbs before reaching the arrow rest and arrow. "I've used Frank Adams' Sidewinder for many years and feel it's one of the best on the market. It's light — the weight with ten shafts is but 1½ pounds — and it's mounted out in front of the bow. The total weight of my bow, quiver and arrows is about six pounds."

When hunting in California, Jensen shuns the use of any scent to cover the human odor. "Most scents are pine or sage, and Southern California has little of this vegetation," Jensen confides. "Using one of these scents would alarm the deer, just as would the human odor.

"What I do is pay particular attention to the direction

Each using a compound bow, Bob and David Jensen were able to score against javelina during Arizona hunt.

and velocity of the wind," says the bowhunter. "I always stalk with the wind in my face."

Jensen has been extremely selective when it comes to hunting partners. He hunts alone or takes his 18-year-old son, David. "Without a crowd, you can hunt the area better, make fewer mistakes and generally have fewer problems," contends Jensen. "Especially when you're packing into a remote area, the selection of a hunting parter must be someone with whom you might have to entrust your life."

Jensen starts his California hunting early in the day; about a half hour before sunrise. He hunts for a couple of hours after sunrise, then quits. "I think the moon cycle affects West Coast hunting to a large degree," he says. "If the moon is full, the best hunting is in the evening, just before dark. With the full moon, the animals will feed all night long and lay up during the day. Hunting in the early morning and during the day usually is poor during a full moon."

For this reason, Jensen schedules his vacations during periods when the moon is not full. "It's too dark for the animals to feed at night, so they'll lay up at night and feed during the day," states Jensen, adding, "which is fine with me."

When hunting in the local area, Jensen surveys the scene long before he hunts, searching for deer and other animal

Jensen poses with his fellow bowhunter, Tim Sizemore, and pair of mule deer racks taken in Colorado in 1974.

Getting close enough to an antelope for a shot can be difficult, but this record class was taken in Wyoming.

This respectable buck, with five points on each side, was taken by Jensen with his favorite bow in Colorado.

signs, plus picking the best areas to work while stalking.

When hunting out of state, he talks with others who have hunted the areas he will cover. For example, prior to hunting in Colorado many years ago, Jensen discovered through conversation that Colorado deer are found on the Western slopes for the most part. For elk, the northern section of Colorado is best. Rarely do elk and deer-hunting areas overlap. Without this information, Jensen could have spent a fruitless hunt where there just weren't any deer or elk.

"When hunting out of state for elk, I use camouflage clothing, scent and spend most of my time in a stand," he comments. "Elk seem to have a keener sense of sight and the bulls can be called into a stand during the beginning of the rut in September.

"I use a high-pitched call, that of a young bull, rather than the lower call of the older bull," continues Jensen. "I do this so the older, bigger bull will come into the stand to teach the younger bull a lesson. I've bagged elk both in 1973 and 1974."

The mule deer he arrowed in 1974 near De Beque, Colorado, was a Pope and Young entrant measuring 188-6/8 inches. It was a forty-five-yard shot after stalking the deer for more than a quarter-mile.

In December, 1971, Jensen jumped four pigs at about seven in the morning. He took a forty-yard shot at the largest of the quartet and nailed a 550-pound boar, one of the largest ever taken with a compound in the Paso Robles, California, area. He was shooting a sixty-pound compound and got full penetration with his two-bladed broadhead.

The ivory tusks of this monster were quite small for the size and age of the boar, measuring only 3½ inches exposed. On Santa Cruz Island, off the California coast, he took a much smaller boar, 150 pounds, during a November, 1974, hunt. Its tusks scaled 4½ inches exposed.

Jensen also has bagged two bear with his compound. Hunting without dogs in 1970 near Eureka, California, he took his first that weighed three hundred pounds. The hunting site is fifteen miles south of the Oregon state border and abounds with the small, California black bear. Most hunters use dogs for hunting in this area, but the real challenge is stalking them afoot, according to Jensen.

He's been active with local, state and national hunting groups. He's an official measurer for the California Bowmen Hunters and the Pope and Young Club. In 1971, he was instrumental in producing a book for the California Bowmen Hunters, that organization's Measurer's Guide. It's one of the most complete books produced on the subject.

All of Jensen's success in hunting might be credited to the natural stalking ability of one man, or simply in knowing the whereabouts of game. This is partially true, but Jensen and his son both shoot the ORANCO Bowmen's field range at least twice each week for several hours. In addition to being one of the state's top hunters, Jensen has won countless honors and firsts in shooting field target rounds for competition in tournaments throughout the state.

It's pretty obvious that Jensen's success as a bowhunter didn't just happen: he's worked at becoming the great hunter that he is. – *Chuck Tyler*

Chapter 12

THE FINE ART OF VARMINT CALLING

BOWHUNTERS have complained continually that they have been placed in the same category as riflemen: They have a short season in which they can be licensed to go after a deer, then they might as well hang up their hunting arrows for the rest of the year.

However, a little investigation shows that this is hardly true. Across the entire nation, there are predators and varmints upon which there is no closed season. Admittedly, varmint hunting with the bow requires a great deal or patience and skill, due to the limitations of range, but it can be done.

For example, Stanley Warner, an Iowa farmer who was a top-ranking midwestern competitor, gave up shooting for trophies a season or so back and now limits himself to hunting. His specialty is fox, and he has killed a number with arrows, but not without a good deal or study and concentration upon these wary little animals. An old rifle shooter, too, he contends that getting a fox with a bow, even when you know its lair, is a good deal more demanding both patience and skill-wise than with firearms.

At Prior, Oklahoma, a nineteen-year-old bowhunter, Charles Gifford, proved that bobcats can be successfully hunted with the bow. He recently stalked a sixteen-pound bobcat to within fifteen feet before he loosed a Razorhead arrow from a fifty-pound Bear Kodiak bow and downed it. This bobcat measured almost three feet from nose to tail. More unlikely, he did it in broad daylight.

These are only two instances; of course, there are hundreds shooting. Still, such authorities as Hiram Grogan have made a hobby of crow-craking with a bow in his native Georgia. He shoots, using calls and decoys, to lure in the crow, although he admits this is "the smartest thing in feathers."

In the East, there are varmint problems. While the coyote is thought of as an animal associated with the far flung prairies and mountains of the West, both New York State and Maine have been plagued in recent years with this species. The eastern areas also have plenty of crows, fox and in some areas, wolves, which have drifted down from Canada.

Jim Dougherty, who won the World's Championship the Varmint Calling Contest in Chandler, Arizona,

The fangs of the bobcat offer indication of the type of predator that can be considered a challenge to the caller.

back in 1957, believes that calling in varmints is a lot easier than stalking them, and most callers will agree. Yet, there are techniques to be followed.

He insists that it is important to be comfortable before starting your call. "Effective camouflage is a must," he says, "and it must be remembered that an animal coming in to the call is going to do his utmost to see what is going on before exposing himself. Since he knows exactly where the caller is located and the caller, as a rule, has not the slightest idea where the animal is, concealment spells the difference between success and failure."

Dougherty says that the gray fox is the easiest to

Mosquito net hood is improved for vision of the bowhunter by sewing frames of a pair of glasses to the fabric, after the glass lenses are taken out.

TO the majority of the varmint calling fraternity, the coyote is king. There are those who like their bobcats and swear that they are the most elusive and canny of the predators, but for thrills and showmanship nothing compares with the hot charge of a worked up coyote; kitty cat is the local dumb bell with four left feet by comparison.

In the twelve years that I have been an avid caller and student of the game of matching wits with the varmints, I have centered my interest on 'ole Canis Latrans and tried to learn all there is about him, but every time I think I've got it knocked, I get shot down. A classic example of this just ended not twenty-four hours ago at the completion of the California State Field Contest. This was based on the actual number of animals taken in a twenty-four hour period. The hunt took place in an area I have hunted for ten years and knew like the back of my hand. My partner, George Wright, who is current co-champion of the World Varmint Calling Contest was likewise educated. The end result was that we took only two coyotes and blew a few others, but all and all, we were left looking like a couple of downright amateurs while Al Abbott, the State Calling Champion and ex-State Field Champ, wiped out everyone by a huge margin.

call in, as it is curious by nature, and will come in to almost any sound of pain which is produced on your call.

When a wolf or coyote is seen approaching, one should stop calling. The slightest movement of the hands, with the sound attracting his attention, can be seen by the sharp eyes of these animals. This explains why these two species are seldom taken with arrows.

However, the coyote will come in close if he does not see, hear or smell the caller. They can often be lured to within ten feet. However, be ready to launch that arrow; unless there is enough wind to deaden the sound, the twang of a bowstring will send them on their way. There are hunters — successful ones — who say that to get a coyote or wolf, one has to second guess the animal and know in which direction it is going to run when it hears that sound.

"Coyotes are best bagged with bow and arrow," Dougherty says," when two hunters work together."

He suggests that you take up positions, well concealed, about twenty yards apart. One hunter then should call, while the other is ready to one side with his bow and arrow. In this way, the working hunter may well go unnoticed as the coyote comes into the man who is doing the calling.

Also tough — possibly the toughest — animals to hunt with arrows are those of the cat family. Unlike the wolf and coyote, they will not run toward a call. Instead, they will crawl, belly down, through heavy brush, stalking the sound. In the case of cougar, although they have been called in successfully, it is not often. Reason, of course, is that they have a wide hunting range and usually are out of range of the call unless one is familiar with the animal's lair, and can stake out there.

And judge your terrain. Most calls can be heard by the animal up to half a mile in flat desert-like country, but in hilly, wooded areas, a quarter of a mile is about tops.

They are there, waiting to be hunted. All it takes is skill, patience and sharp eyes.

In areas where there are chicken ranches, foxes are frequent visitors and will remain close to such sources of food. They can be called up easily during daylight.

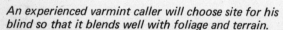

An experienced varmint caller will choose site for his blind so that it blends well with foliage and terrain.

A damper on bowstring will cut string vibration noise.

What's strange about that? This was Al's first experience in this particular country where coyotes react differently from those he was used to hunting.

What does this mean to you? I think it means that no matter what you think you know and who tells you what, there always is going to be a coyote who hasn't read the book and will pass the word around. I am past the stage of saying it's just so.

However, this is not designed to discourage you, but to let you in on some of the tricks that will make you a successful coyote caller — and it takes a lot of tricks.

First, we must understand the critter in question. The coyote is a wide-ranging little wolf that has been persecuted since time began and will probably be persecuted until its ends. Yet when time ends via a big b or whatever, there still will be a pair of coyotes

left to start afresh. To withstand all of this punishment, you have to be quick of mind and nimble of foot — exactly as is our coyote.

Varmint calling has grown in stature to the point where it is big sport and undoubtedly big business, yet callers, themselves, are their own worst enemies. With the armies of callers infiltrating the country, Mr. Coyote has had some big trouble, trying to figure out which rabbit is for real. As soon as he runs into a phoney, which is getting to be about a 50-50 chance, he is pretty much through with bunnies for a long while and he'll restrain his traveling companions from investigating that tempting sound, too.

Coyotes are best called in the fall of the year preceding and during the rut. The late spring is second best, as the pups break away from the main family groups to run for themselves. During the actual denning season, when the pups are born, calling slows down; in some areas it almost stops.

For me, daytime is the best calling period and the one that offers the most in excitement. It also requires a lot of finesse to bring them right up to good bow range. Night calling for coyotes can be good, and for those who really learn the ropes it becomes terrific.

Being a cautious sort, the coyote is not inclined to investigate a night caller who is flashing lights around the desert helter skelter, although I can't say the same for the average bobcat who will stroll in as though everything were grand and stand around on many occasions while people hurl all kinds of missiles at him.

There is quite a bit of difference in the coyote's reaction to a call blown during the day and that blown at night. The records of the California Varmint Callers indicate that the average distance for a kill at night is four to six times greater than those taken during the day.

The secret to night calling is proper and skillful manipulation of the light as the coyote approaches. Many callers also indicate that they change their calling pattern on night stands, too. As a general rule, I call considerably more during the course of a dark stand and the pattern changes a bit to an increasing number of wavering cries ranging in volume from medium to soft. My theory is that the animal must be looking at you to follow the bouncing balls of fire that are his eyes as he comes in; increased calling will keep his attention focused towards you.

Night calling is not a good way to collect a coyote with a bow. You will call up many coyotes before one gives you a good shot inside of thirty yards and then your depth perception is cut down and most shots are missed due to improper range estimation.

In night calling, you are dealing pretty much in eyeballs. This is a thrilling experience but it has hypnotized many beginners on their first hunts to a point where they watch them bounce in and out without ever making a move.

The night caller should dress in dark clothing and remove any articles that will reflect in the side glow of the light; extreme quiet is a must. He also should have a selection of calls on hand, ranging from a loud, long range call down to a fine pitch squeaker.

For daylight calling, the hunter first must be completely camouflaged from head to toe. This requires the use of a head net or face paint and the hands also should be daubed with paint to cut down the flash as

Most of the modern types of varmint calls can be tuned for proper pitch, sound reproduction of an animal cry.

they work the call. A portable blind is a real handy item and can be easily constructed out of a length of chicken wire eight foot. The rear portion of the blind should be as high as the caller's head when he is kneeling, while the front can be cut to twenty inches. When covered with burlap or camo netting and a few native twigs, the hunter's silhouette is completely removed from the landscape. The bow also should be covered with a bow sock or paint to reduce flash as it is brought into play. With such precautions, shots at less than forty feet are the rule rather than the exception.

In picking a stand for bowhunting coyotes, you must select terrain that will work to your advantage, and rolling hill country is not as inducive to close calling as the flats or washes. A wide wash or arroyo is the best bowhunting set up for two to three hunters, but never call with more than three unless you are simply interested in a day's outing. With two shooters at the sides of the wash, the caller should be spotted in the middle and to the rear in order to suck the critter through the slot.

The shooters most often will spot the game from this setup before the caller and it is wise to warn him with a sharp squeak or click of the tongue. This will allow him to work on close-range calling patterns that will bring the dog in hot through the center. As he

Jim Dougherty offers what the well dressed coyote caller will wear, including camouflage paint on face and hands.

passes, take him from a slight rearward angle rather than head on or broadside.

There are few if any animals that can dodge and maneuver with the ease of a coyote. I always have felt when arrowing coyotes that a close running or trotting shot is better than a standing shot as the animal is taking a straight course. When standing you are not sure which way he will go, and if you guess, he most likely won't move. They can see that arrow coming; of this, there is no doubt.

Should a shot be taken and missed, the caller should go into a loud, excited series. This often times will cause the coyote to forget he has been made a target of and he will make another pass to investigate the sound. This appears to work best on a coyote that has come in hard all the way rather than one that approached slower. I have seen as many as eight rifle shells expended on one coyote as he came in and out, then he got away scot free.

If a hit is made, the caller should continue to work on his instrument and the shooters remain motionless

King's Silent Stalker is an example of type of quiver favored by bowhunters for varmints, as it is designed to make arrows easily accessible with a minimum of noise.

As little movement as possible is necessary when one is waiting out a coyote in daylight, but choice of spot to put your blind, as well as camouflage, are important.

George Wright, a champion caller and bowhunter, displays gray fox and a bobcat taken same night on same stand.

and quiet, since daytime stands often produce as many as five or six separate coyotes. One particular stand I recall brought in eleven coyotes, the first appearing within thirty seconds and the last at an even twenty minutes.

Of these, five were grassed and it annoyed the others not a bit. Bill Dudley, two-time world champ, had twelve in on one stand and he and his partner Tom Mills, also a world champ, raised a heck of a ruckus with their .243s before the action was all over.

From June until late September, it is most common to call only single coyotes. From then on, the sight of doubles and triples is not uncommon and nothing will get your blood pressure up as fast.

From early morning until the sun warms up the country side, the vast flats covered with high sage offer excellent calling — especially if they are within a mile or two of thickets or rocky terrain. This type of cover will offer close shooting from the blinds.

Callers should be placed in a line facing the expected direction of the approach. This calls for a lot of know how, as early morning on the flats is generally windless and a surprise attack from the rear is not uncommon.

When calling flats, you always must be ready to shoot from the first blast on the call as a varmint could be working within one hundred yards of the stand. When bowhunting, the only position to assume is on your knees from the blind. If you sit down, you'll never get up in time.

When making any stand a silent approach is an absolute must, and a period of quiet after everyone is situated also is good planning. Any animal made suspicious by your entering the area will forget about it after a quiet interval of five minutes or so.

One of the most common questions is how do we go about finding good areas to hunt. Besides looking over the roads for tracks the best way is to make a "howl count." This is done by being in a suspected area at the times when coyotes are going to howl. Coyotes just don't run around howling like they do in the Westerns. The three best periods to hear coyotes are at moonrise, first morning light, and when the sun actually breaks over the Eastern horizon. By listening closely, you will hear them bark, yap and howl and can get a good idea of the area with the thickest concentration. Nothing is as stirring to me as to hear the little wolves whooping it up at sunrise. I also have used an elk bugle to get coyotes to howl at odd times of the day or night; this is a fine way to locate good country.

Never discount talking to ranchers or farmers about varmint hunting. They seem to be more favorably inclined toward coyote or cat hunters than any other forms of our group, and they are aware of the varmints' points of concentration. Local trappers or wardens make excellent information points and I have found truck drivers to be one of the best sources of information. Drivers see many things cross the roads during their nighttime travels and are happy to be of help.

For calling coyotes, I have settled on the raspy pitched voices that are tuned to imitate the squall of a mature jack rabbit. By and large, most of the coyotes taken in the Southwest are called with this type of pitch. Begin your stand with a loud series of three to six excited blasts. This is called the "surprise" call, and its total duration would be about one minute. From this point we go into what is termed a "scramble," which is a garbled up mess simulating a rabbit thrashing with his antagonist. This will taper into squalls up and down the scale in tone and volume.

Keep this up for the remainder of the stand, but for coaxing, mute it down with your hand and muffle it against your shoulder. Never blow a loud series when a coyote is on the move towards you; if he leaves you can try it, but only then.

For best results, a coaxing squall or two is all that is needed after game has been sighted. With practice, you can draw them around as though they were leashed to your call barrel . . . sometimes.

All of the leading call manufacturers have records available and one of these will help you no end. There is only one way to become an expert coyote caller and that is persistence in the field, trial and error are the best educators in this game.

As I said earlier, you're never going to have it foolproof. If you did, it wouldn't be any fun.

IN AREAS WHERE it is legal, pursuit of predators finds a strange breed of man assembling after dark to go "squealing." Nighttime hunting is an illegal procedure in many states, but where it can be conducted the followers are in for a brand of sport that is entirely separate from its daylight counterpart. Hunting varmints after the sun sets poses many problems, some seemingly impossible for the experienced daylight hunter. For the beginning caller who makes his first attempt at the sport, they can be overwhelming.

The critters are willing, often more so than daytime ever will find them. The hunting activity of the bobcat, coyote, fox and others is at its peak at the setting sun and for several hours thereafter. In California, where night calling is pursued with a glee that borders on the fanatical, it has been observed that the first three hours after dark and the last three hours before daylight offer the best animal activity. Where food is scarce, it is my belief that calling is best from midnight until three. This, I feel, is due to the fact that a hard-hunting animal is reduced to one large rumbling stomach pain by this time. If things have been a bit lean, anything resembling food had best look out. This also can be borne out by the way the approach is made and caution is exercised during the first stands of the evening. Later, they seem to make suicidal charges in order to be there first; one time when being a winner is not all it's cracked up to be...

Of all the predators that answer a call, four of them offer the main action for the night caller. They are fox, bobcat, coyote and coon — and in about that order of vulnerability.

These four critters react a bit differently when being

So as to have almost instant access, if a string should break, some bowhunters carry a spare taped to their bows.

In some areas, javelina are considered vermin, from which the term, varmint, originated, although they are not to be considered predators by their normal natures.

called, and the easiest is the gray fox. The fox is by far the most susceptible, and a call of any type will bring him bounding right into your lap. After a few fox kills, most callers give them a pass.

On one occasion I witnessed a gray fox hunting mice, while I was deer hunting on Liebre Mountain in Los Angeles County. I had no call but there was, however, a Chiclet gum box which I emptied into a pocket. I then proceeded to blow into the open box across the cellophane as we all have done when we were intent upon making noise with anything at our disposal during childhood. The fox crossed the intervening one hundred yards and received a Bear four-blade in the bean for his trouble at the difficult distance of six feet. Almost anything will call a fox.

The bobcat is the prince of the night varmints, not because of his brains, but because he is a trophy well worth the effort. Bobcats come to a call exceptionally

Bobcats are among the most wary of the predators, say experienced varmint callers, but proper handling of the light usually can assure one getting a shot off.

well at night and should be considered the second easiest to call.

The one trait that saves many a bobcat's hide is his general distaste for coming right out in the open. On occasion, they throw caution to the wind and barge right in, a usually disastrous habit.

For instance, Bernie Creamer made a stand one cold winter night on the desert east of the California desert town of Barstow. It was cool, about twenty degrees, and Bernie elected to roll down the window and make a bit of noise from the truck rather than expose himself to the elements. Two hunting buddies in the cab made it

cozy. After several minutes, a small bobcat — but not small enough — came through the window, back legs churning the side of the door, all claws and teeth. A chopping right hook to the teeth managed to dislodge him and amidst the pandemonium, Bernie somehow located his revolver and slew the beast as it readied itself for another charge. The cat was not rabid; just hungry.

Although slow on the approach, (usually, that is), the bobcat seems intent upon getting there and oftentimes nothing you can do will drive him away. I have seen as many as seven arrows and five high velocity rifle rounds

If erecting a blind, be sure to design it in such a manner that shooting is not hindered by construction.

expended on one cat and still he came on. This is not the rule, of course, but it happens often enough to give one the feeling that lynx rufus is a devil-may-care sort.

The coyote is a cagey one. He will give you but one chance to score and it takes a smooth operator to get a crack at him during the dark hours. He's not like the fox and the cat, and when something rings false, he'll be long gone.

Raccoons are easy to call when one locates a meat-eating coon. Once the masked bandit makes up his mind that he's interested, just keep coaxing and bop him with the bow. Down in Texas, Murray and Winston Burnham bring them up close and scoop the buggers up with a big net.

Other animals that can be called up at night — although not as often — are lions, badgers, ringtail cats, and sometimes, skunks and weasels. The nocturnal birds

of prey such as owls come in well, especially the barn owl and the great horned owl. Many a caller has wilted under the noiseless and frightening pass of one of these ghosts using his head for a target. Several years ago, I saw one coming at the last second and snapped the light right into its face. He terminated his power dive on the lens of the light extended in my right hand.

Calling techniques at night are much the same as those used for daylight stands with two exceptions: Night callers generally call a bit more often and the squeaker calls are used a great deal of the time after an animal is located.

Let's go through a night stand step by step: We arrive at a preselected location in the truck, dousing the lights and cracking the doors fifty yards or more from the actual stop. Great pains are taken to make no noise as we get out and take up the equipment including hunting light, a spare flashlight, bows and arrows and the calls already strung up and hanging around our necks.

Generally our clothing is dark. This is not the most important thing, but every little bit helps, especially when bowhunting. A quiet walk from the vehicle to the calling site is preferable on a rise of some sort, especially if the country is thickly covered.

One man will shoot and one will call and work the light. Arriving at the spot, the shooter sits down, while the caller stands. Allow several minutes to pass for all noise to ebb and the night insects to resume their normal chirping. Let us say that I am calling and George Wright will shoot. I take a long range call with a jackrabbit voice. The pattern is the same as always, but not quite so loud, as there may be an animal within scant yards.

We begin at 10:45 and I call for a minute, then allow absolute silence. Your ears play tricks and you imagine many things, but reality is easy to distinguish. If there were an actual noise, you would know it immediately. Taking up the light after a minute and a half, I resume calling softly and point the light straight up into the air and flip the switch. The beam is a wide one and it casts a soft light in the area immediately surrounding us out for fifty feet or so...nothing is within this illuminated area.

Still calling, I drop the light, allowing just the edge of the glow to hit the horizon and make a slow revolution of 365 degrees, I pick up the tempo of the call and the volume just a bit. Two passes reveal nothing, and I flick off the light to switch calls. This one is a bit higher in pitch, usually a coarse cottontail tone with wide range. Still calling I check the watch, it is 10:49. I raise the light and let out a muted series of high pitched excited squeals.

The switch is on, straight up, nothing there and again the glow is lowered to the horizon. Half way around and slightly downwind, a pair of glowing coals are reflected in the soft light one hundred yards out.

George nods his head and squirts a stream of rabbit scent into the air out of a perfume atomizer...that'll fix his downwind trick. From the eyes it looks like a cat and I complete the turn, still calling but soft — squeaks now — nothing violent.

Three quarters around a pair of greenish lights bounce into view coming fast 150 yards out; quickly the ray is raised so that just barely enough light hits the eyes. The bouncing and color indicate a coyote.

He stops and I move the light to the cat, which hasn't moved. He'll probably stay put for awhile, so working one call I fumble for another, a high pitch squeaker, and get it operating. The coyote likes it as he starts in again.

George stays out of the light and raises to a knee to shoot, as the eyes reappear coming hard and bouncing as the dog takes everything in his path.

Now is the moment of the most critical importance. Should I allow too much light, I'll spook him; just the beam's edge, nothing more. Twenty yards out, he skids to a halt. The time is here and the full force of the light illuminates the coyote. For a second he is motionless, then there is a thump as the arrow leaves the bow, its path easily visible in the light like a tracer bullet. It cleaves a part in the hair of his back and the coyote is off and running, zig zag, typical coyote evasive tactic.

I blast out on the call with excitement and distress in the notes; George quietly slips another shaft on the string. Where's the cat? There he is, one eye peeping around a rock seventy-five yards out. It is 10:55 and I keep calling squeaky cries, mouse-like, pleading with the cat, moving him a few yards at a time from rock to rock,

Coyotes are more wary than foxes, but grow exceptionally bold, when hungry and they feel a meal is in vicinity.

twig to twig and the light grows heavy in my hand.

It's 11:00 and fifteen minutes have passed the face of the clock. The cat is at about thirty yards. He would have been a dead duck long ago with the little .222 magnum.

In a sudden change of temperament that always leaves one wondering, that "stubby" is suddenly right out in the open and walking in like the owner about to throw us off the property. He comes full on into the full force of the light which sets him off like Washington Monument at high noon. At forty-five feet, the white feathers merge with the white of his chest and he jumps like a rocket going almost out of the light. Nothing jumps like a bobcat.

The cat has gone out of sight into a ditch and it is weirdly quiet. Then the silence is invaded by a clatter of rocks, and I hear my partner's arrow click across one. There is a slight sigh and all is so quiet that our breathing seems to shatter the stillness. We could perhaps call some more but that seems silly, we whisper to each other. It is 11:10 and with both lights in operation, we check the hit location. Ten feet away is blood. That cat was dead when the arrow hit him; he made ten yards down the draw and piled up. We are no longer quiet.

It was a better than average stand, although I can recall one particular evening when eleven coyotes and three bobcats beat a path to the troubled rabbit noises. That stand lasted thirty minutes and in that time, three of the little wolves were down with one cat. I went out after the last and proceeded to grab him by the back leg only to find out he was far from finished. All the while, Ron and Roy Chesley were calling and stomping around and shooting right and left. Generally one critter per stand is a darn fine average, but it is not uncommon to get doubles in the months of November through January.

The biggest problem in calling is proper light manipulation. A simple flashlight will pick eyes at fantastic distances on dark nights, but they are not adequate to shoot by. The best lights are from 6 to 9-volt jobs that will cut a swath through the dark for up to two hundred yards. Many callers make excellent lights from automobile headlights. The seal beam cigarette lighter types are fine, but limit your ranging around the boondocks. Although they work fine for close order work, they fade away beyond twenty yards.

"Burning the animal" is the biggest problem, so always keep the beam off the game until the shot is to be taken. The shooter lines up with the eyes and he's ready for the big blast.

Night callers are a hardy lot capable of staying awake for hours on end, hoping for the return glow of a pair of bright eyes to answer their call. For the most part, night callers will not call during a full or three-quarter moon but prefer the darker phases or no-moon situations. During a full moon, the animal sees too well and the light is not as effective. Winds in excess of ten miles per hour are a problem but many times the use of scent will change this situation. Animals always seem to want to work downwind when answering a call at night — something they often fail to do during the day.

Little is needed in the way of equipment other than the light and bow with the exception of the arrows. We use white shafts and feathers and place several bands of Scotch-lite reflective tape on each shaft. This makes them easy to retrieve as the tape is luminous with a flashlight at fifty yards or better.

A wide selection of calls is a must, and we usually use three separate calls during a stand, each one progressively higher pitched. The calls should be hung around the neck by a leather thong where they are easier to get at than in a pocket.

I prefer desert calling at night where the cover is not too thick. The usually shy varmints will be working the more sparse terrain under the protective cover of darkness. Toward the beginning of a new day they will work

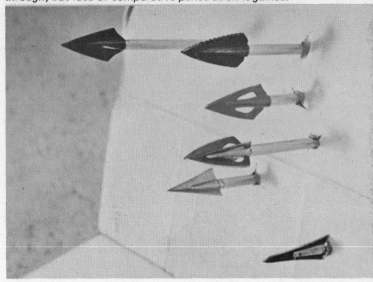

Broadheads, shot into bale of sponge rubber material from a shooting machine for control fact, passed completely through, but idea of comparative penetration is gained.

Charles Gifford called in this bobcat to within fifteen feet in Oklahoma, before he loosed single arrow to take it.

into the heavier cover that is sought out for daytime stands. The smart callers will watch the weather and be in the field just prior to or after a storm or period of high wind. On the desert the wind often will blow for several days, and during this period the animals lay up and do little traveling. Hit it on a dark night at the end of the wind and things will pop fast enough to keep you wide wake all night.

As you drive the roads at night, watch for small rodent life and rabbits. In areas where these seem thicker, you usually will get a hot strike.

Much of the desert country borders ranches and cultivated fields wherein live many forms of varmint food. Work these carefully, taking your stands one mile or a little better apart, and if you know that cats are in the area, make up to thirty-minute stands.

Although their eyes are easy to see, the animals must be looking toward you for the light to catch the reflection. This is one reason for a continuous brand of calling. Many times, though, you will miss a look with each pass of the light, and after thirty minutes, be amazed to have a bobcat looking down your throat at ten feet. It happens.

The most important single thing to me is noise. It seems easier to be clumsy at night and you have more metallic equipment such as lights to bang around. Watch the noise and your odds will increase favorably.

Varmints take a lot of killing, so use big broadheads and make sure they are sharp as razors. I have never seen one go down in his tracks with the exception of one head shot, and as Don Egger puts it, "They can carry more lead than a junk wagon." That pretty well sums it up.

Scout the areas during the day for signs and check with landowners for permission. Then, when the time is right, give it a go. Maybe a bobcat will try and get in your truck.

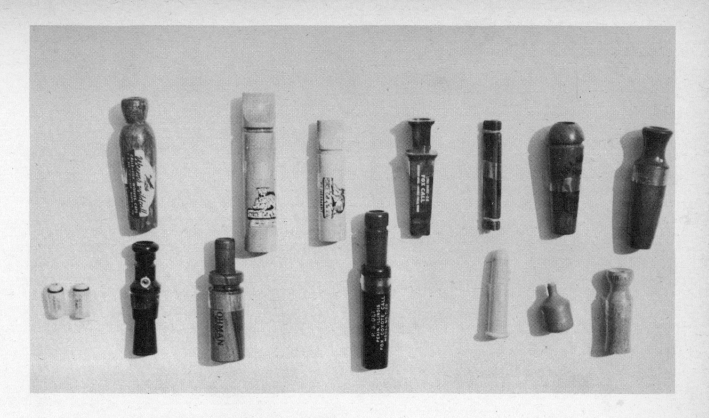

In using the varmint call, proper position of the hands controls tone, although one hand can be used by expert.

ABOUT three years ago I took a beginning caller, Roy Chesley, on his first real varmint hunt. Roy had been calling for a period of six months prior to this memorable event and had noted little success. I should admit here and now that this hunt was made with firearms as we were in the midst of a State Field Contest as well as a large concentration of varmints that were doing vast economic damage to the local ranchers. This hunt was for "blood" so to speak and not for the pure joy of calling-hunting such as bow-hunting provides.

We had quite a time and proceeded to dispatch five bobcats and eleven coyotes. Roy's enthusiasm and excitement as a result of this can hardly be doubted. On one stand we had a coyote come in from behind and actually run right into Roy, throwing dirt and gravel all over him in his paw screeching attempt to put on the binders. When the confusion was over, Roy, with sand running off his hat brim and bouncing onto his nose, was ready to admit that varmint calling actually worked.

Whatever the weapon, or even with a camera, the man with a call properly used is in for action and success previously denied him. In Roy's case, after six months of frustration he found that it really was all it was cracked up to be. Since that time he has gone on the callers trail with a zest, and has taken a second place in the World Championships as well as placing in California State events.

I cite this example as an indication of a particular problem, one of handling the call. Roy had at that time a considerable knowledge of the game in question. He had hunted all his life and trapped, too, and knowledge of trapping varmints does not come overnight. One experienced in trapping the predators has an appreciable jump over the man off the street, who enters varmint hunting with no prior knowledge.

On the hunt under discussion, Roy made a few

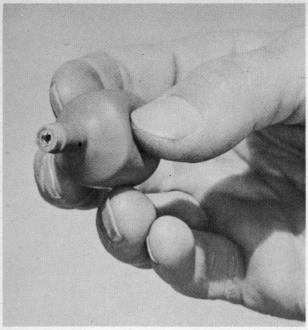

Left: Circe coaxer call imitates squeak of a mouse and is difficult for a bobcat to resist when at close range.

With a tuning rod, the reed is removed from Circe call. Actually, this is three calls in one, each with tone pitched differently. Serious caller can tune his call.

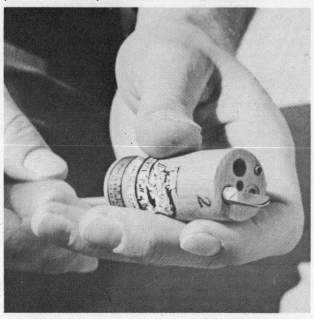

stands throughout the day but spent most of his time in the car, practicing between stands, trying to mimic as best he could the style I was using in the field. By the last few stands he was calling well and demonstrated this by tolling in one cat and three coyotes.

This, to me, is a classic example of a big point: Varmint calling is easy, if one follows a few simple steps and develops a style. Two years ago, Roy called like I do, but today there is very little similarity between our calling styles, yet for the most part he will outcall me in the field. This is a blow to my ego, but gratifying, too.

Over a ten-year period I have been instrumental in teaching hundreds of varmint callers the basic fundamentals of calling. Each individual has, from this point, progressed to his or her own style of calling, one more suitable to his physical abilities.

Burnham Brothers' coaxer call, excellent for foxes, can be varied in pitch simply by pressure of the bite on the mouthpiece. Thus, hands are not necessary to call.

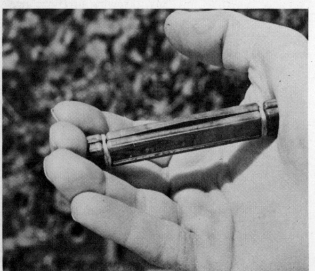

Some bowhunters favor a plastic call of one type or another. This one opens to accept a variety of reeds. They may be changed quickly without tools in the field.

Electronic calls, such as those marketed by Johnny Stewart, use either recordings or tape. This field photo shows that call will bring in unwary varmints.

Reed of plastic-barreled call can be changed in tone by crimping it in predetermined areas of metal. However, due to the thin material, the spoilage factor is high.

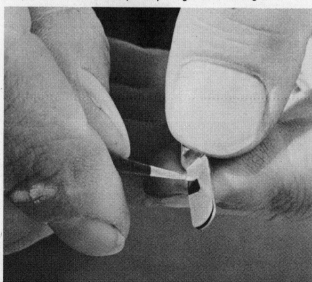

By physical abilities I mean this: Each person has his own blowing capabilities; it cannot be expected that all individuals' wind and endurance are the same. Blowing a call is work, so some callers take it easy where the next will turn fourteen different shades of red and purple while calling. Some callers blow so hard you can actually hear their lungs and diaphragm working where the next will achieve the same volume tone completely relaxed.

You can explain techniques and styles to the beginner but you cannot expect him to mimic completely your style, and there is no need that he do so, because his chances for success are just as good as your own from a call handling standpoint.

Upon developing his calling ability, the future varmint chaser will decide on tones and calls that work best under specific requirments.

The three biggest selling and most popular calls are, Weems, Circe and Burnham Brothers, not necessarily in the order of preference. Each one of these calls sounds a bit different and is entirely different to blow. I personally feel the Weems call is the easiest to blow and the best sounding, but Al LaReau, 1963 California Field Champ, prefers the Burnham, as he feels it is easier to blow. This is a direct reflection on individual physical capabilities.

All of these are excellent and so are the several dozen other brands availables to the caller. Under certain conditions, any of them will work, but under all conditions I feel these three are the ones that do the best all-around job.

Calling patterns vary greatly between individual callers, but no matter what the difference in style, several things remain constant. To be a good caller, I tell the beginning to think of one thing while call-

ing: A rabbit fighting for his life. If this is kept foremost in mind, your style will develop. Each caller must learn to control his call with the hands and the regulation of air pressure. How well he learns, will determine his ability.

Generally, a call is broken down into three parts — surprise, scramble and distress. The surprise call is your first series, and regardless of the volume or intensity, it is the main portion of the call and the part that arouses the critter's interest. This portion of the stand has the carrying power to reach out up to two miles and wake up the varmints.

The scramble is designed to imitate the rabbit

When the air pressure has been built in call to maximum (upper left), it is released sharply. (Above) Hand acts as a sounding board and sound goes in direction in which hand is pointed. High pitched wail carries long way. (Below) Same technique is used with the plastic calls.

This is Dougherty's favorite hand position, as tone can be changed quickly to raspy pitch dear to any coyote. Fluttering hand gives effect of fear, exciting varmints.

fighting with his antagonist and arouses the killer instincts in the varmints. It is the heart of the call and each accomplished caller may handle it a bit differently, yet results are the same if done well. The scramble requires a lot of finesse; just the right amount. Air pressure has to be well controlled with the hands doing the work, as the fingers play the airstream in the same manner that a trumpeter works his horn.

Distress cries are pretty much the same with each caller; wavering cries that go up and down the scale. They should be excited and they should be played out to indicate weakness. Mute the call while using a distress series, especially if you have game coming in. Never launch into a hard series when an animal is coming in hot. You can sometimes do this when one is leaving but, by then, what the heck . . .

Learn to handle the call with one hand, as this will serve you well in the field where control of your wea-

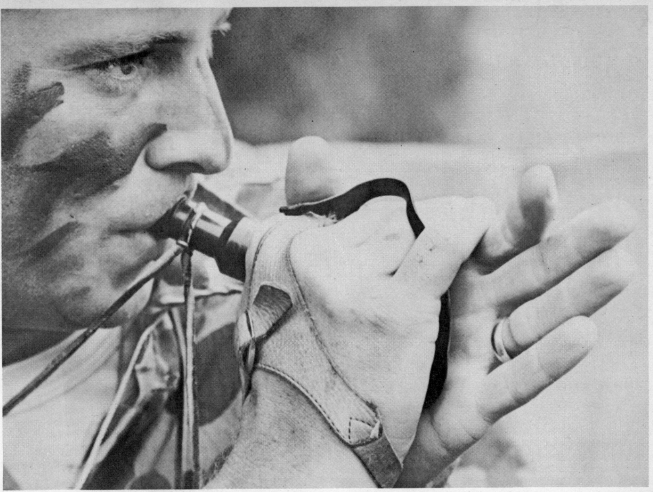

Wearing camouflage paint on his face, protective glove on his hand, Jim Dougherty attempts to draw in coyote.

Weems Dual Tone call is used for surprise series, which is a sqeaker sound controlled by movement of hands.

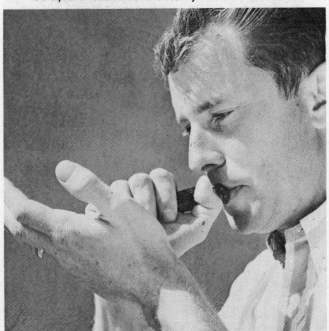

pon is necessary. I usually start a call with both hands, since this is required where volume is the objective. Then I switch to one for most of the balance of the stand.

The sound of the call goes where you point the barrel. For this reason point your call well upward, at about forty degrees when beginning, and face it to all points of the compass on your initial series. Pointing the barrel down is a good way to mute the sound. Muffle it against your shoulder or under your jacket if you like to coax a critter up close.

Muting can be accomplished by terrific air pressure and finger control, too, although it requires practice. Muting the call gives a different effect than switching to a squeaker. A muted jackrabbit voice is better in my mind for coyotes than a squeaker.

Wooden calls may sound excellent to the human ear, yet I believe that animals actually prefer the tone from plastic barrel calls. There is no proof for this other than personal observation but if you're having slow times with a wood call, you may do well to switch. More volume can be obtained with wooden calls and in this respect the Circe cannot be beat. For callers in the windier areas this would be a wise choice.

Check the inside of the barrel of your call. For maximum effectiveness it should have a tapered sound chamber, as these are easier to handle and will give you a third more volume than a parallel chamber.

There is more to it than meets the eye, and trial and error are the best educators. You'll never be good at it unless you spend a lot of time in the field . . . get with it and good luck. – *Jim Dougherty*

Chapter 13

SHARP CARP, NARROW ARROW

This Lowly Fish Can Present Plenty Of Fight And Challenge For Bowfishermen

IF you're a fisherman, you may not go for bowfishing; the same goes for the avid archer. There is something about driving arrows into several feet of water at a two-foot carp, who may or may not be where you're aiming, that leads to major frustrations.

Jim Wallace is both an avid archer and an ardent angler, but never had tried to combine the two until Doug Morgan invited him along for what he promised to be an action-filled weekend on the Colorado River, which separates Arizona from California. The fact that the two states are constantly haggling in court, and out, would lead one to believe that this mass of water divides them emotionally as well as geographically, but that's another story.

The weekend was action-filled as promised, but a lot of it had little to do with impaling carp on the end of an arrow. In reality, it turned out to be a comedy of errors — or, more realistically, a comedy of arrows.

You may immediately wonder why one would choose carp as the targets for his arrows, since this is one of the most unpopular species found in fresh water and certainly is frowned upon for eating. The chief reason, of course, is the fact that this is the only fresh water fish that the California archer is allowed to take with bow and arrow. Also, this particular fish is fast, shifty and gives the archer a good run for his arrows.

In Needles, a California community virtually on the bank of the river, Courtney Boom, one of the town businessmen had told Wallace of the carp fishing potential in the back waters of the Colorado that lie on the Arizona side.

These back waters were formed when the course of the river was changed to channel it closer to the town. A portion of the original stream still seeps through some seventy-five square miles of channels, small ponds and a few small lakes.

Most of these channels, are about fifteen feet in

The carp, considered a rough fish and even a threat to game fish, presents a real challenge to bowfishermen.

Carp are found in most parts of the United States and it takes no special equipment other than a bow reel.

width and from three to five feet in depth. There also are numerous beaver dams, and here the depth will run as much as fifteen feet and the waters bear bass and catfish.

Trying to make as much out of a two-day weekend as possible, Morgan and Wallace drove through the Colorado and associated deserts at night to reach Needles, where they put up at a motel.

The next morning, Courtney Boom and a guide, Kenny Baldwin, met them for breakfast and over steak and eggs the latter told more about the back waters area on the Arizona side of the river. They would be doing at least some of their bow-fishing in small but shallow lakes, he explained, and would be using a twelve-foot flat bottom boat of aluminum. There is little room to maneuver a larger, heavier vessel in the narrow channels, and they probably would have to carry the boat over the beaver dams blocking the way. Also taken along was a five hp. Johnson outboard motor, which he said was well adapted to the area.

The boat and motor had been hauled on a truck. Now began the chore of getting it into the water, and that was where Wallace made his initial mistake of the day — second mistake, if you want to include coming at all. The underwater walls of the channel are steep and slippery, and although the water was deep, it was icy cold!

In launching the boat, he was carrying the front of the lightweight skiff, moving backwards toward the water's edge. Then came that fatal step that sent him plunging into the shallow depths, the full weight of the boat on top. After several moments of breathless scrambling, he managed to get separated from the metallic bottom.

If you have ever tried to get three men, two bows, two sets of arrows, a pair of cameras, assorted lunches and a motor into a skiff this size, you know why they make larger boats.

Moving up the narrow channel, they saw fish moving away. It was almost as though they were herding them; as the boat moved up the waterway, all of the fish would move ahead.

At the first beaver dam, there were about twenty carp swimming in confused circles, and as the boat drew still closer, one huge carp — a leader, if there is such a thing as rank in piscatorial circles — darted through the water, making it past to safety. This started a stampede or whatever it is that fish do when they're in a hurry.

Finally, there was only one fish left and he seemed

in no hurry to escape. This would seem an indication that he was lazy, overfed or just plain stupid. On the other hand, he may have been an individualist, who refused to conform and escape just because the others did.

This carp simply lay close to the bank until the bowmen were virtually on top of him. Then, he shot to the other side of the dam, doing the same thing: Hugging the bank as though attempting to blend with the submerged growth. This went on for several minutes, until they tired of the chase and pushed the dam boat over the dam and into the next channel.

Once back in the water, Ken suggested that one of the immigrants get into the bow of the boat and try a few shots. Morgan scrambled for the position, and as he got into position, Ken cut the motor and used the oars, dipping them as lightly as possible as they slid toward the next dam.

As before, there were carp that moved downstream in a flood of silver scales. Morgan, meanwhile, was having his problems. Perched precariously in the bow, he was having trouble in maintaining his balance.

The largest carp of the expedition started past the boat, still swimming lazily as though daring them to take a shot at him.

Doug was using a reel on his bow, equipped with about fifty feet of line. In the confusion of getting the gear into the boat, his line had tangled on the reel. Now, as the big carp swam past, Morgan took careful aim at what appeared to be a cinch shot. The bowstring vibrated as the arrow was loosed, then pandemonium set in.

The arrow shot downward toward the target — but so did Morgan. The arrow drew the line tight on the reel, and Doug, already offbalance, was dragged into the shallows.

It took several minutes to get Morgan, cursing roundly, back into the boat. The laughter didn't improve his mood any, but it did improve his swearing. The fact that he had missed the fish, too, didn't help.

Several more shots were made with bow-mounted reels, but there was more line than there was pond. And since the water was shallow, dammed at each end by the beaver dams, the reels were unnecessary. They were removed.

Morgan was using a Browning bow with a 64-pound pull and Easton XX75 2020 aluminum arrows. He had drilled a hole near the tip of each of the shafts to release the air and relieve flotation. Wallace was using a Colt *Huntsman* and the same type of arrows. However, his shafts were equipped with standard hunting broadheads, while Morgan used special fish tips.

Moving up the channel, the bowmen could see several fish moving directly ahead of the boat, Morgan had a Kittredge hunting sight rigged on his bow, and came through by making a hit with his second arrow, then his third — and so on into the night.

Fish heads come in varying shapes and designs, but the primary need is a barb so that the fish won't wiggle off.

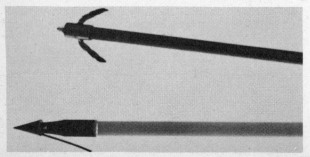

Doug Morgan looses a shot after wading in on a bit carp. (Below) Aluminum shafts tend to float, so this one was drilled to take on water and a line was rigged in hole.

It may have been his use of the sight, or simply the fact that he had not done more of this type fishing, but Wallace found that scoring was not easy, and made several shots before hitting the first carp.

Depending upon the angle at which the sun is hitting the water, there is a deflection of light rays; they tend to "bend" upon hitting the surface. As a result, the fish is not actually where you see it. One has to learn to compensate or "lead" his game. Also, they found that, as the arrow hits the water, it deflects upward; the deeper one is shooting, the more the arrow will deflect until it stops traveling.

Shooting most of the time into about three feet of water, they found that if one aims just under the fish, he is most likely to get a hit.

At the end of the second channel, the skiff entered a small pool that measured thirty-odd yards across and was about two feet deep. Here, Morgan and Wallace clambered from the boat and tried wading and shooting. Considering the deflections, et cetera, earlier discussed, this may sound like a damn good way to get one of your arrows through your own foot, but it turned out to be a ball.

The boat handler joined them and the trio spread out

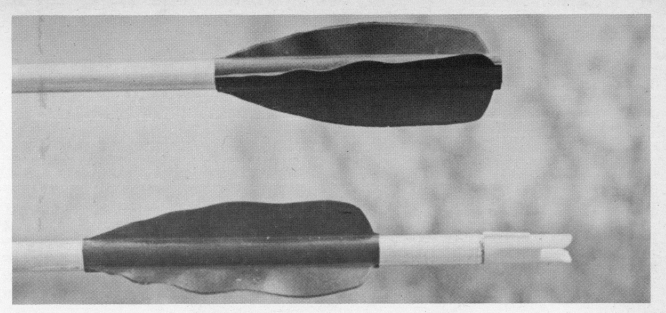

Rubber fletching that simply slips over the featherless shaft is available and is affected in no way by water.

across the lake on a frontal line and began to move across the lake, maintaining interval to drive the carp ahead. Near the bank, there were perhaps thirty fish swimming about, trying to find a way between the three, but not daring to make the run.

One carp tried to make it, and Wallace made a quick draw with the bow but missed. The entire school of fish

A variety of bowfishing reels is available today, most of them designed to be installed without marring bow.

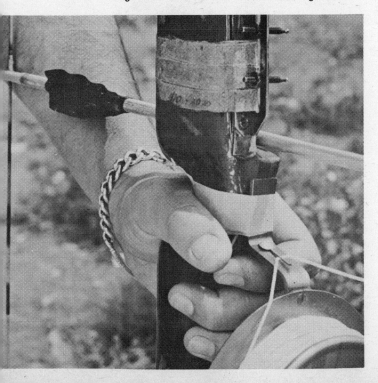

followed this leader. Jim drew another arrow, missed again, then looked up in time to see Doug Morgan sink a shaft through a carp's head. The latter quickly nocked another arrow, drew and pasted a second one to the bottom.

By this time, the water was so thick with fish making for safety that it was hard to pick a specific target. Standing there, knee deep in water, they could feel fish bumping their legs as they waded.

One carp tried to make it, and Wallace made a quick draw with the bow, but missed.

Another channel led into a deep pond, where Wallace spotted some of the largest bass he had ever seen. There were carp here, too, but they were running deep. The few shots tried were to determine how the arrows would react. The conclusion was that the shafts offered good penetration only through about six feet of water. But it also is harder to judge your aim and your chances of hitting one beyond five feet are virtually nil.

Heading back to where the truck had been left, they attempted to keep the carp on one side of the channel and crowded against the bank. Although the fish proved less than cooperative, they managed to get in several shots. The arrow usually would go completely through the fish and imbed itself about a foot into the sand of the underwater embankment.

Once on shore, they found that they had gotten an even two dozen fish. It was 102 on the river by then, and our heroes were in favor of finding the tallest cool beer in that vicinity of the desert.

But suddenly there was a sound within yards of what sounded like a gunshot. Not knowing what was happening, both men hit the ground, accusing some idiot of sniping in the surrounding brush.

But they raised their heads high enough at the next sharp report to see the guide standing knee deep in the water, an oar in his hands. After he slammed it down against the surface once more, he reached down to pull out three giant carp — all larger than any previously taken. – *Jack Lewis*

Chapter 14

HOW TO BECOME ANTI-ANTELOPE

Techniques For This Type Of Bowhunting Vary From One Hunter To Another, But These Experiences May Help You

Hunting the pronghorn with bow and arrow is an experience that every archer interested in matching wits on an equal level with his quarry should try.

To begin with, the antelope is not really an antelope; he is a goat. Antelope have been accurately clocked at speeds up to seventy miles per hour, and they have the largest set of eyes of any North American game animal. This means that they see well too. They make a variety of sounds by blowing through their nose, from a bark to what I would describe as a whistle; this means that they can — and do — laugh at you when you miss. They send heliographic messages to each other across the open prairie by extending the long white guard hairs on the rump patch causing them to flash rapidly in the sun. While warning each other with these visual messages, they also emit a powerful scent, which when carried downwind, serves as a danger signal to others of the breed up to a mile away.

But they don't hide from you; they stay right out in the open all day long and tantalize you into thinking there might be a way.

A man does not have to buy a .243 rifle to kill an antelope; however, it would certainly be the easiest way. Those of us who hunt with the bow have obviously decided that the easy way was not for us. To make a kill is not the all important thing. The kill should be the climax to a contest between you and

the game; a hard fought contest of nerves, skill and intelligence; of knowing the game — and of having a super grade rabbit's foot in your pocket.

Most antelope hunts in Wyoming, which is the capital of all antelope hunting, fall in September. At this time, the rut is getting started or reaching a full pitch, depending a bit on the weather and the latitude. Romantic pronghorns will offer a bowman certain advantages in hunting. Bucks often are busy warring among themselves. This often gives the bowman a chance to slip up unnoticed for a shot. The herd buck is a pugnacious critter, ready to do battle with any upstart who challenges his privacy and supremacy or casts a coveted look at one of his does.

Here lies an angle to pronghorn hunting that will definitely require more investigation. While in quest of the prongies last season, my hunting partner, George Wright, hit upon a diabolical plot to do in one old fellow who had half of the available ladies under lock and horn.

Returning to the ranch house, Wright set to work with great vigor, bent on becoming a buck antelope. First, he cut a pair of record class pronghorn horns from cardboard and secured them to his hat. A fast application of shoe polish made them quite presentable. A perfectionist, he also darkened the center of his face to give himself the appearance of a truly magnificent and romantic buck. His fervor was infectious, and the rest of us dashed around the house searching for items to transform him completely. A throw rug was discovered of perfect color and shape; Cinnamon brown and oval. This was attached to Wright's back and fixed to his trophy type headgear. A freshly laundered tee shirt was attached to his rear so that it hung off his rounded posterior, simulating a sparkling rump patch.

Wearing a white tee shirt over his torso and white levis tinged with more shoe polish, George Wright became the first buck antelope — pseudo or otherwise — to cavort about the living room of Maycocks' ranch while sipping a beer. At two thousand yards he would have fooled me completely. Assuming a bent position, arms dangling to the ground, George perfected his barks and snorts, while bouncing up and down in the best antelope tradition. Crude as it was, I was convinced that he might have something.

We put the plan into gear.

Wright, Leo Farley and I drove past the pasture where dwelt the monarch of the ranch. His does were at rest, while he stood off some distance riding herd on any desire they might possess to try and investigate some distant youngster who lacked courage to come calling.

Out of sight over the crest of a low swell, George disembarked while we turned and raced to a distant

The Little Shaver broadhead is one of several marketed that utilizes a razor blade inserted as a cutting edge.

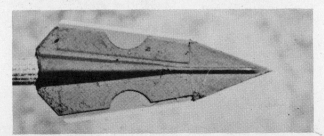

With razor blades inserted in the head, it becomes an instantly sharp instrument. Blades can be changed, too.

hill to observe what might well be the end of a dear friend. It very nearly was.

Farley and I had been sitting only a few moments, eyes glued to our field glases, when "Pronghorn" Wright hove into view over the hill. He bent over, turned broadside, bounced twice and snorted a challenge to the buck in the valley below. The buck, at least three hundred yards away, couldn't believe it. He spun around and pawed the ground, cast a suspicious glance at the girls, who were looking at George, snortin' with open admiration. Then the buck lowered his head and charged.

At this point, George informed us later, he was experiencing some mild regrets. The buck came at a dead run across the valley and up the hill but at fifty yards, he seemed to experience some misgivings. He skidded to a halt, pawed the ground, then lowered his head again for the final lunge. At this point, Leo gave a startled cry. Another buck was making off with the big boy's does.

For the next five minutes, the pasture's green carpet was covered with dust as the big buck charged back and forth, trying to save his herd from these two challengers. It was a wild melee of grunts, false charges, actual contacts and a few scattered arrows. But, the plan had worked and a new concept of bowhunting pronghorns was born.

The main disadvantage in shooting an antelope with an arrow is the reactions of the targets. Possessing magnificent vision, they can see the arrows coming at them. Possessing better coordination, they can side-step, duck or outrun the arrow as it pursues them. This is a pure and simple fact: Antelope are tough targets.

The pronghorn is not a large animal, but his bright coloration against the drab background makes him appear larger — and therefore closer — than he actually is. The archer will find that most of his misses will be on the short side, often by as much as twenty yards. In the open country that these critters love so dearly, range estimation is a real problem. This is even a problem for the man who attempts to flatten one with his favorite smokepole.

Antelope can be stalked successfully, though. It requires a vast amount of patience and the utmost in determination. The Wyoming country has many little draws along which one can crawl; slight ridges that one can use for what little cover it will offer. Using these means, it is not too difficult to close to within sixty-five yards. Most often you will be shooting from a low position — kneeling or even lower, if possible — the prongies generally will let you get off the shot, being somewhat inquisitive. They are not so inquisitive as to wait to see if you scored a hit. Sometime between the release and contact, they decide to move. Radio-controlled arrows would be a real boon here.

In stalking, camouflage is a big help. The coloring of the clothing should blend well with the countryside. Remember those eyes; they probably saw you get out of bed in the morning. I recall one incident when I crawled across a low ridge bent on sticking the buck in a small band with a 2016. All the eyes of the band were elsewhere as I made ready to shoot.

The buck was about sixty-five yards away, and by this stage of the game I was shooting more and enjoying it less. In keeping with most of my past performances, I missed him cold, shooting high for a change. This, in itself, was some sort of mental victory. The buck turned his gaze up slope and fixed his huge brown eyes on me. I shot four more arrows and I firmly believe they were good ones, but with each shot his muscles tensed, he dropped his head a bit, and leaped out of the way. I did manage finally to skewer a fine buck while stalking him. However, I have to admit, I cheated. I shot him in the back!

There really is only one excellent way to bowhunt antelope. This is from a blind at a waterhole. I have run into those pure-type people who scream indignantly at the suggestion of such an uncouth ambush, but let them scream. Crawling on your belly is a great way to study the local flora and insect life, to meet up with certain unsavory reptiles and to develop excellent calluses; it is not the best way to fill a $25 antelope tag.

Antelope drink several times during the course of the day, although the weather will have a bit to do with this. The hotter it is, the more they will drink. During a dry year, this can offer the choicest of situations. Blinds should be constructed in such a manner as to blend well with the low sage. This is done by digging a hole which allows the hunter to sit well below eye level, the blind also should be quite roomy as you are going to be there quite awhile; allow ample room to straighten your legs and shift positions. Build the blind up with sage or whatever is natural growth all around, making it somewhat higher in the back, but not so high as to draw attention. Several openings should be left through which to shoot, if the blind will allow you to shoot without

For hunting, Dougherty uses aluminum shafts, but due to cost, he paints them red and uses a five-inch white feather fletch, which makes them easier to find in brush.

standing up. Most of the waterholes in the prairie country are behind dirt dams at the lower end of a natural draw.

The best blinds I have seen for shooting with a minimum of movement are those built right into the side of the draw, sort of a cave affair. Antelope are very cautious when coming to drink, and take a lot of time to study the situation. When they make up their minds, however, they all gang up and come in at once. This is not the time to shoot. Generally the buck will drink alone, most often in advance of the does, but I have seen many cases when the entire herd drank simultaneously. This stage of the game is why you have been sitting there all day, yet, it is without a doubt the most nerve-wracking of emotional experiences and it is here that most setups become goof-ups.

Never shoot at the game the first time his head goes down; it goes down and comes up immediately. An Indian told me once, "The first time they kiss the water; the second they taste it; the third, they drink." When an antelope finally goes down, he plunges his head into the water up to his eyes and sucks it up like a hose, and this is the time to take your shot. Veteran antelope busters have told me that if you have to raise for a shot, do it now. Not too slowly, not too fast . . . they might see you but they won't bolt all at once. Their theory is, they didn't see you when they came in, and they can't really believe it. Here again is a classic example of how much they depend upon their eyesight.

Sitting in a blind can offer a variety of excitement, too. I spent one long, long day in a fine blind and spent several hours with a flock of mallards that zoomed in at sun up and spent the day with me. For better than an hour they were within scant feet, and it was a great occasion to listen to their conversational chatter and store it away for later use during the duck season. I am not the sort who can sit too long

Outfitted for a try at the wily antelope of Wyoming, Jim Dougherty pauses to consider approach to problem.

Dougherty stalks an antelope, creeping up behind a small hill, hoping to get close enough for telling bow shot.

in one place, but a blind at a waterhole, I can tolerate, because something is always going on.

One of the finest aspects of hunting pronghorns is that you can always see game. In almost every direction you can see one or more of the beautiful animals feeding, bedded down or playing. At least you know they are around, which is not so often the case when deer hunting or in pursuit of other specimens for the den wall.

The archer who goes after a pronghorn will have an unparalleled ball. He will get lots of shooting if he is not too particular as to what he is after in the way of a head. The real trophy bucks come harder. Long shots for the stalker will be the rule, and you will do well to brush up on this phase of skill. But not at the local field range, as this will not help you a bit. Get

out in the open — the wide open — and shoot . . . and shoot.

Several states have a fine antelope program, but Wyoming has the best set up. For $50 the non-resident can take one antelope and two deer. Deer hunting is fabulous for bucks grow huge and the does will average 140 pounds field dressed. It is not uncommon to see deer on the plains with the antelope, although they generally seek out the bigger draws and coulees adjacent to the antelope range. Nothing will startle you more than to bust out a big-four point from a ditch hardly able to conceal a jackrabbit. The majority of the land is privately owned, but the ranchers are more than willing to allow you in to hunt, although a slight use fee usually is charged.

Cheap for the thrills that await. — *Jim Dougherty*

Chapter 15

TALES OF A SMALL GAME ADDICT

Success Here Can Lead To Bigger Game Trophies

Ron Chesley poses with his take of jackrabbits after a
bowhunting session in desert of Southern California.

DOUG Kittredge has an expression that I always felt
was aptly put: "Small game is big game, when you
hunt it with bow and arrow." When you stop and think
about it, Doug has smacked the ol' nail right in the
center.

Doug was the guiding light, when I was first en-
ticed into my often rewarding and more often frustrating affair with archery. We made a deal a long
time ago. I would teach him to fish, and he would
teach me to shoot a bow.

Doug became a superior angler, while I really never
did learn how to shoot. This had nothing to do with
who was doing the teaching. I think fishing must be
easier. Doug and I busted a lot of arrows and a fair
amount of fishing tackle as we roamed the country in
pursuit of trout, bass, deer and small game.

It was, incidently, because of our interest in small

game hunting, and the great amount of time we spent
at it, that we became involved in varmint calling.

Doug thinks that practice on the field range is not
going to produce a great shot in the game fields. We
got prepared for the venison season by hunting venison
country (minutes from home) for small game. That
way we got in a lot of good hunting, and kept abreast
of what was going on in the deer woods. As far as I'm
concerned, it paid off. There were few seasons that
Doug and I didn't collect some meat right promptly.

This habit of small game hunting has been ingrain-
ed in me and the majority of my hunting partners.
Although practice is undoubtedly of value when one
talks small game, the real selling point for this type
of hunting is the fact that it is downright exciting.

Within fifty miles of my home in the metropolitan
Los Angeles area, I can hunt the following: rabbits,

squirrels, frogs, varmints, racoons, carp, sharks, all kinds of game birds, deer and even bear. That's just a smidgin, and all of this right in close to town. Many places where we hunt, we can see downtown Los Angeles and observe the freeway rush from the top of a suburban hill. My point is that small game hunting is available wherever you may be and shouldn't be passed up.

The gathering together of a group of bowhunters, for a week end of jack rabbit shooting, is just as exciting as a deer hunt. In the east, the fellows hunt woodchucks, a challenging pastime. Down in Texas, Arkansas and Louisiana I was introduced to a big sport, as much fun as anything I ever tried, hunting armadillos.

The armadillo can be duck soup or tough. In some woods they run rampant and have created a serious problem by sheer weight of numbers. Until you have seen an armadillo on the run, with three or four archers flinging arrows at him, you haven't seen one of bowhunting's craziest sights.

Small game hunting offers a fine supplement to a major big game trip. Rabbits are found in one variety or another wherever you may go. Cottontails, brush and

Also demanding when it comes to serving as a target is the fox; few are taken even by varmint callers at night.

The raccoon is another type of small game that is legal in most areas with a bow, but which presents a challenge.

swamp rabbits go well in the pot. Most of the small game is edible. I can recall many a memorable meal in camp made up of some critter.

Stalking rabbits or squirrels is not easy to pull off successfully. The training is excellent. Many mornings Doug and I stalked the elusive and tasty cottontail for hours, around cactus beds and woodpiles. The same shooting conditions encountered when pitted against bigger game are experienced.

The type of equipment used by the small game hunter should be the same used against bear or deer in the fall. Even the broadhead can be used, although most hunters prefer blunts or field points of a weight the same as the broadhead.

Blunts are used on small game. Arrows, with rare exceptions, set up a shock wave like a bullet on big game. Rabbits and other small game are tough, but a blunt takes a lot of the fire out of them, pronto.

One enjoyable small critter hunt involves plunking frogs at night along the banks of a slough or marsh. The hunter must exercise care in the approach and pinpoint accuracy in the shooting. The bag of frogs, after an evening's sport, contains a delicacy that could cost ten dollars a plate in a restaurant. Broadheads are ideal, unless the frogs are in the water, then a bowfishing rig should be employed.

Sneaking along a frog bank in the dark with a headlight can give a hunter chances at other game. We have run across coons, muskrats, bobcats and fox, while hunting big green bull frogs.

Varmint calling is the ne plus ultra of small game

pursuit. A coyote or bobcat can be placed in the same category as a deer or elk, when hunted with a bow. Foxes are the easiest to bag. Coyotes are the most difficult to lure up and place in contact with an arrow. Razor keen broadheads are all that will bring them down quickly and humanely. Racoons come well to a call and can be hunted with dogs or by slipping along on foot in good coon feed areas, where waterlife is abundant.

Bowfishing can take on many shapes. Carp offers the best spring season hunting. In most areas you are doing game fish a favor by removing carp from the lakes and rivers.

In the Pacific Ocean, as the waters grow warm,

All of the techniques of bowhunting, whatever the size, can be practiced and exercised in stalking small game.

sharks move in following the game fish. They are uncommonly easy to take with a bow and arrow. When dealing with the big ones, the smart hunters run a line from their arrows to conventional salt water tackle and reel in their prize.

In California a law has been passed making it permissible to pursue ocean game fish with a bow. Although I haven't tried it, I know from experience this can be productive on surface fish such as yellowtail.

Small game hunting certainly helps out the dealer's arrow sales. Thousands of arrows are lost and broken annually by small game hunters. I have developed a habit of saving old arrows, arrows with broken broadhead and other remnants which make excellent throwaways for the wild, carefree small game hunts. If you have a son or daughter who likes to shoot, small game hunts are ideal. Dad's broken arrows are often long enough to re-point for the kids.

My son cut his teeth on lizards. He stalks them carefully and blasts them consistently, anytime he gets inside of thirty feet. That's good shooting. It has helped him collect some bigger game and more trophies on the range than any ten year old should rightfully have.

Birds fall into the small game category, although they are difficult to collect with a bow. We hunt quail, doves, bandtail pigeons, ducks, geese, coots and pheasants every year with our bows and blunt tipped arrows. California established a trial run for bowhunters with a special pheasant season after the regular season. The success ratio was good. It made believers out of a lot of skeptics, and was a major step for bowhunting in California.

There is nothing wrong with field and target ranges for the aspiring bowhunter; they are necessary Small-gaming it, however, is the ideal way to get ready for a crack at the big stuff. Like ol' Doug once said, "small game is big game when you hunt it with a bow and arrow." –Jim Dougherty

Chapter 16

BOWHUNTING FOR DISTAFFERS

Wives Have Been Known To Outdo Their Husbands; This May Help You Avoid It

ONE facet of archery in which women are becoming ever more evident is one that leaves no trophies to collect dust, no scores to be tallied at the end of the shoot — and leaves no doubt as to ability with the bow.

The only score in hunting is the game you bring back. Many a doubtful husband, out of kindness of his heart, has allowed the wife to tag along on the annual hunt. He even goes so far as to get her a heavier bow so she can compete. To some of these men has come a rude and abrupt awakening. Some have been completely blanked by the wife, bagging nothing, while she brought home the game.

Some women become interested in hunting with the husband, but the husband makes the mistake of overbowing them and they become easily discouraged. This usually is not intentional, since most states require a minimum bow weight for hunting big game.

Most women make better hunters than men since they have more patience. Tell a woman to sit on a stump by a deer trail, and that a deer will be along soon, and she will sit on that stump and wait. Women are not as fidgety as men, and when it comes to stalking, they are more cautious than any of the husbands encountered. Women will walk along, watching the birds, the trees and all the wildlife around and take their time. They aren't as impatient as men to see what lies over the hill.

The girls get as much enjoyment out of a good stalk as getting their game — well almost as much. They feel the challenge lies in getting as close as possible to the game and they do a good job of it. When a wife takes up hunting with the husband, she usually becomes another member of the hunting group. The girls join in the bragging sessions after a day's hunt, talking about the shots they made — and missed.

One problem, as indicated, is getting the proper weight bow. Arizona, for example, requires a minimum of forty pounds draw weight for hunting deer and javelina. If a woman is systematically conditioned to the heavier bow, she can manage it with little difficulty. When they get their form developed, they have little trouble keeping in condition.

Many hunting archers are not interested in target shooting. Instead of going to an all-day shoot at butts and targets, they will take a picnic lunch and go where they can get some hunting practice. Jackrabbits are always a good target in many states and they are fair game all year, if you have a license. The greatest challenge for most hunters is the ground squirrel. Take a look at a ground squirrel sitting on his rock and see the size target you have to hit. It can provide many hours of enjoyable hunting — and many broken shafts from missing.

Women usually start hunting to be with the man of the house when he takes off for a weekend of shooting and to join him on the family vacation which he usually spends hunting big game. One such participant is Rene Giardina.

She's almost as tall as her hunting bow and shorter than her target bow, but Rene places an arrow where it counts. Two years ago she was the first to bring in her deer among the hunters in the Elk Ridge country out of Monticello, Utah. Her barren doe field dressed at one hundred forty pounds, a good deal heavier than Rene.

The Giardinas are an archery family. Husband Nick is a hunter with good deer to his record and daughter Sandy is now old enough to take her try at deer.

Relating the incident of Rene's first deer hunt in Utah, Nick Giardina admits, "It was a thrill to see her get her deer, but still exasperating. Hunting together, we saw this doe at about forty-five yards. We both shot at the same time, we saw a hit and I yelled, 'I've got my deer!'

"When we went to look for the blood in a foot of new snow, we saw where the doe had jumped a log about forty yards from the hit. The doe was giving her last kick when we saw her a few yards away, but it wasn't my arrow in the deer. Rene's arrow had severed the femoral artery, I had shot under her neck and found my arrow in the snow by a tree. Most exasperating."

The doe was so big they had trouble loading it onto a *Tote Gote* to get it into camp. Five days later, Nick bagged his deer.

The tackle Rene Giardina uses for hunting includes a forty-one-pound, fifty-six-inch Drake bow. Her ar-

Betty Farmer shot this buck at thirty-eight yards on a Utah hunt. She was only one of thirteen hunters to score.

rows are custom made by her husband and are 21/64 Port Orford cedar with a three-feather helical fletch. The broadhead is a two-bladed Black Diamond with the total weight of the hunting arrow adding to 450 grains.

While waiting for big game season, Rene maintains her hunting eye by shooting jackrabbits, ground squirrels and targets, both the American and field rounds. For target shooting, Rene uses a thirty-five-pound, sixty-six-inch Fasco bow and Easton 1616XX75 aluminum arrows. When there are no rabbits and the squirrels are underground, the family packs up and heads for the Colorado River and carp shooting.

Nick claims that he would be the best hunter in the world if he had the patience and stalking ability of his wife. She is ninety percent more patient and is as good, if not better, at stalking than he. Nick starts on a hunt and sends Rene around the other way. He stops, looks and listens and purposely kills time, feeling that he will meet her at the designated spot. He has yet to succeed.

When he arrives, he can see Rene, still off about a quarter of a mile, looking at trees and cautiously moving forward. "There's nothing to do but sit down and wait. She'll get there in her own good time."

When Rene shot at her very first deer, she started out that day with a new pair of slacks on. They spotted a deer and Nick moved up close to it. He would make hand signals to Rene since he wanted her to make the kill. When the deer put its head down to browse, Nick would motion Rene forward, and when the deer's head came up, he would motion her to wait. This stop-and-go technique brought Rene within forty-five yards of the buck. It was impossible to get closer, since there was a shale slide between them and the deer. Rene had made the one-hundred yard stalk on her stomach. She got her shot at the deer but went between the deer's legs. After such diligent crawling, she had big holes in the knees of the new slacks.

This family plans vacations around the hunting seasons as much as possible.

"I enjoy hunting. Camping out is fun and even when I don't get my deer it is almost as much of a thrill to stalk them and see how close you can get. That's fun and takes some patience, too. When I shot my deer,

Dixie Sharman shoots an arrow that is intentionally longer that her draw, as she feels this keeps razor-sharp broadhead from coming too close to her fingers.

I was thrilled to know I had made my kill but was a little sorry, too. But I got over that," Rene says.

She takes great pains with her stalking since she wants to be as close as possible when she shoots. "A hit in the leg would worry me since it wouldn't do more than cripple the deer. With good equipment, it is up to me to make the best possible shot. When I miss, it's me, not the tackle," she concludes.

Another modern Diana with a deer trophy hanging in her home is Bettye Farmer.

"Charles started me out right by giving me the right tackle. Too many husbands give their wives discarded bows and mismatched arrows. With gear like that they lose interest."

Bettye took up archery to be with her husband, Charles, on weekends and during vacations. She started target shooting seven years ago with a thirty-pound Corky bow and fiberglass arrows. When hunting interest was aroused, Charles bought a heavier fifty-four-inch Browning forty-pound bow.

Bettye's first javelina hunt amused and vexed the group she was with. They spotted a herd of javelina and Charles made her stalk on all fours for about thirty feet to get close enough to shoot. The pigs were in front and Charles kept telling her to stand up and shoot. After several minutes, it finally registered and Bettye jumped up like a jack-in-the-box and spooked the pigs so no one got a shot.

Bettye had better luck in 1960 when a group from San Diego went to Northern Kaibab in Arizona for deer. Thirteen hunters packed into this deer rich country. Bettye operated under a time handicap since she had to be back at work in 4½ days. They hunted the first four days and saw nothing but some mangy looking does which they passed up. On the fifth and final day, Bettye allowed herself until one o'clock to give it a last try.

All during the hunt, they had been plagued by a group of joiners who would cruise the road and when they saw parked cars, they would stop to hunt. They figured there must be deer if there were hunters. This had gone on for the previous four days.

On the fifth and final day, the hunters decided to outwit the joiners, so got out earlier and picked an area. But right on schedule, the joiners appeared and started slamming car doors.

Bettye and Charles went their way and Charles told her to whistle if she got a hit. She carries a police whistle to signal when she gets a hit, so he can help her track and clean the kill.

Bettye was moving through the timber when she saw some deer ahead of her. She went down to one knee to look the situation over. Suddenly an arrow whistled by, and when she turned toward the sound, she saw two does coming up the hill. These had been startled by another hunter below her. Following behind the does was a nice forked horn buck.

There were two pines along the trail and, even though she doesn't like a moving shot, she decided to shoot when the buck cleared the largest pine, regardless. As the buck passed the marked tree, he stopped and turned his head left. Bettye made her shot from the kneeling position and scored a hit. Not waiting for the deer to go down or do more than jump, Bettye jerked out her police whistle and started blasting with it.

After the initial excitement of hitting her game, she decided to nock another arrow. Reaching over her shoulder, she discovered she had left her quiver in the car and had no more arrows. She marked the line of her shot, and still whistling, started to track her buck. Another hunter came up and asked her if she had seen any deer.

"I shot a buck," was her calm reply.

By this time there were hunters converging on the kill from all directions. One hunter asked her if she had been blowing the whistle and she admitted she had.

"Do you know you have been blowing the international distress signal of three long blasts?"

Her enthusiasm with the whistle had turned the hunter into the hunted.

Investigation showed she had taken the buck with a lung shot, from a distance of thirty-eight yards, using a Black Diamond broadhead on a cedar shaft. Her buck was the first to be shot during the first five days in Kaibab and dressed at one hundred and forty pounds.

Still pressed for time, Bettye returned to camp,

Whether male or female bowhunter, there is nothing like getting those boots off after return to camp, followed by a cup of hot coffee and an opportunity to unwind.

then started home. The worst part of the hunt was not being able to stay in camp after making her kill and be in on the bragging sessions. She was the only one in the group of thirteen archers to get her deer that year, hubby included in the blanks. The mounted, forked horn head of Bettye's buck has a corner of the wall in the Farmer residence.

Since her one arrow kill and the incident of the forgotten quiver, Bettye has switched to a bow quiver that holds seven custom-made arrows.

When Bettye started archery, she tried a shooting glove and a tab but had little success with either. Now she uses a bow lock. There is some argument among archers about the noise this device makes but she has had little trouble. She stalked a deer and it stood and calmly watched while she shot seven arrows at it, missing each time. Then the deer bounced out of sight.

She did miss a shot at a buck because of the bow lock, however. She and Charles were resting in a draw when deer appeared right above them. Charles kept telling her to shoot but she couldn't find her bow lock and didn't think of a bare-fingered shot. Charles missed, too.

They seldom hunt together since Charles prefers to move faster than Bettye. She likes to take her time and as seems to be the case with women, makes a better stalk. This husband and wife really work as a team. They both carry a compass to prevent getting lost. Bettye carries her police whistle to signal a hit. When they hunt javelina they carry walkie talkies. They take off in different directions and when one spots game, they use the modern communications system to call the other one to it.

Bettye gave up target shooting about two years ago and concentrates on hunting. She and Charles go after rabbits, ground squirrels and carp. Occasionally they will go to a broadhead shoot since most of these are similar to hunting conditions.

Perseverance is one of the attributes of all hunters, Still hunting for her first big game kill is red-headed Dixie Sharman.

"Perhaps the best thing about hunting, other than the camping fun and excitement of hunting, is the fact that I can buy all my vacation clothes in a surplus store, mostly Marine green dungarees."

Like other wives, she started her archery to be with her husband on weekends and vacations. A comparative newcomer to the field, she has been shooting about four years and three of the four has gone to Utah and Arizona for deer.

Her husband, Les, started her with a thirty-three

Nick Giardina offers pointers to his wife, Rene, and daughter, Sandy. All three practice for big game season by practicing through year on jackrabbits and varmints.

Rene Giardina poses with her first deer kill, which dressed out at 140 pounds. It was taken in Utah hunt.

pound Fasco target bow and glass arrows. The two of them would go on picnics and Les would shoot squirrels. Dixie didn't join in the hunting at first but went along for the outing. Soon she started carrying her bow and the hunting interest took claim of another victim. Les bought her a forty-four-pound fifty-four-inch Fasco hunting bow and equipped her with broadheads and blunts. Now when they go picnicking on a weekend, she participates in. the shooting.

Dixie has made two trips to Utah and one to Arizona for deer. Her first deer encounter came when she and one of the other women were casually walking down a road outside of camp, when they became aware that a buck was standing broadside in front of them.

Dixie just stood there with a true case of buck fever, too excited to do anything but look back at the deer. The other woman kept telling her to shoot but she couldn't get her bow up. Finally the deer moved away and neither hunter got a shot.

Dixie hunts with Les and doesn't like to have him more than a hundred yards away. During one of their hunts, Les put her on a stand by a trail and told her to wait until he came back. Dixie waited for two hours and didn't see a deer. She worried that Les would get lost.

Her first reaction to the idea of hunting was without enthusiasm, but the campfire bragging sessions and the talk about the missed shots soon aroused her interest. Then her first encounter with buck fever showed her the challenge of hunting.

When the Sharman's took their hunting vacation in 1962, they went to Utah to join a group from San Diego. Dixie was determined to get her deer. She made several trips through the area with Les without success, so decided to do her hunting in the area around camp. There were deer tracks all over the camping area that morning. The other hunters headed out bright and early and when they had gone, Dixie took the hunting gear and found a log. She sat down to wait. She stayed on that log for two hours, ignoring ants that were crawling over her and kept her mind on hunting. Her wait seemed fruitless so Dixie lit up a cigarette and started walking back to camp, dangling her bow and daydreaming. Four beautiful bucks bounced from the timber about twenty yards from her, but she didn't even get a shot — and within a "half block of camp," as Dixie puts it.

Women suffer the same problems of buck fever that men do. One lady hunter spotted her buck but didn't have an arrow on the string. She frantically reached to her back quiver, pulled all the arrows out one by one and threw them on the ground, never getting one arrow near the bowstring.

But we all know of male hunters who have suffered similar reactions at sight of that first deer.

Don't we?

Chapter 17

BOWFISHING'S TOUGHEST TROPHY

The Alligator Gar Of Our Southern States Is A Destroyer Of Game Fish, A Tough Target

THE big alligator gar were taunting me, daring me to shoot. They lazily rolled their six foot long armor plated bodies insultingly near the bow of the boat where I was poised, bow in hand, praying for a chance to loose an arrow. But they were either too far away, too fast or broke water under my nose just after I relaxed my vigilance long enough to slap at a persistent mosquito. The frustration was growing unbearable.

"You might as well give up," calmly advised my host, guide Charles Alter of DeWitt, Arkansas. "You're never going to sink an arrow into a gar that way. And it's probably a good thing. With the rig you've got, a hefty 'gator would yank you right out of the boat."

I relaxed, looking sheepishly at the standard bow reel, ninety-pound test line and forty-pound bow that had always been so formidable on small scissorbill gar. He had a point.

We were anchored off a long sandbar on Arkansas' famous lower White River, deep in that tangled green bottomland wilderness where the White, Arkansas and mighty Mississippi Rivers merge. This trackless country looks today much like it did when French explorer DeTonti traveled through this region in 1686 and established the first permanent white settlement in the Mississippi Valley . . . Arkansas Post, now a national monument.

"It takes special archery tackle to nail the big 'gators," Alter explained, adjusting his tall, rawboned frame to a more comfortable position among the heap of gasoline cans, tackle boxes and assorted gear gar fishermen must have to function.

Alter's two clients, Chicago business executives, perked up from the long wait between battles, showing interest. They were fishing for alligator gar with rod and reel, an exciting enough business as it is. The idea of bagging these fresh water brutes with bow and arrow must have seemed to them like a tough nut to crack.

Charles Alter probably knows as much about the

Texas youngster moves through shallow waters of bayou in search of alligator gar, which feed in such shallows.

habits of alligator gar as any man alive. A DeWitt rice farmer by occupation, sportsman by avocation, Alter was one of the original guides on the lower White River during gar fishing's heydey in the 1950s.

Large alligator gars are becoming scarce these days. Back in 1950, it wasn't unusual for a party of gar fishermen to land eight or more one hundred-pound plus 'gators in a day's time, day after day. But, a combination of extensive commercial and sport fishing, pesticides, cold water from upstream hydro-electric power dams and other factors, soon trimmed the gar population.

However, the alligator gar's comparative scarcity has made it even more a prized trophy, especially among bowfishermen.

Arkansas contains some ideal bowfishing territory for gar in the lower White, Arkansas, Mississippi, Ouachita, Saline and Red Rivers and their numerous tributaries and ox-bow overflow lakes. Four species of gar are found in Arkansas: Shortnose, native to clear mountain streams; longnose, spotted and alligator gars, ranging throughout southern Arkansas.

Naturally, bowfishing is a popular sport with Arkansans, who consider their state to be the Bow-hunting Capitol of the South, because of its liberal archery hunting regulations. But most of the bow-fisherman's attention is directed at the smaller long-nose (scissorbill) and spotted gars, which abound throughout the southern part of the state. However, the alligator gar, which can weigh over three hundred pounds and reach a length of eight feet, remains the bowfisherman's top trophy ... The Holy Grail.

"The ordinary bowfishing rig just isn't suitable

Bowfishermen are an inventive lot, which results in the variety of arrow points as well as gigs used for gar.

As arrow strikes it, gar fish breaks water. These fish feed on game varieties and are considered to be pests.

for taking large alligator gar," continued Alter, who is president of the White River Bowmen's Club and past president of the Arkansas Bowhunters Association. "One must have a flexible rod to play a big gar or he'll break the line, even fifty-pound test line with a steel wire leader. Playing a large 'gator with a bow held in the hands just won't work, and it could be dangerous."

An archer can get by with attaching his line directly to the bow when fishing for smaller gar. But this technique isn't recommended for taking a fish as powerful as an adult alligator gar . . . The archer may take an unexpected swim.

Alter and his long time bowfishing companion, Dr. Rex Hancock of Stuttgart, have evolved a technique for taking big gar that is safe but effective. The braided bowfishing line, usually of at least ninety-pound test, is not fastened to the bow reel, but to a small cork. The cork then is taped lightly inside the hollow of a standard commercial reel. If a big 'gator is hit and churns for the bottom, he will pull the cork free instead of yanking the bow from the archer's hand or hauling him overboard.

"Then you follow the cork in your boat until the gar stops his running," Dr. Hancock recommends. "When the gar slows for a rest, quickly tie the line to an ordinary gar fishing rig — short deep sea rod and sturdy star drag reel — and play the gar in the con-

ventional manner until it is tired enough to bring alongside for the *coup de grace*."

Alligator gar never are brought into the boat alive. These fresh water carnivores have a jawful of razor sharp teeth capable of ripping a man's leg to shreds. Accidents have happened, although gar aren't known to attack intentionally. If a trophy is wanted for the den, a .38 Special slug through a gar's forehead will loosen him up enough to make him sociable.

In some cases, Alter doesn't use a bow reel at all. The line is carefully coiled in the bottom of the boat, making sure that it will not foul on any equipment as it unwinds.

A rugged arrow and special point is needed to penetrate the layer of tough garnoid scales that protect an alligator gar's body. These scales are so hard they will turn a pistol bullet fired at an angle. Indians used to make arrow points from them.

"I prefer to use a solid fiberglass fish arrow with a single barbed point," Alter says, "The long single point we use is homemade and has a nail for a barb. It will penetrate the thick scales and sink deep enough into the body to hold. Gig-type points are fine for

small gar, but the prongs are too short to penetrate inside a large gar's body and hold him while he thrashes around."

Alter, Hancock and other veteran bowfishermen

use heavy hunting bows, fifty-five pounds draw weight and over, to propel these necessarily heavy glass arrows. Since the hot sun in the Arkansas Grand Prairie region often causes laminated glass and wood bows to warp and "swap ends," inexpensive solid fiberglass bows are popular. Also, if you drop such a bow overboard during the melee, it doesn't put such a crimp in the family budget.

"Since the alligator gar hasn't been a commercial species of much value, at least, until recently, few scientific studies have been made of them," Alter says. "I believe his reputation as a destroyer of game fish is largely undeserved. One summer, I cut open and examined the stomachs of over one hundred alligator gar. I found portions of partly decomposed longnose gar, but no game fish.

"If there are any depredations on game fish that amount to anything, I lay the blame on the smaller scissorbills and immature alligator gar, not the adult 'gators."

Alter and Hancock have long waged a two-man war to have the alligator gar classed as a sporting fish, not a pest, and protected by law. So far, however, their efforts have been unsuccessful.

"It's the small gar," Alter contends, "that feed on the fry of game fish and cause most of the damage. The adult alligator gar feeds on the scissorbills. Without the alligator gar to act as a controlling factor on smaller gar, game fish will really have a rough time of it."

It was October during our trip and the 'gators had ventured upstream out of the Mississippi and Arkansas rivers into White River to "bed down" for the winter in their ancestral hibernation holes.

The gar were on a final feeding fling before hibernation. Their giant bodies surged upward out of the

O.K. Jones draws on gar during a night hunt in southern area of Arkansas. In some areas floodlights are allowed.

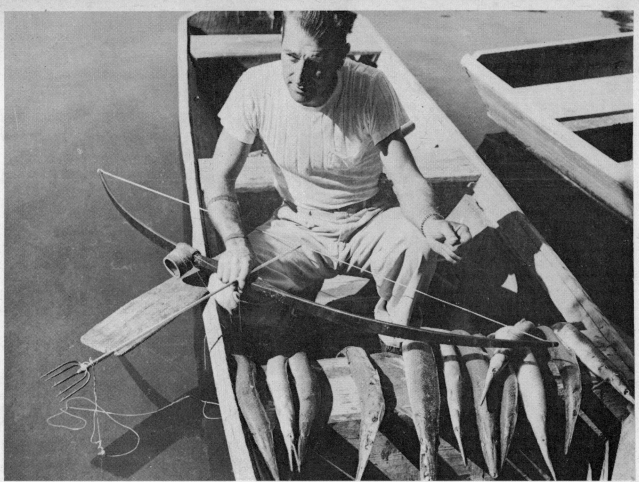

*Max Zeiner, former Arkansas instinctive field archery
champion, uses homemade reel, gig point to take gar fish.*

river at frequent intervals for as far as the eye could see. It's an impressive sight to see an alligator gar tailwalking across the blood red waters of the White, leaving a geyser of white water behind.

October is a fine time for watching gar, but it's no time for taking them with bow and arrow. Hitting one when it's rolling is largely a matter of luck, not skill.

A hot summer day is the best time to tangle with the 'gators. Gar have a functional lung and will "float" near the surface on muggy days and nights. But, alas, night shooting of gar is prohibited by law in Arkansas without special permission.

Anyone holding a valid Arkansas fishing license can take gar anywhere in the state during daylight hours. A non-resident annual fishing license is $5 and a fourteen-day trip license can be had for $2.50.

One of the special occasions where night gar shooting is permitted is the annual White River Gar Shoot, held at Jack's Bay in the White River National Wildlife Refuge of southeast Arkansas. This colorful outdoor event, sponsored by the Arkansas Bowhunters Association and hosted by the White River Bowmen's Club of DeWitt, attracts archers from throughout the South every July 25.

Archers compete for prizes given for most, biggest and smallest gar and between bouts tangle with heaping plates of deep-fried froglegs, catfish and hush puppies. Last year, archers consumed over two hundred pounds of catfish. Gar shooting works up quite an appetite.

Bowhunters are by nature an independent lot and the gar shoot attracts the cream of the South's crop of bowmen. The varied, and sometimes bizarre assortment of homemade bowfishing gear displayed by the contestants is a highlight of the shoot. Wicked looking gar fishing points, concocted by do-it-yourself craftsmen, are found in profusion.

Boats are converted into floating battlewagons and altered to suit the archer's fancy, such as lanterns and lights strung from poles for night shooting and soft drink bottle caps nailed upside down on the boat to provide a non-skid surface for the shooter.

All this is done in the hope of lancing the biggest gar ever taken with the bow. Some big ones are taken during the contest, but none even approaching one hundred pounds, or even fifty.

"The biggest gar I've ever seen that was actually taken with the bow, without first catching it on rod and reel, weighed 116 pounds," said Dr. Hancock, a frequent winner of the contest. "It was killed by Charlie Alter and me on one of our trips.

"You can shoot scissorbills until your arm trembles from weariness . . . Not so with large alligator gar," Hancock explained. "It takes patience, skill and perseverance to sing an arrow into a really big gar. I'm still trying.

"But if I ever do, I'll know I've done something and will have a trophy anyone can be proud to show off."

And that possibility is what lures Arkansas archers back to the bayou country. – *John Heuston*

Chapter 18

BAD CAT OF RELIZ CANYON

Cougar Now Are Considered An Endangered Species, But In This Pre-Ban Hunt, The Hunter Found Himself Outclassed Most Of The Way!

STEVE MATTHIS was only fifty feet ahead of me but it might as well have been fifty miles; the brush between us was as solid and impregnable as a cast iron wall.

When was this picnic going to end? With this thought I took a sound shot on Steve's general direction, steeled my legs, bowed my head and wrenched my firmly entangled **Kodiak** bow free for another assault that would gain me precious yards. A headlong craze-filled charge brought me crashing face down into the tiny clearing. From my prone and pleasantly relaxed position, I cast my gaze up the long straight frame of my guide. "Hiya, seen any mountain lions lately?" I asked, tone dripping sarcasm.

Steve squatted beside me on his haunches, blood trickled down his cheek from a cut issued by one of the billions of grabbing, slashing miserable branches we had crashed through. "Well, what do you think now?" he asked with a slightly amused glint in his grey eyes. "Man, I haven't had so much fun since I broke both my arms high jumping."

The most important item for a good lion hunt is a good guide and I had the best in the business. Steve Matthis is without a doubt one of the best lion hunters ever to put a dog on a track. His reputation in the West is one of unquestionable excellence. At forty-nine, Steve feels he is at the peak of his career, putting to use the lessons learned in a lifetime of following the killer cats throughout the Southwest and Mexico.

Our arrival in camp had been late of a Saturday morning and the drive up the long valley was highlighted by the sight of a bountiful and varied supply of game. Deer were everywhere, an indication to my uneducated lion savvy that this would be fine country for the big cats to earn a living. Near a creek bed we jumped a small band of wild boar. Dove and quail scattered in all directions and long-legged blacktail jackrabbits pulled down their ears and tried to become invisible with our passing. The camp consisted of a small trailer and tent at a green oasis consisting of a spring under a canopy of large live oak. This would be home for the next ten days. The dogs set up a clamor of welcome as we stepped out of the trucks. Steve had brought them in a day earlier and set up housekeeping in readiness for my arrival. He pointed out a pair of lion tracks made by a female and medium kitten within four hundred yards of home. Things looked like they were going to be right nice.

We made a short look-see hunt that morning, as the summer sun was warming the land and actual hunting was pretty much out of the question. Summer lion hunting is a rough operation due to the heat. Most lion hunters simply will not seriously attempt to hunt lions during the summer due to the hardships involved and the slim chance of the dogs sticking to a track. Most

Dougherty pauses during hunt to attempt to make friend of one of his guide's especially trained lion dogs.

lion hunters don't have Steve's dogs; most wish they did. Our actual hunting time would be a few hours each morning before the heat erased the good scent left by the cats. Steve advised me that this would entail early rising. In the course of this orientation ride for the dude, we located the tracks and scratches of several cats. This looked like lion heaven.

Lions leave their sign by scratching in loose dirt, pine needles, rotted logs or similar places. The amount of sign in one canyon indicated, as Steve put it, "There was a prospective love match in the making." Scratches of a female and a big tom were in evidence, as well as those of a medium-size romeo.

"That's the dude we want. He's a fine, big lion and he'll leave lots of scent," offered Steve. The males leave more scent than the ladies, which makes it a bit easier on the dogs. Whether we'd be lucky enough to tangle with him was yet undealt in the cards.

Other than the little scout, we did nothing constructive until dusk. Then we went for a drive and did a little draggin'. Lions were working the roads above camp and there were several crossings below, a large batch of limbs tied to the rear bumper eliminated all old game sign from the dusty road. In the morning a track would show clean and bright, easy for us to see. Now there was nothing to do but wait.

Three hours after full daylight found us in the ear-

lier described garden spot of the California brushlands. Steve's lead dog, Brave, had opened on a track shortly after we had begun a walk up one of the three canyons on which we were to concentrate our attention. The long bawl of this noble dog sent a charge down my spine that I never before had experienced. At heel, the other two selected for this first hunt whined and strained to be off. Brave's voice lined out up canyon and to the ridges, and with a word of encouragement, Buck and Goldie leaped from restraint as though propelled by an unseen catapult.

I had been warned of the famed Matthis endurance by those who had hunted with him. I'm in darn good shape due to constant hiking and hunting but this was unbelievable. I could do nothing but force from my mind every other thought than that of simply keeping up with this man. Unless you have seen the brush covered mountains that make up the coast range of California you cannot fully understand the scene.

Briefly they are virtually impregnable, unless you're Steve Matthis. He went through that stuff with a speed and a violent force that few men half his age (which is about what I am) could equal by half.

There are no trails, game trails or otherwise; only occasional little openings, a barely discernible line of travel offered in the pattern of growth.

For the hunt I had selected as my bow one of fifty-

One method of detecting whether a cougar is in the area is to wipe out tracks with brush drawn behind a truck. Then, the next day, check the road, seeking new signs.

four pounds with an eight arrow bow quiver attached. This was fully loaded with Easton 2018 Durals pointed with Little Shaver heads which I had altered into four-blade affairs. Generally speaking, this is an easy bow to handle, maneuverable and pleasant in the hand. Within an hour I wouldn't have given you a nickel for every other similar model made in this — or any other bow. Burdened with this stick that managed to tangle with every other living sitck, my progress was sorely hampered and the foulness of my thoughts startled the mind that gave them birth.

The cat had naturally gone over the highest ridge, and the dogs never did jump him, as they had begun on what turned out to be the long end of a long hard track and conditions eventually became too much for them. They made a lose in a pocket that was so thick that I experienced a mild case of claustrophobia. It was so thick we were lying on our bellies, our mode of travel for the last half mile. Steve looked at me with that same good natured air and indicated that at least we were getting the worst part of the hunt over first. I looked at him, at the dogs and up and around me at the nauseating brush. "I don't care what Smokey the Bear says. Burn it."

By sheer will power I made it back to the truck, a torn and shattered remnant of my former self. The flame of desire to add a lion to my list had ebbed and fluttered to the point where the pilot light barely burned. My nice new shirt had a vague resemblance to a hula skirt, a good portion of my lower anatomy was

being air conditioned by a new system of allowing maximum air circulation by free and easy passage through a highly complex arrangement of holes and my arrows —let's not try and describe my arrows.

ON THE THIRD MORNING, I somehow dragged my skinny frame out of the sack at Steve's bubbly, enthusiastic greeting of "breakfast is ready." An hour before daylight, we hit the road, driving slowly and looking for tracks in the headlights. We checked the crossings — nothing. Jackrabbits scampered in all directions, we saw several legal bucks but couldn't be bothered now. Made a long walk up two canyons, nothing doing. Bones loosened up, I kept up with the mountain man — a surprise to me. Back in camp early, as we couldn't get anything going, I missed a fox four times. Swell omen!

Steve's dogs are the results of long and studied in-breeding and are his own breed. Some of the original strain dates back to the pack of the legendary Ben Lilly, last of the mountain men.

The cats work in a pattern; like all wild life they have a system. Steve understands this system and has taken five hundred or so of the big cats in his career.

He also has attained a reputation as one of the finest jaguar hunters alive today. His lion hunters have one hundred percent success. It is interesting to learn about the big cats from one who is an authority, as there are so many so-called lion hunters and trappers often erroneously referred to as lion hunters.

Steve was a hunter for the California Fish & Game for thirteen years, and if he says we'll get one, he is serious.

Steve has noted over seventy percent of the lion kills he finds on deer are bucks. This makes an appreciable dent in the huntable deer population. During the hot summer months, the cats will make a couple of kills a week, and that adds up to a pile of venison.

FOURTH DAY: It is not so hard to get up, as the memories of the "death march" have faded sufficiently to give me heart. Breakfast is always ready when I arise. Steve is a good cook, offering nothing fancy but good, solid food of proper balance. Proper nourishment is essential for this type of endeavor, and too many hunters eat nothing but fried starches while hunting hard. This will take a lot out of you in short order.

I have come down with a first class case of poison oak, and am totally, thoroughly, completely covered except for my face. Steve calls it the Reliz Canyon Rot and there is nothing to do but accept it.

On a hunch, we head right to the canyon where Brave opened Monday and hike to the head. Nothing doing here. We then go to the Point, a finger ridge where lions cross when they are in the area. Here, we walk up the trail to find a scratch and right in the middle, the brightest track I ever saw.

For once Steve shows excitement, as he dashes to the truck and opens the hutch. Brave and Goldie bail out and run toward where I'm sitting looking at the track. On a dead run, Goldie about turns inside out as she hits the track. Recovering, she opens with a bawl and Brave joins in. They're off like a shot and this looks like the real thing.

Steve is cursing and stomping the ground. We are late, the sun is high and the dogs may not be able to do anything with it. Steve is mumbling about why he couldn't have been here at sun up. Up on the ridge the dogs suddenly become confused. They cannot move the track, although they are trying so hard to take it out of the pocket. They want that cat.

Steve decides to go up and help them out if he can, but it looks pretty grim. I stay below to give him a line on the dogs should they go out of his hearing. Up on the sidehill it is hotter than the hinges of Hades' front

Brave, the guide's lead dog, is descended from stock raised by Ben Lillie, termed last of the mountain men.

The dogs are off like a shot. They are on the long end of the track but Brave and Buck think it is pretty fine. Naturally, the dogs go over the mountain, so we have to follow. By now, I can keep Matthis in sight, as great an accomplishment as I can ever hope to achieve, the brush is still bad but it no longer appalls me. Duck your head and charge. We have four dogs on the trail, as Frisco and Goldie also have been turned out, but when we get to the top of the first mountain we cannot hear Frisco.

"If Frisco is out ahead, he'll be on the cat," says Steve, but it is hard to tell, since the dogs are a long way off and deep in the next canyon.

Of course we have to go to the top of another mountain. Onward and upward. I have developed a new mode of travel to reduce the complications of the bow hanging up. The string is in my pocket, I take the bow and throw it ahead, arrows and all, then I crash to it and repeat the operation. Fred Bear makes a tough bow, as it also serves as a walking stick, and in some cases, I club poison oak out of the way, although by now this is really a bit late.

We have been following for two hours, and finally are above the dogs which we can barely hear far below. To go down is a bad scene, as we can never come back out the same way and to go around is mucho miles. But it's all in a day's lion hunting.

We head down, taking it easy, trying to hear the dogs and learn the story. Faintly I can hear them, then I can't. Puzzling. We go down some more, not wanting to sacrifice all of our hard won height.

This is the type of mountain terrain favored by cougar and which must be traveled in search of the elusive cat.

door, and the dogs cannot do anything but bawl their discontent.

Steve finds where the cats were bedded, leaving much sign of their presence and the fact that they have been eating much fresh meat. There are two cats.

If we had only been there, but if is a very big word, and the world revolves around it.

The cats won't be far; somewhere along the long sidehill, probably right up in those rocks. Tonight I'm going to try and call one up with the varmint call. I know it will work as I've called up three in the past, all sad experiences that I hate to think about, but we will give it a try.

It is three hours after dark when we pick the spot to make our stand, the moon is full, bright enough to read by, which is not good for calling animals up close.

We call for half an hour and no lions. A couple of fox give us a pass and the owls go nuts, but no lion. For some reason, we both think tomorrow is going to be the day.

FIFTH DAY: I hit the **Ziradryl** bottle to relieve my itching, but my legs are swollen badly enough to make getting into the Levis a problem. When I walk the blisters break, proving poison oak is something anyone can do without. For five days I've been in the obnoxious stuff over my head and cannot understand why I still don't have any on my face. I've got a sexy beard by now, because my buddy, George Kili, grew one and killed two lions. I'll try anything. Maybe the beard keeps off the Rot. An interesting thought I'll have to pass on to medical science.

We hit the road about first light and drive down to where we made the stand with the call. Less than one hundred yards past the spot, lion tracks hit the road.

Deeper in the canyon, we cross a dog track on top of a big lion track. Steve is puzzled, one dog here, one lion here, different track than we started. Then we can hear the dogs clamoring. In the rocks of the canyon sound is tricky, but it is only one dog.

"Sounds like he is trying to tree," Steve says, but I can tell he is not sure and doesn't want to offer false hope.

The side hill opens up and it is easy going. We make good progress and suddenly there is Frisco under a bunch of oaks, walking around a tree. The dog looks pretty calm. I look again and Frisco barks.

"Don't look up. He thinks you see something," Steve mutters. So I don't look up, but I peek under my hat brim; still nothing.

"Well, you got one."

I look and there is a tawny blob amid the thick growth, and a head the size of a wash tub is suddenly thrust down through the branches. If looks could kill, I'm stone dead. Face to face with this beautiful lion, he is big, really big. The whole thing was so quiet and uneventful that it doesn't seem right. I somehow expected more commotion. The head is pulled back and I can hardly see him, it is a bad tree; very bad.

Steve urges him to talk to the cat and Frisco complies by barking vigorously. I'm trying to take pictures, but the cat is impossible to see from any angle, and he is nervous, uncomfortable on a small limb. The tree is on a steep side hill with perhaps a sixty percent grade, so the footing is rough. The only possible shot is straight on and not very good, so neither of us wants to take it.

As I walk around, I look at this animal as best I can, taking a few poor pictures. A truly superb animal, absolutely beautiful, it is a sight I'll never forget. I can't locate a good path for an arrow. Steve wants me to shoot, because old Tom is quite edgy. We discuss trying to kick him out and trying for another tree, but the cat is fresh and the day getting too warm. Bad odds. This would have to be it.

Finally I find a spot, not good, but I'll have to try, about a five-inch hole through to his ribs. I have to clear the brush to allow room for the bow and this is a bad deal, as the noise upsets the cat. I can find no footing and finally balance on one foot on a pointed rock. I start to draw and quit.

"I'm nervous," I tell Steve, my stomach suddenly doing a few flips.

"Sure you're nervous," Steve nods. Then I settle down. This is what all the hard miles were for. The

At times, the hunter found himself in brush such as this and had to proceed almost on belly, dragging bow.

Dougherty's glove, placed on ground beside paw print of mature lion, affords comparison to the size of the cat.

Kodiak draws smooth, the razor blade-loaded head is lined up and I sight through the hole towards the patch of tawny hair that covers the lion's rib cage and release. The arrow hits a twig, a tiny twig reaching upwards through that hole toward the sun. There is a clang and a crack as the arrow hits and then all billy hell breaks loose!

"Give him another one. He's coming out!" Steve takes a firm hold on Frisco as he hollers.

For a moment, I can't take my eyes off the cat, as with the utmost grace it swaps ends and heads out of the tree. The cat comes right toward Steve, and as I get on him, the guide is in my line of fire. I leap off the rock toward the cat, as he hits the ground and goes twenty-five feet in a bound. It is a running shot but I can swear it takes him right in the chest. Then he is going out of sight up the other canyon, covering ground in huge leaps.

Suddenly it is so still, until the silence is broken by Frisco's whining. Steve turns him loose and off he goes, hot on the track.

My arrow must have hit a bone, allowing no penetration. The second was a miss, passing just beneath the lion's chest. The first apparently was deflected by the twig enough to cause it to strike on an angle into the hip bone through which nothing would penetrate. We still have hopes, but inside I am sick. Never have I been so discouraged. Steve is encouraging and not in the least resentful. He knows and understands the breaks and I guess he knows the agony that I am going through.

The cat is gone — in the heat Frisco could not pick up the scent, though God knows he tried until his poor nose was raw. He looked at me like I was some sort of bug, I swear.

It was a long hard walk out, with the sun high and the temperature pushing 100 degrees. Late afternoon found us just making it to the truck. Although the terms of the hunt had been fulfilled as far as Steve's obligation is concerned, he insisted that we keep at it in the hopes that we will strike the big tom again. He says I deserve a lion but he is wrong there. I blew the party.

THE SIXTH AND SEVENTH DAYS are spent hunting for the big tom. Steve feels that if he is the slightest bit sick, we can cut his track at water. This is not too bad, as water is located in but a few spots. We check it all out and find nothing but trout. The streams are drying up but many deep holes remain. In these are many beautiful native rainbows of four to twelve-inch size. I am amazed at the fish population, as the streams would not be large when filled with water. With hand made rigs fashioned on the spot, we take a few of the beauties as a pleasant diversion.

On the seventh day we find the tom's track. He is traveling easy and we track him for a good distance by sight as the scent is so old the dogs are able to get nothing but an occasional whiff. In one respect I am happy, as the cat is not hurt and will be alright.

Maybe some other day we will tree him again. I hate the thought of someone else catching him. I feel as though he is my lion and that he deserves his freedom if I can't take him.

BY THE EIGHTH DAY we are branching out, hoping to run across another cat in the other locations, but the sign seems to have disappeared, as though all the cats have left the area at once. This they could have done, but in short order they or others will move into the range for a stay. This area is a natural lion funnel from the vast reaches of the coast range, during the course of a year many many lions use it. Steve feels that the lions are increasing in California, as there has

Dougherty relaxes for a few moments, while the hounds sniff the bobcat between his feet. It took a great deal more time for hunter, guide and dogs to corner cougar.

been no full-time hunting by State agencies for quite a few years.

The loss of the cat has done something to my normal high level of confidence. Confidence is essential, I feel, and if you don't have it you're beat before you start. I told Steve that maybe I had it coming, as the breaks had been falling my way for quite awhile. I had started to believe I couldn't miss. Now I knew I could.

NINTH DAY: Late in the morning, Goldie tries to start a day-old track. There is a good female in the canyon loop and things are looking up, again. She cannot do much with this scent but we know the cat will be on the mountain. With one day left, my spirits rise a bit, when Steve says we'll get her. Never in the course of ten hard and sometimes extremely bitter days has he lost faith in the hunt nor in me, which is encouraging. He has consistently tried to buck up my spirits after the fiasco of the fifth day. I am his first bow-hunter and responsible for his first loss of a cat, I would have expected him to put me out, but they threw away the mold when they made him.

TENTH DAY: We are at it bright and early, heading up the canyon where the female should cross. I have some confidence, as I have a reputation as a "come through in the clutch type" with my hunting buddies. On many a hunt I've scored in the last moments.

Suddenly the dogs open and almost instantly tree, but something is phony. During the long hunt they have ignored the many bobcat tracks, a sign of superb training, but this one was too much and they run into each other literally. I am in a killing mood and the bobcat is a suitable end to my homicidal instincts.

The first arrow knocks him spinning from the tree into the waiting dogs as confusion reigns. The cat dives out and up another tree. The next time he hits the ground he is stiff as a board and the dogs get in a few licks. It's not a lion but it is something to chew on.

The hunt is ended and we are about ready to wrap it up. We both feel badly to some extent but it has been a trip worth taking and an experience I shall take with me. Not all hunts can have successful endings, but one never hears too much about the ones that got away.

Back at Steve's home in Paso Robles, we shook hands goodbye. He agreed that we should do it again, that he will get me a lion. That is reward enough.

Maybe on that future hunt the lion will tree good, with no interfering little twigs. And maybe — if we are lucky — it may be the big tom of Reliz Canyon. It's a big **if**, but then **if** is a big word. *–Jim Dougherty*

Bonus of the hunt was this bobcat. It was treed by the hounds after they lost scent of the cougar, a rare error.

Chapter 19

THE TANGLE TRAP

Alaskan Caribou Follow A Herd Instinct And May Charge The Bowhunter's Blind!

To say that a caribou is less than magnificent would be an injustice. In the opinion of many — and I share that view — the caribou is one of the most beautiful animals that walks anywhere on this earth.

To a deer-oriented hunter making the scene in caribou country for the first time, even the sight of a scrawny bull with immature antlers is an impressive sight. Witnessing a mature, white-maned bull rolling across the tundra with those almost unreal antlers laid back along his withers is staggering by comparison.

Many a hunter, fortunate to hunt both caribou and elk, will argue long and hard around the cocktail lounge campfires as to which is the greater trophy. I do not feel that there is a real argument, as the two are as different as peas and corn, although generally in the same category. The elk has to lead the list in the trophy department, as he is more of an adversary than the jogging ghost of the muskeg flats.

But when beauty becomes the topic, I would be quick to change my affiliation. The caribou is no whizz kid in the smarts department. He relies upon fair eyes, long legs and the safety of numbers rather than a quick wit to survive. Were he to possess the canny traits of even a first year whitetail, hunting him would become a demanding problem.

This is not to say that anyone desirous of a caribou rack to adorn his den can simply stalk off across the tundra and subdue the bull of his choice with a strong right arm and stout cudgel. But if he exercises certain basic tactics, he should have no trouble getting within a hundred yards before bending too severely at the knees.

The only hair in this particular pot of soup is that most bowhunters like to get considerably closer than one hundred yards. If you shoot like I do, it is always best to reduce that figure by seventy-five percent, if possible.

Alaska is generous to non-residents who wish to chase caribou. For every twenty-five dollars — up to

three times — they will give you a caribou tag. I felt that a couple was good enough for openers. By the time I had a non-resident license, one moose tag and the caribou goodies, it was almost Tap City.

My destination was a small cabin on the Mishak River via Seattle, Anchorage and King Salmon on the Alaskan Peninsula. There were several reasons for selection of the peninsula as the place to make my first Alaskan hunt. Primarily, the area had been producing the bigger heads over the years: caribou and moose might be a little scarce, but they were reportedly bigger.

Another reason involved a guide to lead me on this quest. Ed King came to me highly recommended by a pair of bowhunters whose opinion I value quite highly. Dick and Rick Cooley had hunted with him two seasons earlier. They had collected some fine animals, but more important, they had found the kind of guy you trusted, respected and wanted to hunt with again. Rick Cooley, incidentally, was the first woman accepted into the Pope & Young Society.

Over coffee, King was filling me in on the situation, while we waited for my luggage in King Salmon. He had just returned from leading another hunter to a moose that taped sixty-nine inches. The lucky hunter had rifled the critter at what King considered good bow range: about forty yards. When you consider that the Alaska-Yukon moose stands well over six feet at the shoulder and is better than eight feet long, that's just my kind of target at forty yards. Big!

Besides being a first rate guide and one of the most experienced pilots in Alaska, Ed King is a good photographer with a movie camera. One of my major projects was to secure footage of this adventure and we hoped to get into a good photographic situation for both moose and caribou. Making movies of a hunt really compounds the problems, adding another chain of elements to worry about. King's prognosis was that caribou were going to be tougher than moose to come

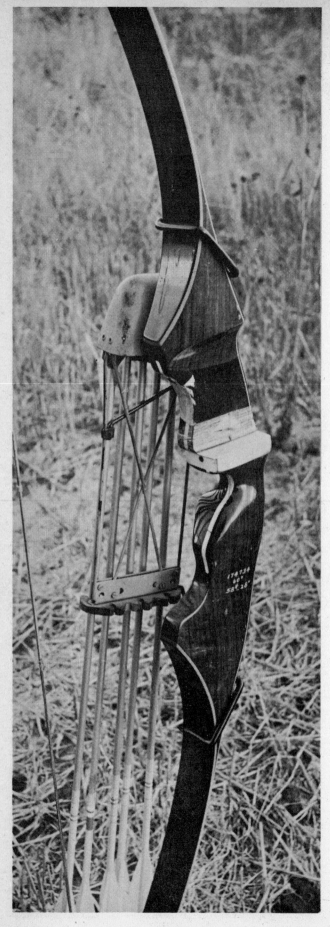

Bow used for the caribou was take-down Mercury Hunter by Ben Pearson. Sixty inches in length, it drew 58 pounds at 28 inches. Dougherty's 29-inch draw adds three pounds.

by, adding that sparse cover and too many caribou in most instances would be our major obstacle.

I saw my first caribou from fifty feet a few hours later, as we skimmed across the vast flatness of the peninsula enroute to our base camp on the river in King's *Super Cub*. It was a small herd of young bulls and cows that threw their heads back and stamped irritably with their feet as we buzzed them.

I had a fleeting glance of dilating nostrils as I looked the largest bull squarely in the eye, while we zoomed past. Then they were gone in the purple distance behind us.

It was enough to raise my spirits and by the time we reached the river we had seen quite a few caribou. The herds were visible in the distance working their way across the lush green landscape; ten here, twenty there, with the occasional single or cow and calf. It reminded me of antelope on the plains of Wyoming — always in view but not accessible.

The terrain of the peninsula is like a great billiard table surrounded by water with a range of mountains running down the center. Rivers come down from the Peninsula Range to the great complex that is Bristol Bay. Along the river beds there is a certain amount of cover, but once away from the rivers, the country becomes a broad prairie of deep grass that is ninety percent swamp. Walking through this is virtually impossible, and stalking is out of the question. Our strategy would be to hunt the river beds in hopes of catching caribou in the heavy cover or by lying in wait for a band that was heading for the river.

Ideally, we hoped to find small bands of bulls or old solitary monarchs, for they would be far easier to stalk than the great bands.

It was amazing how the caribou simply began to materialize on their great trek to the winter range. For the first few days we saw plenty of caribou, but the bands seldom numbered more than fifty. By latter days of the hunt, it was not uncommon to see a herd of caribou that stretched out for two and three miles. It was a virtual sea of moving animals, a wave of towering antlers following the trails that the caribou had used for thousands of years to walk the length of the peninsula.

It was also frustrating to see so many and be unable to get a good chance at them. It was no problem to get within a hundred yards, but cutting this distance in half began to be a real challenge. The long plodding line would shift to a new bearing and continue on,

leaving you far behind. I always had wondered about the stories that one could not catch up to walking caribou. There is no way that a man can keep up or catch up to a herd of these beautiful animals as they simply walk across the tundra. A caribou is a well designed critter made for negotiating his homeland with ease. Men just do not have the equipment.

Shooting at great distances is not the best way to employ archery equipment, yet I, like any hunter, will

There was plenty of water with which to contend during the Alaskan trek, as seen on surface of the bow. Arrow is XX75 aluminum; broadhead is Dougherty's design.

take a long shot if that is all that is offered, especially after several days of coming in second in the great caribou race. Eventually I tried a couple of long shots and learned it's a great way to lose arrows.

In the soggy bog that makes up most of the real estate, arrows simply disappear, although we had a pair of good bulls out in the vicinity of ninety yards. I was ready for anything, and I figured maybe I would get lucky. The first arrow was low, the second high, the third high but just barely.

The caribou had become alarmed and, heads high, antlers laid back and with knees churning, they vacated the area.

The search for arrows lasted quite some time, because I didn't believe that they could vanish so completely. It is almost like walking on a carpet laid over a pool of water; stand in one spot too long and, before you know it, there's water up to your knees. The arrows simply drove into the goop and were gone.

We finally got a break on a pair of bulls bedded down in some tag alders near the river. Our stalk was a thing of beauty, we even circled twice to keep the light perfect for the movie camera. It was the type of situation about which every bowhunter dreams. We had slight elevation, as they lay in the river bed, while we had the advantage of the bank. There was adequate cover, good light, perfect wind. Unfortunately, the hunter did not fully understand the mind of the caribou. It was my thought, as I crept those last remaining yards, that the caribou would leap to their feet and stare in utter disbelief, giving me ample time to shoot as they made themselves really photogenic.

Ed King could not see the caribou well as they lay, so it was necessary that they stand. They finally saw me when I was about twenty-five yards away. They apparently did not understand just what we had in mind. With churning legs and popping knuckles they exploded from their beds and took off. I shot, and the miss is recorded for all to see in living color. The arrow passed right between their majestic forms. I shall always recall that episode as a classic example of a dumb animal's triumph over the crafty human mind.

If opportunities were scarce for openers, the situation seemed to change with the blown chance on the two big bulls. By noon of that same day, we were up to our necks in caribou. We had managed to get ahead of a large herd, when suddenly we found ourselves right in their path leading through a tangle of shoulder high alders. This was a good situation on the surface, but our problem was to see just what kind of caribou were stomping past us. Caribou were passing me on all sides. They must have winded us but in the confusion of heavy cover, they apparently couldn't collect their thoughts any better than I. We were having problems trying to get lined up for a shot at a good bull, synchronizing our movements in order that King could cover the action with the camera. Sometimes this movie business is for the birds.

We were rapidly running out of caribou. For all of their supposed lack of brains, they were the ones making the most definite move, beating a hasty retreat for the security of the wide open spaces.

Through the brush I saw a bull coming. He looked big enough, so camera be damned, I was going to take a poke at the first close caribou with something on his head.

Stepping around the brush I drew on the bull that was walking through another thicket of alders. The arrow made the twenty-five yards in a blur, terminating with a resounding crack in the caribou, which promptly dropped as if the weight of the world had landed on his shoulders. He was a nice little bull, with

There appears little doubt that this trophy is down for keeps, but bowhunter advances, arrow ready, with caution.

beautifully proportioned antlers that were sub-minimum. In the shifting mess of stepping around the brush, I had shot the wrong bull or the bull was not as big as I had imagined. When you are used to seeing good mule deer, a small caribou looks plenty big, particularly in this moment of making a snap decision. But this was an ice breaker that served to ease the pressure somewhat. We could use the meat in camp, and the antlers were a darn nice trophy.

In the days following we had interesting experiences hunting both caribou and moose. We had looked at a pretty fair bunch of moose but so far had not found

Dougherty replaces in his bow quiver the arrow that was responsible for downing this trophy caribou. His expression offers indication of post-hunt weariness.

one we felt was good enough. As a change of pace, we would fish for salmon in the river right at the front door of the cabin. These slashing silvers averaged nine pounds each, and it was all but impossible to make more than three consecutive casts without a hookup. We took only three or four for food, releasing the others to continue their long journey to the headwaters.

Anyone making an Alaskan hunt should take his fishing tackle. I had slipped a four-piece spinning rod that is convertible to a fly rod amid my gear, along with a handful of assorted lures and flies. Light tackle is all you want in this fishing paradise.

In a way, caribou reminded me of Catalina Island goats, because of their habit of following an old herd leader and walking single file along the trails that they could nose out in the swamps.

We lay ahead of a good bunch at the edge of a finger of tag alders. As they drew closer, I could distinguish a variety of groans, grunts and coughs. Popping of the knuckle cartilage as they walked added an unreal note.

This looked like a good situation with caribou stretched out as far as we could see. Their course looked as though it would be right over the top of us. The only problem was that the biggest bulls were a long way back in the line of spindly antlers of cow caribou and frisky calves. All of these undesired ones were going to have to pass us before we could go to work on the big boys. The wind was straight from them to us, and on they came, popping, slurping, grunting and coughing. The caribou split the finger of cover where we hid and continued past us. We were literally surrounded by caribou and not a shootable bull!

Eventually we split the herd into three groups. Each major bunch would get by us some distance before the wind carried our scent to sensitive nostrils. The groups following still wanted to follow even though something had spooked the leaders ahead. On they came, group after group, then the big bulls for which we had been waiting.

The wind shifted but perhaps perserverance has its rewards. The band of bulls were within forty yards when the wind slowly began to shift. We had been waiting until they were as close as possible, but they spooked, leaving the scene as fast as possible.

As the bulls moved out in their rolling gait, we went to work. There was no time to tell which was which. All of them were more than adequate in my book and the last one in line was the closest. That made him the candidate. They were angling away, turning to the left to head in the direction the rest had gone. It seems that once they make up their mind to start the migration, nothing changes their course.

The arrow and the bull came together as the herd continued on, then the bull staggered. He slowed to a trot, took a step sideways and went to his knee. The herd stopped as the big bull went all the way down for good. It was as though they stopped to say goodbye or pay their respects. They waited for a moment and went on. It was a sight I shall never forget.

He was the caribou I had come for; one for the book with a rough score, over 370 points. He will long remind me of the vast tundra plains and knee deep swamps of the peninsula. As I look at him I can hear the wind and the cry of the emperor geese, see the salmon rolling in the riffles. — *Jim Dougherty*

Chapter 20

TAKE TO THE TREES

If It's Game You Want, The Possibilities Of Tree Blinds Are Outlined Here!

L. J. MacKool is called "Mac" for obvious reasons. I had reason to believe "Crazy Mac" would be more apt, and was voicing this observation, while reaching for the bottle of Scotch he slid across the table between us.

"Jim, I'm telling you. Your shot won't be more than thirty feet, and you won't shoot anything less than a ten-point the first day." Thirty feet is my distance, but I have a tendency toward sober skepticism, when someone is guaranteeing a bowhunting situation that good.

I had arrived in McAlester, Oklahoma, for my indoctrination in the art of bowhunting the wily whitetail deer From all that I've been told and read, people just don't go calmly about clobbering ten-points at thirty feet. Mac, however, knows his business. More whitetails have wound up on the short end of an encounter with him than you could count on all your fingers and toes. You would have to borrow several sets of nearby feet to get half a total.

"Well, I came here to be shown. Just how are we going to get me a whitetail at thirty feet? But before you tell me pass the soda."

"A tree, my friend. You are going to sit in a tree and the deer will walk right under your tree. Just don't shoot anything under ten points," he confided.

"I shot a big buck once, from a tree, back in my formative years. I got so shook afterwards I about fell out. Very dangerous business, this hunting out of trees."

"We have a rope so you can tie yourself up in. You are up about twelve feet, a high blind."

To be perfectly honest, at this point I wasn't the slightest bit concerned about shooting a whitetail. After all, they couldn't be that much tougher than mule deer. If this place was such a hot spot, I'd just go out and give them the old western stop-and-go tactics and tag a deer. Ignorance is bliss and the Scotch was pretty good.

Hunting whitetails, I was to learn quickly, is not at all like hunting mule deer. The only similarity, as far as I'm concerned, is that they both have four feet. They put bigger springs in the *virginianus* models, however.

The next morning, I greeted the day with a sore head. Mac took me in tow. Off we went to the Naval Ammuni-

tion Depot to meet Colonel Robert Jones of the USMC garrison based there. The NADS site is chocky jam full of whitetails and the surplus has to be harvested on an annual basis.

This is carried out under the direction of Game Manager Jim Hodge, who works for the state, and Fred Lowry, whom everyone calls Davy Crockett, if for no other reason than he is a hell on wheels hunter with a middle name of Crockett.

These fine gentlemen gave me the inside on the program and filled me in thoroughly on security regulations and precautions. The base is open to bowhunters for two week ends, and believe me, they flock in. I was to soon see why.

The day was spent putting up tree blinds. In between locations we ogled the deer, conspicuous by their abundance. I also spent some time slipping about in my best western tradition, trying to practice sneak the whitetails with a camera. No way!

Mac had several portable tree stands, some he had designed himself, and a couple of commercial models. We utilized one-by-twelves, and nailed several platforms in trees, that were built properly in good locations. My blind, which we set up last, was a commercial model with a little, teeny folding seat, and we did put it up twelve feet in the air. On a trial run, the twelve feet looked pretty foreboding. The platform was about the size of an index card. There was no room for extras, barely enough for my size tens. I got the impression it would be no problem at all to fall off.

Setting a tree blind is tricky business. The shooter has only a limited field of maneuverability for a shot. Knowing just where the target will be is crucial and care must also be taken to give the hunter as much cover as possible, without restricting his necessary motions and to avoid silhouetting him. We did all these clever things that day. I was pretty impressed, and after my trial stalks, I was beginning to see the logic.

I sat in my blind the evening before the season with my camera and a handful of acorns. By dark, fourteen deer had passed by. I saw four bucks, one that I estimated as an eight-point. I had vivid intentions of jabbing him on

opening morning. Never in my born days had I seen goosier animals.

The following morning, seated on my postage-stamp platform, I awaited full light to the rhythmic chattering of my teeth. It wasn't that cold. I was either excited or scared that I might fall off.

The promised rope with which I could secure myself was nowhere to be found. It may sound like the chicken-hearted way, but I have become a firm believer in a safety rope in a tree blind.

With full daylight, I suddenly was looking at a deer slipping silently straight to my position. A bald headed deer. Within the hour, an even dozen had come along, most of them passing on the appointed trail, just as we had planned. I was impressed. Not one deer ever was aware of my presence. They were all does and one little forked horn. The promised ten-pointers were elsewhere.

When I first saw the big buck of the evening before, he was on the bad side and I was sitting. There was no way to shoot and I dared not move, as a doe and fawn were feeding almost straight below. The buck took off in a stiff-legged trot after another doe.

About eight-thirty, a buck hopped out in the clearing in

Left: An adequate tree stand can be constructed from the materials at hand with little effort, yet it affords the archer plenty of freedom of movement, if planned well.

Fred Lowry carries a portable tree stand into the field so he can install it before beginning of his hunt. Most commercially made models are lightweight, easy to handle.

front and headed right to me. He was a six-point, pretty and alert. He stopped right under me and, raising his head, looked me right in the eye. We carefully studied one another, then he dropped his head to the ground to feed. It was a trick. He popped those two eyes right back up, as if he intended to catch me in an impardonable act.

Half torn between the desire to shoot and the desire to let him go, I was undecided. His big brother who hopped up, made up my mind for me. This one sported an honest eight and was twice the body size of the six-point. He trotted straight across the opening and came to a halt on the other side of my tree. He was twenty feet away and safe. There wasn't a thing I could do but wait.

I could hear him chewing up acorns behind me, and all the while the six-point was moving in his direction. Soon I was going to be reduced to a zero potential situation. I decided to shoot the six and the heck with MacKool's ten points. As I slowly raised the bow to bear on the little buck, I had to turn slightly in the direction of the big buck. Out of the corner of my eye I could see him studying the whole program. He kind of grinned and let go a snort that about knocked me out of the tree. So much for that. The six-point's first bound carried him off about eight hundred yards.

After I climbed down, MacKool greeted me with what I can only say was a nasty grin. He had collected one of the NAD's famed fallow deer, an old timer with a huge palmated rack. Besides everything else, there went five bucks down the tube. Conceivably I could still best Mac, but I wasn't making any more bets. None of this double or nothin' jazz.

The big buck had come by Mac's tree blind in heavy cover, passing an opening about twenty-five yards. The first shot took him in the hip, angling forward, and as the confused buck circled the blind in his dash, a second slipped through his ribs.

There are a lot of disadvantages to being in a tree. The advantages of height, wind and concealment are obvious, but the advantages are about equalled by the restrictions. Twenty minutes into my watch of the afternoon, I heard the unmistakable sound of something chewing up acorns. One eye wrapped around the tree trunk at my back clued me in on the culprit. This was another eight-point that had made no sound in his approach and was in a vulnerable position. His path was headed right up the slot along the little creek that was ten yards from my blind. As he came along the trail behind me, I could hear each step. The bow was ready, arm extended covering the spot on the trail.

Casually he turned to his right, still short of the tree and bounded across the creek. Unspooked, he sauntered away looking for does and gobbling acorns. He passed a small opening at forty yards and out of desperation, if not frustration, I turned the arrow loose at the hole filled by his golden hide. The shaft hummed through like it had eyes - - - after the hide had passed beyond.

The McAlester hunt did result in my first whitetail, a button buck that came late on the afternoon of the last day of the season. That happens to be the way my luck runs. Less than magnificent, he was nonetheless a whitetail and I felt some satisfaction in adding one of these creatures to my collection of sub-standard representatives of North American big game.

My education in hunting monkey-style wasn't to end there. A few weeks later, I was in Louisiana sitting in another tree. My blind on this hunt was a portable step ladder arrangement with another comfortable postage stamp at its peak. Butted snugly to a towering pecan tree, I had a commanding view of several deer trails and a field dotted with new green rye tops. It was here that I found the best use for a safety rope.

It was impossible to shoot sitting down from this blind as a full draw could not be made against the steep downward angle. I was to find out another complication of tree blinds. It was an hour earlier than the deer were supposed to be moving, so I was sitting on the platform, bow across my lap, sucking on a jaw breaker the size of a new Dunlop golf ball.

A big doe stepped out twenty yards away and began to feed daintily on the new sprouts. We were allowed a handful of deer apiece in Louisiana. Carefully, I brought the bow up, after first depositing my jaw breaker. A jaw breaker filling your entire mouth is hard on your concentration. My left arm stretched back drawing the string — for about fourteen inches — before my elbow ran into the tree trunk.

I kept jamming my elbow into the tree, hoping for a spot that would allow me to finish the draw. Naturally, my commotion aroused the deer's attention. She was now standing half cocked, watching me bang my elbow repeatedly into the pecan. Something had to give, so Molly made up her mind and became absent.

From then on I stood. I drove a nail into the tree and hung my bow, with the arrow nocks pinched tight on the string and an arrow within easy reach.

The rope was looped over one shoulder and around the tree. I allowed enough slack so I could lean way out over the edge at a relatively steep angle. This made shots straight below easy to cover, once you convinced yourself the rope would hold. When another big doe walked under that

Hunters check in a deer taken from a tree stand during open season on naval installation in the Oklahoma hills.

Louisiana pecan, I was leaning almost flat out over her back when I turned the arrow loose.

The angle of a shot from a tree blind makes heavy tackle necessary, in my opinion. If the shot will be taken at a relatively flat angle, then medium weights would suffice. Other times you happen to be in a spot where you need a lot of stuff on the arrow to drive it clear through from the top. With a high wound and no low exit, trailing can be difficult at times.

Most tree blinds are restrictive. Mac has the right idea with his homemade stands. His platform is larger than most, padded with rubber and vinyl-coated for additional warmth. They are extremely quiet. With his portable ladder arrangement the blind goes up in minutes, is secured with chains and solid enough for two big men.

MacKool puts up his portable blind. Note clamp-on ladder that makes mounting tree, future access a simple matter.

Accommodations may be limited, but they offer a degree of comfort as Jim Dougherty illustrates, awaiting game.

Picking the proper tree is the secret. A tree with a big crotch up over eight feet is excellent.

The best thing about a tree blind is the elevated vantage point. You really can see what's going on and chances at a greater variety of game are easier to come by. Sitting in a blind never has been my strong suit, but in a tree it seems as though more is going on. I think it's easier to stay in a tree blind after you get in, if for no other reason than the problem of getting up and down.

Where it is legal, more hunters are taking to the trees for the big, wide-racked bucks than in the past. It's not as simple as it may sound. In areas where deer have been hunted from trees for several seasons, a lot of deer, particularly wise old does, walk along and spend a lot of time looking up.

I talked to one fellow, who had missed a big doe from a tree on two successive days. On the third day, he watched her come along, slowly checking out each tree, until she saw him. She made a wide circle, snorting and blowing all the way. The next day, she did the same thing; spotting him, circling, and telling all the world about it, until finally she walked under him and he drilled her. The sneaky guy had put a dummy in his old blind and relocated on the deer's new trail.

Camouflage is a must in a tree, especially on the face and hands. It is easy to match up to the foliage and shadows of a tree to hide the body.

It may not seem ethical to lie in wait of game, hidden from eyes that seldom look up. I have talked to some who consider it less than sporting. Perhaps they have a point. However, things are never that good or simple when you are hunting with bow and arrow. I have to go along with the tree hunters. It is a good way to go about the fine art of bowhunting, for whitetails in particular. If it was all that easy, then what ever happened to that Oklahoma ten-point at thirty feet?

Chapter 21

OF BEARS AND BLONDES

This Honey-Colored Bruin Was An Oddity That Sent The Bowhunter To Plotting Strategy For A Rug

Once you have hunted with hounds, it gets in your blood. If the hounds belong to Orville Fletcher, this is particularly true, since he has some of the best and you know your chances are good.

I watched them now as we worked out way up the juniper-covered ridges. In a way they reminded me of good bird dogs, ranging out, nosing likely looking spots, then returning to check with Fletcher. It had been almost a year since I last rode the beautiful mountains of southwestern New Mexico and I was glad to be back. The interlude had eased the memory of the aching muscles and creaking bones. Time in the saddle probably would refresh the memory, but for now all was comfortably pleasant.

Our little group had begun riding as the sun lightened the sky over the Continental Divide. It was one of those clear, sharp mornings, the kind with a tang you actually can taste. It was almost a reunion, and once you have made a trip with Fletcher, it's a hard thing to put out of your mind. You keep longing to go back.

Jack McDowell of the New Mexico Game and Fish Department had made it possible. I met Jack on a deer hunt in northern New Mexico. He took it upon himself to be my guide on the famed Jicarilla Apache Reservation and his second act had been arranging my trip with Orville Fletcher in quest of a mountain lion which we eventually collected about twenty miles out of Reserve, New Mexico.

Now this magnificent three was working up the side of a big New Mexico mountain, looking for fresh bear sign. In the distance, the sky was beginning to fill with ominous clouds, as the wind steadily increased, whispering through the trees, bending the long stalks of knee-high grass.

In the discussions the night before, I had learned that the bears were "poor," as Fletcher put it. Lack of fattening feed had them unusually lean for this time of

Jim Dougherty used the 003 broadhead, which he designed and which now is being produced, marketed commercially.

year. The bears were taking the majority of their diet from juniper berries and cactus apples in the lower country. A lean bear is built for speed to lead dogs on merry little romps all about the country before treeing or coming to bay. This is hard on the dogs, as a bear in this condition may be more inclined to fight than one packing a full winter's supply of fat.

Halfway up the mountain the dogs opened in a frenzy of bawling squeals and yelps. One minute you are riding along, enjoying the scenery and easing your rear with various relocation maneuvers about the saddle, then you find yourself in a wild melee of activity. The suddenness of this transition always has been shocking to me. The joys of riding the horsies were waning suddenly.

When everyone takes off on one of these little rides, problems develop. First is staying together. The country in which we rode was covered with thick cedar and juniper. Each horse would pick his path, and the rider soon was separated a bit from the man in front. One turn around a cedar and the man in front is out of sight. When this happens, you head for the dogs as best you can. Each time it happens I experience the same troubled thoughts. Jack was making a film for his TV show, *New Mexico Outdoors*. He also had my arrows. I had some of the movie film in my saddlebags but keeping up with Fletcher was the really important item; he had the lunch.

It is no real problem to regroup. There are always tracks to follow and you learn to head in the right direction either by the lay of the land or the distant baying of the hounds.

The race covered ground rapidly. Once the dogs got lined out and off, they could cover the miles in a hurry. By shortcutting and utilizing main ridges to stay within hearing, the horsemen pretty well keep up. Generally, the country was thicker than that in which

we had hunted lions but it also was easier to ride in, as it wasn't so broken up.

Three hours later, those distant clouds were descending upon us and already had washed the scent away for the dogs. Had it been a hotter track they could have stayed with it, but Fletcher reckoned that it was better than a day and a night old and prior thundershowers pretty well had obliterated it.

We sat munching our sandwiches under a sheltering ponderosa, watching a huge cloud bearing straight

Arrowheads were not inserted with screw-in ferrules until actual hunt began, saving sharpness for hunt.

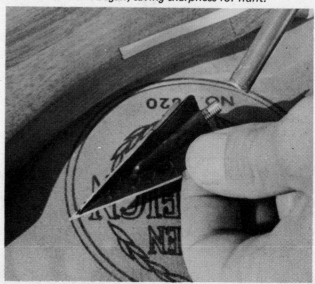

at us from across the valley. My poncho was in my suitcase about fifty miles away. It hit us like a breaker in the surf off Hawaii. One moment we were discussing the rain-laden cloud, the next it swamped us all in an airborne tidal wave. As a futile gesture of defiance, I zipped my levi jacket up half way. I have no less than six good waterproof jackets. There are three two-piece rain suits in my closets, two pair of suitable wet weather footgear, a half dozen weather resistant hats, warm clothes of all styles. But there I stood on the wind-swept face of a New Mexico mountain in one pair of leather boots, one pair of levis, one shirt and one levi jacket.

If nothing else, this day we did prove out a new bunch of equipment for horseback hound hunters. After my last trip with Fletcher, I had come away with

The Pearson Mustang model was used in developing the take-down prototype, but the production style differed. Note method used for connecting sections.

Using a short case with the take-down bow in its divided parts, it was found simple to lash to saddle to carry.

the knowledge that the ordinary hunting bow is a real pain to transport on a horse. I speak of the hell-for-leather dashes through some of the roughest country in the Southwest; country that rips and tears at man and beast alike; rides that require your sole concentration to stay aboard with no time to worry about equipment.

I took my bow problem to the Research & Development Division of Ben Pearson, Incorporated, where Dick Karbo already had been doing some experimenting on a new type of take-apart bow. When Karbo presented me with a left-handed bow incorporating this new design, I knew I had the answer to my horseback problem.

The next concern was the arrows, which had to be carried in some sort of quiver that would totally protect them from the brush, weather and general abuse.

The solution here was the installation of threaded broadhead adapters by Hughes-Smith Company. These are a standard broadhead insert manufactured for aluminum or glass arrows. The five-degree taper unscrews while the ferrule remains in the shaft. It was ideal. After mounting all the heads I unscrewed them, installed razor blades and taped each head to protect the blades and myself. These were carried in a small pouch on my belt; an erector set for bowhunters. The equipment rode beautifully on the horse, as the bow broken down was no longer than the arrows. Each quiver or case was tied by saddle thongs and off we went. The durable, waterproof cases withstood all that New Mexico could throw at them.

By the end of that first day we may have been a bit worse for the wear physically but our spirits were high. A gentle rain continued to beat steadily through dinner but the report was for clear skies in the morning. Still, I threw my poncho atop my gear as we settled down for the night.

The day began with a thirty-mile drive back to the camp where we had left the horses and gear. Those last six miles down into Devil's Park were treacherous with axle-deep mud, and I believe we slid most of the way.

Dougherty found the angle at which he had to aim for his blonde bear somewhat uncomfortable, still effective.

giving Fletcher and his dogs fits. This bruin was extremely large and not afraid of the dogs, a combination that had spelled disaster for several of Orville's best hounds. Only a week before, a fine dog had died in an encounter with this bear.

The color of the black bear can vary greatly and not all are black. Many black bear rugs run from auburn to cinnamon and in some cases lighter. It was my hope that, should we eventually tree a bear, it would be one of these lighter colored examples.

Surprisingly enough, when I had tightened my cinch, attached my take-down Pearson bow and made sure my poncho was tied behind the saddle, I did not

Our hunt would be in the general area of the previous day's ride. Orville figured that this was a good piece of bear country, as the juniper berry crop was excellent.

I imagine that more bears are taken over baits and by accident than with the use of good dogs. In the Southwest, however, this is one of the best ways to add a bear to your collection and one of the most exciting. In a year such as this, the bears come down to lower elevations to forage. Black bears are great thieves and, at night especially, will lumber into a camp or cabin site in quest of something to put in their constantly growling stomachs. Such situations get a lot of bears reduced to rugs and can prove a contributing factor to the few bona fide cases of bears molesting humans.

The sizes of black bears vary but the average mature bruin will weigh around two hundred pounds. Some are on record that tipped the scale at close to five hundred and one hears stories of the six hundred-pound bears. In my opinion, however, bear weights are exaggerated much in the same manner as the weights of wild boar. New Mexico produces her share of whopper bears and there was one in our area that had been

Jack McDowell (right) admires the blonde trophy. This is considered a most unusual specimen among veteran hunters.

experience that familiar reluctance to swing into the saddle. It was a half hour after daylight when we lined out into the junipers across a yellow meadow and up to the ridges above. The long ride took us over one small mountain and into Devil's Creek along a cattle trail in country that just had to have bears. We rode for three hours, peaking out at last at the head of the creek. The only action had been a brief opening on an old track and the dogs quit almost as fast as they had begun. By the time we peaked out it was raining again.

Fletcher had just made mention of lunch, when the dogs opened with an insistent note that spelled a hot track.

At the spot where the dogs had struck we could not locate a track, but four hundred yards further down the mountain, we found it. Orville split the air with an oath as he swung off the horse, there in the trail was a track made by the bear's forepaw fully eight inches long and going in the opposite direction as the dogs.

"It's that big bear and the dogs are heading the wrong way!" He remounted, ordered us to wait, then took off in the hopes of turning the dogs, an almost impossible task. This, incidentally, is a common enough problem in hunting hounds. When a track is struck it is impossible for the dogs to tell which way is the front, getting them straight is one of Orville's primary concerns.

As we waited, we marveled over the track. McDowell never had seen a bigger one. Great credit has to be given Fletcher's ability to handle his dogs. In short order, he was back with all of them save two pups. The race was on for sure.

That was the last time we saw Fletcher for two

hours, so the search began for bear, dogs and guide. Naturally we went up the wrong mountain, forsaking the intelligent method of tracking in our haste to close the gap. We finally picked him up on a ridge, where without a word, he led us over the side on foot, leading the way down the vertical face of the canyon.

Halfway down, we could hear the cries of the dogs from beyond a turn in the canyon bottom. Orville turned as we neared the bottom with instructions to keep quiet.

A hundred yards from the tree and still out of sight, we tied up the horses and began to assemble the gear. Jack unscrewed the points and slipped off the tape covering, while I fitted the two parts of the bow together and locked them into place.

The only sound as we slipped up to the tree was the baying of the dogs, but no indication as to whether the bear was bayed on the ground and fighting. Orville's first concern is his dogs. Were the bear bayed and I began punching it with arrows, things could get messy and Orville would drag out the .44 he carried on his hip. I didn't want any large round holes in my bear, but I wanted cut-up dogs even less.

The huge ponderosa was growing in the base of the canyon. I peered into the tree, a patch of tawny blonde fur visible through a hole in the branches.

We caught a lion, was my first thought. But sitting astride a limb in a ball was a beautiful blonde bear.

Fletcher picked up a rock and chucked it at the bear, the bear moved cat quick to another part of the tree. Twice the bear started out of the tree but the waiting nine dogs changed her mind. We could see now that it wasn't a huge bear, not the bear that we had imagined it to be. Apparently the dogs had hit the big bear and run into two splitting off on the smaller blonde, I was happy as hell because I couldn't have had a written order for color filled any more perfectly. All I had to do was shoot it and by the time we decided to collect it the bear had left the branches down low and was now way to heck and gone up in the tree bouncing around and making funny *woofing* noises everytime someone came close or connected with a rock.

Finally Fletcher yelled, "Shoot it and let's get out of here."

I looked at Jack, he nodded. I yelled back to Orville, "It's pretty high, let's try and get it lower."

"Blast it!" was Fletcher's only comment.

The bear, covered with foliage, was on the end of a limb, looking down. Then it began to turn.

"When it gets to the base of the branch," I said and nocked the Easton 2020 with the razor-sharp 003. The bear walked the length of the branch and reached her right leg for the trunk, it was about twenty-five yards from my spot on the sidehill.

I never in all my experience saw anything like what happened next. The arrow caught the bear, angling up right behind the leg. The bear reached with her left leg, jumped and died all in one motion. It came crashing down through the branches like a runaway locomotive. It landed on its head in the middle of the dogs.

She was not big but one of the most beautiful bears and in prime condition. Orville said he never had seen but one other that color. A post mortem revealed that the arrow had centered the heart and passed completely through the off side, taking out two ribs. I don't think she will measure up to the Pope & Young minimum, but the hide, with its six-inch fur, will be reward enough.

Chapter 22

BOWHUNTING AFRICA'S BIG GAME

This Famed Hunter Turned In His Rifle For Archery Tackle To Seek Some Of The Dark Continent's Most Dangerous Trophies

AFRICAN SAFARI! These words spell magic. They suggest stalking wild game in unfamiliar surroundings, waiting for just the right moment to release a feathered broadhead and bring down a magnificent trophy — the dream of all bowhunters.

The fun began soon after I landed in Nairobi, the capital city of Kenya, in East Africa. Going through customs at the airport, all of my equipment had to be unpacked and inspected. The native porters at the airport were of the Wakamba tribe, great bowmen themselves and as soon as they spotted my equipment they began jabbering excitedly and examined the bows and arrows with delighted grins. One persistent native — after interpretation by my white hunter, wanted to trade a leopard skin for one of my bows.

I was pleasantly surprised to find that my white hunter was an archery enthusiast, himself. His farm in the Kenya highlands is located on the edge of the great mau forest and he keeps several families of Wanderobos on his property. They are without peers when it comes to tracking and bow hunting. From the time they are able to crawl, a tiny bow and arrow is put in their hands. Their very life is spent hunting in the forest.

My first trip into the forest with them was a revelation. My white hunter and I and two of the Wanderobo warriors with the unlikely names of Meesta and Wambua set out about 4 p.m. one evening armed with bows and arrows. I had examined the Wanderobo equipment with great interest and although quite crude in comparison to my own, it was quite effective as I was soon to find out. Their bows were about 5½ feet in length, completely round and tapered to a point at each end. They were pre-set by being strung all the time, but averaged about forty pounds pull. Their arrows were carried in a skin quiver about two inches in diameter which was slung at the waist and was capped with another piece of skin. The arrows were of all different lengths, diameters and weights with no two being the same.

The feathers were about 4 inches long and about a quarter-inch in height and extended all the way back to the nock. They were bound to the shaft with hair from a giraffe's tail. The tips were soft barbed iron or hardwood fitted into a hollow socket at the tip

Among the first African game animals taken by Gates was impala ram that didn't see arrow coming, he says. Secuma tribesmen (facing page) use crude bows, poisoned arrowheads, as they cannot always depend on making a killing shot.

of the shaft. When shot into an animal the point would remain embedded while the shaft dropped away.

I wondered about the accuracy they achieved with this crude equipment, but after watching them operate I noticed two things which indicated that neither accuracy, trajectory nor penetration were of any importance. First, their arrows were tipped with poison, fatal within minutes to man or beast. Secondly, they are such clever stalkers that their arrows are fired from distances averaging fifteen to thirty feet.

The poison they used was black and sticky like tar and was carried in a little pouch around their necks. Certain members of the tribe make the poison from a formula handed down from generation to generation and the hunters either buy or trade for it. I watched Meesta test the potency of his poison by putting a little daub on the palm of his hand and then, holding his hand in an upright position he made a little cut with a knife on his index finger. As the blood trickled down on the poison I could see the black stain creeping up the blood. Just before it reached the cut in his finger he wiped it off and grinned. The purpose of this maneuver I learned was to find out how fresh or active the poison was. The speed with which it melts and mixes with the blood tells the story. After the poison is exposed to the air for some time it becomes rather firm and will not melt and act as rapidly as when fresh. As we walked along they would breathe on the poison every few minutes to keep it soft and moist. When introduced into the bloodstream it affects the heart, and even though the arrow makes only a scratch on an animal the exertion of running causes the blood to circulate faster and as soon as the poison reaches the heart, down he goes!

They offered some of their poison for my broadheads and were disappointed when I declined.

In addition to their poison arrows, they are master stalkers and trackers. They can look at a single track and not only identify the animal that made it but tell how long since it passed and whether it was a male or female.

We eased along through the forest with the two Wanderobos about fifty feet ahead of us. After about a half mile of silent stalking, Wambua suddenly froze with one foot in the air like a bird dog. A split second later a bushbuck burst out of a clump of undergrowth in front of him with a shrill bark. As quick as a flash Wambua, who had been carrying his bow at half draw, and while still on one foot snapped an arrow that caught the bushbuck in the neck. It was a pure instinctive reflex action, but a marvelous shot just the same. A hundred yards further on we found him. The poison had acted almost instantaneously.

On the way back we spotted some colobus monkeys high in the trees. This time my superior equipment held an advantage for their arrows were not accurate at that distance — about 75 to 80 feet. We all started shooting and I missed twice then brought one down with the third arrow and another with the fifth. Wambua and Meesta missed several shots each. Later when we hunted the plains country of Kenya and

In hunting African game, Gates was accompanied by the professional hunter and guides, who were equipped with big bore rifles to back him up in case of any dangers. This is a requirement for professional African guides.

The cartridges in the belt loops were for bigger game than Elgin Gates planned to take in what amounted to this introduction to the problems, rigors of bowhunting.

Tanganyika I had ample opportunities to use the bow and great sport it was, too. My equipment consisted of two Bear bows of 40 and 75 pounds pull and the arrows were fiberglass and aluminum tipped broadheads.

After leaving Nairobi, we drove three days down into northern Tanganyika and finally arrived at our first hunting camp late one afternoon, which was located near a small stream. While camp was being set up the cook's helper went down to get some water and I went along with my bow. My white hunter had mentioned that we needed some fresh camp meat and told me to shoot a reedbuck if I could, as the high grass along the stream was full of them.

As we reached the stream bank which was about a hundred yards from camp I saw the head of a reedbuck sticking up out of the high grass on the opposite side. It was an easy shot at about twenty-five yards but with only his head visible it was impossible to tell whether his body was turned to the left or right. I guessed right and dropped him.

A few days later, I had an interesting encounter with an impala ram at the same place. He was standing in a little open spot right on the bank of the stream as we came up. The distance this time was about forty yards. When I drew back and released the arrow he jumped stiff-legged about ten feet and froze, still watching us. The arrow passed through the space he had occupied a split second before. He had actually seen the arrow coming and leaped out of its way. I shot twice more with identical results. It was an amazing yet frustrating experience. After the third

shot, I decided he had earned the chance to go on living and didn't shoot again. With his attention concentrated on me, I doubt If I would have ever hit him anyway.

Later that afternoon, I stalked another impala and got him with a fifty-yard shot when his attention was concentrated on two other rams that were coming towards him. I soon discovered also that the performance of the first impala wasn't unique. Most of the antelopes could — and did — dodge arrows in flight, usually with the same stiff-legged bounce. In a country inhabited by lions, leopards and other predators who were masters at the art of stalking, most of the antelopes had developed hair-trigger reflexes.

Warthogs were an exception to this rule and provided a lot of sport with the bow. One belligerent boar used to come to a water hole near our second camp every day and would raise a big fuss snorting, grunting and charging any of the smaller animals that came along until he had finished drinking and grubbing in the mud.

Several stalks failed until I caught him pushing another boar around one day and pinned him down with a heavy fiberglass broadhead from the seventy-five pound bow. He struggled a little and the other boar, not realizing what had happened but knowing an advantage when he saw it, pressed the attack. He slashed his dying enemy unmercifully then stepped back and grunted a challenge. When it wasn't answered, he gave him a final slash and stalked away the victor.

Warthogs are like ice cream to leopards, so we

Among the native archers of Africa, varying shooting techniques are in evidence; note holds on equipment.

hung this old boy in a tree for bait. Three days later when he was getting ripe and tasty, I shot a big leopard out of the tree just as he was reaching for his second mouthful.

Another source of sport was the flocks of guinea fowl and francolin we encountered everywhere. I had brought along two dozen flu-flu arrows and managed to keep the table supplied with these birds.

There was one animal in Africa that I hated with a great passion, the hyena. The natives call him *fisi*, a fitting name for this ugly animal. In recent years the hyena and other scavengers have been put on the protected list, but on this safari they still were classed as vermin. I could not stand the sight of these slope-backed, shuffling, horrid, stinking, carrion-eating creatures and I never missed an opportunity to do one in.

Fisi will follow a calving antelope, and when the mother lies weakened by birth pangs, will snatch the baby and make away with it. He will follow the great herds, waiting for a sick or lame animal to drop out, then he will pull it down, tearing out and eating chunks of flesh from the still living animal. He has carried babies out of native huts and eaten them. He eats the old and mortally ill natives that are put out in the bush to die. He will eat other scavengers when

he can. In short, he eats anything. He is a cannibal that devours his own mother, brother or sister when they weaken. To the natives he represents all that is evil, dirty and rotten in the world. He is the symbol of death, this destroyer. Sooner or later, everything in Africa ends up in his belly from the mighty elephant down to the lowliest reptile.

Now the average African native simply cannot understand a white man's joke, and while they will not shoot or even touch a dead hyena for superstitious reasons, just let something happen to a hyena and they will scream with laughter and roll on the ground in ecstatic delight. I shot hyenas with the rifle, but enjoyed it more with the bow. A razor sharp broadhead was better medicine for these slimy, arrogant, cowardly beasts.

They would gather around the camp at night attracted by the smell of the skins and horns we had drying in the trees. Early in the safari, they made away with a choice set of kudu horns one night that the boys had forgotten to put up in the trees. We never did find them. The war was on then with a vengeance!

The next night they were back as usual and more arrogant than ever. They thought they had found easy pickings, but I waited patiently until a big dog *fisi* sidled up about thirty feet from the camp fire and sat down licking his chops then I shot him with a broadhead. He snarled and snapped at the arrow and rolled on the ground in a frenzy. In a few seconds the rest of the pack was on him slashing and tearing. Within a few minutes they had devoured him, hair, hide, guts and all. The boys went hysterical with laughter over the whole affair.

A rifle shot would scare them away for about an hour, but with the bow they never quite realized what was happening and as soon as they had disposed of their luckless brother, they would be back for more and I did not fail them. It meant the loss of an arrow for each *fisi* as they would chew it to bits in the scramble, but the price was cheap.

One day, coming back to camp, we caught a *fisi* on the open plain. I got out on the hood of the Land Rover as we followed him and placed an arrow square in his behind. He rolled over snapping at the arrow then ran about fifty feet and repeated the process. We followed him for two miles trying to get in another shot to put him out of his misery. The two gun-bearers and trackers with us simply cracked up with laughter over this performance. For four hours after we returned to camp they kept the boys in an uproar by acting out the whole thing in pantomime over and over again.

This African vulture, another of the less appreciated species, was taken with a single arrow from hunting bow.

Anything *fisi* did while in pain was a colossal, side-splitting funny to them. When an arrow bit into his vitals and he screamed in pain, they would scream with laughter. When he snapped madly at the arrow they would slap each other on the back. When he rolled on the ground in mortal agony, they would roll on the ground in a delirium of delight. When the rest of the slavering pack mobbed him and slashed him to ribbons they would be reduced to incoherent, eye-streaming ecstasy.

It was the Saturday night carnival, the three-ring circus come to town, the Bob Hope, Milton Berle, Jerry Lewis and Jackie Gleason shows and every other funny thing in the world all rolled into one. They danced and snickered in anticipation when *fisi* came to the bait. They giggled, hee-hee'd and yowled when *fisi* was eaten by *fisi*. Afterwards, they chuckled and chortled with glee and when one would pantomime *fisi* in his death throes they would go through it all again until finally they would all be stretched out on the ground exhausted, helpless, quivering, sniggering, blubbering wrecks.

Personally, I thought it was more nauseating than funny, but however and wherever the source of African mirth and comedy was dammed up. the flood was released and all inhibitions with it the minute they saw anything bad happen to *fisi*.

The second night I used the seventy-five pound bow instead of the forty. Quite by accident, the first arrow I released cut through the vitals of one hyena and went on to impale another one behind him. Thereafter the seventy-five pound bow became the object of the boys' affection. They fell in love with it on the spot. Where previously they had called it *"Uta M' kubwa,"* the big bow, they named it *"Uta m'kubwa mungu kufa fisi mbile ya m'shale moja."* The great king bow, killer of two hyenas with one arrow. It became a magic, supernatural weapon, a *fisi* fetish. They would rub it with respect, roll their eyes in reverence and croon incantations over it. Seldom, if ever, has a bow received so much attention or adulation. Wangi, our number one tracker, appointed himself personal guardian and cared for it like a baby.

In the days that followed it became a ritual. We would finish supper at dusk just as the hyenas began to appear, and the boys would build up the camp fires so there would be light enough to see. Their own fire was about thirty feet away from ours and they would put some of the horns and skins in the ground between the fires as bait. The hyenas would edge slowly closer and closer, licking their chops all the while. When Wangi, our head gun bearer and camp boss, decided they were close enough he would string my seventy-five pound bow and bring it over with some arrows.

"Bwana" he would say with a grin, *"Piga fisi pamoja uta m'kubwa."* Shoot a hyena with the big bow.

"Eko ni mingi?" I would ask him. Are there many?

"Ndio Bwana, mingi kama inzi" he would answer. There are many, like flies.

I would shoot one and the fun would begin. The boys never tired of it and they appreciated seeing *fisi* shot with a bow and arrow. This was something they understood better than a rifle.

At the end of the safari they expressed their regret at my leaving, mainly, I think, because they never had seen their hated enemy *fisi* disposed of in such a delightful way. They would miss all the fun and pantomime and laughing they said, and urged me to come back again and be sure to bring *Uta m'kubwa* — the big bow.

All things considered, it had been a wonderful safari and I assured them I would be back. The elephant, rhino, buffalo and other game I wanted had been bagged, and not counting the hyenas, I had taken sixteen of Africa's big game trophies with the bow.

IT HAD seemed like a good idea early that morning — now I wasn't so sure. There were buffalo on three sides of us, and if they kept grazing in our direction, we would be completely surrounded in a few more minutes.

The crossbow in my hands seemed rather inadequate. If it hadn't been for the assurance of the .470 double rifle my white hunter was carrying and the prospect of losing face, I would have called the whole thing off. But it was too late now; we were committed.

We have begun the stalk two hours before and now were crouched in a small patch of thorn bush that barely provided cover. We were both frozen statues, for even the slightest movement would have betrayed our presence. Any second I expected to hear a snort of discovery and the exploding, churning stampede as the herd took off. The point was which way would they take off? An old cow and her calf had walked by a few minutes before and now were feeding almost directly behind us less than fifty feet away. If she caught our scent, she would obviously take off in the direction she was heading and the whole herd would pour over us like a tidal wave.

The big black herd bull we had spotted when we started the stalk was about sixty yards in front and slowly moving closer. He was the target I had picked out. We had reached the last bit of bush about twenty minutes before and I had knelt with the crossbow cocked and a fiberglass broadhead snugged against the string. There was only the open plain ahead that was slowly filling with buffalo coming out of the brush on the other side.

Fortunately, the air was dead still or we would have been scented long before when some of them began to pass on both sides of our meager cover. Even so, we had left our scent where we had belly-crawled through the grass from bush to bush and, as soon as one of them came to our trail, all hell was going to break loose.

For my money, the African Cape buffalo is the most dangerous animal in the world. Usually he will run at sight or scent of a man, but with a herd as big as this one, which I estimated to contain at least two hundred animals, there was no telling what was going to happen.

When wounded or suddenly come upon, he is a cunning, vindictive enemy. He will wait in ambush until you get close enough, then burst out of cover and pulverize you. During many safaris to Africa I have shot some thirty buffalo. The first two I ever encountered charged me and several have since. The net result is that I have a healthy respect for these crafty beasts.

The morning coolness was gone and the heat was building up. Perspiration was running down my back and I could feel a tick crawling over my face, but I dared not move. The big bull was within thirty yards now and we couldn't afford to wait any longer.

I glanced at my white hunter. His knuckles were white where he grasped his rifle. His eye caught mine and he nodded his head almost imperceptibly. The bull was broadside now and slowly, scarcely daring to breathe, I raised the bow and took dead aim just behind his shoulder. I had previously come to the conclusion that the only place to shoot an animal as big as a buffalo was to try and get an arrow through his ribs behind the shoulder and into the heart or lungs. Almost anywhere else was too much meat or the bones were too big and heavy. The odds were that he would run after being hit and I hoped the motion would cause the arrow to work back and forth inside causing more damage.

I released the arrow and a split second later there was a whump as it struck home. Then there was pandemonium.

The white hunter jumped up, fired a shot over the herd and yelled like a banshee. There was a thunder of hooves as the stampede started. We both yelled again and jumped up and down waving our arms as the buffalo on both sides of us turned to follow the herd. Some were headed directly towards us, but they turned off when they saw us.

"That's about the only way to save your neck when

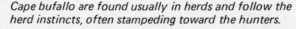

Cape bufallo are found usually in herds and follow the herd instincts, often stampeding toward the hunters.

Elgin Gates is one of the world's foremost big game hunters, but the crossbow as a weapon was totally new.

you get caught in the middle of a herd," said my white hunter. "Yell like hell, jump up and down, wave your hat, shoot in the air and pray a little. Usually they will turn away from you."

"Yeah," I said, "but what happens when they don't turn?"

He grinned. "Well, you climb a tree if one is handy and, if not, you shoot a couple and hope for the best."

"Did you see where the arrow hit?" I asked him.

"It was a good shot," he answered. "Just behind the shoulder. Perhaps a bit high, but it should be right in his lungs."

There was no use trying to look for the blood spoor since the stampeding herd would have obliterated it.

From past experience I knew that any time a buffalo was hard hit, he usually would stop in the thickest patch of brush he could find and wait there. We decided to wait a couple of hours ourselves to let the arrow do its work before following the tracks. It had been about 10 a.m. when I shot, so we walked back a half mile to where the Land Rover was parked and drove the five miles back to camp for lunch.

It was only the second day of the safari, and I had wanted to use the crossbow on some of the less

dangerous game to get the feel of it before tackling something as big as a buffalo, but the opportunity had presented itself, so we had stalked buffalo the second day out.

A little after noon we got into the Land Rover and drove back to where the herd had stampeded. This time we had Nzumi, one of our Wakamba trackers with us. The big mass of tracks was easy to see, so we followed them in the car for about a half mile. Then we saw where the herd had plunged through a dense patch of thorn bush some two hundred yards long and about one hundred yards wide. We drove around the patch and saw where the herd had come out the other side and gone on.

"I'll give you ten to one he's in there" said the white hunter.

"I agree with you," I answered, "so we might as well get on with it."

We parked the car at one end of the patch and the three of us got out. We stayed about fifty yards away from the edge of the brush for elbow room and slowly and silently eased along with all eyes on the lookout for any movement or sign of a wounded bull.

Stalking a wounded buffalo is no child's play,

especially when he has four good legs under him as this one did. I've seen buffalo shot several times in the chest and body cavity with heavy caliber rifles, then run a mile, wait in ambush and still have enough adrenalin-hypoed energy to charge with a full head of steam when tracked up. I saw one shot squarely in the heart that disappeared into a thicket and an hour later charged like he hadn't been touched at all. They charge with head up, nose outstretched and eyes wide open. They will hook, butt and stomp a man to bloody rags. Only a brain shot through his outstretched nose will kill him or a shot that smashes the shoulder bone will turn him. When they come they mean business, and under these circumstances, a bow and arrow is rather useless.

We circled the patch once without seeing anything, then moved in closer for another look. This time we went half way around the patch. We were right on the edge of it when Nzumi suddenly froze and pointed. I moved over to look in the direction he pointed, but could see nothing. He silently moved up about twenty feet and pointed again. This time I saw a slight movement and a moment later I made out the shape of a bull lying on the ground about fifteen yards inside of the brush. He was still alive for the movement I had seen was his tail switching. The crossbow was cocked and ready. The white hunter was at my elbow with his .470. We had agreed that I would finish him off with the crossbow if possible, but that he would use the rifle if there was a charge.

He must have sensed our presence or heard us, for although he was lying with his head away, he suddenly struggled to his feet and turned to face us. I took quick aim and shot an arrow into his neck. He grunted and took two or three steps in our direction, then went down. The white hunter had been holding his rifle at ready position with the safety off. He lowered it with an indrawn sigh.

"That was a close one," he said. "For a moment there I thought he was going to have a go at us."

"I think he was dead on his feet," I answered. "Let's go have a look."

This time I had been lucky. When we did a post-mortem we found that the first arrow had indeed done its work. During his running, the razor-sharp broadhead had practically cut his lungs to ribbons. He had burned up his last ounce of energy getting to his feet and I am dead certain he would have gone down again without charging even if I hadn't shot the second arrow. Just the same, you never take anything for granted with a buffalo. He's never dead until his eye doesn't blink when you jab a stick in it and I never feel completely relaxed until his head is off.

A few days later, we were sitting on the bank of a dry ravine having lunch when I spotted a big boar warthog coming our way along the bottom. He was carrying the biggest tusks I've ever seen on any boar anywhere in the world including trophy collections, museums, record books or otherwise. My crossbow was leaning against the log I was sitting on and it took but a few seconds to cock it and place an arrow on the track. I had learned long ago always to have a weapon within reach in hunting country, whether attending a call of nature, taking a stroll or eating lunch. More than once this habit has given me a chance at a good trophy.

It was almost too simple. I crawled over to the edge, waited until he was directly below me at a distance of about thirty feet, drew a bead and let fly. He fell over as the arrow penetrated his back, got to his feet again, ran

Arrow went completely through rare and beautiful red leshwe, a swamp-dwelling creature that rarely is taken. The arrow with which it was shot was lost in the swamp.

about fifty yards along the ravine and scrambled up to the top and collapsed there.

A warthog carrying big ivory is considered a first class trophy even in Africa, and let no one get the idea that because of the small size of the animal — a big one will weigh less than a hundred pounds — that he is not a dangerous foe. I've seen much bigger animals give way to them on trails and at waterholes. They can use their tusks with great dexterity and can slice the belly out of a horse as quick and easy as a Spanish fighting bull. I would as soon face a lion or a leopard as an enraged warthog at close quarters. In fact, one of the neatest shellackings I've ever taken from an animal was at the hands — or rather the tusks — of a warthog.

A few years back we were driving through the plains country and caught a warthog out in the open. I thought it would be fun to lasso him and the white hunter fell in with the idea. There was some rope in the back of the Land Rover, so I quickly fashioned a noose while the hunter maneuvered the car alongside the running warthog. After a couple of misses, I succeeded in getting the loop around his neck. I snubbed the end of the rope around the gun rack on my side and we stopped. When he hit the end of the rope, he was flipped over on his back. He got to his feet and staggered around for a minute or two, then made another lunge with the same results. We were convulsive with laughter and slapping each other on the back as the Zuwamba gun bearer in the back suddenly pointed.

"Angalia!" he exclaimed. "The warthog is coming!"

The frenzied animal had identified his tormenters and was charging the Land Rover with tusk-chopping, mouth-frothing rage.

When traveling through hunting country, we would remove the two side doors from the Land Rover and fasten military gun racks on the door hinges. The rifles were carried here so when game was spotted you could grab the rifle and bail out in a hurry if necessary. With the doors thus removed our feet and legs would have been within easy reach of his tusks, so our first reaction was to scramble over the back of the seat into the rear compartment. He hit the side of the car about the same time we went over the seat and he proceeded to slash it from one end to the other. He would slash four or five times, back off a few feet, grunt a challenge and attack another place.

He had us cold. When we tried to reach across the front seat for the rifles he would come boring in and slash like crazy. I wasn't about to climb over into the front, for with one little hop he could be right in the car.

Sometime during the action, the loop around his neck loosened up and he got a lower tusk in it, cut the rope clean and freed himself. Even then he didn't leave but walked around and around the car. Every time we moved he slashed it. Finally we got the idea and remained motionless for about fifteen minutes until he cooled down. When his rage subsided he trotted off with his tail in the air. We waited until he was of sight and climbed down to survey the damage.

One tire was punctured, another one was slashed to the cord and had to be replaced a few days later. There were numerous scratches, grooves and dents in the body and several holes in the fender where his tusks had gone through the metal like a knife through cheese.

One of his slashes had caught my rifle stock just above the recoil pad and there was a beautiful precision groove about three-eighths of an inch deep that came out at the pistol grip. The edges were as clean as it had been cut with a sharp wood chisel. Our funny little joke had back-fired, but still, I was thankful for one thing: Warthogs can't climb.

There were three more trophies I wanted to bag with the bow and arrow that I hadn't taken on previous safaris. Namely a lion, a greater kudu and a sable antelope. These three, with the buffalo, elephant, rhinocerous and leopard, are the top trophies in Africa, and are known as "the big seven." I still wasn't ready to tackle an elephant or a rhino with a bow and arrow, but I was going to work hard at bagging five of the big seven. I had taken most of the common game previously, including a leopard, so now that the buffalo was in the bag there were three to go.

Kudu and sable are considered to be two of the top antelope trophies in Africa. Recently I received a newsletter from one of the largest outfitters in Africa. Druing the two previous seasons they had put eighty-nine safaris into the field with all the clients using firearms. Only fifteen kudu and nine sable were taken, which will give some idea of how difficult these trophies are to come by. A total of eighteen lions were taken during the same eighty-nine safaris, which also indicates how tough lions are to come by.

We broke camp and drove fifty miles south to a permanent water channel the white hunter knew and which he told me would offer the best chance to collect these trophies. After a long, hot, dusty drive across country, we reached the channel and set up camp near the lower end. Late that afternoon we went down to the water to get the lay of the land and check for tracks.

On previous safaris, I'd heard all the usual excuses: Either there was too much water and the game had scattered or there wasn't enough water, so the game had gone somewhere else, or the grass was too green, so the game was spread out far and wide or it was too hot or too cold or wet or something. This time everything was right.

There was plenty of good water in the channel, but no other permanent water within forty miles. All the water pans between were dried up. The game was concentrated here and came to drink every day. The soft ground at the edge of the channel was stiff with tracks of elephant, buffalo, kudu, sable, lion, zebra, eland, wildebeeste, roan, sassaby and everything else that lived in this part of Africa.

There was a thin fringe of brush and some high grass — mostly tramped down — along the edge of the channel. There was open country for about four hundred yards, then the thick niombo forest of mopani and teak trees. Most of the game watered early in the morning, then spent the day back in the forest. It was a perfect, ready-made set-up and I was anxious to start hunting.

At daylight the next morning we were ghosting along through the brush at the edge of the channel. Game was everywhere: Reedbucks, waterbucks, zebra, wildebeeste, sassaby and others. There were some easy shots offered but I had my mind set on the exotic trophies and passed these by. About a half mile from camp, we saw four female kudu drinking but no bulls were with them. A little farther on, we surprised a small herd of sables in the edge of the water. They were mostly cows and calves with a few young bulls, so we continued on.

About two miles farther on we rounded a bend in the channel and there they were, five kudu bulls one hundred yards away and one of them was a beauty. I estimated his horns would measure fifty inches plus, which is a good trophy anywhere in Africa. The tip to tip spread of his horns was tremendous. The other four were between 40 and 45 inches.

Luckily we were behind a screen of brush and they didn't see us. They were just entering the water to drink and I quickly appraised the possibilities of making a stalk. About seventy-five yards back from the edge of the water there was a small sand ridge about six feet high. There were a few thorn bushes growing on the top of it and I reasoned that the kudu would go directly back to the forest after drinking. If I could get behind one of those bushes near their line of travel there might be a chance for a shot.

When stalking with a bow and arrow, the fewer the better, so I whispered to the white hunter to remain where he was with the tracker, while I went back a ways to see if I could work my way behind the sand ridge. I eased back and soon found enough cover to cross over and within three or four minutes I was behind the sand ridge and moving as rapidly as I could without making any noise. I had picked out a lop-sided bush on the ridge as a landmark and which seemed from our original observation point to be where the kudu would pass on their return to the forest.

The plan went off like clock-work with one good piece of luck included. I reached the lop-sided bush just as the kudus left the water and started walking slowly towards the forest. I saw they were going to pass very close and the luck was that the big bull was leading. The bush was too thorny to get inside of and there was no other cover available, so I lay down behind it and checked the crossbow to see if the arrow was snug against the string and straight in the groove. The first kudu that came over the ridge would spot me and there would be only that first second of hesitation before they leaped away. My only thought and hope was that the big bull would stay in the lead and be the first over the ridge. I had removed my hat and checked the wind when I arrived at the bush. The slight air movement was coming from the water so everything was perfect so far.

I raised my head once and peered through the lower branches of the bush. They were coming on and would pass within twenty feet if nothing spooked them. Kudu are among the smartest, cleverest, most cunning, most difficult animals to stalk in the world and I imagined fifty things that could go wrong before they reached the ridge. I had been out-smarted by them in the past so many times I've lost count.

After what seemed like an eternity, but could have been only a minute or two, I saw the tips of two horns appear and knew instantly it was the big bull, because of the tremendous spread. I raised the bow slightly and aimed it where I thought his shoulder would be in a few more seconds. More of the horns came into view, then the big ears, the head and then the body. The distance was less than thirty feet. He saw me at that instant and hesitated for one fatal second before leaping away. I released the arrow in that same second and saw him stagger from the impact. He recovered and bounded toward the forest with the other four bulls close behind. At the fifth or sixth leap he folded up and went down like he had been poleaxed. Later we found that the broadhead had cut into the spine and the few leaps caused the arrow point to actually sever the spinal cord.

It was a moment for rejoicing for here was one of the finest trophies in all Africa and so far as I know it was the first time that a bowhunter had ever taken a greater kudu. His horns just shaded fifty-four inches which was more than I had dared to hope for and the spread was a whopping forty-three inches. He was a fine trophy and it was a stalk to remember.

That same afternoon I shot a reedbuck for camp meat and we had a celebration that night with sizzling steaks and Scotch on the rocks.

Three days later I collected a big sable antelope. As with the kudu it was the first sable ever collected with a bow and arrow so far as I know. In any event, it was a piece of cake on a silver platter.

We were stalking through the forest that afternoon when the white hunter spotted him in a clearing ahead. They are easy to see anywhere, because of their beautiful coal-black coat and vivid white face markings. Through the binoculars I could see that something was wrong with this bull. He was walking slowly around in a circle in the center of the clearing and kept shaking his head. We eased up to a screen of brush at the edge to take a better look. He was about sixty yards away. I waited for a few minutes hoping he would stop so I could get a still shot. Shooting at an erratically moving target at sixty yards isn't the easiest shot to make. I was afraid to step out in the open to get closer, for I've seen animals acting goofy before, then when they scent or see a man they will take off like a flash in full control of their faculties.

When he was broadside I released an arrow that went under him, a clean miss. He didn't even look up, so I quickly reloaded and shot again. This time he turned just as I released the arrow and I missed again. I waited until he momentarily turned in his circle and was moving towards me. This time the arrow struck fairly in his chest and penetrated his heart as we discovered later. He swayed back and forth a few times, took a few steps and slumped down. When we examined him we found a horn wound near his left eye and several other wounds in his body. The churned up earth told the story. He had been in a terrific scrap with another bull before we came on the scene which accounted for the daze he was in.

He was a tough old warrior with a magnificent set of horns that measured 47½ inches over the curve. This measurement beat the old East African record by three-fourths of an inch. In a way, I felt sort of sorry for the old boy and I don't believe I would have shot him

had I known he had been in a battle royal. There was no doubt he was the victor, for he was still occupying the battleground, while his antagonist had been driven away.

As the animal was being skinned out by the natives, my white hunter picked up the crossbow and looked at it with distaste. "You're determined to get a lion with this monstrosity?" he asked cautiously.

"I think it can be done," I told him.

"I hope you don't bring this bloody thing with you again," he said. "I've had enough cheap kicks to last me the rest of my life."

"Well," I said, "I've had a few thrills myself, but next year I'm going to bring some real high-powered gear. There's still elephant and rhino you know. Maybe we can try it with spears or slingshots."

He groaned, and for a minute I thought he was going to wrap it around my neck.

Nzumi, the file-toothed Wakamba gun bearer and tracker, carries a pair of rare trophy heads taken by bowhunter.

IT came again. The awesome, spine-tingling roar of a full grown African hunting lion. If there is one sound in the world that acts as a catalyst to start my emotions churning, this is it.

My usual reaction is one of adrenalin-pumping anticipation. But this time a new element was added: Fear! Not the dry-mouthed paralyzing fear, but the sweaty-armpits, butterflies-in-the-stomach-kind of fear. It was induced by the fact that I was going after this particular lion with a crossbow rather than a high-powered rifle.

Lions usually will roar several times at daybreak just as they are settling down for the day. I had heard the first roar about twenty minutes before, just as the first light streaks of morning appeared in the sky. Nzumi, our African gun bearer, stuck his head in to my tent just as I finished lacing my boots.

The safari camp from which bowhunting adventures were
launched was far from palatial by some standards of
African hunting, but it was functional, easily moved.

"Bwana," he said, "simba m'kubwa ngruma." The
big lion is growling.

"Simba eko ya nyama?" I asked. Is the lion on the
bait?

"Ndio, Bwana, ya nyama," he said. Yes, he is on the
bait.

Six days before, I had shot a fine greater kudu with
the crossbow and we had hung the carcass in a tree on
the edge of the forest as lion bait. Every morning we
checked the carcass hoping to find a lion on it, but so
far, there was only the usual gang of scavengers hanging around; my old friend Fisi, the hyena, jackals, and
a cluster of big, ugly vultures hunched in the trees. The
carcass had been hung by the hind legs so that the
front part of the body was about four feet off the
ground. The hyenas and jackals couldn't get at it but a
lion could easily rear up and take what he wanted.

On the fifth morning, about one third of the carcass
had been devoured. I looked closely and found a few
long, dark hairs caught in the bark of the tree. They
were from a lion's mane. Under the tree we found his
tracks and those of a lioness. Without disturbing the
area, we quickly left.

Back at the Land Rover, we worked out a plan. One
third of a kudu carcass could hardly fill the belly of
one hungry lion, let alone two. The odds were that they
would be back during the night to eat some more, so
we decided to be in position to stalk at the first light
of morning. Lions usually will stay on a kill until the
sun comes up, then they will go find a patch of thick
brush nearby to lay up for the day.

The African lion is called the King of Beasts with
good reason. He is a lightweight alongside such animals as the buffalo, rhino, and elephant, but if wounded, he shows no fear and can hide in a place where a
rabbit would have trouble concealing himself. Whether
gaunt with hunger or with his belly almost dragging
the ground from eating seventy-five pounds of meat at
one sitting, he still can cover the ground with incredible
speed. His powerful forearms that can break a buffalo's
neck with one wrench, can smash every bone in a man's
chest with one slap. The jaws that can disjoint the same
buffalo carcass can bite through a man's skull like an
egg shell. If that isn't enough, his curved talons can
slice his victim to bloody ribbons or disembowel a man
with one stroke.

Last year, two American big game hunters were killed by
lions they followed into the brush after wounding them.
One well known white hunter was crippled for life and
others have been savagely mauled, their lives being saved
only because someone on the scene had enough courage to
stick a rifle in the lion's ear and blow his brains out as he
crouched over his victim.

White hunters as a whole would rather follow any

other wounded animal into the dense brush than a lion. Most of them have a healthy respect for buffalo, are careful with elephants, sometimes contemptuous of the blundering rhino, and are extremely wary with lions.

I already had taken a buffalo, a sable antelope, and the kudu we were using for lion bait with the crossbow and now the supreme test was soon to come.

With a lion you never know exactly how he will behave. I've driven up to within twenty-five feet of them in a Land Rover and they have just given me a curious look. The next one you see is liable to come right down your throat. Then the next will run like hell when you get within half a mile of him. A lioness with cubs is usually mean and surly and not to be tampered with. The only thing to do is play it by ear and be ready for anything.

My white hunter classifies lions as approachable and unapproachable and a funny thing is this: If a lion is the approachable type, the best thing to do is just walk up to shooting range and bust him. If you try to sneak-stalk him, and he spots you, he will either disappear or he will counter-stalk you. Frankly, I'd rather walk up to a lion in the open and take my chances than to be crawling through the brush on my hands and knees while he is stalking me. I bow to my superiors at the art of stalking.

After a quick breakfast of toast and tea, we drove the Land Rover to a point about three-quarters of a mile from the tree where the bait was hanging and started walking when it was light enough to see. There was a vantage point behind some thorn brush about two hundred yards from the tree. We reached this just as the first rays of sunlight appeared.

The lions were there all right, and through the bi-noculars I could see the big male lying down at the foot of the tree while the lioness still was worrying the carcass.

We had decided earlier that to get close enough for an arrow shot we would have to assume and hope they were approachable lions. We actually got about eighty yards before the lioness spotted us and dropped down from the carcass. She growled a few times, crouched down facing us and began lashing her tail. We stopped. I double checked the arrow in the crossbow and heard the faint click as the white hunter released the safety on his double rifle.

The big lion was lying broadside to us and at first didn't pay any attention. Finally he turned his head and watched us. Actually, both of us were concentrating our attention on the lioness, for as long as her tail kept lashing, everything was in the green. It is when a lion's tail stops lashing and sticks out as stiff and straight as an iron bar that you are living on borrowed time. This is the signal that they are coming.

We waited at the ready for a few minutes and finally this old girl lowered her chin to the ground with her eyes still fixed on us. Her tail was still moving but not as violently as before. With a rifle it would have been a dead easy shot at eighty yards but I wanted to get closer to try to place the arrow as accurately as possible. I didn't want to go after a wounded lion in thick brush if I could help it. Particularly with a crossbow!

Slowly we edged closer, a short step at a time until we had narrowed the distance to about forty yards. The male was still lazily watching us but the lioness began to get nervous. Her head came up, as she showed her fighting fangs and began growling down in her throat. Her tail still was lashing but I knew we had reached the invisible line beyond which we could not

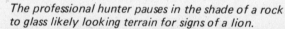

The professional hunter pauses in the shade of a rock to glass likely looking terrain for signs of a lion.

Gates scored on this African lion, bringing it down with
a bolt from his crossbow, an especially demanding event.

go without having her charge.

I slowly kneeled down and rested my left elbow on my left knee to get as steady a rest as I could. At the same time, the white hunter raised his rifle and drew a bead on the lioness. I was fairly steady but I could feel perspiration from my armpits running down my sides and my palms were damp. Aiming just behind his shoulder, I released the arrow. It flew just over his back, a clean miss. He got to his feet and stood there, still broadside, watching us, while the lioness hunched down a little lower and snarled horribly.

"For gawd's sake shoot again and hurry!" whispered the hunter. "She is going to have a go at us pretty quick."

Holding the stock of the crossbow in my stomach I cocked it again from the same position and placed another arrow on the track. Taking rather quick aim, I shot again and this time the arrow struck him low in the shoulder, barely missing the leg bone. He made a big leap in the direction he was heading and piled into

the lioness knocking her sprawling. He continued running broadside to us and the lioness was so startled, when she got to her feet she followed him without another glance at us. The lion went down thrashing after running about fifty yards. Without even pausing, the lioness zipped by him and ran on into the forest and disappeared.

Although I had hurried the second shot, I couldn't have made a better one. The arrow had gone through his leg muscles and penetrated into the chest cavity. The movement of his leg while running had caused the arrow point to cut a six-inch swath through his vital organs. It had snapped off about four inches back from the point but not before making several deadly cuts.

He had a full mane that was turning black on top and he measured out at nine feet, ten inches, a heck of a fine lion in anybody's language. I had taken several lions on other safaris and while this was the first one I had ever taken with a bow and arrow, I had a strong feeling it was going to be the last. – *Elgin Gates*

Chapter 23

BUILD A SHOOTING MACHINE

One Way To Test A Bow's Speed And Consistency Is To Build A Machine That Can Draw, Hold And Release The Same Way Every Time.

Components for the shooting machine: an I-shaped rail, three lengths of galvanized pipe, a U-bolt and winch.

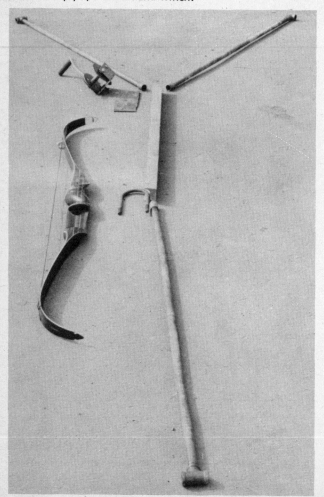

GETTING THE HUMAN element out of archery is the only way to decide the issues and arguments that tend to come up between archers when they sing the praises of their personal bow favorites. Variables in release and form can greatly affect an arrow's performance out of any bow.

About the only way to solve this problem is to come up with a mechanical device capable of holding and drawing a bow and releasing an arrow the same way each time. This done, the only variables left to deal with are those of arrow weight, spine, point and fletching, and, of course, factors such as wind and weather that also can affect arrow flight and performance.

Building such a machine isn't all that difficult, though certainly the job can become complicated, depending upon the approach the would-be builder chooses to take. For example, I faced the dilemmas of what kind of material to use for the construction, how to make the monster high enough so that I wouldn't have to bend over, and how to make it strong enough to handle any bows with draw weights in excess of seventy pounds.

When we bought our present home, the former owner left many sections of galvanized pipe in a corner of the back yard. Over the years, I've found a great many uses for bits and pieces of this pipe but haven't really made much of a dent in the pile. When the shooting machine idea came along, the old pipe struck me as perfect construction material. The machine could have been built with two-by-fours, but the cost of the pipe — nothing — made it my choice for this project.

The old pipe was laid out in the shop and some calculations made for measurements. The legs were forty-six inches long. The machine was to be three-legged, and the legs were at an angle, so the machine isn't that high, but does stand at a comfortable shooting height. The height also allows for any length of bow to be shot from the machine.

The front leg has to be adjustable. There are several ways

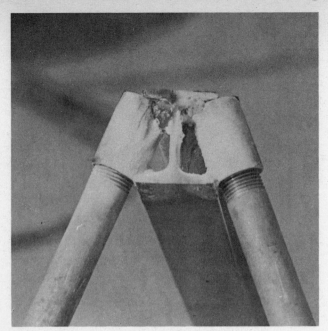

After U-bolt is welded into position, clean to remove scale from welding operation.

The machine's bow-holding attachment was made from a six-inch stripped thread U-bolt. If you save things like that, as I do, you'll have all you need to make the machine.

The drawing system puzzled me for a time, but while fishing at a local lake, I watched a boat being winched to a trailer. I didn't have a boat winch but found one second-hand that was in good shape. They sell from five bucks up, and you don't need a large one.

I cut the legs and threaded the ends with a pipe threader borrowed from a neighbor. The bottom tips of the legs were fitted with T-connectors from the pipe pile to prevent them from digging into the ground when the machine is being used. The wider base also made it easy to drive a stake into the ground to anchor the machine down.

I cut the front leg at forty-eight inches, longer than the other two, to allow for range adjustment. The main rail was cut forty-one inches long. With the four inches or so for the winch plate, this gave me a draw length of thirty inches, about as long as anyone draws a bow. If you want to draw farther, you can extend the bow in front.

All the legs were to be attached with pipe couplers from the junk pile. Three couplers are needed, one for each of the three legs, along with three T-connectors for the bottoms of the legs.

After I got all of these components assembled on the floor of the shop, it didn't look as bad as I thought it would. The pipe, rail and U-bolt were loaded into the back of my old station wagon and carted off to Bill Duff's welding machine. Duff spends his days making custom knives along with his partner, Don Collum, and they humor me on many of my hairbrained ideas.

After I unloaded all the pipe and parts and had them in an exploded view for Duff to check out, he scratched his head and remarked, "Just how is this all to go together and what am I supposed to have it look like when I finish with the torch?"

A few minutes of scribbling with paper and pencil and he had an idea of what I was trying to assemble. He took

of doing this. My method was to weld a coupling to the front of the bar. A variation of this is to use a pipe clamp which one buys for clamping wood or furniture while it cures in a vise. These pipe clamps can be purchased in any hardware store, and I would have used one instead of the coupling because it makes adjustments faster and easier, but I already had a coupling in stock and decided to keep expenses to a minimum.

For the main section of the monster, I used an old fence rail — the type used for woven wire. These can be found in stores or in an extensive junk pile like the one in my shop. I chose a large fence rail that would make the machine strong enough for any bow. Just make sure you get the I-beam rail, not the round-type style.

Large U-bolt is heated and formed around already welded couplers at front of rail.

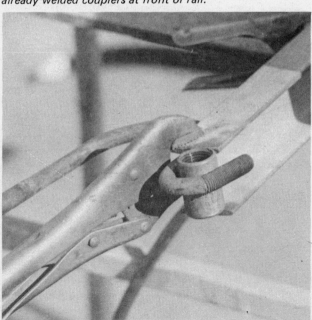

Rear legs are welded at an angle to make sturdier and to prevent bow limb interference.

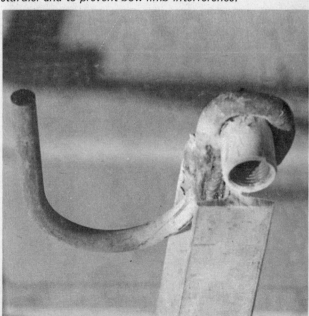

out his arc welder and in a few minutes had the three couplers welded to the main I-beam rail. He angled the two at the rear to my specifications. Luckily, the top of the coupler that was set into the underside of the top metal of the I-beam gave me the right angle and also made the welding much faster and stronger.

He torched and arced all over the rail and asked what was next. I explained how the winch was to be used to draw the bow. He went into his shop, came out with a piece of light plate steel and welded it on the bottom at the back of the rail. The height of the winch on top of the plate made it perfect for the drawing height of the bow.

When the couplers had cooled and the plate had been drilled to fit the holes on the winch base, we attached the legs to the rail and put the winch in place. All that remained was the U-bolt to hold the bow in front. Duff took his torch and heated the bolt to bend it for fitting around the front coupler and welded it to the coupler and the side of the rail. This made it solid.

After cutting off a part of the U-bolt that protruded too far, we had the basics of my iron monster. Duff stood back, shook his head and made me promise to let him witness the monster in action. What he welded in minutes would have taken me hours.

The unit was disassembled and put back into my wagon.

When I returned to the shop I used gasoline to clean all the parts. They were then assembled and painted a bright red enamel left over from a former project.

When the paint dried, I took the front leg to the local hardware store and had the threads turned down about ten inches from the top. This gave me plenty of adjustment for distance.

With that, I had the assembled platform for the machine. All that was needed was the method of holding the bow and the release system.

The bow should have a wrist-type action. If it is bolted in place, it can't move as it does in the hand. I also wanted the bow to be out from the side of the main rail to prevent scratching. My bows are scratched but someone else might not like the scratched look.

I put sections of sponge rubber in the open U-bolt and the biggest-handled bow I had in the shop was placed in the unit to see how it fit. Most bow handles today are quite small, so if I made the unit big enough and snug on the biggest-handled bow, it would fit any bow.

The padding was checked, the bow braced and pulled partly back to draw by hand to see if the string and lower limb would clear the unit. It looked good, so the handle was taped with duct tape and that gave me a good soft, yet solid, rest for the bow with no scratch problems.

The boat winch is bolted to the metal plate which has been welded to the main rail.

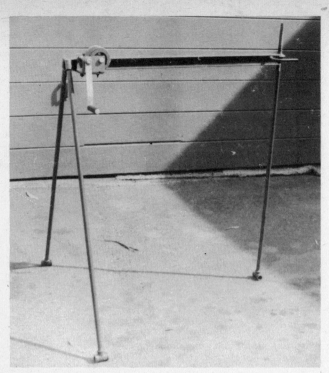

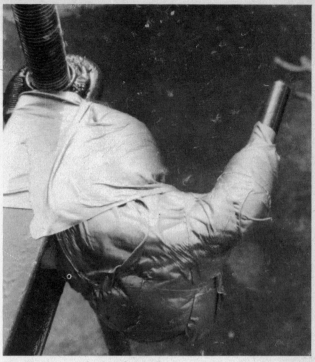

The unit after assembly — all that now remains to be done is to pad the U-bolt.

The U-bolt as it looks after being padded with sections of sponge rubber.

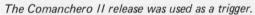

The Comanchero II release was used as a trigger.

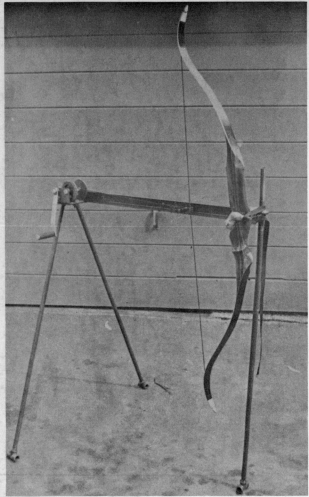

The unit is completely assembled, ready for testing.

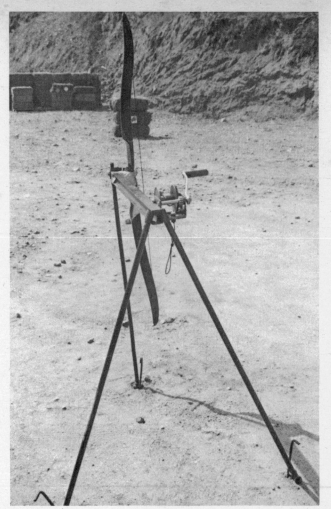

The unit seemed to function well on the test range.

The release took some thought. While shooting with a group of archers, I noted the different releases they were using. The Comanchero II looked like it would fill the ticket, so I picked one up at the local equipment shop to put on the iron monster for my release mechanism.

The drawing system almost can be any strong line, but it shouldn't be too big. At first I toyed with the idea of using nylon-coated steel fishing leader, but it was too hard to make a simple attachment to the Comanchero release. I used a six-foot section of the black six-hundred-pound test nylon line instead. This can be bought in backpack stores and many hardware stores.

The Comanchero is gripped by the two first fingers and tripped with the thumb. I used a simple loop tied into the nylon line and over the top of the release.

The bow was put in place, the Comanchero snapped onto the string and the bow was drawn back with the winch. It drew evenly and certainly held the bow solid. Now I was anxious to see if it would fire the bow as I wanted it to.

What I needed was a big stack of straw bales. The San Diego County Fish and Game Association has put in a new archery range next to their pistol and trap ranges, and that made an ideal place for the test firings. I immediately dismantled everything and took it to the range along with some tent stakes to anchor the monster down.

The unit was reassembled at the range after I paced off thirty-five yards. I had intended to shoot at thirty yards,

since that is the average deer-killing distance, but the ground at thirty yards was too hard to drive stakes. I anchored the unit and strapped a fifty-pound Bingham bow into the U-bolt handle with a section of nylon strap from an old backpack. I selected arrows that were three-fletched, four-inch feathers on Easton 24SRT-X in 2016 size. I thought they'd probably be perfect for the weight of the bow. This done, the final testing began.

The bow was winched back and the arrow placed on the string just under the nock. I tripped the Comanchero with my right hand. The arrow flew low, so I screwed the front leg up higher. The second arrow hit a bale, but not high enough, so I raised the front again. The third arrow hit the midsection of the bale.

When the elevation had been locked in, I picked the arrows from the bale and fired four more for a hopeful group. All of these stayed in the bale but were scattered high and wide. To adjust for this, I placed the drawing loop over the top of the Comanchero and each time held it as close to the same spot as possible.

I had taped a measure on top of the rail to make the draw length the same each time without having to guess. The erratic grouping came from the side and the up and down movement of the release. I had made no positive stops for the release to come to as I had on most everything else. The test firing was to determine problem areas and it showed that weakness in the system.

I continued firing four arrows at the bale but the wind

The shooting machine at work with the bow at a full twenty-eight-inch draw. Ruler on top of rail keeps draw honest.

Initial groups left something to be desired for tightness. A simple remedy of release position will improve them.

came in gusts down the draw where the range is and I still had erratic groups. The wind was an irritant but I had wanted field conditions and I had them.

I spent several hours working on the groups, but none really came to my expectations. I should be able to split nocks with this machine and it will do it with a few more additions of positive stops for left to right and top to bottom on the release.

The Bingham had been drawn to the same spot on the tape each time, but next time that will be marked with a template of plastic or light metal so it can be clamped to the top rail and be more positive. The draw line was changed from top to bottom on the Comanchero release and that did make a difference in the grouping, but was the same if the line was used the same way. The release worked either way.

The arrows will be renocked with Bjorn nocks or some type that will grip the string as Bjorns do. Speed nocks don't allow drawing the arrow back on the string because they fall off. I pinched a couple and, naturally, broke them.

With the addition of the shooting position mark and a plate at the bottom to make the same draw and hold each time, the machine will drill them very tight. I have plenty of range adjustments, so that is no problem. A few refinements will give me tighter groups. After I make them I'll call Duff and ask him to come witness the iron monster in action. I can see him smiling now. – *C.R. Learn*

Chapter 24

RACK 'EM UP

For Straight Shafts, Protected Arrowheads, These Simple Constructions Are Necessary Items

Bob Learn checks his arrow rack for the proper types of arrows he wants for a specific shooting mission. In this chapter are ideas for target and broadhead racks.

You bought 'em, now what are you going to do with 'em? I'm talking about those shiny new shafts clutched in your hot little hand. They may be a dozen woods for rabbits, a batch of new glass by Gordon or Microflite or did you go all the way and get those long dreamed of XX75s? They might be a special order of Forgewoods.

Now that you've got them the problem of where to keep them becomes just that: a problem. You could leave them in the box — if they came with a box — or you could put them in your quiver to let them hang against each other and ruin the fletch, or you could build, in a matter of only a few minutes, a rack to hold your new and your old shafts.

The arrow rack can be made from almost any material. Many take ordinary peg board, merely drill out the holes and use this to make a rack. If you have the patience and know-how, plexiglass can make an attractive arrow rack but you have to have a drill of the right pitch and the speed of the drill can't be too fast or the plexiglass will shatter. So why not do it the easy way?

Hunting through my clutch pile, I found a piece of good pine 1x10 and some scrap sheets of 3mm hardwood ply left over from some forgotten project.

Another short piece of 1x2 and I had most of the materials needed for a good arrow rack. The needed material was some decorator plastic that is made in sheets 24x24 with square holes one-half-inch wide. This saves all the drilling and makes an attractive rack when finished.

The size of the rack depends upon how big you want to make it. For a few shafts or a rack in which to put unfinished shafts while you work them, a small size works up just as well as a larger one. The only thing that governs the size is your need. If you think big and keep a large supply on hand you can cut the plastic sheet in half and make a big rack. **This size will hold eight hundred shafts!** For more practical reasons the 1x10 will make one large enough. Once again the size of the rack in width is governed by the size board you use but the length is up to you, it can go the full twenty-four inches if you like.

I picked a mid-point and cut the decorator plastic to fit the width of the board, then cut the length of the plastic in half to give me two finished pieces that measure 9x11 inches. This size will hold 288 shafts; large enough for most of us, I believe.

One thing I have found with the plastic materials is that they break easily. Care must be taken when handling them and especially when cutting them with a saw. If you plan to use each hole in the rack it works well for unfinished or partially finished work but I found that by spacing my fletched shafts in every other square and alternating on the next row it left plenty of air around the fletch to keep them from bunching and getting pushed out of shape.

A

B

The tools for this project would include a fine-tooth saw for the plastic, a standard saw for the wood, a hammer, a few nails and glue. If you have a portable saw or saw attachment for a drill, or better yet, a bench saw, you can dado a cut the width of the plastic and slide it into the grooves, put a section of ply on the bottom and one on the back and you have a finished arrow rack.

If you can't dado, the small strips of 1x2 will work as well or perhaps some quarter round left from that last project might be better. There is no weight on the plastic so all you need is something to support it and hold it in place.

Cut two pieces of the 1x10 fifteen inches long. Mark each piece from the bottom so the plastic will be parallel and at right angles to the sides and back. If you dado, cut at the marks and don't cut all the way through. Stop about a half inch from the end. Take a wood chisel and cut the end of the dado cut square and to the same depth.

If you are using the quarter round, nail it on at the marks. Take the ply and cut a bottom for the rack to fit the plastic after it is inserted in the dado grooves. The best procedure is to assemble roughly the sides and plastic, then make some quick measurements. The same goes for the quarter round. Cut the bottom from the ply, then take the 1x2 and cut two pieces to fit the length of the bottom ply between the sides. These will be glued and nailed to the sides of the rack to form a support for the bottom and to keep the sides in place.

Insert the plastic pieces that have been measured and carefully cut with the fine-tooth saw — a coarse saw will break the plastic — into the dadoed grooves, then measure another piece of ply to be used for the back of the rack. This will give the rack support and also keep the plastic in place. If you prefer, you can stain the pieces before assembling with the plastic or assemble first, then stain or paint.

When the back is in place and nailed on, the rack is complete except for the addition of the arrows you have purchased recently. There will be room in a rack of this size for many more dozens of arrows and for unfinished shafts as well. I keep finished shafts in one rack and have another for the raw materials of Port Orford cedar, glass and Forgewood. When I need an arrow I have a straight shaft that hasn't been warped by having it in a box with something heavy placed on top of it. It makes it faster to work since they are at hand when you need them and can be placed back in the rack as you finish one operation such as cutting the nock taper, then the tapered broadhead cut.

The size of materials and type of construction can be with your own modifications but this gives a fast, convenient arrow rack for storing maximum numbers of shafts in a small space.

C

A Simple tools, plywood sheet, lumber and lattice-work decorator panel of plastic are all you need to build an arrow rack. The job should not take more than a single afternoon. B Wide dado cuts are grooves for the plastic separators, and narrow cuts are for thin plywood sheet forming the bottom of the rack. Be sure to mark boards so dado cuts will be even when assembled. C Note that dadoes are not cut all the way. Grooves are squared and trimmed with a chisel, forming a tight shelf into which the plastic separator will fit. D Use only a fine-tooth saw or the brittle plastic will break. Support the work firmly on both sides of the cut while sawing. E After assembly the author applied red maple stain to the pine board sides and the plywood back and bottom, rubbed with steel wool and stained again. Any finish is suitable, including paint or no finish at all. It is best, however, not to attempt painting the plastic lattice-work grid.

D

E

An adequate rack to hold and protect broadheads can be made from memory type plastic hose. This type material can be cut easily with ordinary metal or garden shears.

After the section of plastic hose has been cut to the proper length, cut down side, take out small section.

A BROADHEAD rack that will hold your broadheads out of the quiver and ready for the hunt can be built easily and quickly. There are several types that can be made, if you specialize in two-blade heads.

The first rack goes together in a matter of minutes. Take a piece of plywood, one-by-four scrap wood or an old section of panel. We picked one that measured thirty inches long and three and one-half inches wide. This was rasped to remove the sharp edges, then sprayed with green spray paint.

Next, make a straight line one inch from the bottom edge for a guide. Measure intervals three-fourths of an inch apart on the guide line and make a pencil mark. Tap a carpet tack into each mark. When you get to the end of the board you are at the end of your project except for the nail to hang the board on the wall.

This fast, simple rack will hold up to twenty-four broadheads. It isn't elaborate, but it is effective. If you mount your broadheads vertically, turn your cock feathers out from the wall and no feathers will touch.

If you like the idea and want to elaborate, you can take pine with similar dimensions and screw right angle drapery hooks into the board.

The second rack involves more time, but is equally simple. Take a piece of plywood; we used a panel scrap measuring thirty-six by four and one-half inches. These dimensions are flexible.

The mounting will be done with flexible tubing such as a neoprene hose.

Cut sections one one-fourth inch long from the hose and set them in a pile. Take small tin snips or heavy scissors for this, as the hose cuts with difficulty. If you have a section of tubing on hand, cut a piece, split it up the middle and check to see if it will hold by inserting a shaft. Tygon works well as the plastic grips the shaft whether it is wood, aluminum, or fiberglass.

After you have the sections cut to length, slit each one up the middle to allow the shaft to go in. You can stop here, but we found that by cutting a small section from the side and rounding the corners, the shafts fit easier.

When you have all the sections slit, cut the corners rounded and take a small tack hammer and some carpet tacks to mount the sections to the board. Carpet tacks work fine, as they have a large head that prevents the tubing from cutting though. Too large a tack head won't allow the tubing to return to shape.

Pound the tack into the tubing and into the board. By using a small shop anvil and bending the points over with this as a backstop, the tacks won't work loose or pull out. When you finish, you will have a sore finger or two from cutting the tubing, and when you start tacking, send the wife and kiddies to another section of the house or to a movie. You will hit a finger once in a while, as the tubing is tough and wants to curl. You hold the tubing apart and hit gently against the tack head to get it mounted.

These tubing sections were mounted 1¼-inch on centers to allow for the big heads such as the Ace Super Express and the Deadheads. The board is high enough to prevent most of the heads on the market from sticking above. My rack holds twenty-eight broadheads. This is an odd number, but we used scrap wood and didn't cut for any specified number of shafts.

For the archer who has lots of shafts with heads mounted and wants them to stay that way, two, three and four-blade heads will go in this third rack.

We save everything, and in a cigar box we found many cut ends from the last batch of fiberglass shafts we made. Not many archers use the thirty inches of fiberglass tubing supplied in the raw shaft form, so when you cut off those ends, save them and make an arrow rack from the waste. The sections we saved were about four inches long.

Find a two-by-four in the pile. The length is not

This particular broadhead rack, made with the plastic hose, will hold twenty-eight arrows in orderly fashion.

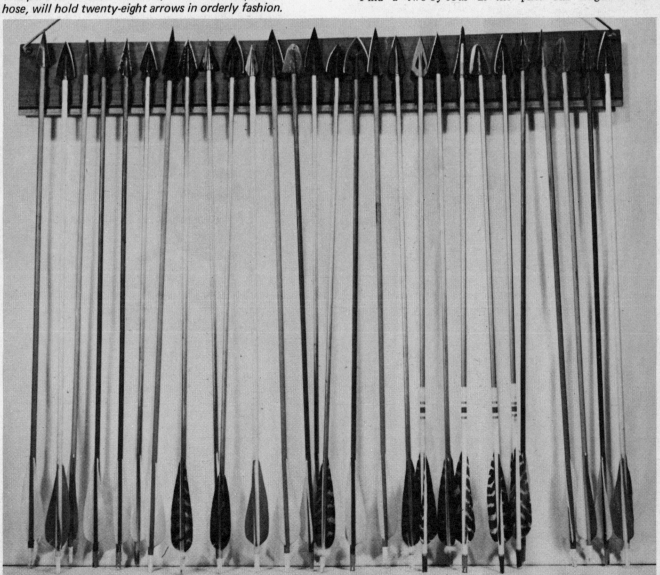

important, unless you are aiming at a specified number of shafts to be mounted or a particular area in which to mount the rack. Our section measured twenty-four inches. A bit of sanding revealed a nice grain pattern hidden beneath, so we smoothed one side and leveled the ends. A bit of oil stain brought out the grain.

The two-by-four is marked with a straight line. The shafts are mounted by drilling holes into the pine just a bit smaller than the OD of the shaft. The drill size will depend on your shaft or dowel material. A five-sixteenth-inch drill made a snug fit, so we marked the board with three-fourths-inch intervals, determined by one test drilling in another piece of scrap and mounting extra dowels to be sure. The different shaft materials fit nicely between the dowels.

When drilling these holes, it will help if you have a drill press of some type. The holes should have a slight upward tilt on the board to prevent shafts from sliding off. This is easily accomplished by tacking a piece of molding onto the back of the two-by-four. This gives a constant tilt to the board.

Drill the holes with a stop on the drill, so they will all be the same depth. Take the dowels to be used, and tap them into the holes using a soft hammer. Tap them gently until bottomed.

Hanging can be done with a wire or cord or by drilling holes in the corners and nailing or screwing to the wall.

The dowels we used were two colors of arrow shaft material. The shaft racks were alternated between a set of red dowels and a set of yellow dowels. As an added touch, we tipped the dowels with plastic broadhead adapters to make them more presentable.

This rack will hold assorted heads. With the heads mounted and full hunting fletch, six shafts mounted with the Black Copperhead Ripper fit into one section. It will

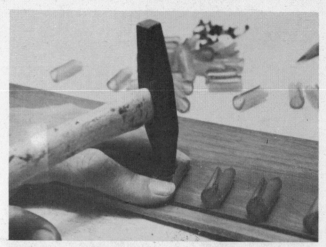

Split tubing is held apart and nailed to beam with a tack hammer. Interval of two inches is left between.

An equally simple type of arrow rack can be built by driving dowels into pre-drilled holes to act as hangers.

When the holes have been drilled in board, tack piece of molding to back so as to afford an angle to better hold the arrows, not allowing them to slip from pegs.

hold a minimum of eight Ace or Black Diamond heads mounted on hunting shafts and an equal amount of two-blade heads, regardless of make.

There are sixteen sections for mounting broadhead tipped shafts; a minimum of ninety-six shafts ready to go. That is a lot of shafts and even more broadheads. You can cut the length down and keep the other dimensions and have fewer sections, and it will work equally as well. By using the two-by-four section the shafts won't hang back against the wall and mash the feathers.

If you like, you could make a small version of the dowel rack to hang your multi-blade heads, and a small version of the carpet tack, drapery hook, or tubing rack to hang your two-blade heads. They are all simple to make. The dowel type went together fastest and looked the best. —*Bob Learn*

Rack built with plastic tubing will handle broadheads
of varied design, including two, three, four-blade types.

Better for multiple-bladed arrows is rack
built of dowel material, as the longer
length tends to hold bulkier broadheads.

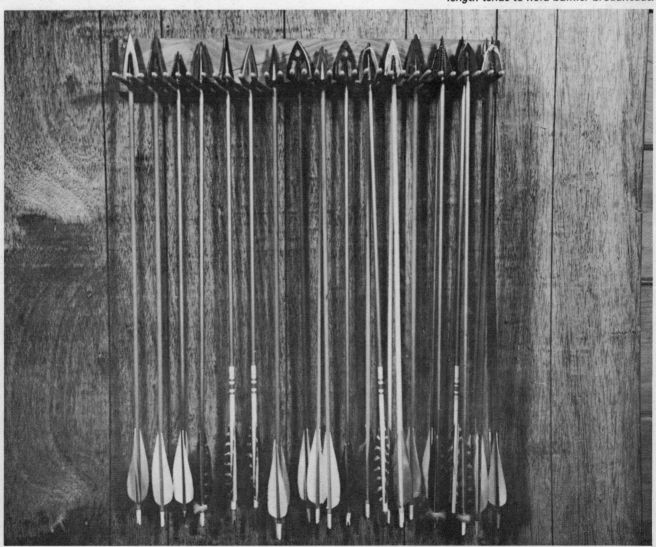

Chapter 25

ANYONE FOR YABUSAME?

The Ancient Japanese Sport — Given A Modern Twist— Can Be Duplicated In The Pasture Or Boarding Stable

In Japan, in spite of modern glasses worn by archer, yabusame continues as an ancient ceremonial sport.

THE pounding of horse hoofs on hard ground! The twang of a bowstring! A short rebel-like yell and the soft swosh-h-h as an arrow heads straight for its target!

The archer on horseback quickly places a second arrow in position, draws, aims, and releases...

No, this is not a classic Apache, Sioux, or Mohawk attack — circling a terrified group of white settlers perhaps for the benefit of TV or film cameras! It is a Japanese archers shooting Far East style at an annual yabusame shoot — somewhere in Japan!

To the American, Japanese sports conjure up a hazy vision of judo, karate, swimming and ping pong. Or a veteran of World War II with shrieks of "banzai" still ringing in his ears will visualize the Japanese warrior with swinging samurai sword in hand, and waves of human attacks!

The student of Far Eastern history and modern-day Japanese art films, will likewise visualize the Japanese warrior as a sword-wielding figure — such as the Japanese actor Mifune Toshiro in the award-winning *Rashomon*.

However, archery is very much a warrior's arm in the battling history of the Japanese — and the yabusame ceremonial meets which are just as popular in Japan today as a judo or sumo bout are held under rigid standards nearly a thousand years old.

English written historical records of Japan carry little of the history of Japanese archery — that is, in comparison to the much more publicized sport of judo or kendo (sword play, or fencing). However, Japanese language histories record the specific ceremonial sport of yabusame as having been started during the reign of the Emperor Temmu (the fortieth emperor), which would

In American West's version of the Japanese type of archery,
Jean Learn places full attention on shot, forgets horse.

place the event close to a certain event in a manger at Bethlehem.

Definitely the ex-Emperor Shirakawa (the seventy-second emperor) did, in the fourth month of the year 1096, hold a yabusame event. Yabusame means literally "shooting from a running horse!"

This means it is highly possible that certain unclear legends of Japanese warriors riding with the legions of Genghis Khan several centuries later may have been true. The Mongol conqueror was famous for archery-cavalrymen.

What is true is the definite ability of the Japanese archer on horseback. He would have been a formidable foe to meet on a field of battle. He was both an excellent horseman and excellent archer.

Unfortunately (or fortunately) due to the geopolitical confines of the Japanese islands, Japanese archers were never in combat except against other Japanese. However, in the Thirteenth Century, the archers were mounted and ready to meet the expected invasion of the Mongolian hordes under Kublai Khan who were sailing in a vast armada towards the Japanese islands. A typhoon destroyed the armada — and became known as the divine wind — or "kamikaze" — to the Japanese.

The classical ceremonial shooting of yabusame had 16, 10, 7, or even 36 shooters in former days — a grouping which could be symbolic of a cavalry troop. However, nowadays there are generally three shooters dressed in appropriate costume and mounted on horseback.

A yabusame shooting course of two cho is laid out. One cho equals approximately 119 yards — a little over a football field's length. The three horseback archers work as a team.

At a given official signal, they gallop along the course in tandem — or one after the other. They shoot at three targets, two feet square each. Each target is put on a pole three or four feet high, and posted at approximately thirty-yard intervals.

Notice, of course, the similarity of a two-foot square target atop a three or four-foot pole to the body of a man. Also, to test yourself for sheer archery skill, employ one horse, saddle, three targets, a stretch of ground equal to 238 yards, and a box with a quiver of arrows on your back. Then, set said horse a-gallop in a direction somewhat parallel to the three targets, then aim! shoot! re-string! aim! shoot! re-string! aim! shoot!

If you can imagine yourself doing the above in the time it takes you to deliberately read aloud the "aim! shoot!" sentence, than you know just how fast on the arrow-draw you have to be to hit the yabusame style target. Naturally, expert yabusame horsemen rarely miss.

Students of Japanese cinema — the films usually shown in art houses — will recall seeing some Japanese costume drama where horseback archers do engage in combat. As indicated in the original "platoon" arrangement of yabusame, and the present three-man team shoot, the archery-cavalrymen did have cavalry values for battle.

However, most of the individual glory has gone to the sword-wielding samurai who meets his rival at sun-up or sun-down in the wide open paddy fields or deserted village main street.

But the ceremonial yabusame shoot has more historical and costume value than a judo meet.

The ceremony itself was adopted by Minamoto, one of the two military families of feudal Japan. In uniting the various Japanese clans, Minamoto obviously used his archery-cavalrymen to distinct advantage. Then, for many generations the Minamoto clan held the annual yabusame ceremonial shoots.

In 1266 it became an annual affair at the famous festival of Hachiman Shrine at Kamakura. Kamakura is the ancient seat of the Bakufu, or "camp" government about sixty miles below Tokyo on the seashore. It is most famous in travel folders of Japan for the huge bronze statue of Buddha pictured there.

These Japanese characters designate the yabusame and are translated literally as "shooting from a running horse."

This ancient Japanese print illustrates the running course for the Japanese cavalry, used for centuries.

Sketch illustrates glove used in the Japanese archery sport. Of leather, there is a thong to tie about wrist. The thumb was thicker than fingers and was padded.

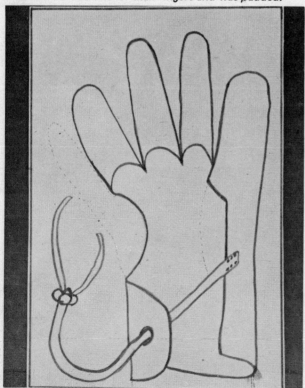

Visitors to Japan lucky enough to be at Hachiman Shrine at Kamakura in mid-September may see this exotic display of ancient archery skills any given year.

The ceremony also was held by Ashikaga about the same time that Yoritomo, the first Shogun of Minamoto, in 1186, was holding the festival at Kamakura. But the Nara ceremony fell into disuse during the latter part of the Ashikaga Shogunate (1338-1573).

When Lyeshige, the Shogunate heir, fell victim to small pox, his father ordered yabusame to be restored after the style given in the old records, and the ceremonial shooting was performed as an offering before the shrine at Takada, Edo, on the fifteenth of the third month, 1728, with a prayer that the Shogunate heir might be restored to health.

In 1875, seven years after the Restoration of 1868, Viscount Masanori Honda restored yabusame, which had all but died, and Prince Tokugawa gave it at his private residence in 1887 when the Emperor Meiji — often called by historians the "Lincoln of Japan" — was present at the performance.

Other than at Hachiman Shrine at Kamakura, yabusame is also held throughout Japan on certain felicitous occasions or at the yearly festival of any given local shrine. It is a ceremony-shooting match of great interest, typical of ancient Japan, and many foreigners make a special visit to shrines to see it.

For the archery-historian-linguist who would be accurate, we offer the definition of the word, *ya* — an arrow. In the illustration, one will notice the obvious similarity of the character of a man with a bow. As explained: "shooting an arrow from horseback."

Sirs, we took up the gauntlet and we did yabusame or whatever you may call it in the western world, or at least we did a western version of same.

Now we didn't just run out and gallop off with this little game; it took time and careful research. We got together at various times and one would ask how the horses were; they were fine but none available yet. How about the research on the course?

Occasionally the wife and I go to one of the you-rent-and-ride stables, fork a barn sour nag, and after an hour or so of fighting the critter's head to keep the crow bait from returning to the barn, we give up, give the monster its head and to the barn we go. When we have gone on these infrequent rides, I have managed always to get some odd looks from the owners by asking if they would mind if a group of archers came out and tried to shoot bow and arrows on horseback. They politely smiled and said sure. They immediately go to saddle or unsaddle a horse or to help someone out but they get away from me in a hurry.

"Nags wouldn't run anyway I bet" and we go back to the city and report at the next session of the erstwhile archers who want a ride and shoot club that it is nonexistent except for die-hards like me.

When I manage to attend a shoot and bring up the subject of ridem-shootem, the archers react like the stable owners. They go to find arrows in the north forty, but they always smile as they leave. This was beginning to give me a complex. I found many archers who stated that they were excellent riders and had ridden for years. Of course, being pro shooters on the range, they could hit any old target from a galloping horse. Naturally.

Sometime in the near future, the wife and I and our three-year-old tiger hied ourselves out to a stable for our yearly outing, and for a change, found a stable with decent horses. They had plenty of acreage, good horses, and the urge hit me again to do the yabusame bit. The wife groaned, and when we rode back in and headed for the office, she headed for the car and rolled up the windows. She's heard the groans and moans before when I hit people with such an idea.

These people didn't even bat an eye! I asked if they had horses that would allow a bow to be shot from their back at full gallop and not leave the rider in the dust?

"Sure, we've got horses here that have had shotguns fired from their backs." This stopped me, I knew they were trying to throw me off the track. Would they object to a group of archers, at their own risk, of course, attempting to shoot at three targets with a bow from the backs of galloping horses?

"Certainly not. You bring the archers, we'll provide the horses."

Six months later, I looked at the list I had compiled of the archers who said they would like to try the event. I finally had the horses. I hadn't checked but figured the stable was still there, and all we needed now was the time. Three weeks ago, we rolled into the ranch office again and explained that I wanted at least three, maybe four, horses for Sunday.

"Well, that's usually our busy day but if it were in the morning and we could have the horses after a short time, I guess it would be all right."

At last the green light; the hay burners; the works!

That night, I started calling. The list dwindled rapidly, as my cohorts suddenly were going out of town on a long weekend, relatives were coming down, or up, and they couldn't make it. At the finish I had the wife,

At a full gallop, one of the western-oriented yabusame experimenters prepares to loose an arrow at the target.

Ranch hand Don Schultz tried his hand at the unusual sport, managing to hit bale from running horse with his first shot.

This was the typical yabusame course used in ancient Japan, although distances were made to differ when a more difficult challenge was sought by competitors.

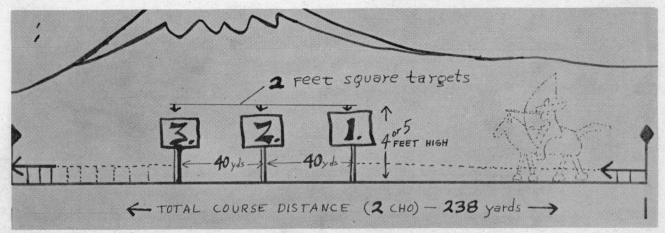

Jean, myself, another archer and his friend and an archer who had put up with my nonsense before and was willing to try again. As a clincher, a former six-goal polo player wanted to come along and try the game. He vowed he could hit the target with the sticks since it was more a matter of riding ability than archery ability. Now we had anarchy in the ranks. A rider who hadn't shot in his life, should prove interesting at any rate. Now all that was left was to lay out the course and shoot it.

Somewhere in the clutter of bows, 1929 *National Geographics,* pocket editions, broken arrows, arrow racks, camera equipment and other clutter that composes my den, I ferretted out that valuable copy of B&A from the year 1963 and checked the distances for the course. Saturday morning, I called Chuck Pelletier and asked him if he could help me lay out the course that evening.

"Sure. When and where?"

I loaded the tape measure, the copy of B&A and some marker stakes into Chuck's pickup and we headed out to Rancho Tierra on Highway 76 north of El Cajon, California. We drove into the yard and Billie Cope, the owner-operator, asked where we wanted to set up the course. I pointed to what looked like an area on the south side of a hill and she said there was a small ditch that wouldn't be too good but maybe we could bypass it.

Now this sport requires two *cho* as the Japanese measure, which with careful computation and calculation and a quick look at the conversion factor in B&A proved two *cho* to be equal to 218 yards, American style. That is almost half again as long as two football fields. The field I had in mind measured out to be one and one half *cho* before he hit the ditch.

*Chuck Pelletier releases an arrow while at full gallop. Arrow landed in bottom of the bale in spite of the fact that the horseman had **passed** target before he released.*

Next on the list was a narrow strip along a road, flanked by a grove of eucalyptus trees. We did a quick eye measure and saw it wouldn't be long enough either. It wouldn't give the rider time nor space in which to turn or stop his horse after the target run. I had a feeling that after all this time and research, the whole thing was going to fizzle due to lack of *cho* space.

We bumped across the next field, through a gate and over the top of a ridge into a level — well it had a slight rise — area that our trained eye knew had enough room to start the horse, shoot the course and stop or turn the horse in time to regain control.

Chuck and I jumped out and started leap frogging up the field with a fifty-foot tape, marking off the course. We found three excellent spots where we could place the targets at the prescribed forty-yard distance apart and have a good background to retrieve missed arrows.

No sooner had we finished marking off the course than Don Schultz, a ranch hand at Rancho Tierra, came bouncing over the now beaten path with a pickup loaded with six bales of hay. We off-loaded these and placed two bales at each marked spot.

We put one bale on the ground flat and braced the other bale in an almost vertical position on top of this with the two-foot side out and the long way up. Anyway, we had a two-foot surface to hit and some to spare for the near misses. The bale on the bottom, combined with the upright bale, gave us the four to

Bob Learn illustrates the technique found best for shooting one arrow, being ready for others, while riding the course at the horse's full gallop.

five-foot height required for all regulation yabusame shoots. One thing lacking in the article was the distance of the target from the course for the horses to run. We started with the bales at twenty yards from the horsepath but later changed this to about twenty feet. This bit of handiwork completed, we rode back to the ranch and reminded Billie that we would be out in the morning about 8:30. This would give us at least two hours before the crowd hit to take their weekly ride and would allow time to get good and saddle sore while we proved that we could do the game.

That night, I called another archer and asked him if he would be interested in this little game. He had to work but said he might show up and get some footage for the local newscast on KOGO TV, in San Diego where he works, if the news desk liked the idea.

Sunday morning, I headed for the ranch loaded down with bows, cameras, arrows, quivers and other tackle. Jean was going to follow with the polo player, Jack Ross, after the baby sitter showed up. When I darted into the ranch gate, Chuck was already there, sitting in the cab of his pickup, staring at the fog that enveloped the area in a white shroud. You could see about one hundred feet in front of you. Of all days to get fog!

Chuck had headed out to the ranch early since he had been intrigued by the number and size of the jackrabbits around the ranch.

"Got two," he remarked.

We headed on to the office and Don greeted us and said Billie was already over at the course. I took my wagon and Chuck took his pickup, since we both had too much gear to transfer. We bumped across the tracks made the night before and when we got to the course, Billie was dragging it with a log drag behind a truck. "Makes a better track for the horses to follow," she said. We were up early but she had been up earlier. Billie's husband, Marshall, had been grooming the horses and checking the saddles, so the horses came over almost immediately.

Chuck and I went down the course to double check the bales. Nothing had eaten them overnight, so we waited for the others and did our fog dance. Jean showed up with Polo Ross and a welcome thermos of hot coffee. Next to appear were Frank Eicholtz and Jimmie Davis. Don't let the name Jimmie confuse you, as she's a blonde archer-type female.

The four horses that Marshall brought over looked good. A white, a pinto, a grey and a bay. I'm partial to solid colors, so I struggled up on the grey's back, took a fast run at the course and found she was more than willing to run. Now, what would she do when I shot a bow from her back? I rode back to the wagon, reached over and picked up my fifty-one pound, fifty-four-inch Drake Hunter-Flight and an arrow out of the quiver. If I got thrown, best to have the arrows on the car and not in me. I rode up to the first bale, stopped Blue Bell — that's her name, Blue Bell — drew the bow, braced in the saddle, since I had dropped the reins on her neck in order to draw my bow and had no control on her at this point and let the arrow fly.

Nothing, absolutely nothing. The horse didn't flinch and I didn't hit the target, the bale or anything but the ground beyond. Nerves, you know. I rode back to the group since I now knew I had a horse that would cooperate. I loaded my quiver and decided to make a true run at yabusame, western style.

At this time, a white station wagon came bouncing over the hill. Jack Moorhead of Channel 10 had arrived. He would do his shooting with a 16mm camera, not a bow today. He wandered down the course and waited for the shoot to start.

I put Blue Bell into a fast gallop, reached back for an arrow from my quiver, but this proved quite a trick in itself. When I sat forward in the saddle, the arrows were forward in the quiver, but when I sat up and reached back for an arrow, they fell to the back of the quiver, making it a longer than normal reach. There I was, fumbling for an arrow, there went number one target, astride a galloping horse, bow in hand and the reins free. To ride and shoot, you have to drop the reins on the horse's neck. Finally I found an arrow, as number two target went bouncing by, nocked it and managed to get a fast going away shot at number three bale! This might not be so easy!

We all made runs at the targets, but they remained clean and clear, as we went into a war council. Moorhead was smiling, Don was smiling, and Billie was smiling.

Ross, who isn't an archer, had been getting some fast instruction from Jean, Frank, Chuck and Jimmie. He took the white horse, Crystal, galloped down the course and nonchalantly placed an arrow in the number one bale! He lost the other shafts so couldn't get any more shots off.

We went into another council and then Moorhead came up to ask how the course was laid out. We explained the problems of converting *cho* and the trouble of finding field long enough until someone shouted, "Forward, *cho*!!!!!"

That newly coined battle cry moved us all and we decided to move the targets closer to the running course and make some further attempts at yabusame.

This time, Frank tried one arrow nocked on the bow and the other two in his hip pocket. He just missed with the first and the other two fell out of his pocket. Next Chuck got an arrow off at the first target, starting with an arrow nocked, then got another shot at the third target.

"The bow was bouncing so badly I couldn't hold the arrow on it," he remarked when he returned. At least he had shot two arrows. Jean mounted the grey and streaked down the course, managing to get a couple off, sinking one in the third bale. Jimmie got up on the white and started down at a gallop, neared the first target and when she rose in the saddle to shoot, the horse stopped. Forward motion or pressure in the saddle brought Crystal to a stop each time. We decided she had been a roping horse at one time.

Ross had the pinto, Chubby, off to one side and was bending his ear, literally. He was explaining the course, what he wanted to do, what he wanted Chubby to do.

"I always did that with the polo ponies and it helped a great deal to explain these things to them." He booted Chubby into a gallop, the pony took off for the first target, ran straight up to it, then stopped and started to eat the bale. Ross hadn't made his instructions quite clear enough.

The fog was starting to lift; you could see the road along the field now. Cars would pass, screech and come backing up to find out what was going on. The drivers invariably smiled and drove off.

I dispensed with the back quiver, pocket quiver and all quivers. I nocked the first arrow on the string, took the other two in my bow hand and started my run. The first shot hit the side of the bale, the second missed the bale but I did get it off, and the third could be counted as a hit, since I barely pierced the bottom of the two-foot square cardboard face we had mounted on the bale.

Several others started getting hits. The second bale remained clear throughout the day but we did manage to get three shots off toward the targets, one at each, usually hitting the first and last bales. There is a minor problem with our style though. The yabusame start at full gallop, draw from the quiver, shoot, draw, shot and draw and shoot again, all from the back quiver. We had to hold an arrow on the string, and generally two others in the bow hand to get three shots off with perhaps a hit in the first and third bales. This was not according to yabusame techniques.

Moorhead shot quite a bit of footage, got into his

Jimmie Davis mounts up on unfamiliar horse to try her luck on the Japanese equestrian course that's updated.

staff car and stated that it might be used in the Monday night news feature spot. He smiled as he drove away.

Don Schultz thought it looked like fun, so he rode up and Frank gave him some instructions in archery and Don decided to make a run himself, with one arrow though, not three. He was mounted on a registered four year-old quarter horse that was a beauty. When he booted her, she literally jumped into a gallop and went flat out. Don drew as he neared the first bale and planted the shaft in the target face! Not only that time but on each occasion thereafter. He didn't try more than one arrow but he did far better than we had. For that matter, so had the former polo player, Jack Ross. This brought up the question, is it necessary to be a good archer to score in this game or a good rider? We weren't sure. Once we got our riding straightened out, we started hitting but the experienced riders had hit on the first attempt with no knowledge of archery.

Another problem was the length of the bow. The average bow used was sixty-six inches long. When one of these recurves lets the arrow go, it could come back and hit the horse a good whack in the side or shoulder and prove interesting for the rider. The Japanese use a seven-foot bow, with three feet of this length below the handle which would be a little longer than our 66 inch recurves. I had taken my fifty-four-inch hunter to see if the shorter bow made it any easier. We found no problem with any of the bows.

Monday I got a call from Moorhead. His news editor had liked the film and it would get about two minutes during the evening newscast. Sure enough, there it was, and this time we smiled. When you look at it from the other side, it is rather amusing.

Want to try it yourself? Lay out a level field with enough room to get a horse into full gallop, place three targets forty yards apart at a distance of about fifteen to twenty feet from the track, and have enough room at the end of the course to get control of your horse. To shoot, you have to drop the reins and just sit there, at full gallop. After you finish shooting, you start fumbling for the reins to bring your horse under control, all the time trying to keep your bow from digging the horse in the side and pitching you off. That's all you need to break the routine, and perhaps your foolish neck if you should be unlucky.

"Forward, *cho*!!!!!" —*Bob Learn*

Mounted samurai warrior pictured in ancient Japanese print wore, as protection, plated armor, a special protector over his back, as well as a horned helmet.

Chapter 26

SECRETS OF FLIGHT SHOOTING

The Turks Started It, But Modern Techniques And Materials Have Made Mile-Long Shots Not Unusual

MAHOUD EFFENDI was the secretary to the Turkish ambassador in London. Around or about 1794, just outside of London, Effendi shot an arrow 482 yards. The witnessess were amazed — that distance with a bow and arrow was unheard of. But Effendi shrugged modestly and told the admiring crowd that the Turkish sultan of the time, Selim III, could do infinitely better. And four years later, true to Effendi's word, the sultan shot an arrow 972 yards.

That was almost two hundred years ago, and, as it is considered a remarkable feat today, imagine the amazement of the people who saw it happen — if it did happen. You see, since the sultan was using a bow of unrecorded and unknown weight, and since we're really not too sure about the distance-measuring methods and unit (the gez) of the time, this 972-yard shot really isn't documented. But until September of 1976, even as today's flight shooters were suspicious and doubtful of the record, they were still feeling twinges of irritation that with today's sophisticated and improved flight equipment, the Turk's alleged record surpassed the current world record by far. Even as late as 1939, the record was only 517 yards. In 1947, the six hundred-yard mark was finally reached by the now-famed flight shooter Harry Drake. Drake, in 1958, went on to surpass the seven hundred-yard mark.

Year by year, flight shooters steadily inched closer to the Turk. Meanwhile, in 1971, Drake, who designs and builds most of today's flight equipment, shot his unlimited

Besides his record-breaking 1000-yard-plus shot, Bruce Odle also set new records in the amateur men's compound bow divisions.

footbow the incredible distance of 2028 yards — 268 yards more than a mile. But in the hand-held bow divisions, the sultan's "record" remained unchallenged. Then, in 1975, a young newcomer to the sport, Bruce Odle, shot one of Drake's bows 922 yards — a mere fifty yards from the Turk. Flight shooters held their breaths in anticipation of what just might happen in 1976.

The Bonneville Flight Range, adjacent to the Bonneville Salt Flats in western Utah, was muddy as the dawn broke on September 11, 1976, which was the first day of the National Flight Championships, sanctioned by the National Archery Association. It had rained heavily during the night, and though the sun was rising alone in the cornflower-blue sky, the air was cold.

An hour later, 23-year-old Odle shot a hand-held recurve bow 1077 yards and three inches — making him the first person ever to shoot a hand-held bow over 1000 yards. Even seconds after his release, the atmosphere turned from one of nervous expectation to excitement: Many, including Odle, himself, sensed that this shot might have pulled the Turk down. The small but dedicated group of flight shooters began the long, now-historical trek through the mud, eyes on the ground to avoid stepping on the arrows of other competitors — the long, thin arrows blended well with the gray-white salty ground of the flight range.

When Ike Hancock, the NAA Flight Chairman, first spotted the record-breaking arrow, many yards beyond the 1000-yard mark, he jumped nearly six feet in the air; Odle's wife Betsy was heard to remark, "The Turks have nothing on us now."

So what is flight and why haven't we heard much about it? Well, it might be said that flight shooting is the most specialized form of archery. It is so specialized and takes so much patience and work that there are only a limited

Equipment designer and builder Harry Drake adjusts Odle's 119-pound regular flight bow.

number of archers in the United States — and in fact the world — who shoot flight.

The flight archer's only concern is distance; his or her equipment and actions are based wholly and solely in the interest of getting the arrow to fly the maximum distance possible.

Procedure-wise, the National Flight Championships begin at dawn because of better shooting conditions — most importantly, the wind is usually down at that hour. If

Record breakers Irv Ambler and son R.J. begin the long trek out to retrieve flight arrows.

the equipment is available, the temperature, velocity and humidity at the time of the shoot are recorded.

The championships must be conducted in an extremely flat and barren area to avoid injury; the desolate Salt Flats of western Utah — where countless car commercials and Westerns have been filmed — were perfect for this. California's Death Valley was also used at one time.

Currently, there are two events at the championships — amateur and nonamateur — with various weight classes and types of bows in each event. The tournaments for compound flight and broadhead flight are also conducted — these two are separate from the rest of the championships because FITA, with whom the NAA is affiliated, does not recognize the compound bow. But the compound and broadhead flight tournaments are registered with the NAA and the records are recognized.

Whenever entries permit, there are also classes for regular flight footbows and crossbows.

Before the shoot, all arrows are registered: The arrow clerk takes down the serial numbers of the contestants' arrows and records them on his scorecard, together with the class to be shot and the code mark, if there is one, used for the event. The name of the contestant and the serial number of the arrow must be clearly marked on each arrow.

Next, the bows are officially weighed on the scales. A one-pound excess is allowed if the temperature is below seventy-two degrees Fahrenheit. In all events, a competitor may shoot six arrows and the farthest arrow shot by each competitor in each event is identified by a wire marker where the arrow entered the ground. The official measurer measures the distance of the arrow at a right angle to the C-line, which has been laid out in advance by the flight committee, with stakes placed every one hundred yards. Measuring the distances of the arrows is by far the most time-consuming part of the championships.

Extremely heavy bows must be used for achieving such distances as Odle's 1077-yard shot, and this fact immediately culls those of us who can't pull a·one hundred-pound-plus bow — at least culls us from ever hoping to take Odle's world record away, even though thirty-five, fifty, sixty-five and eighty-pound classes are available.

Odle's Drake-designed and constructed bow was 41½ inches in length and had a weight of 119 pounds at Odle's draw length of twenty-nine inches. As previously mentioned, Drake — working at Browning in Morgan, Utah — builds most of today's flight equipment, and currently holds all of the records in the nonamateur men's division, including the aforementioned 2028-yard unlimited footbow shot. Aside from Drake, the one remaining competitor who makes all of his own equipment is Vernon Godsey, who, with an amateur standing, currently shares with Ike Hancock the record for the amateur fifty-pound class and also holds the title in the amateur eighty-pound class.

Irv Ambler shot 459-2-8 with his compound to set a new record in broadhead flight.

R.J. Ambler gets last-minute pointers from NAA Flight Chairman Ike Hancock.

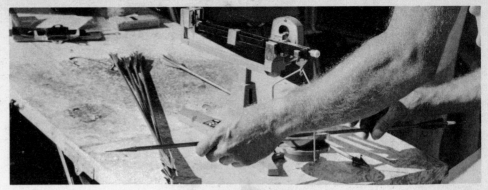

Arrows are weighed and then recorded preceding each class in the broadhead competitions.

Flight equipment is extremely specialized, with exaggerated features for ultimate distance efficiency. The conventional flight bow, from thirty-six to forty-two inches in length, is of composite construction — with Gordon Plastics' Bo-Tuff on the back and belly. The tips of the limbs are reinforced with synthetic material such as Micarda, to prevent breakage. The extended handle on the bow enables the flight archer to achieve a normal draw and to utilize the power in his back. The overdraw permits the shooting of a shorter, lighter, more efficiently designed and stable arrow. An elastic band is stretched across extensions on the sides of the overdraw as a safety feature to prohibit the arrow from being shot into the arm or hand if it is overdrawn off of the arrow rest. The centershot keyhole construction eliminates torque and any contact between the bow and arrow, and also distributes the energy of the bow to the center and allows precise alignment of the arrow.

A toothbrush arrow rest, three bristles wide and three bristles deep, is used on the flight bow, with the center bristles trimmed slightly to hold the arrow in place during the draw.

Kevlar string is now being used because of its proven strength — it eliminates the bow breakage that was due to string breakage. Flight bow tips must be reinforced in order to shoot with a Kevlar string, as this string has many times pulled through the nonreinforced tip. Ten to eighteen strands of Kevlar are used, depending on the weight of the bow.

Odle's record-setting flight arrow was made by Drake from Sweetland Forgewood — compressed cedar injected with resin — and was 18-3/8 inches in length from the tip to the floor of the nock. Most regular flight arrows are between seventeen and 18-3/8 inches in length; compound bow flight arrows are twenty-three to twenty-five inches in length. Besides Forgewood, flight arrows also are made of fir, lodgepole pine and Magnamite — which is solid graphite-resin dowel. Much experimentation with the Magnamite arrow is being conducted, and Flight Chairman Hancock believes that this material may make all other shafting for the conventional flight bow obsolete.

"Although a Forgewood arrow set Odle's new world record, the Magnamite arrow has been performing more consistently and at greater distances than Forgewood," says Hancock.

The arrow design for all conventional flight arrows is tapered at both ends, with a small (.013-inch diameter) point of brass or aluminum. The nocks usually are made of plastic, with a diameter of three-sixteenths of an inch. But for the unlimited bow, a nock of aluminum or brass must be used because the plastic nock will not take the force and breaks — which may result in a broken arrow or even a broken bow. While the fletching on most flight arrows

Above: Close-up of the heavy flight compound bow handle. Below: Odle's 119-pound regular flight bow and Drake-made 18-3/8-inch arrows.

usually is plastic, Drake used razor blades on Odle's and some of the other flight bows.

According to the official tournament rules approved by the National Archery Association Flight Committee, mechanical drawing and release aids are prohibited from the flight competition because they are prohibited in all NAA tournaments and NAA-sponsored events. According to the rules, "mechanical" means "...any method that embodies a plurality of interacting parts, capable of cooperatively acting to affect bowstring release by a separating motion of at least one such part relative to another."

To be legal, the flight release must be held in the hand. No attachment or anchor of any kind above the hand is permitted. For these reasons, three types of releases are used exclusively in flight shooting. The first is a double-strap release with rubber backing on one side that is stretched so that the outer strap will flip away from the

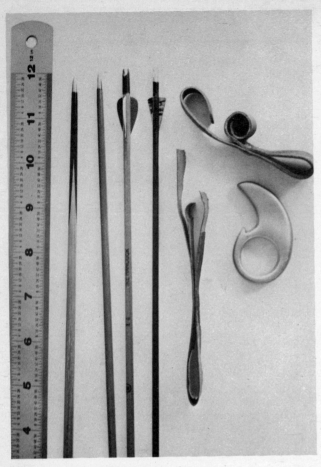

Above: First three flight arrows from left are Forgewood; fourth is Magnamite. Releases are only types allowed in flight. Below: Compound and regular flight bows — both are of composite construction.

string upon release. The shorter inner strap is first placed around the string and then the longer rubber-backed outer strap is positioned over the first strap. The archer's thumb and forefinger hold these straps together around the string with the thumb placed against the rubber backing.

The triple-strap release is made from thinner material, such as synthetic woven strapping, with no rubber backing. First, the shortest strap is placed around the string, barely overlapping it. The second, slightly longer strap is put over the first and then the third and longest strap is placed around these two and the string is held between the thumb and forefinger, pressing against a strip of medium emery cloth glued to the release in order to obtain the necessary grip.

The third legal release is the commercial metal, one-piece Six Gold used mainly on the heavy bows due to the more positive grip it affords. The index finger is placed in the hole of the Six Gold and the forefinger hooks over the extension. The hook on the Six Gold holds the string until the forefinger is released.

If the equipment sounds complicated, it is — and shooting it is possibly even more so.

"One psychological factor in flight archery that most archers are not aware of until they try it is being able to obtain the maximum draw from the bow, which requires bringing the tiny brass point of the arrow back into the one-quarter-inch toothbrush arrow rest and releasing at that instant," Hancock explains. "Those who can accomplish this with smoothness and perfect timing are a sight to behold. The brief flash of the arrow point into the brush rest often brings a gulp of appreciation to those watching. The inability to accomplish this necessity might be compared to the target archer freezing off the target. And those flight archers who cannot do this without recklessness should not attempt it."

There's another misconception about flight archery — that all one needs is strength to pull back that heavy bow and get that arrow to fly those incredible distances.

"The flight archer who can draw the one hundred-pound

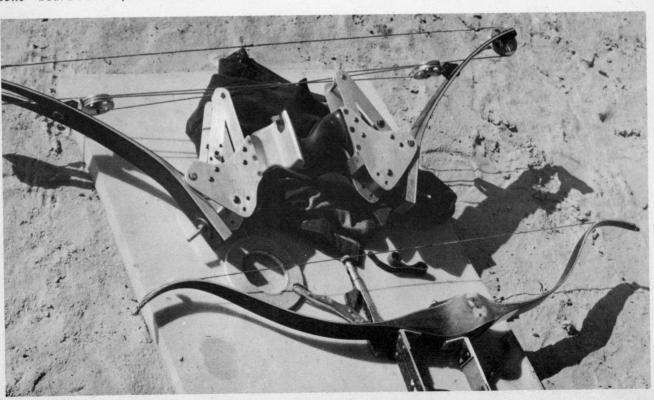

Besides holding the record in the fifty-pound class, Myrna Ambler shot a new record in the amateur women's thirty-five-pound class.

Bob and Arlyne Rhode set new records in the nonamateur men's and women's divisions. He shot 885-0-2 in compound flight, while she shot 675-1-6 in unlimited regular flight.

bow is looked upon with envy by many archers," says Hancock. "This capability does not, however, mean that the archer who can draw this weight will attain phenomenal distances such as Odle has. As a novice in 1974, Odle showed great promise. And in 1975, shooting Drake's equipment, Odle broke Drake's own world record. Since that time he has exceeded Drake's hand-held conventional flight bow record — which was 856 yards, one foot and eight inches — with the 1077-yard three-inch shot at the 1976 National Archery Association Flight Championships." In other words, strength is not the only requirement — it also takes skill and practice.

While Odle, alone, appears in the 1977 edition of the Guinness Book of World Records — with his 1975 record, due to an early print deadline — many other records were broken at the 1976 Championships. Among those not already mentioned, new records were set in both the nonamateur men's and women's divisions by the husband and wife team of Bob and Arlyne Rhode. He shot 885 yards and two inches in compound flight, while she shot 675 yards, one foot and six inches in the unlimited regular flight. In the broadhead flight competition, Irv Ambler set a new record in the eighty-pound compound bow class with a distance of 459 yards, two feet and eight inches, while his sons Bob and R.J. set new records in the junior boys' regular flight divisions. Myrna Ambler continues to hold the records in the amateur women's division in both the thirty-five and fifty-pound classes. Ted Roeder set a new record in the amateur men's sixty-five-pound class. So the awards ceremony on the final day of the 1976 Championships was a happy one — everyone heaped praise on everyone else, particularly Bruce Odle.

When asked how he felt to be the first person in history to shoot a hand-held bow over 1000 yards, Odle modestly remarked only that he was very honored. Later, after what he had accomplished sunk in a bit and most of the shock wore off, Odle expounded further.

"I owe a lot to Harry Drake," he says. "He got me interested in flight shooting. He and I both work at Browning — I'm the production manager for the fishing rod division — and shortly after I started working there, somebody pointed out Drake to me and said, 'That man shot a bow over a mile.' They were talking about his 2028-yard unlimited footbow record. Anyway, I was intrigued, and I started visiting his shop. Finally, I got him to agree to make an unlimited flight bow for me and I started to shoot flight in 1974...." We all know the rest of Odle's story.

Flight shooting is an exciting and challenging sport. But even as it grows in popularity, it is still grossly ignored in most archery circles. Flight shooters are eager to admit other interested archers into their ranks — there's much speculation and a lot of hopes about the future.

"An 1100-yard-plus conventional hand-held flight shot would not be surprising with Odle shooting Drake's equipment," says Hancock. "Although this 1100-yard-plus shot may never happen, Odle's current world record for the conventional hand-held bow may last as long as the Turkish one." And if anybody is interested in attempting to break this record or in simply getting into flight for the fun and excitement he or she should write to Ike Hancock, NAA Flight Chairman, at 2782 McClelland Street, Salt Lake City, Utah 84106 for more information. — *Jacqueline Farmer*

NATIONAL ARCHERY ASSOCIATION FLIGHT RECORDS

Title Holder	Bow Weight or Class	Distance (yards, feet, inches)	Year
Amateur Men			
Ike Hancock Vernon Godsey	50 lb.	729-2-6	1976
Ted Roeder	65 lb.	786-0-2	1976
Vernon Godsey	80 lb.	892-2-6	1976
Bruce Odle	Unlimited	1077-0-3	1976
Danny LaMore	Footbow	937-13-0	1959
George Alevekiu	Crossbow	1313-2-0	1967
Amateur Women			
Myrna Ambler	35 lb.	554-2-10	1976
Myrna Ambler	50 lb.	649-0-10	1975
Norma Beaver	Unlimited	718-0-8	1967
Norma Beaver	Footbow	881-1-1	1967
Intermediate Girls (age 15-17)			
Peggy Dunaway	35 lb.	418-1-1	1946
Peggy Dunaway	50 lb.	427-2-9	1946
Peggy Dunaway	Unlimited	393-1-10	1946
Junior Girls (age 12-14)			
April Godsey	35 lb.	425-1-3	1969
April Godsey	50 lb.	397-1-7	1970
April Godsey	Unlimited	468-0-10	1969
Intermediate Boys (age 15-17)			
William Mendels	35 lb.	548-1-6	1970
William Mendels	50 lb.	647-2-0	1969
Kelly Reynolds	Unlimited	667-2-5	1975
Junior Boys (age 12-14)			
Bob Ambler	35 lb.	470-1-3	1976
R.J. Ambler	50 lb.	579-0-4	1976
R.J. Ambler	Unlimited	655-2-6	1976
Nonamateur Men			
Harry Drake	50 lb.	754-1-10	1976
Harry Drake	65 lb.	780-2-0	1976
Harry Drake	80 lb.	851-0-3	1967
Harry Drake	Unlimited	856-1-8	1967
Harry Drake	Footbow	1048-1-0	1967
Harry Drake	Crossbow	1359-2-5	1967
Harry Drake	Unlimited Footbow	2028-0-0	1971

Title Holder	Bow Weight or Class	Distance (yards, feet, inches)	Year
Nonamateur Women			
Monica Wildenberg	35 lb.	495-1-7	1968
Monica Wildenberg	50 lb.	566-0-11	1967
Arlyne Rhode	Unlimited	675-1-6	1976

UNLIMITED COMPOUND BOW REGULAR FLIGHT

Amateur Men			
Bruce Odle		977-0-2	1976
Amateur Women			
Myrna Ambler		351-2-11	1975
Nonamateur Men			
Bob Rhode		885-0-2	1976
Nonamateur Women			
Arlyne Rhode		612-1-5	1976

BROADHEAD FLIGHT RECORDS

COMPOUND BOW

Amateur Men			
Irv Ambler	80 lb.	459-2-8	1976
Bruce Odle	Unlimited	493-0-1	1976
Amateur Women			
Myrna Ambler	80 lb.	193-0-9	1975
Nonamateur Men			
Bob Rhode	80 lb.	428-2-5	1976
Bob Rhode	Unlimited	467-2-7	1976
Nonamateur Women			
Arlyne Rhode	80 lb.	333-2-0	1976

CONVENTIONAL BOW

Amateur Men			
Bruce Odle	Unlimited	433-0-10	1976
Amateur Women			
Myrna Ambler	80 lb.	239-2-8	1975
Nonamateur Men			
A. Reynolds	Unlimited	398-1-4	1975
Nonamateur Women			
Arlyne Rhode	80 lb.	315-2-10	1976

Chapter 27

A CROSS TO BEAR

Today's Crossbow Fancier Is A Member Of A Small But Enthusiastic Group Of Sportsmen!

The women crossbow champs at the 1976 Nationals were, from left, Grace Kremer, third place; Carol Pelosi, first place; and Barbara Sacco, second place. Photo by Bob Cacace.

In the men's division, George Hall took first prize with a comfortable margin over his closest competitors, Thomas Phipps and Charles Sacco. Photo by Bob Cacace.

Zaphyrus, A RESIDENT of the Greek city of Tarentum, is usually credited with the invention of the crossbow — and that was way back in 300 B.C. But the crossbow gained its eminence as the deadly weapon of terror in the Middle Ages. It is said that the crossbow was introduced into England by the Normans during the invasion in 1066.

Since then, the crossbow has had a long and turbulent history and today, while it is illegal to hunt with a crossbow in most states, crossbow enthusiasts are hoping that their sport will begin to play a bigger role in target archery.

There were over three hundred longbow archers at the 1976 championship tournament in Pennsylvania's Valley Forge State Park. There were nineteen crossbowmen. How better to describe the state of the art than this? But let's look at the brighter side: The figure nineteen represents the largest contingent ever to take part in a national tournament, dating back to the Amherst, Massachusetts, contest in 1947, where the crossbow shooter was first allowed to participate in this gala event.

You can carry this a step further. Archery is often described as America's fastest growing sport. The National Archery Association has a membership of 5000 — three hundred of them participated in the 1976 championships. That's only six percent. There are only 150 members in The National Crossbowmen. Nineteen of them participated in their national tournament. That is over twelve percent!

Membership turnover in organized crossbow archery is greater than that in the longbow group, although it is disturbingly great for both. It takes longer for a novice longbow archer to peak out, or reach his probable potential, than it does for a new crossbow enthusiast, and when it happens many start looking for something else to do. In those few cases where the levelling-out plateau turns out to be a lofty peak, they stay longer — and as often as not they are hooked for life.

Credit for getting target crossbow competition into the National Archery Association family belongs to Henry L. Bailey, who was from Elizabeth, New Jersey. Those who knew him called him Gran'pa Bailey, and the crossbow he designed held most of the records for many years. Today, one would be hard pressed to find that style of bow in serious competition anywhere in this country. A bona fide Bailey Crossbow has become a collector's item.

There were other pioneers, besides Gran'pa Bailey, who should be mentioned whenever the history of crossbow target archery is discussed. Colonel Francis Pierce, USMC ret., was the first and only first captain of the National Company of Crossbowmen, forerunner of The National Crossbowmen. Mrs. Murvil (Fannie) Brumble was first lady — a Company office — for many years, although Ms. Verrel Weber from Colonel Pierce's home state of California did precede her in that position. Fred Isles was the first Company scribe. Then, in 1959, the colonel severed his and the Company's relations with the NAA and The National Crossbowmen — today's target organization — was formed to fill the breach.

Isles became the first president of TNC, Paul Eytel was named vice-president and Fannie Brumble became secretary-treasurer — a position she held until 1976 when

TNC roving awards placed in competition each year at the Nationals — Championship cups plus King's Dagger award, Karl Traudt International Round Trophy, Queen's Scepter and Crossbow Clout Trophy. Photo by Bob Cacace.

she asked to be relieved of the assignment. Her husband, Murvil, also pioneered in the sport — he helped in the development of the crossbow itself, improving upon the original Bailey design.

Several exceptionally fine marksmen appeared in those

Hot competition between the women at the Nationals. Photo by Bob Cacace.

early days — Paul Eytel was one of them, shooting scores in the Fifties that are seldom equalled to this day. Stanley Turner, from England, was another. Turner is still active, heading The British Crossbow Society and is Great Britain's crossbow champion for 1976, a title he has held on many past occasions as well. Years ago, there usually was a big gap between the scores shot by these two gentlemen and those of other contestants, but this gap is now just a crack and today's top crossbow scorers have to scramble for it to stay out in front. The excitement of close competition is where it belongs — right at the top.

The crossbow has changed significantly since the days of Gran'pa Bailey, and still other changes are being planned. Basically, a crossbow is the product of the crossing of a rifle and a bow — using the trigger stock and sights of a rifle for firing and aiming, and the design and mechanics of the bow for its shooting style and power. A short but powerful bow is attached at right angles across the front part of stock.

Earlier model crossbows had the bow, or prod, mounted underneath the barrel, which caused an energy-draining drag on the bowstring as it pushed an arrow down a grooved guiding tract. This was thought to be necessary as otherwise the string would jump and flutter down the track when an arrow was released. It turns out that this phenomenon doesn't matter that much, or perhaps the flutter is exactly the same for each shot. At any rate, most target crossbows today have the bow mounted on top of the barrel and the string just kisses the barrel surface or rides entirely free.

Many crossbowmen now rely on a front arrow rest, similar to those used on longbows, instead of the grooved arrow track of yesteryear. The squared-off flat arrow nock is also fading into disuse, and either full longbow-type nocks or a half-nock, with the lower "ear" snipped off, are taking its place. The probable reason for squared nocks in the first place was the diameter of crossbow strings in Medieval Days — a longbow nock would not fit. Otherwise, this change might have taken place then, instead of now.

Another innovation many crossbowmen have adopted is a string loop at the exact center of the bowstring, which hooks over the release latch or finger. The loop absorbs much of the violence that takes place when a taut bowstring parts company with a metal-holding finger. It has been shown by high-speed photography that a latch that breaks down into the stock causes considerable string jump; a latch that breaks up causes less jump; and when a string loop is used in conjunction with either, no jump at all can be detected.

Until quite recently, crossbow archery carried the stigma of being a game played by over-the-hill longbow archeritics. The original charter developed by the National Company of Crossbowmen, at their founding meeting during the Los Angeles national competition in 1951, suggested as much:

"...This company is composed of members of the National Archery Association of the United States, who either from desire, or force of circumstances, shoot the crossbow rather than the longbow."

Some longbow archers still think of crossbowmen in that light, but if they do they haven't been watching crossbow activity very closely in recent years. The NAA's 1976 indoor crossbow champion was Randi Kremer, from Rydal, Pennsylvania, and at that time Kremer had just turned 16. The women's champion in 1976, for both indoor and outdoor competition was Carol Pelosi from Greenbelt, Maryland — an attractive young miss who had never shot a longbow in her life.

No distinction between men and women is made at some crossbow tournaments, such as the annual Eastern Championships or the contest for the coveted Karl Traudt International Round Trophy that is held in conjunction with the national championships each year. A number of women have won these contests — Lillian Eytel, Margaret Breneman and Carol Pelosi, to name a few. All of today's records, by men as well as women, were established with crossbows having a pull weight of less than fifty pounds, which was considered quite light in earlier years. Perhaps the greater violence that a heavier weighted bow imparts on an arrow is the reason for this. It is also possible to match

Barbara Clapham, (Second from left) shot a modified Whamo Powermaster crossbow, as second-placer Barbara Sacco (Second from right) shot a modified Bailey-style bow. Photo by Bob Cacace.

*Shooting and spotting — common crossbow procedure at the 1976
Nationals in Valley Forge, Pennsylvania. Photo by Bob Cacace.*

one of today's bows with a lighter weight arrow, thus retaining almost as much speed as before. Most crossbowmen weight the points of their arrows to offset their fifteen inches or less length, the shortness of which gives a more critical missile than their longer cousin shot from a longbow.

One question often is asked — where can one find competition if he takes up crossbow archery? You have a choice of moving to where the action is, building up your own local competition, or resigning yourself to rather extensive travel. In addition to two national tournaments — one indoor, one outdoor — and the aforementioned Eastern Championships, you can find some serious crossbow competition at such places as the Brown County Open in Indiana, and at a number of state archery championships including Pennsylvania, Maryland, New Jersey, New York, and others, with Ohio planning such an event for the future.

Each year, crossbowmen also hold one or two international mail matches with their counterparts in countries such as Sweden, Ireland, England and Canada. At this writing, a live international event is being planned in Dublin, Ireland, at which time those who participate will have the opportunity to meet some of their mail-match friends in person.

Then there is an annual TNC-sponsored tournament in Tell City, Indiana, during the second week in August, when that Swiss-colonized community holds its yearly Sweizer Fest, commemmorating the legendary crossbowman Wilhelm Tell and his son Walther. The crossbow tournament is listed as one of the feature attractions at this festival.

Many local archery clubs include competition for crossbows, and others probably will if they are approached about the subject.

There also are two national organizations that emphasize the hunting aspect of crossbow shooting. The American Crossbow Association is one of them, and was founded by veteran crossbowman George Stevens. Although the ACA places most emphasis on hunting, they do sponsor two target events each year: Their Duster Shoot — i.e. dust off your equipment and start shooting — is held in the Spring, and their annual championship is the second weekend in October. Both events are held in Huntsville, Arkansas.

The more recently formed crossbow-hunting organization is the National Crossbow Hunters Association, with present headquarters in Ohio — the latest state to modify its hunting regulations to permit crossbow hunting.

Arkansas has allowed hunting with the crossbow for some time — thanks to the efforts of George Stevens. A number of states permit the use of crossbows during the gun hunting seasons, while Kentucky, Arkansas and Ohio have designated special areas and separate seasons for them. Although Arkansas has one of the most liberal crossbow seasons of all, it is against the law to shoot the lowly carp fish with it. You can use a longbow for this, but not a crossbow. In North Dakota, Louisiana and Oklahoma, only persons with severe disabilities are allowed to use crossbows. In South Carolina, crossbows may be used only on land not under control of the state. Texas only allows their

Nineteen crossbow competitors took part in the four-day 1976 Nationals in Valley Forge. Photo by Bob Cacace.

use in thirty of that state's 254 counties. Crossbows are banned in Alabama. And finally, you won't see any crossbow hunting or even crossbow tournaments in West Virginia — it is illegal for residents of that state to possess a crossbow.

Those seeking additional information about organized target crossbow archery should contact G. Frey, correspondence secretary, The National Crossbowmen, 203 Laytonsville Road, Gaithersburg, Maryland 20760. For information about organized crossbow hunting, write to George Stevens at the American Crossbow Association, P.O. Box 72, Huntsville, Arkansas 72740 or J. Michael Watkins, president, National Crossbow Hunters Association, Incorporated, 201 Citizens Bank Building, Wadsworth, Ohio 44281. – *Gil Frey*

Barbara Clapham and Barbara Sacco at the Nationals. Note crossbow construction. Photo by Bob Cacace.

Chapter 28

BUILDING A RECURVE BOW AT HOME

Bingham Archery in Ogden, Utah, offers several methods for the novice or pro bowyer to build a bow at reasonable costs.

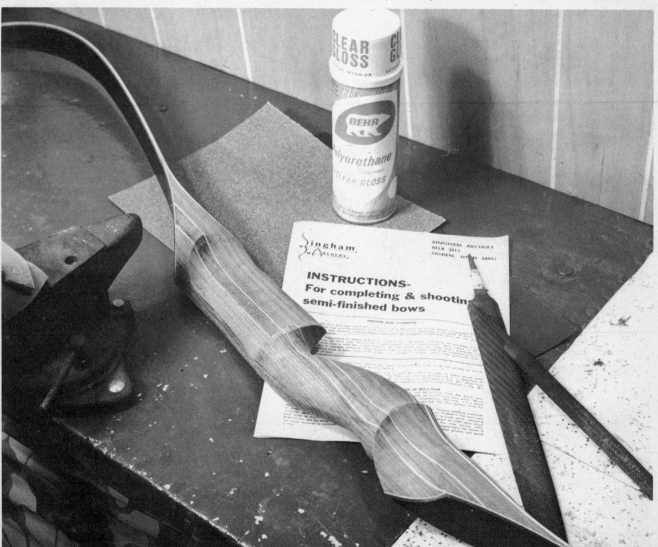

This Model Is Offered — Semi-Finished — In Three Different Stages Of Production

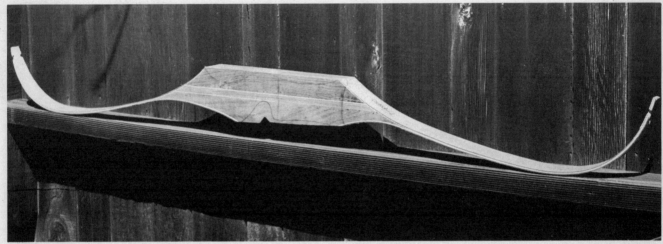

Bingham's Basic model comes with the sight window and handle marked off on the riser, with limbs tillered and nocks cut.

SOONER OR LATER you have to try it; many have wanted to, but just didn't feel quite up to the rather demanding project. Occasionally, while thumbing through archery-oriented magazines, they'd see ads offering all the raw materials needed to build a homemade bow. But to build a bow from scratch, using the laminates and riser materials offered, requires the fabrication of a jig and forms, and most simply lack the time and, perhaps, the inclination.

Bingham Archery in Ogden, Utah, has taken these factors into consideration and offers several routes for the novice or pro bowyer. One can buy the components and go

This Deluxe model comes with the sight window cut out, the handle cut and also some shaping on the riser.

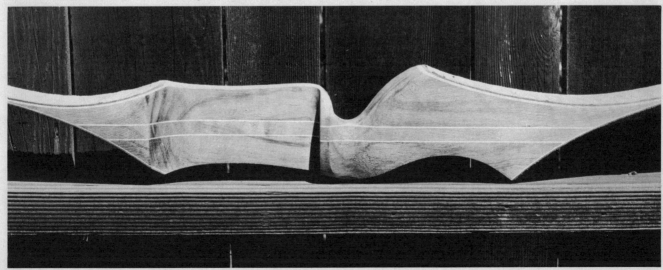

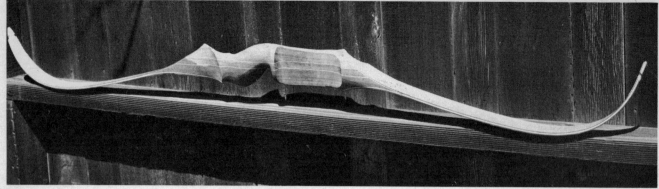

The Custom model has nocks cut, tapered and handle shaped for its final fitting. It only needs final sanding and painting.

from scratch — as most would like to try, but it usually requires more shop tools than are accessible. A simpler approach is to buy the semi-finished bows offered by Bingham Archery.

After considering several of their products, the decision was made to build their Custom Super 62-inch Hunter.

Available in lengths from the short fifty-two-incher to the sixty-two-inch model, the complete listing includes bows of fifty-two, fifty-six, fifty-eight, sixty and sixty-two inches. Each bowhunter has a favorite bow length, and Bingham caters to just about all needs; including a take-down hunter model.

After determining the length desired, the decision must be made as to what stage of production you want the bow to be in, and three choices are available.

The first model is the Basic, and it is just that. It has the limbs tillered and the string nocks cut in, the sight window marked on the riser block, as well as handle contours, plus some shaping of the riser itself. To finish this bow requires a band saw to cut the sight window and handle sections properly. This possibly could be done with a saber or hack saw, utilizing great care, since a good clean cut is essential for this finishing process — and plenty of time to do it properly.

Second choice is the Deluxe bow, which has the sight window and handle sections cut in, and the contours of the riser shaped but not finished. The limbs are tillered and string nocks cut, so all that's needed is to finish the bow in choice of style. This can be accomplished with hand tools or power sanders, as the majority of the critical work already is done.

Naturally, the cost is higher than for the Basic model, but if shop tools are limited, this is an excellent choice.

The third model is the Custom Bingham bow. This model has the riser cut, fluted and shaped with power sander, limbs are tillered, string nocks cut and tapered, and the string guide cut into the limbs. This is the most expensive of the three models, yet still a great bargain. All that's needed to finish-out this bow are some rasps, sandpaper and time. If new to the game of bow making, this might be the best model with which to begin.

Costs are extremely reasonable, plus there's a three-year guarantee against any material flaws.

When the Custom arrived, it had the sanding from the power equipment in evidence, but the basic shape of the bow was a beauty to behold. The fluting and contours were, at first, considered too much for a hunter and the idea of cutting the contours down was considered. But just because it was to be used in the hunting field didn't mean it had to look like a brute at the same time, so they were left.

This Custom model handle, offered by Bingham Archery, comes pre-sanded and requires only final sanding and painting.

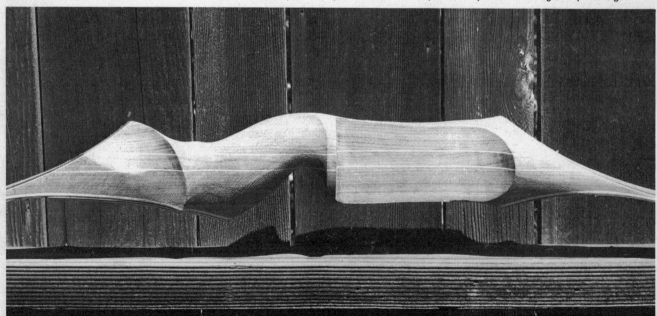

A package containing the bowstring, shooting rest and side plate were included, along with a pack of sandpaper and a can of polyurethane spray finish.

The first step in finishing-out the Custom Hunter was to work the raw fiberglass off the limbs. Bingham makes their bows with Gordon Bo-Tuff fiberglass facing and backing. The limbs are wide and the laminates are tapered.

All that's required is to remove the masking tape from the glass, starting at the riser and peeling toward the tip. If a sliver of glass should come up with the tape it will diminish rather than increase, since the limbs are tapered toward the tips.

To check out the bow weight, the bow was braced using a DEI bracing unit and it trued at fifty-three pounds at twenty-eight inches, just as marked on the limbs. Don't try to use any push-pull or other system at this point or you will get a handful of fiberglass slivers — the limb edges are still raw from the band sawing.

After unbracing the bow, the unit was clamped in a vise — with padded jaws to protect the wood — and the limbs were rasped from the inside toward the outer edge to keep from raising slivers.

Start the rasping with a medium rasp, and move from the riser toward the tip. Do both sides of the limb and both sides of the bow, face and back. Don't try to take so much as to lighten the draw weight. All that's needed is to bevel the edges so they won't catch on the bowstring or hand when bracing. Move from the riser to the tip and from the inside-out at an angle, rasping until the white of the maple laminate used in the midsection of the limb is visible.

After the medium rasp, follow-up with a fine rasp or go to medium-grit sandpaper. Sand the entire face and back of the limbs and don't worry about scratches; but take it easy with the coarser grits.

The final finish is with 400 grit sandpaper on the facing and backing and around the edges of the limbs. This gives the finish a surface to adhere to and removes any epoxy that might be on the limb edges.

Once the limbs have been finished, move to the riser section. The sight window is simple; just use sandpaper or a medium rasp to remove the sanding marks from the factory. The same rasp can be used on the entire riser to the same degree. About all the shaping required is to fit the handle to one's style of shooting. This is the big advantage

The tip is tapered and nock cut for final sanding. Protective masking tape (white area) is later removed.

Models are shipped with fiberglass facing and backing. First step is to work it off of the limbs.

To take the tape off, start peeling from the riser and peel toward the tip.

of finishing-out your own bow. The handle shape can be of any style.

Work the entire riser section with one grit of sandpaper at a time, moving to successively finer grits to remove marks left by the other, and so on until the final finish of 400. The hardest parts are the cross-grain sections just under the sight window and above the handle grip area. Where there's a cross grain, more care must be exercised to get the area sanded smoothly for the next grit.

When sanding sharp contours or fluted areas, sand up to and follow through, never going over the edge or it will become rounded; unless, of course, rounded edges are wanted.

During sanding of the riser section and handle the bow can be field tested by putting on the string and shooting a few arrows. This confirms the grip as to fit and enables changes to be made before applying the finish coat.

All the sanding could be done in one long evening or, better yet, over a weekend, and checking for fit and finish at each step.

After the final 400 grit was finished, my bow was taken out for a final shooting before the finish was applied. A glove was worn on the bow hand to keep body oils from getting into the wood. The handle felt great, it fit the way I wanted, but in the sunlight a few marks from the coarser paper were noted. These were removed once back in the shop, using 400 true grit. This left nothing to do but wait for the sun to warm the riser and limbs before applying the spray finish.

The riser and limbs should be covered with a protective coating of either epoxy or the newer polyurethane finishes. A rifle stock epoxy finish could be used, but I used the Behr polyurethane spray as supplied by Bingham. This bow will be camouflaged later, but the full protective coat is needed to prevent moisture from getting into the riser or the limb laminates.

A clean, dust-free and dry area should be selected for spraying. I chose a back section of the patio where there was little or no wind and good light to see by, plus the drying factor of sunlight. If there are any marks on the riser or limbs they will show up in bright sunlight. The bow was hung by one end, the spray can moved according to instructions on the can, and a fine, light coat was applied. The bow was reversed and the other end done in the same manner. Don't try to apply one heavy coat; it is better and easier to apply about three light ones.

The bow was left until midafternoon, then removed from the rack and 400 sandpaper used to finish-out runs that developed plus some bubbles on the finish. These were sanded smooth, the limbs, riser and entire bow wiped clean of dust with paper toweling. Rags usually have detergent or oil in them, so I use the always present paper towels for dust removal with great success. The bow was checked over again and the spray procedure repeated that afternoon.

You can't rush the finishing procedure. I waited a minimum of four hours before sanding and apply the second coat of polyurethane. This was left overnight, again sanded with the 400 grit and the final coat of spray applied when the sun became warm. The third coat brought out the lustre and depth of color in the woods of the riser, and the finish stayed smooth as it should.

The finished bow looks as the pictures said it would and shoots well. To check the bow weight of fifty-one pounds, suggested as the finished weight by Bingham, I reweighed the bow. It trued at fifty-one pounds, so I finished the limbs properly. If too much is hogged off the edges, draw weight of the bow will be lightened.

One final tip: Before applying the finish, place the serial number and draw weight on the bow for future reference. I placed this data on the white fiberglass overlay below the handle section on the riser, using a permanent marking felt-tip pen. Although the bow will be camoed, that information is there if I ever need it.

After the final coat had set long enough, the mohair pad, cut to fit, was placed on the shelf of the bow and the side

plate of the same material placed on the sight window. This finished the bow except for the final shooting. My range will give me forty-eight yards maximum and the bow placed the arrows as well as I can shoot them from that distance — and much better at closer ranges. The bow will be shot-in and the finish allowed time to cure before it is camoed for the hunting field. With the poly finish on the limbs and riser, I can't hurt it with any of the camo processes, so the bow is fully protected.

This made an enjoyable weekend project, but could be accomplished in a shorter time. Since this initial effort turned out so well, I plan to order the Deluxe unit of the same style, do more work on it and make my own shape on the riser; ending up with a matched pair of hunting bows. You can't hardly beat the price, plus having the personal satisfaction of doing it yourself.

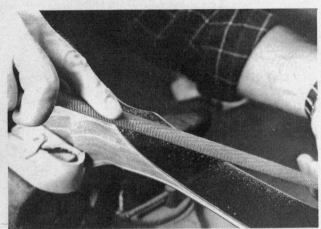

Rasp edges to remove fiberglass slivers and give beveled finish. Then bevel until white maple laminates are visible.

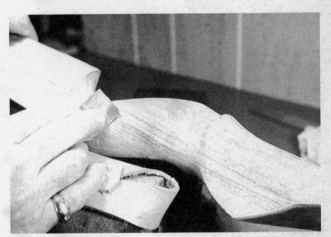

After handle is shaped to fit, use sandpaper to smooth out. Drop to finer grit each sanding and use 400 grit for final.

Author tests partially homemade Bingham Custom bow. Elated with initial results, he plans to try finishing a Deluxe model.

Chapter 29

Test shooting was benchrest style for accuracy. The hard part was bracing the 125-pound bow for firing many rounds.

MAKE A CUSTOM CROSSBOW

IT'S ILLEGAL TO hunt with a crossbow in many states, so why bother building one? For me it was the challenge of trying to put together an instrument that's accurate for more than one shot and customizing it beyond the commercial models.

Components were collected from many sources. The bow was made by Harry Drake some years ago for a crossbow, but never was mounted on a stock. The limbs, including the center core, are of laminated fiberglass; there is no maple laminate as usually is found in limb construction. The limbs are on a keyhole setup that allows the bolt to be shot through the center. One must feed the bolt through the center, but that's a mild inconvenience.

The limbs measure thirty-six inches from string nock to string nock. With a brace height of four inches and drawing it back fourteen inches from the belly of the bow, it generates 125 pounds in draw weight. The accuracy so far has proved exceptional.

The maple stock is a Royal Arms second thumb-hole style with a high, rollover Monte Carlo cheekpiece. High-comb stocks for crossbows give the shooter enough eye height to see what he's shooting at. The high, rollover comb on this rifle stock is designed for telescopic sights and has a similar principle behind it.

I added a recoil pad. This is mostly for conversation but does have a utility function since it prevents the stock from

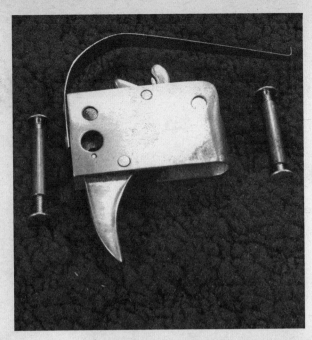

The trigger system was supplied by Dave Benedict. Upper bolt spring was later removed.

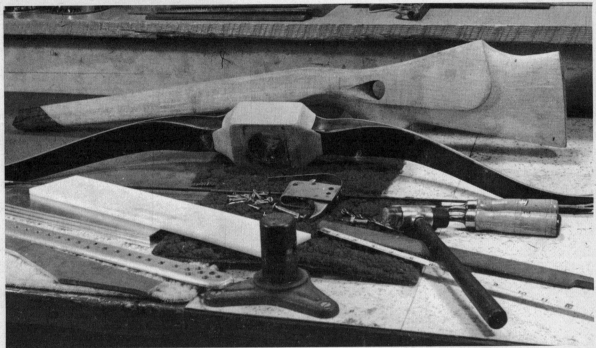

Tools and materials include measure, chisel, wood rasp, drill, screwdriver, hammer, crossbow, trigger, metal bolts, screws, Du Pont Delrin, and sandpaper.

slipping when placed on the butt end. It also provides a cushion when cocking the bow.

The first step was to finish the stock with rasps, sandpaper and time. After the thumb-hole had been shaped to fit the hand and the finish perfected, the entire unit was coated with a two-solution epoxy finish supplied by Royal Arms for rifle stock finishes.

After the first finish coat had been applied, actual fitting of the crossbow limbs began. Before I could do any cutting for length, the bow's draw had to be determined. And before I could measure the draw, a trigger assembly had to be inletted into the stock.

A trigger assembly was obtained from Dave Benedict, who's been building commercial crossbows for many years. This was beefed up with a heavier metal housing for the trigger mechanism.

Any trigger requires a trigger guard, so Bill Duff of Rigid Knives fashioned one out of brass to fit my rifle stock/ crossbow conversion. They use brass on the finger guards and butt sections of their knives, so it was simple for him to cut and shape what I needed.

After the trigger assembly had been waxed, the epoxy was mixed and the trigger assembly imbedded into the wet epoxy, then allowed to cure; keep in mind that the trigger, itself, should be removable. When the epoxy cures, you have a form-fitting base for the trigger system that will

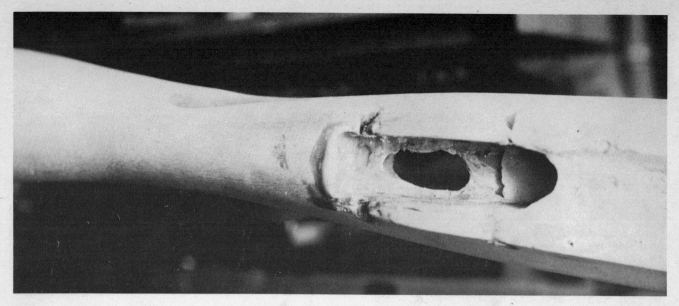

Trigger opening was roughly inletted with wood chisel and drill unit.

withstand tremendous pressures. It's similar to stockmakers bedding a rifle barrel. It's done for strength and often to cover some unsightly gashes such as those I had when I finished tooling the trigger slot.

There is one area in which many commercial bows leave me cold: the string drag created by downward pressure on the stock or its barrel section. This supposedly is done to make the string track to the stock and follow the bolt to the end. A tremendous amount of the bow's power is lost by this drag on the barrel of the stock, however. After having seen some of the equipment used in flight shooting over the years, I decided to have my string ride as close to the surface of the barrel as possible. This would be simpler due to the keyhole bow.

This decision caused further problems, since I wanted as smooth a surface as I could find for the string to slide on. The slickest material I could think of was Teflon, but it also is soft. Du Pont's Delrin was the answer. A sheet gave me more than I needed for my track.

The brace height of the bow is four inches, maybe a fraction less, and the maximum needed for draw would be ten inches beyond that brace height, to give me more than enough power from the bow. The stock was cut squarely at a distance of twelve inches from the end of the trigger housing. The extra inch would be supplied by the draw back of the rollover block of the trigger. This cut is permanent, so this point is critical — you can't add more forward extension without creating a monster.

In the next step, the inletting is bedded and crossbolts positioned in the stock to prevent the unit from riding up on continual firing.

Top view of the trigger unit. The Delrin will overlay the crossbolts much like the bedding in a rifle barrel.

Rough-measure at least ten inches and cut off stock forend. Allow ample stock for final assembly.

This now gave me a stock with a fitted trigger and a grooved center channel needed for the cock feather which faces down on a crossbow bolt to clear the wood of the stock.

The problem now was to mount the keyhole bow to the front of the stock in a solid position. A piece of one-inch aluminum channel material was cut nine inches long. A section of hardwood was cut and sanded to fit into this one-inch channel for rigidity.

A hole was drilled one inch from the end of the metal channel and this was centered on the bottom of the stock, five inches back from the end. This hardwood-filled metal channel was bolted to the base of the stock with one bolt. Another hole was drilled through the metal channel and the stock in proper alignment to center the channel with the upper groove in the stock. This second bolt hole was drilled 1½ inches from the end of the stock itself.

After checking the alignment, the nuts for these bolts were countersunk into the center channel of the stock and epoxied into place. This makes them solid and hopefully I never will have to remove them. This forms the base of the mounting system for the crossbow on the front of the stock.

The metal base bolted into position, I had three inches protruding over the end of the stock, below it and on center with the upper groove in the stock itself. A piece of one-inch aluminum right-angle stock was cut 3½ inches long. Two of these placed with the edges together formed the base section for fitting to the two-inch keyhole base.

To attach the crossbow limbs to the cradle, formed from the metal straps and angles, two holes were drilled through the base of the cradle and through the one-inch, hardwood-filled channel below. Matching holes were drilled through the base of the keyhole on the bow and the bow was attached to the end of the stock with bolts. They hold the bow in a solid position vertically, and the end screws prevent the cradle from moving forward.

The limbs placed into the cradle, the bolts snugged

The crossbow is placed on the front of the stock, draw to trigger. Remember to make correct measurements as stock cannot be lengthened.

A one-inch channel of aluminum is filled with hardwood and then drilled to accept the crossbow and stirrup. The bow holes are visible at the top, stirrup hole at the side.

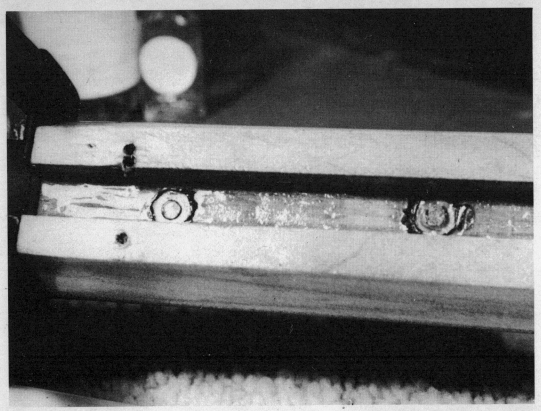

The channel is then fitted to the stock by means of epoxy-embedded nuts in the upper section of the stock. Note the extreme depth of the channel for the feather to ride down.

The Delrin is cut and placed on stock for fitting. Cut for length and drill, because cement won't hold.

down, the bow is almost ready to shoot. With a bow of sixty pounds or less, one can place the butt of the stock in the stomach, pull the string back with two hands and cock the crossbow. Try that with one hundred-plus pounds and all you'll end up with is a sore stomach. What is needed is a foot stirrup as a bracing or cocking aid.

A stirrup was fashioned from strap aluminum, bent to fit over a hunting boot and fastened to the one-inch support base section with one bolt. The hole for the stirrup happened to fall right between the two vertical holes for the limb.

Washers were placed against the support so the stirrup would pivot for extra usage. If you've ever tried to shoot a crossbow from a prone position, you know it's awkward. This stirrup will pivot to a vertical position and act as a forward base section, resting on rocks, posts or the ground. For an extremely steady hold on the crossbow, pull the stirrup back even farther and use it to pull the stock into the shoulder, giving a solid shooting stance.

Storage of a crossbow often is a problem and the folding stirrup is an aid here, too, since you can get the entire unit into a smaller case or drawer.

The unit was fully assembled, the Delrin tracks checked for clearance of the twenty-strand string. The clearance above the track was about a cat's whisker high. This would hopefully allow a fast movement down the track and still

The cradle is built from one-inch angle aluminum and one-inch aluminum strap. The back is rounded to fit keyhole, front square to fit stock channel.

keep the bolt in tow as it moved. The trigger was checked and all seemed ready.

With a bow of this power, a dirt embankment is one of the best backstops. A cedar bolt with field point was placed in the Delrin track, pulled snug against the string in the rolling block and the trigger released. The bolt still was there, but the base or cock feather was flying all over the yard. The blunt nock of the bolt had fit too tightly in the trigger rollover and the string had passed under it, stripping the feather like a razor blade.

One word of caution: Keep your fingers below the track when shooting a crossbow. If you get the tips along the edges or above the track, you'll have some tender, if not bloody, fingertips. The Delrin track had been made extra wide to act both as a reminder and preventive measure for this problem.

Another bolt was checked for trigger clearance and found to be free fitting. It was placed in the cocked system and the bolt smacked into the dirt about eight inches deep. Several more were shot. Using the tip of the bolt as the

Crossbow in the unpainted cradle. The cradle will be attached to the stock at the two holes seen at its base.

Cradle has been painted flat black and the bottom brace rod is now in place. Metal screws hold the cradle to forend.

aiming point or front sight, all were in a five-inch area at thirty yards.

The entire unit was taken down again and fine sandpaper used to remove any scratches and runs from the first coat. Two more coats of epoxy finish were applied to all sections of the wood stock. The center channel was epoxied for as smooth a finish as possible to prevent any feather drag in this area. It is three-fourths of an inch deep and the fletch will not exceed one-half inch.

The brass trigger and guard were polished and everything was reassembled. The forend cradle and the base metal support system had been sprayed flat black to minimize reflections. The stirrup soon will be flat black.

Two reasons for the efficiency of this bow are the free-floating or barely touching string/track relationship (so I gain full power from my bow but still retain some slight, down pressure to keep the bolt on the track), and the smooth Delrin track, allowing the bolt to travel only with two points touching it for minimun friction.

To take this unit into a legal hunting area, one must set

Bolts from the bottom brace channel are brought up, aluminum section is placed on keyhole and nuts are affixed.

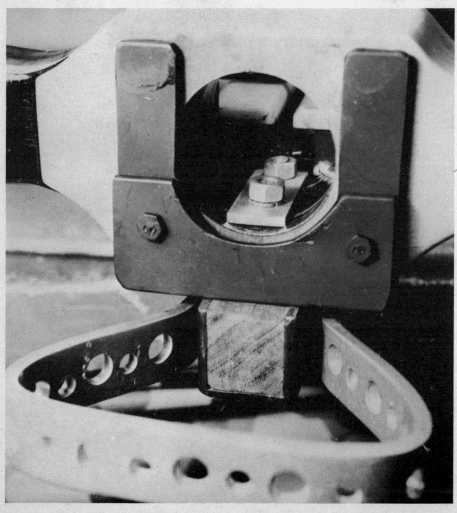

Stirrup is fitted into the hole and allowed to swivel on brace channel for use in firing and bracing.

up a sight system. In some states, this bow is required to have a full safety lock on the trigger system when in a full-cocked position.

The simplest sighting system is to hold the crossbow stock in exactly the same position on the cheek each time, sight over the tip of the bolt and use it for an aiming point.

This is not the most accurate system, but once you find a point-on distance — that distance where the tip of the bolt held in alignment gives you a zero elevation — you should be able to hit consistently in the same area. We are basically concerned with a four-inch kill area; you have much more area than that on a deer, but a varmint has a smaller area of vitals. If the bolts vary in length, that will change the point-on distance due to the type of point or actual length of the bolt.

Adding a rear pin to the system will give a constant rear reference point and one can raise or lower the head on the stock, but the pin will give the same relative distance. The pin could be any height, but the shooter would only be on for that particular distance. For longer shots, hold the rear pin on the bolt tip and judge how much to hold over or under the target. Here again, one is dependent on bolt length for consistent accuracy.

A better, and still simpler system is to add a front-sight pin to the underside of the keyhole. This provides constant

Rigid Knives' Bill Duff made slightly inletted brass trigger guard — fastens to stock with brass screws.

Delrin channel of this trigger unit will make a slick track for the bolt. It is held in position by three countersunk brass screws.

reference for the front section of the sight system and the rear pin offers another constant. These are fixed pins and the length and height of the front and rear pins may be set for any distance required.

For fifty-yard accuracy, you make the rear pin X inches high, the front pin a flexible height and start shooting for fifty yards. When you put them consistently into the target at that distance, cut the pins and glue or affix them in some permanent manner.

Since you have two constants, learn to judge how much to hold over or under for different distances. You could make the rear pin adjustable and mark it with scratches for a calibrated sight system, but there is one already on the market that can be found in any gun shop.

Look for an old military .30/06 rear spring sight. It has a double bar that lifts up from a spring-loaded base and is fully adjustable — with positive stops all along the side bars. The base unit can be clamped or screwed to the crossbow stock and the front-sight pin permanently fixed. All you need do then is go to a range and find which setting gives you what yardage.

My collection of rear sight systems runs to the exotic. One has a good, center peep hole for a sight picture and also has side arms that fold out from the sight bars. The bars have two notches and an end mark with numbers from one to three. They came off an old machine gun and the side arms were used to calculate lead for flying objects or fast-moving targets.

This is a good working sight. There are two constant

Weaver Qwik Point sighting system was the final sight choice. The sight does not magnify the target, but places red dot on target when alignment is proper.

View of sight picture with pin at rear of crossbow for sight system. Adequate, but limited, as much Kentucky windage is still needed to get on target.

references for sighting and I merely judge distance and set the proper rear-sight elevation. There is a basic problem: It is impossible for the eye to focus at the same time on three different distances. You can focus on the rear peep, then the front sight and let the rear peep fuzz out on you, or the target you are aiming at. You can't see all three in sharp focus simultaneously.

Optics are used to keep the front and rear sights and target in focus at the same time. Dave Benedict has been offering a good telescopic sight on his crossbows for some years.

Weaver has a sighting system they call the Qwik Point. This optical system doesn't magnify the image, but places a red dot on the target when you are in proper alignment with the target. The most I could hope for with this crossbow would be one hundred-yard accuracy, and perhaps seventy-five might be more realistic. At any rate, here was a sight system that put all phases in one image, gives a nonmagnified image and the red dot would help in shaded areas.

A Qwik Point was purchased, but when the unit was placed at the back of the barrel, it was too low. A double-laminated block system was used by epoxying a rosewood, then a maple block to the rear of the Delrin bolt track to raise the base mouth.

The Qwik Point mounts on standard Weaver bases used for rifle scope mounting. These were placed on the mount

Left: Another view of rear pin sighting system for comparison and evaluation with the Qwik Point sight.

Alternatives for rear pin or relatively expensive Qwik Point sight are shown here. Obtainable at just about any surplus outlet.

block at the rear of the barrel and the Qwik Point set up prior to mounting. The sight picture put the red dot midway between the tip of the bolt and the top of the keyhole. All it needed was a permanent, solid mount, but another problem developed.

The Qwik Point comes with three different base units. One is for a rifle mount, another for shotguns and a third for .22 caliber rifles. The R-1 unit for rifles was at least two inches too long and protruded over the rolling block of the trigger where it would be in the way when loading the bolt — and possibly be hit if a bolt misfired. A check with the Weaver people and it was determined that the mount unit I had would need modifying.

I called in my resident engineer, Gene Chandler, who agreed to lop off the excess mount bar and tap and thread for the forward spring clamp system so I could use the R-1 mount. It worked beautifully. There still is a bit of overhang on the trigger system, but the bolts slide forward, then come back to the trigger and string without problem.

The Weaver bases were set up, the hardwood blocks drilled and screws used to attach the bases to the stock. The Qwik Point slides over the front spring clamp and has a thumb nut at the rear bracket that can be hand-tightened or really snugged down by using a coin. The sight system was checked for alignment by placing a metal rod down the bolt channel on the barrel of the bow, over the trigger tangs and up to the block on the back. This puts the sight in alignment with the track of the barrel.

Sight picture through machine gun sight, which even provides a system for leading a moving target, but is more than a little difficult to get used to due to side arms that can cause focusing eye difficulty.

First attempts to mount Qwik Point failed because the system was too low.

The optical sight was mounted and the red dot showed up like a beacon. There are no batteries with the unit, but it has a light-refracting system.

I had made up a variety of bolts that ranged from light Port Orford cedar to heavy fiberglass. I picked up three of the cedar shafts tipped with field points and headed across the yard. Straw bales won't work with this unit, as the bolts are too short and they usually either go partially through and have to be pulled out or become lost in the middle. My Korky targets will stop the bolt, but on repeated occasions I have pulled the inserts out of the fiberglass. I now use an embankment for most of my crossbow bolt shooting.

I placed a one-pound coffee can lid on the bank and stepped back thirty paces. The first shot out of the bow hit center, but about four inches right, off the lid. The second shot hit well, but left. The third was beside the first. You could lay a ruler across them — they were that good for elevation. They were off from left to right, but any of the three would have dropped a deer if held on the chest cavity area. This proved that the sight system would work, although it needed some setting that could be done only after the bolts had been refined.

There are many variables when it comes to accuracy with one of these ancient weapons, regardless of how sophisticated you make them by adding optics and all that. When you brace the bow, you have to be certain the center of the string is in the same spot each time on the trigger system. If a bit to the right or left, the bolt will go accordingly.

Crossbow bolts can be made from any current arrow material. This includes Port Orford cedar, fiberglass and aluminum. I decided to make some from each of these materials.

When I looked in my rack for short shaftings to make the bolts, I found two sets of commercial crossbow bolts made from Port Orford cedar. They had two different fletchings — both feather but of different heights. A set of Grodon Glashaftings had been cut many moons ago for this project. There was a set of 24SRT-X 2020 Easton shafts in the rack also.

The cedar shafts were red and green. The green weighed 300.0 grains and measured fifteen inches. The red shafts were the same weight but only fourteen inches long. These would be all right for basic testing but I planned to keep most of the bolts at least sixteen inches long since the state of Wyoming, where I hope to hunt, has strict rules regard-

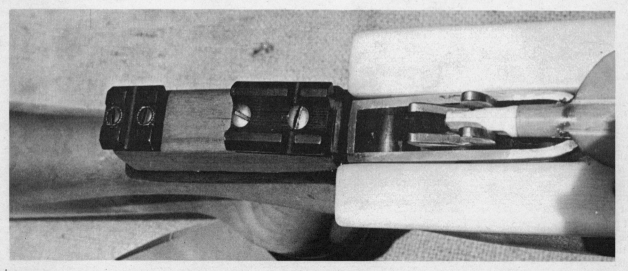

Mounting problem was solved with a double-laminated block on which the sight system could be mounted; mounting didn't present a problem but it was then found that the scope was too long, projecting over the rolling block in the way of loading. Solved by shortening and rethreading mount bar to reduce overhang.

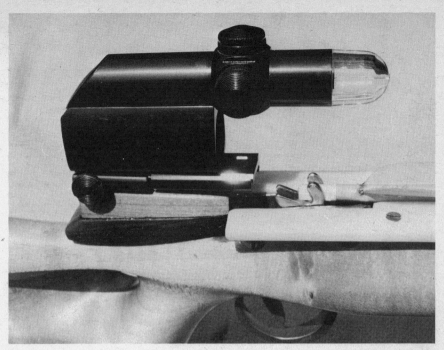

Laminated hardwood blocks were used to raise system up to level allowing proper functioning.

ing bolt size.

The Gordon shafts were sixteen inches and fletched with three-inch feathers weighed 365.0 grains including the point. These bolts were ready to shoot with the nock in position, fletched and with a 125-grain Sweetland field point in place on the tip.

The aluminum shafts were fletched differently. There were eight of them set in groups of two. One set had the small black mini-balloon Plastifletch by Arizona Archery. These were short but high and if they worked well as a guidance system they should be fast.

The second pair of aluminum shafts were fletched with bright orange Plastifletch about 2½ inches long. These were lower but longer than the balloon fletch. These two types were the hard, rigid plastic used by target archers.

The final two pairs of aluminum were fletched with four-inch soft plastic fletch. One pair used four-inch Ultra fletch and the other had Plastifletch of 4½ inches. This should give a cross section as to bolt flight and steering capability. The less mass of fletch the faster the bolt, or so goes theory.

All aluminum shafts were tipped with Sweetland field points at 125.0 grains. The nocks were Plastinocks and the notch of the nock was retained. Most bolts, like my cedars, have the nock cut and made blocky at the base for the string to ride on. I wanted to try the regular nock since it would make fletching easier on damaged shafts. Also, if the nock would fit, it would save the problem of having a keeper on top of the stock to hold bolts on the track when loaded. Most crossbows have a steel finger holding the bolt down from the top. This could be eliminated if the bolt would shoot from the twenty-four-strand string I now have on my bow. The Plastinock fit snugly, wouldn't fall off and came free with a slight nudge.

All fletchings were straight down the tube since a hellical or spiral makes it difficult to allow the bolt to move down the bolt groove in the stock.

These bolts were weighed and the balloon came to 380.0 grains, the orange was 385.0 grains, and the Ultra and four-inch Plastifletch were 400.0 grains. All were sixteen inches long and tipped with 125-grain field points — legal hunting bolts in most states that allow crossbow hunting.

I wanted the test shooting to be simple but accurate. This eliminated any offhand holding. A benchrest was the best bet, so I loaded an old patio bench into the back of the wagon and hauled it to a sandpit along with some laminated cardboard to stop the bolts. Also, I threw in some small sandbags.

Rear view of Qwik Point sighting system. Red dot in sight shows up like a beacon.

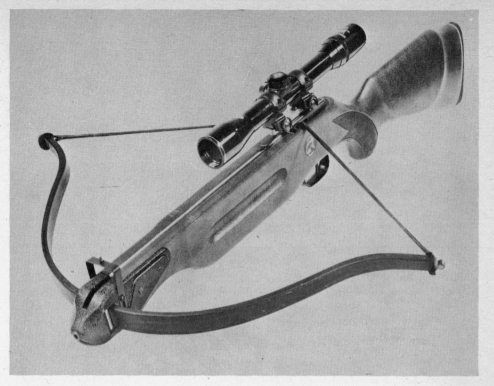

Commercially built Wildcat hunting crossbow has a safety catch that sets automatically when string is drawn. Available with telescopic sight as shown.

The bench was placed on the open tailgate of the station wagon after pacing off and double-checking a distance of fifty yards with a Rangematic distance finder. The bow was placed on the bench, two clamps placed on the front end of the bench as a stop for the stirrup and a bag placed

under the stock to elevate or depress as needed. My sight hadn't been touched except to make visual alignment in the back yard.

A twenty-four-inch laminated target was placed in the sand at the base of the bluff. A large red circle the size of a coffee can lid sprayed in the center of the face offered an aiming point.

The first bolt went low into the sand at the base of the target. The next went right, and so it went for the first round. My bolts were all over the embankment, still within a few inches of the cardboard face but hardly accurate. All had flown more or less as predicted — the heavier bolts dropping low, the lighter bolts going higher. There didn't seem to be much difference initially as to the fletching style and length.

The sight adjustments can be made internally on the Qwik Point, so the caps were removed for the second round. The red aiming point was put on the center of the target. The bolts of the first round mostly had hit right and low, so the azimuth ring was turned and the dot raised.

When the string was braced on the trigger, it was grabbed with the first fingers against the Delrin track. I held this to make certain the string wasn't loaded with an uneven tension on one side or the other to throw the bolt in that direction.

The nock on the bolt was seated as tightly as allowed by the unit. The blunt-ended bolts were snugged back into the trigger claw to fit up against the string to prevent jumping when shot. The Gordon shafts were tipped with the Nocksert nylon unit, and were a bit tight on the thick string.

An aluminum shaft was chosen and snugged up to the string in the claw. It flew downrange and thunked into the paper face, still low. The adjustment on the sight was raised a few more clicks. Another bolt hit in the red circle. Again all bolts were shot with the adjusted sight. They were a

The Qwik Point sight system with the internal adjustment covers removed from sight system for fine tuning.

Completed crossbow, with Weaver sight, ready for the field and test firing.

much better grouping but usually some oddball would defy the system and dive low or fly to one side or the other.

Several rounds were shot using the different bolts. What I wanted to do was come close to hunting systems using the field point. These tests proved that I could guide the "black balloon" fletched aluminum shafts with target point. They were tough and only one feather fletching came off after repeated firing, which is good considering the impact on firing and hitting the target.

There were three casualties: Two aluminum and one glass bolt were bent when they hit buried rock. The glass broke at the ferrule base; the aluminum curled the insert at the junction with the shaft. Anything must give when slammed into a solid object with the force put on it by that 125-pound bow.

The fletching on the aluminum bolts was giving the best performance. This was of soft or hard plastic.

The field points were removed using a propane torch and a variety of broadheads placed on the shafts — the lightest heads on the smallest vanes and the heavier heads on the bigger-vaned bolts. These were spun for true alignment and had no wobble that was visible.

The light head selected was the Bear Razorhead without inserts, which weighs 110.0 grains. The next, heavier head selected for toughness, was the 110-grain two-bladed Black Diamond Eskimo. It was placed on the next-sized orange-fletched bolt. The 125-grain Black Diamond was fitted on the Ultra-fletched bolt. The biggest head — the Black Diamond Delta — was put on the four-inch Plastifletch. These all are two-bladed heads.

I had no three-bladed heads along. My belief is that they might just peel apart on impact, because most are laminated. The same goes for the four-bladed heads with one exception: The Black Copperhead Slicer is the only four-bladed head with full-length blades on each surface. It has a solid ferrule.

Insert blade heads usually have a brittle steel cutting edge and, although they probably would do the job on game, it makes them rough to handle when pulled from laminated cardboard. Except when using a dirt target, any

multi-blade is tough to pull from a target — there is no way to move or wriggle them since the blades are in opposition to this.

I decided to shoot all units in twos as a check. The first broadhead-tipped bolt was the Bear with the balloon vane. When the trigger was pulled, the bolt headed in the direction of the bank. But after a short distance it flipped, made some wild contortions in the air and thunked into the bank twenty feet from the target. This was a pure case of planing caused by a combination of factors. First was the improper alignment of the broadhead when mounted on the shaft. These had been spun but needed more of an alignment check than that. Second, it was the smallest vane and I'm sure the broadhead took over the steering of the bolt. This proves that the small vane shoots target or field points, but forget broadheads.

The orange vane tipped with the Black Diamond repeated the Bear's performance. The Ultra vane with the 125-grain Black Diamond came in beside the target. The big heavy Delta heads with the four-inch Plastifletch grouped low and to the right but not where I wanted them.

I learned from these tests that the bolts require the biggest fletching I can put on them for guidance with broadheads. These can be the regular five-inch hunting fletching used on regular arrows or the larger fletching.

My tests proved the head must be mounted with extreme care; much more is required than the simple spin test I used in the field. It must have no wobble or it will take over and become the guidance system and you'll have the same problem I had — bolts into the blue.

The crossbow system works better than I had hoped. The sight system is good and when you move the head you move the dot — but it diminishes to let you know it isn't centered.

I achieved fifty-yard accuracy — not as good as the target people get, but I was using much heavier bolts than their target arrows. If I ever consider using this crossbow for targets, I would use a light, small bolt with a weighted point and the "black balloon" Plastifletch. — *Bob Learn*

Directory of the Archery Trade

BOW MANUFACTURERS

Allen Archery, 805-E Lindberg, Billings, Missouri 65610

American Archery, P.O. Box 100 Ind. Park, Oconto Falls, Wisconsin 54154

Arrow Archery, Incorporated, 19706 E. Arrow Highway, Covina, California 91722

Bear Archery Company, Rural Route 1, Grayling, Michigan 49738

Bingham Archery, Box 3013, Ogden, Utah 84403

Bradshaw Bows, Rural Route 1, Box 641W, Tarpon Springs, Florida 33589

Browning Arms Company, Route 1, Morgan, Utah 84050

Carroll's Archery Products, 59½ South Main, Moab, Utah 84532

Cravotta Brothers, Incorporated, Third Street, East McKeesport, Pennsylvania 15132

Cupid Archery, 2716 2nd Avenue North, Lethbridge, Alberta, Canada T1h 0C2

Eicholtz Archery, 3640 Ruffin Road, San Diego, California 92123

Graham's Custom Bows, P.O. Box 1312, Fontana, California 92335

Groves Archery Corporation, 3116 Karen Place, Colorado Springs, Colorado 80907

Herter's Incorporated, Rural Route 1, Waseca, Minnesota 56093

Howard Hill Archery, Route 1 Box 1397, Hamilton, Montana 59840

Jack Howard, Washington Star Route, Nevada City, California 95959

Damon Howatt Archery, Route 8, Yakima, Washington 98902

Hoyt Archery Company, 11510 Natural Bridge Road, Bridgeton, Missouri 63042

Indian Industries, Incorporated, Evansville, Indiana 47717

Interstate Archery, 7179 West Grand, Chicago, Illinois 60635

Jeffery Enterprises, Incorporated, 821 Pepper Street, Columbia, South Carolina 29209

Jennings Compound Bow, Incorporated, 28756 North Castaic Canyon Road, Valencia, California 91355

Longbow Manufacturing Company, 858 Shoshone Loop, Hamilton, Montana 59840

Martin Archery Company, Route 5 Box 127, Walla Walla, Washington 99362

Old Master Crafters Company, 130 Lebaron Street, Waukegan, Illinois 60085

Outers Astro Archery, Onalaska, Wisconsin 54650

Ben Pearson, Box 270, Tulsa, Oklahoma 74101

Plas/Steel Products, Incorporated, Walkerton, Indiana 46574

Precision Shooting Equipment, Incorporated, Main Street, Mahomet, Illinois 61853

Rigid Archery Products, 445 Central Avenue, Jersey City, New Jersey 07307

Robin Hood Archery, Incorporated, 215 Glenridge Avenue, Montclair, New Jersey 07042

Sabo Archery Company, Westminster, California 92683

Staghorn Archery, Merrill, Wisconsin 54452

Wing Archery Company, Division of AMF Voit, Route 1, Jacksonville, Texas 75766

Woodcraft Equipment, (York Archery) P.O. Box 110, Independence, Missouri 64051

ARROW MATERIALS, EQUIPMENT

Acme Wood Products Company, Box 636, Myrtle Point, Oregon 97458 (Port Orford cedar shafts)

Arrow Manufacturing, Incorporated, 1365 Logan Avenue, Costa Mesa, California 92626 (screw-on inserts, aluminum and fiberglass arrows)

Bingham Archery, P.O. Box 3013, Odgen, Utah 84403 (arrow shafting, feathers, points, nocks)

Henry A. Bitzenburger, Route 2, Box M-1, Sherwood, Oregon 97140 (fletching jigs)

Bohning Adhesives Company, Limited, Route 2, Box 140, Lake City, Missouri 49651 (vanes, arrow repair kits)

Copperhead Manufacturing, 30259 Calahan, Roseville, Michigan 48066 (broadheads)

Easton Aluminum, Incorporated, 7800 Haskell Avenue, Van Nuys, California 91406 (aluminum shafts, arrows)

Vic Erickson, 1295 Ada Avenue, Idaho Falls, Idaho, 83401 (aluminum arrows)

Frontier Archery Company, 3440 La Gande Boulevard, Sacramento, California 95823 (vanes)

Gordon Plastics, Incorporated, 2872 South Sante Fe Avenue, Vista, California 92083 (fiberglass and graphite shafts)

Max Hamilton, Route 2, Box 333, Flagstaff, Arizona 86001 (plastic vanes)

Hunters International, 26422 Groesbeck Highway, Warren, Michigan 48089 (stainless steel shafts, broadheads)

Lamiglas, Incorporated, P.O. Box 148, Woodland, Washington 98674 (graphite shafts)

Little Shaver Company, Box 543, West Unity, Ohio 43570 (two and three-blade broadheads)

M.J. Log Corporation, 1921 14th Street West, Billings, Montana 59102 (aluminum, fiberglass and cedar arrow shafts)

Mark V Industries, 4 Hyder Street, Westboro, Massachusetts 01581 (fletch waterproofing compounds)

McKinney Arrow Shafts, Oakland, Oregon 97462 (cedar shafts)

Mohawk Archery Products, 228 Bridge Street, East Syracuse, New York 13057 (broadheads)

New Archery Products Corporation, 370 North Delaplaine Road, Riverside, Illinois 60546 (five-blade broadhead)

Norway Archery, Norway, Oregon 97460 (cedar shafts)

Pacific Archery, Route 3, Box 912, Coos Bay, Oregon 97420 (hand-spined cedar arrow shafts)

Pioneer Sporting Goods, Route 12, Bloomington, Indiana 47401 (Game Tamer hunting points)

Rose City Archery, Incorporated, Box 342, Powers, Oregon 97458 (cedar shafts)

Savora Archery, Incorporated, 11039 118th Place NE, Kirkland, Washington 98033 (broadheads)

Sweetland Products, 1010 Arrowsmith Street, Eugene, Oregon 97402 (arrow points, other arrow accessories)

Texas Feathers, Incorporated, Brownwood, Texas 76801 (fletching feathers)

Tofco, 1842-44 Dorchester Avenue, Boston, Massachusetts 02124 (Tourney-Flite fletches)

Trueflight Manufacturing Company, Incorporated, Manitowish Waters, Wisconsin 54545 (feathers)

Ultra Products Limited, Box 100, Fairfield, Illinois 62837 (vanes)

Utah Feathers, Box 396, Orem, Utah 84057 (feathers)

Wasp Archery Products, P.O. Box 760, Bristol, Connecticut 06010 (broadheads)

Zwickey Archery Company, 2571 East 12 Avenue, North Saint Paul, Minnesota 55109 (broadheads)

MAIL ORDER DEALERS

Anderson Archery, Grand Ledge, Michigan 48837

Archery Wholesale, 2007 High Street, Alameda, California 94501

Arrow Manufacturing,1365 Logan Avenue, Costa Mesa, California 92626

Cabela's Incorporated, Sidney, Nebraska 69162

Deercliff Archery Supplies, 2852 Lavista Road, Decatur, Georgia 30033

Feline Archery, 220 Willow Crossing Road, Greensburg, Pennsylvania 15601

Finnysports, 9571 Sports Building, Toledo, Ohio 43614

F/S Arrows, Box 8094, Fountain Valley, California 92708

Herter's Incorporated, Waseca, Minnesota 56093

Kittredge Bow Hut, P.O. Box 598T, Mammoth Lakes, California 93540

Martin Archery Company, Route 5, Walla Walla, Washington 99362

S. Meltzer and Sons, Archery Department, Meltzer Building, Garfield, New Jersey 07026

PGS Archery, 46 Almond Street, Vineland, New Jersey 08360

Robin Hood Archery Company, 215 Glenridge Avenue, Montclair, New Jersey 07042

Saunders Archery Company, Columbus, Nebraska 68601

Southeast'n Archery, 4718 S. Orange Avenue, Orlando, Florida 32806

T.J.S. Distributors, 110 2nd Avenue, Pelham, New York 10803

Vick's Archery Center, 938 S. Cooper, Memphis, Tennessee 38104

Western Direct Sales, Box 1270, Moab, Utah 84532

West Hills Sport Shop, Box 28, Corapolis, Pennsylvania 15108

BOW, ARROW CASES

The Allen Company, Incorporated, 2330 West Midway Boulevard, Broomfield, Colorado 80020

Challanger Manufacturing Corporation, 94-28 Merrick Boulevard, Jamaica, New York 11433

Gateway Luggage Manufacturing Company, Incorporated, 820 W. Tenth Street, Claremore, Oklahoma 74017

Gun-Ho, 110 E. Tenth Street, St. Paul, Minnesota 55101

Paul-Reed, Incorporated, P.O. Box 227, Charlevoix, Michigan 49720

Penguin Industries, P.O. Box 97, Parkesburg, Pennsylvania 19365

Protecto Plastics, Incorporated, Box 68, Wind Gap, Pennsylvania 18091

Sloane Products, P.O. Box 56, Saugus, California 91350

Sportscase, Incorporated, 204 Central Avenue, Osseo, Minnesota 55368

Sylvester's Archery Supplies, 212 Hawthorne Circle, Creve Coeur, Illinois 61611

VARMINT & GAME CALLS

Burnham Brothers, Box 110, Marble Falls, Texas 78654

Electronic Game Calls, 210 W. Grand Avenue, Grand Rapids, Michigan 54494

Faulk's Game Call Company, Incorporated, 616 18th Street, Lake Charles, Louisiana 70601

P.S. Olt Company, Pekin, Illinois 61554

Penn's Woods Products, Incorporated, 19 W. Pittsburgh Street, Delmont, Pennsylvania 15625

Scotch Game Call Company, Incorporated, 60 Main Street, Oakfield, New York 14125

Johnny Stewart Game Calls, Incorporated, 5100 Fort Avenue, P.O. Box 1909, Waco, Texas 76703

Thomas Game Calls, P.O. Box 336, Winnsboro, Texas 75494

Western Call & Decoy, P.O. Box 425, Portland, Oregon 97207

LEATHER GOODS

J.M. Bucheimer Company, P.O. Box 280, Airport Road, Frederick, Maryland 21701

Hobby-Horse Crafts, 1811 Sixth Street, Wyandotte, Michigan 48192

King Sport-Line Company, 328 S. Cypress Avenue, Alhambra, California 91801

Kolpin Manufacturing, Incorporated, Berlin, Wisconsin 54923

Swiss-Craft Company, Incorporated, 33 Artic Street, Worcester, Massachusetts 01604

BOWSIGHTS

Accra Manufacturing Company, 717 N. Sheridan, Tulsa, Oklahoma 74115

Eryleen Products, 361 Cambridge Street, Burlington, Massachusetts 01803

Full Adjust Products, 915 North Ann Street, Lancaster, Pennsylvania 17602

Golden Key-Futura Archery, 1851 South Orange Avenue, Monterey Park, California 91754

Goodyear Company, Box 265, Lincoln City, Oregon 97367

Merrill Bow Sights, 3830 Orleans Lane, Minneapolis, Minnesota 55427

Moto Miter Company, Prairie du Chien, Wisconsin 53821

Scanner Products, 3 Hawthorne Road, Gibbsboro, New Jersey 08026

Schneider Enterprises, 11245 S. Thompson Drive, Wind Lake, Wisconsin 53185

Sprandel's Bowsight Company, 19 Brookside Drive, Monroe, Connecticut 06468

Toxonics, Incorporated, P.O. Box 1303, St. Charles, Missouri 63301

CROSSBOWS

Benedict Crossbows, P.O. Box 343, Chatsworth, California 91331

Chriskim Company, Box 1782, Tampa, Florida 33601

Classic Crossbows, Eagle Rock Distributors, P.O. Box 131, Fordyce, Arkansas 71742

Midwest Crossbow Company, 9043 S. Western Avenue, Chicago, Illinois 60620

Stevens Crossbows, Box 72, Huntsville, Arkansas 72740

MISCELLANEOUS ACCESSORIES & EQUIPMENT

Aladdin Laboratories, Incorporated, 620 S. Eighth Street, Minneapolis, Minnesota 55404 (deer lure)

Al's Fish Slick, 7828 West Lorraine Place, Milwaukee, Wisconsin 53222 (fishpoint)

Ambusher, 2515 Magnolia Street, Texarkana, Texas 75501 (tree stand)

Archer's Arm, Payne Street, Elmsford, New York 10523 (armguards, releases)

Avery Corporation, P.O. Box 99, 221 N. Main Street, Electra, Texas 76360 (varmint calling lights)

Auto-Quiver, P.O. Box 771, Wayne, New Jersey 07470 (bow quivers)

Baker Manufacturing Company, P.O. Box 1003, Valdosta, Georgia 31601 (tree stand)

Belke Company, 2308 Pleasant Avenue, New Holstein, Wisconsin 53061 (tree stand)

Joe Bender, Stoddard, Wisconsin 54658 (No-Glove finger protectors)

Bonnie Bowman, 1619 Abram Court, San Leandro, California 94577 (complete line of archery accessories)

Brownell, Incorporated, Moodus, Connecticut 06469 (bowstring material)

Buck Knives, 1717 N. Magnolia Avenue, El Cajon, California 92002 (hunting knives)

Buck Stop, Incorporated, 3015 Grow Road, Stanton, Michigan 48888 (insect repellent, deer lure)

C/J Enterprises, 410 S. Citrus Avenue, Covina, California 91722 (one-piece aluminum release)

Camillus Cutlery Company, Camillus, New York 13031 (hunting knives)

Camouflage Manufacturing Company, 9075 Atlantic Boulevard, Jacksonville, Florida 32215 (camouflage hunting clothes and accessories)

Camp-lite Products, Incorporated, 1408 W. Colfax, Denver, Colorado 90204 (lightweight back pack and camping tents)

Camp Trails, P.O. Box 14500, Phoenix, Arizona 85031 (back packing and camping equipment)

Colorado Outdoor Sports Company, 1636 Champs Street, P.O. Box 5544, Denver, Colorado 80217 (lightweight packing equipment)

Cutter Laboratories, Incorporated, Fourth and Parker Streets, Berkeley, California 94619 (insect repellents, snake bite kits, first aid kits)

D&D Rods, Box 206, Comstock, Michigan 49041 (stabilizer rods and weights)

Deer Me Products, Box 345, Anoka, Minnesota 55303 (tree steps, tree stands, deer drags)

Deer Run Products, Incorporated, 166 Granite Springs Road, Yorktown Heights, New York 10598 (game lures)

Dolch Enterprises, Incorporated, Box 606, Westlake, Louisana 70669 (telescopic bowstringer)

J. Dye Enterprises, 1707 Childerlee Lane, NE, Atlanta, Georgia 30329 (arrow guide)

Dyn-O-Mite Archery and Sports Accessories, Division of Rogue Basin Developers, Incorporated, 225 SW Western Avenue, Grants Pass, Oregon 97526 (releases, arrow rests)

Federal Instrument Company, 99-36 65th Avenue, Rego Park, New York 11374 (range-determining devices)

Game Winner, Incorporated, 2940 First National Bank Tower, Atlanta, Georgia 30303 (camouflage and hunting clothes, accessories)

General Recreation Industries, Fayette, Alabama 35555 (sleeping bags)

H&W Tree Grabber, P.O. Box 4026, Burlington, North Carolina 27251 (tree stand)

Hobby Haven, 2 Pine Street, Wheelwright, Massachusetts 01094 (release aid)

Hunter's Hideout, 1817 McKeon Road, Box 31, Kenosha, Wisconsin 53140 (tree stand)

Impact Industries, Incorporated, 7020 Packer Drive, Wausau, Wisconsin 54401 (tree stand)

Indian Ridge Traders, P.O. Box X-50, Ferndale, Michigan 48220 (hunting, skinning knives)

J.C. Manufacturing Company, 6435 West 55th Avenue, Arvada, Colorado 80002 (nock point)

Jet-Aer Corporation, 100 Sixth Avenue, Paterson, New Jersey 07524 (insect repellents, game lures, fabric and leather treatments and waterproofing)

Kelty Pack, Incorporated, P.O. Box 639, 10909 Tuxford Street, Sun Valley, California 91352 (pack bags, pack frames, soft packs)

Killian Chek-It, 12350 S.E. Stevens Road, Portland, Oregon 97226 (competition string release)

Kwikee Kwiver Company, 7292 Peaceful Valley Road, Acme, Michigan 49610 (bow quivers)

L&M Cork Products, Mokena, Illinois 60448 (cork target backstops, mats)

Len Company, BJ-101 Brooklyn, New York 11214 (survival knives)

Loc-On Company, Route 1, Box 711, Summerfield, North Carolina 27358 (tree stand)

Mac's Archery Supplies, Incorporated, 6336 W. Fond du Lac Avenue, Milwaukee, Wisconsin 53218 (bowfishing reels, arrows, points)

Mini Bow, 1880 Century Park East, Suite 315, Los Angeles, California 90067 (novel system for living room archery)

Mountain Products Corporation, 123 S. Wenatchee Avenue, Wenatchee, Washington 98801 (lightweight camping gear)

National Archery Company, Route No. 1, Princeton, Minnesota 55371 (bow quivers, tabs)

National Archery Supply, 602 Neal Avenue, Salina, Kansas 67401 (arrow rest)

National Packaged Trail Foods, 632 E. 185th Street, Cleveland, Ohio 44119 (freeze-dried camping foods)

Natural Scent Company, 1170 Elgin Avenue, Salt Lake City, Utah 84106 (animal scents)

Nirk Archery Company, Potlatch, Idaho 83855 (bow hangers)

Nock Rite Company, 3720 Crestview Circle, Brookfield, Wisconsin 53005 (bowstring attachments)

Old Master Crafters Company, 130 Lebaron Street, Waukegan, Illinois 60085 (bow laminations)

Precision Shooter Company, P.O. Box 201, Flushing, Michigan 48433 (release)

R&D Products, P.O. Box 154, Euless, Texas 76039 (arrow holders and bowfishing points)

Rancho Safari, Box 691, Ramona, California 92065 (bow quivers, string silencers)

Ranger Manufacturing Company, P.O. Box 3386, Augusta, Georgia 30904 (camouflage clothing)

Ranging, Incorporated, P.O. Box 9106, Rochester, New York 14625 (range-determining devices)

Richmond Sports, 56 Spartan Avenue, Graniteville, New York 10303 (compound clicker)

Ron's Porta-Pak Manufacturing Company, Box 141, Greenbrier, Arkansas 72058 (tree stand)

Rorco, Box 1007, State College, Pennsylvania 16801 (shaft spiders)

Sagittarius Martin Incorporated, 114 East 11th Street, Medford, Oregon 97501 (bow quivers)

San Angelo Die Casting Company, Box 984, San Angelo, Texas 76901 (bow racks and holders)

Saunders Archery Company, P.O. Box 476, Industrial Site, Columbus, Nebraska 68601 (complete line of archery accessories)

Shockalator, 12122 Monter, Bridgeton, Missouri 63044 (mercury bow stabilizers)

Schrade Cutlery, Ellenville, New York 12428 (hunting knives)

Selector, P.O. Box 1588-VHFS, Warrenton, Virginia 22186 (release)

Smith's Sports Products, 925 Hillcrest Place, Pasadena, California 91106 (bow holder)

Spectre Archery Enterprises, 17th & Northampton Streets, Easton, Pennsylvania 18042 (complete line of archery accessories)

Swede Seat, Box 471, Pelican Rapids, Minnesota 56572 (tree stand)

10-X Manufacturing, 100 S.W. Third Street, Des Moines, Iowa 59309 (camouflage and hunting clothing)

Trail Chef Foods, P.O. Box 60041, Terminal Annex, Los Angeles, California 90060 (lightweight foods)

Trueflight Manufacturing Company, Incorporated, Manitowish Waters, Wisconsin 54545 (string silencers, nock locators and assorted accessories)

Warren & Sweat Manufacturing Company, 4121 Aldington Drive, Jacksonville, Florida 32210 (tree stand)

L.C. Whiffen Company Incorporated, 923 S. 16th Street, Milwaukee, Wisconsin 53204 (bow quivers)

Wilson-Allen Corporation, Box 302, Windsor, Missouri 65360 (bow tip protector, arrow nock lock)

R.C. Young Company, Incorporated, Manitowoc, Wisconsin 54220 (feather trimmers)

TODAY'S BOWS

TODAY'S TREND in choice of archery tackle is away from the tried-and-true recurve and long bows, with the emphasis on compounds, although manufacturers admit they do not know how long such interest will last. Currently, however, the compound appears to have the greater part of the market.

Prices for bows listed in this section are based upon the manufacturer's suggested retail prices, although many of them do not quote retail prices at all, leaving it up to the retailer to determine how much he feels the bow should be worth. Investigation shows that there is a wide range in retail prices, some models varying nearly one hundred percent from one area to another.

Compounds

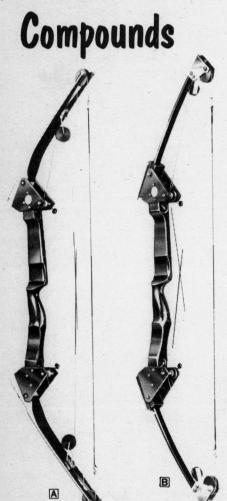

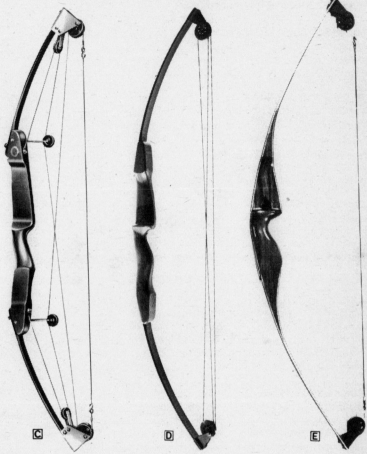

A ALLEN MODEL 7303 HUNTER

Length is 48"; draw length, 23 to 31"; draw weights, 25/35 lbs., 35/45 lbs., 45/55 lbs., 50/55 lbs.; mass weight, 3½ to 4 lbs.; maple core laminated limbs; hardwood riser. **$250**

Model 7303-15 is target version with draw weights of 25/35 lbs., 35/45 lbs.; blue hardwood handle, white laminated limbs, stabilizer bushing, panic button. **$275**

B ALLEN MODEL 7306 HUNTER

Length is 48"; draw lengths, 23" to 31"; draw weights, 40/50 lbs.; black hardwood handle, black solid glass laminated limbs; mass weight, 3½ to 4 lbs. **$115**

Model 7306-2 is the same as above but designed for ladies and juniors; draw weight, 25/35 lbs; green hardwood handle. **$115**

Model 3706-10 has same general specifications as Model 7306, except for draw weight of 50/60 lbs.; brown hardwood handle; black solid glass laminated limbs. **$125**

C ALLEN MODEL 7507 SPEEDSTER

Length is 48"; draw length with 2" eccentric wheel, 27 to 29"; with 2¼" wheel, 29 to 31"; mass weight, 3 lbs.; window clearance, 3/8"; 40% letoff; laminated all-glass limbs; maple handle; textured nonslip grip. **$79.50**

Model 7507-4 has same basic specifications, but with 2" eccentric wheel, 50 lb. draw weight at 27/29" draw length; 35 lbs. with cables unhooked from handle idlers; with 2¼" wheel, provides 50 lb. draw weight at 29/31" draw; 35" at 27/29" draw with cables unhooked. **$89.50**

Model 7507-6 with 1¾" eccentric provides 45/55 lb. micro adjustable weight at 25/27" draw or 35 lbs. at 23/25" draw with cables unhooked from handle idlers. With 2" eccentric, it provides 45/55 lb. micro adjustable weight at 27/29" draw; 35 lbs. at 25/27" draw with cables unhooked. With 2¼" eccentric, provides 45/50 lbs. micro adjustable draw at 29/31" draw; 35 lbs. at 27/29" draw with cables unhooked. **$99.50**

D AMERICAN PENETRATOR

Length is 48"; draw length, 27/28", 28/29", 29/30", 30/31"; draw weight ranges, 35/50 lbs., 45/50 lbs. maximum; mass weight, 4 lbs.; break reduction, 50% maximum cable clearance for all arrows; stabilizer insert; arrow rest; straight length, 38"; right or left-hand model; aluminum alloy riser. $69.95

E AMERICAN AM-MAG

Length is 48"; draw length, 27", 28", 29", 30"; draw weight ranges, 35/40 lbs., 40/45 lbs., 50/55 lbs., 55/60 lbs.; mass weight, 2½ lbs.; break reduction, 50% maximum cable arrow clearance; stabilizer insert; arrow rest; 38" string; right or left-hand model; wood handle, Super-Flex core. $99.95

F BEAR VICTOR TAMERLANE II

Lengths are 50 and 56"; draw weights, 30 to 55 lbs.; draw lengths, 25/31, 27/31"; takedown capability; magnesium handle; glacier vein metallic epoxy finish; 33% to 36% letoff; bristle rest, adjustable nylon arrow plate; drilled, tapped for accessories; right or left-hand models. $300

G BEAR VICTOR ALASKAN

Length is 50"; draw weights, 35 to 70 lbs.; draw length limit, 25 to 33½"; 33% to 36% letoff; takedown capability; micrometer click adjustment assembly; magnesium pistol grip handle; silver vein metallic epoxy finish; bristle rest; adjustable nylon arrow plate, cover plate for bowsight; drilled, tapped for accessories; right and left-hand models. $275

BEAR POLAR LTD

Length is 44", axle to axle; features six adjustable peak weight settings from 25 to 65 lbs.; draw limits, 28½ to 30½", 26½ to 29"; magnesium pistol grip handle, silver vein metallic epoxy finish; 50% letoff; drilled, tapped for accessories; right and left-hand models. $190

H BEAR WHITETAIL HUNTER

Length is 44", axle to axle; adjustable draw weights of 50, 55, 60 lbs.; draw length, 20 to 30½"; 50% letoff; magnesium handle, brown metallic epoxy finish; bonded fiberglass limbs; predetermined locator for Berger button, Check-It bowsight; drilled, tapped for accessories; right and left-hand models. $108.50

BEAR KODIAK HUNTER

Length is 60"; draw weights, 40, 45, 50, 55 lbs.; special order to 70 lbs.; draw length, unlimited; handle of green Futurewood; laminated limbs; green fiberglass face, back; Futurewood tip overlays; hand-contoured grip with thumb rest; camouflage finish at no added cost; right or left-hand models. $60

BEAR GRIZZLY

Length is 55"; draw weights, 30, 40, 45, 50 lbs.; special order to 70 lbs.; draw length, unlimited; handle of Futurewood in random color combinations; laminated limbs; fiberglass face, back; hand-contoured grip; tip overlays; camouflage finish at no added cost; right or left-hand models. $77.50

BINGHAM COBRA X40

Length is 40"; draw lengths, 28 to 31"; draw weights, 45/50, 51/60 lbs.; 40% letoff weight reduction; exotic wood riders; laminated black glass/maple core limbs; right or left-hand models. .$77.50

I BROWNING EXPLORER

Length is 40½", axle to axle; mass weight, 3 lbs., 11 oz.; draw weight, 45/60 lbs.; draw range, 28/29, 29/31"; 2 or 2¼" eccentric pulleys; 5¼" sight window; hardwood handle; high-gloss black face, back; 40% letoff; full pistol grip; right or left-hand models; accessory insert bushings. $169.95

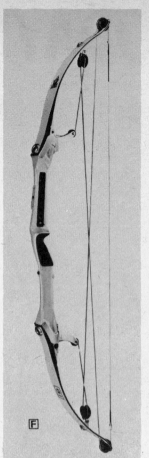
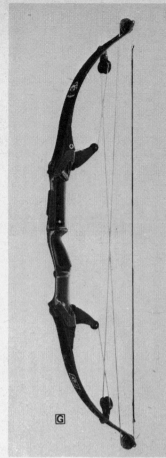
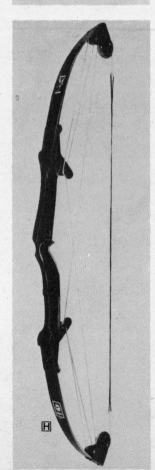
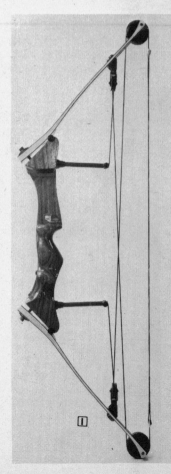

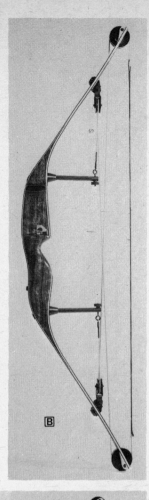

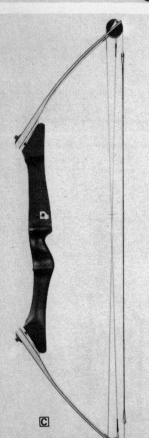

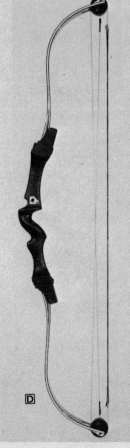

Ⓐ BROWNING BUSHMASTER

Length is 40½", axle to axle; mass weight, 4 lbs., 6 oz.; draw weights, 45/60 lbs.; draw range, 27 to 31"; 2 or 2¼" eccentric wheels; 30% to 40% letoff; 4" sight window; laminated hardwood pistol grip handle; hunter black limbs; accessory insert bushings. **$75**

Ⓑ BROWNING STALKER I

Length is 40½", axle to axle; mass weight, 3 lbs., 6 oz.; draw weight, 50 lbs. peak; draw length, 28 to 31"; 38" custom black dacron string with monofilament center serving; 4½" sight window; full pistol grip shadua handle; left or right-hand models; black face, back; accessory insert bushings. **$157.95**

Stalker II has the same general design; length is 47½"; mass weight, 3¾ lbs.; draw weight 50/60 lbs.; draw lengths, 28 to 30"; 1¾", 2" eccentric wheels; 35% to 50% letoff; custom black dacron string, monofilament center serving; 3¾" sight window; other specs those of Stalker I. **$159.95**

BROWNING DELUXE MODEL

Length is 41¾", axle to axle; mass weight, 2¾ lbs.; draw weight, 45/60 lbs.; draw length, 28 to 31"; single pulley design; custom black dacron string with monofilament center serving; 5½" sight window; handle of selected hardwood, full pistol grip; insert bushings; olive drab handle, high-gloss black limbs. **$114.95**

Nomad model has the same general specifications as deluxe model, but is sans draw length adjustment feature, insert bushings.
. . . . **$99.95**

Ⓒ BROWNING WASP

Length is 48½", axle to axle; mass weight, 3 lbs., 6 oz.; draw weight, 45/60 lbs.; draw range, 28/31"; 1¾ or 2" eccentric wheels; custom black dacron string, monofilament center serving; 7¾" sight window; selected hardwood handle, full pistol grip; right or left-hand models; accessory insert bushings; hunter black limbs. **$134.95**

BROWNING COBRA

Length is 43", axle to axle; mass weight, 2 lbs.; draw weight, 50/60 lbs.; 35% to 50% letoff; draw length, 29 to 31"; 2 or 2¼" eccentric wheels; custom black dacron string, monofilament custom serving; 4¾" sight window; select shedua handle, full pistol grip; right or left-hand models; accessory bushings; black face, black limbs. **$77.50**

Ⓓ BROWNING CAM-LOCK

Length is 48¼", axle to axle; mass weight, 4½ lbs.; draw weight, 45 to 60 lbs.; draw lengths, 28 to 31"; 1¾ or 2" eccentric wheels; 40% to 50% letoff; 5½" string window; handle of cast alloy, full pistol grip with thumb rest; custom black dacron string with monofilament center serving; accessory insert bushing; predrilled for hunting sights, bowfishing reel; hunter black limbs. **$75**

CARROLL CAP 1200 HUNTER

Length is 45", axle to axle; draw weights, 20 to 70 lbs.; 20% to 35% letoff; mass weight, 4½ lbs.; draw length, 22 to 31"; cast magnesium handle; black or white limbs; right-hand model only.
. . . . **$237.60**

Ⓔ CARROLL CAP 900 HUNTER

Length is 47½", axle to axle; draw weights, 30 to 65 lbs.; 35% to 50% letoff; draw length, 25 to 32"; metal alloy handle; drilled, tapped for hunting sights, adjustable rest, cushion plunger; all black.
. . . . **$175**

Ⓕ CARROLL CAP 1500 HUNTER

Length is 45", axle to axle; available with 1½, 1¾, 2 and 2¼" eccentric wheels; draw weights, 20 to 70 lbs.; 20% to 35% letoff; black handle of cast magnesium; drilled for arrow rest, sight; limbs are laminated glass, hard core maple, in white or black; slotted swept-wing side plates. **$244.50**

G CARROLL CAP 2000 TARGET

Length is 49", axle to axle; draw weights to 70 lbs.; 20% or 35% letoff; eccentric wheels available in 1½, 1¾, 2 and 2¼" sizes; cast magnesium handle in custom colors or Plastic Fantastic paint; laminated glass, hard core maple limbs; hardened steel axles; aircraft-type cables; stabilizer, cushion plunger furnished; handle drilled, tapped for target sights. **$310.95**

CRAVOTTA BLACK HAWK JUPITER B-0

Length is 40¾", axle to axle; 2-wheel style; standard draw weights; draw length, 27 to 30"; cast aluminum alloy handle; drilled, tapped for sight, bow quiver, stabilizer; hard rock maple, fiberglass limbs. **$100**

CRAVOTTA BLACK HAWK CHIEF SCOUT B-01

Length is 44", axle to axle; 2-wheel style; standard draw weights; draw length, 27 to 30"; handle section is laminated contrasting hardwoods; hard rock maple, fiberglass limbs; optional eccentric wheel sizes; rug rest with leather side plate. **$110**

CRAVOTTA BLACK HAWK SATURN B-3

Length is 40¾", axle to axle; 2-wheel style; standard draw weights; 50% letoff; mass weight, 2½ lbs.; designed primarily as hunting bow; laminated hardwood handle, laminated wood/glass limbs; rug rest, leather side plate. **$100**

H CRAVOTTA BLACK HAWK WARRIOR B-4

Length is 40¾", axle to axle; 2-wheel style; standard draw weights; optional eccentric wheel sizes; mass weight, 2 lbs.; laminated oak handle; limbs are fiberglass, hard rock maple lamination; rug rest, leather side plate. **$90**

DARTON HAWK 40RC

Length is 44"; draw length 24 to 27"; peak draw weight, 30 lbs.; 50% letoff; laminated wood riser; continuous cable; arrow rest, plate; right or left-hand models. **$85**

DARTON HUNTSMAN 46M

Length is 46"; draw lengths, 24/27", 27/30", 29/32"; peak draw weight, 45/55 lbs.; 50% letoff; wood riser; laminated limbs; continuous cable; arrow rest, plate; right or left-hand models. ... **$110**

DARTON FALCON 45GL

Length is 45"; draw lengths, 24/27", 27/30", 29/32"; adjustable draw weights, 40/55 lbs.; 50% letoff; spring-tension adjusting screws; center-shot magnesium handle; continuous cable; arrow rest, plate; drilled, tapped for bowsight, stabilizer, plunger, quiver, counterbalance; right or left-hand models. **$85**

DARTON TRAILMASTER 45K

Length is 45"; draw lengths, 24/27", 27/30", 29/32", adjustable draw weights, 45/65 lbs.; 50% letoff; spring-tension adjusting screws; center-shot magnesium handle riser; laminated limbs; drilled, tapped for stabilizer, plunger, sight, bow quiver, counterbalance; right or left-hand models. **$130**

DARTON REGAL 50KH

Length is 50"; draw lengths; 24/27", 27/30", 29/32"; adjustable draw weights, 40/55 lbs., 55/70 lbs.; 50% letoff; spring-tension adjusting screws; center-shot magnesium handle riser; extra-long window; drilled, tapped for stabilizer, plunger, bowsights, quiver, counterbalance; right or left-hand models; designed for hunting.
.... **$145**

Regal 50 KT has same specifications as 50KH, except for adjustable draw weights of 20/35 lbs., 35/50 lbs.; designed for target archery. **$150**

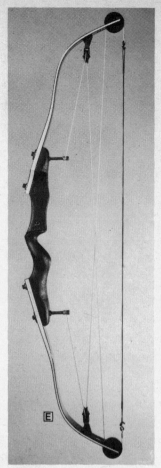

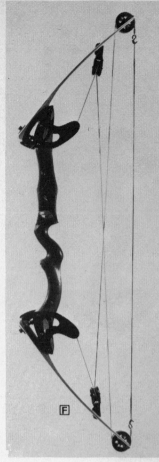

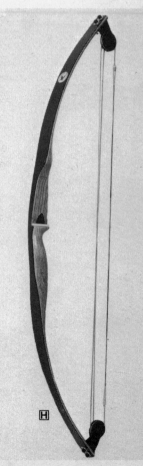

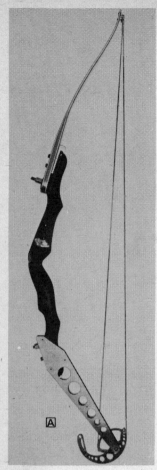

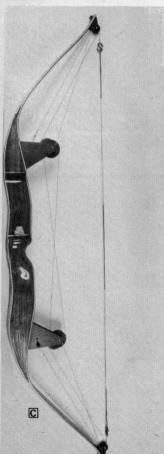
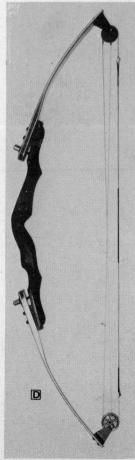

GRAHAM CUSTOM

Length is 50", axle to axle; draw weights, 25/40 lbs., 35/50 lbs., 45/60 lbs., 55/70 lbs.; magnesium handle section; limbs are wood/fiberglass laminated; has 15-lb. adjustment; noncritical to tune, adjust; novel design features; stabilizer inserts; drilled, tapped for bowsight; letoff ranges of 20%, 33%, 40% and 50%. **$250**

A GRAHAM DYNABO

Length is 44", axle to axle; adjustable draw weights of 25/40 lbs., 35/50 lbs., 45/60 lbs., 55/70 lbs.; letoff ranges of 20%, 33%, 40%, 50%; aluminum alloy handle section; upper limb is laminated wood, fiberglass; lower limb is adjustable alloy; noncritical tuning; drilled, tapped for bowsight. **$180**

B GRAHAM KING GEORGE

Length is 48", axle to axle; adjustable draw weights of 25/40 lbs., 35/50 lbs., 45/60 lbs., 55/70 lbs.; letoff ranges of 20%, 33%, 40%, 50%; aluminum alloy or magnesium handle section; laminated wood, fiberglass limbs. **$180**

C GRAHAM "JG" MODEL

Length is 48", axle to axle; draw weights of 25/40 lbs., 35/50 lbs., 45/60 lbs., 55/70 lbs.; letoff ranges of 20% to 50%; aluminum alloy handle section; laminated wood, fiberglass limbs; arrow rest, plate. **$160**

GRAHAM DURO 4-WHEELER

Length is 44", axle to axle; draw weights, 20/40 lbs., 35/50 lbs., 45/60 lbs., 55/70 lbs.; letoff ranges of 20% to 50%; aluminum alloy handle section; critical adjusting, tuning; arrow rest, plate. .. **$150**

GRAHAM DURO 2-WHEELER

Length is 44", axle to axle; draw weights, 20/40 lbs., 35/50 lbs., 45/60 lbs., 55/70 lbs.; letoff ranges of 20% to 50%; aluminum alloy handle section; noncritical adjusting, tuning; arrow rest, plate.
.... **$130**

HERTER'S BLACK MOUNTAIN HUNTER

Length is 44"; draw weights, 45/50 lbs., 50/55 lbs., 55/60 lbs.; 50% letoff; 28 to 30" draw length; aluminum alloy handle; laminated wood, fiberglass limbs; spring arrow rest, string replacer; 4" sight window; right or left-hand models. **$57.95**

Black Mountain Hunter Youth Bow has the same specifications as model listed above except draw weights are 25/30, 30/35, 35/40, 40/56 lbs.; draw length is 24 to 26"; also available in right or left-hand models. **$57.95**

HERTER'S MODEL G.L.H.

Length is 51"; draw weights, 45 to 60 lbs.; 50% letoff; one-piece bow with full-working recurve limbs; handle of imported exotic wood; fiberglass backing in desert tan; facing, black; finished with high-gloss urethane; 7" sight window; spring arrow rest, string replacer; left or right-hand models. **$79.95**

D HERTER'S POWER MAGNUM

Length is 44" in hunter model; draw weights, 40/55 lbs., 50/65 lbs.; 50% letoff; draw lengths adjustable from 27 to 32"; handle of exotic imported woods; 7½" sight window; laminated wood, fiberglass limbs; high-gloss urethane finish; right or left-hand models.
.... **$110.97**

Power Magnum target model has same general specifications as hunter version, except draw weights range from 38 to 48 lbs.; right or left-hand models. **$144.97**

E ROBIN HOOD CANTERBURY

Length is 44¼", axle to axle; mass weight, 3½ lbs.; adjustable draw weights, 20/30 lbs., 35/50 lbs.; draw lengths, 23 to 26", 26 to 29", 28 to 31"; 35% to 50% letoff; magnesium riser, glossy white;

black moulded replaceable grip provided; new offset riser design to reduce limb twist, bowhand torque; 7" sight window; limbs are double-core maple laminate, white fiberglass; Flipper two arrow rest; Accra plunger; custom nonserved bowstring; custom weight adjustment bolts; drilled, tapped for stabilizer; bushings for limb adjustment bolts. $175

F ROBIN HOOD LITTLE JOHN

Length is 41", axle to axle; mass weight, 3 lbs.; adjustable draw weight, 45/65 lbs.; 35% to 50% letoff; draw lengths, 23 to 26", 26 to 29", 28 to 31"; 5" sight window; offset riser; black magnesium riser with replaceable moulded grip; double-core maple laminate limbs with black fiberglass; drilled, tapped for plunger, bowsight, stabilizer; flexible plastic rest with plunger access hole; left or right-hand models. $130

ROBIN HOOD SAXON

Length is 33¾", axle to axle; mass weight, 3-1/8 lbs.; adjustable draw weights, 50/55 lbs.; 50% peak letoff; draw length, 28 to 31"; 5½" sight window; gray solid fiberglass limbs; black magnesium riser; drilled, tapped for plunger, bowsight, stabilizer; replaceable offset grip; right or left-hand models. $85

ROBIN HOOD SQUIRE

Length is 37½", axle to axle; mass weight, 2 lbs.; peak draw weight, 30 lbs.; 50% peak letoff; continuous cable system, no bowstring; draw length, 24 to 27"; one-piece imported hardwood riser; twin-core maple/fiberglass laminated limbs; 5½" sight window; hair shelf, leather side plate arrow rest. $80

DAMON HOWATT 2430 WARTHOG Model A

Length is 45½", axle to axle; peak draw weight to 65 lbs.; 50% letoff; draw lengths, 25 to 33"; handle riser has seven layers of hardwood, including bubinga, shedua, maple; reinforced limb caps; hardened steel axles; inserts for stabilizer, bow weights; right or left-hand models. $169.50
Warthog Model B has same specifications as Model A, except for handle riser of maple with hunter black finish; black fiberglass limbs. $149.50

DAMON HOWATT 1234 SUPER DIABLO TAKEDOWN

Length is 47½", axle to axle; mass weight, 3-7/8 lbs.; peak draw weight to 65 lbs.; 50% letoff; handle riser of shedua, bubinga; black fiberglass backing, back on limbs; hardened steel axles; Dura Flip rest; pro string; draw lengths, 25 to 32"; right or left-hand models.
.... $175

DAMON HOWATT 2400 LITTLE JOHN

Length is 35", axle to axle; mass weight, 1-3/8 lbs.; draw weights, 15 to 35 lbs.; 50% letoff; draw lengths, 22 to 27"; handle riser of assorted hardwoods; limbs laminated with black fiberglass; hardened steel axles; pro string; right or left-hand models. . . $79.50

DAMON HOWATT 2410 GAZELLE

Length is 45", axle to axle; mass weight, 2½ lbs.; draw weights from 25 to 65 lbs.; 50% letoff; draw lengths, 25 to 33"; handle riser is shedua, East India rosewood; black fiberglass limb laminations; hardened steel axles; stabilizer insert; pro string; right or left-hand models. $135

G INDIAN GOLDEN COMANCHE TROPHY

Length is 34", axle to axle; mass weight, 3-15/16 lbs.; adjustable draw weights, 40/55 lbs.; standard draw lengths; 40% to 50% letoff; checkered moulded grip with wood-grain finish; 7" sight window; tapered walnut burl-finished fiberglass limbs; adjustable 3-pin sight; window-mounted arrow rest; nylon-coated steel cables. . . . $135.95

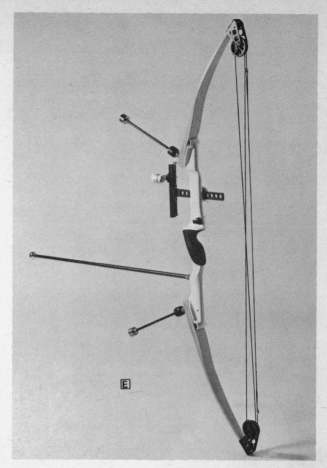

E

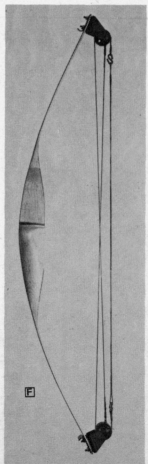

F

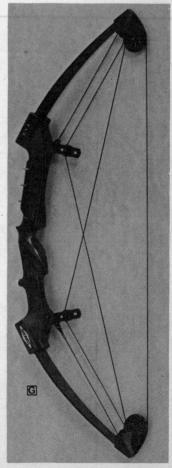

G

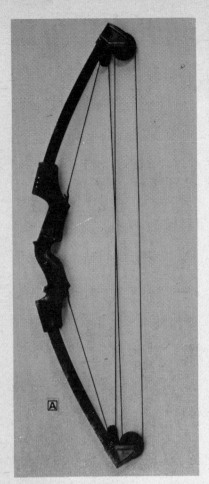
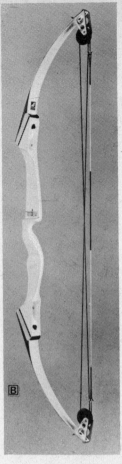

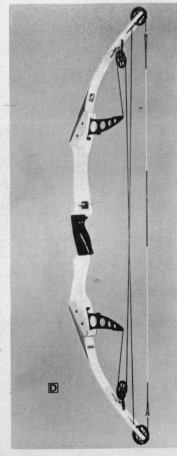

A INDIAN GOLDEN COMANCHE
Length is 38", axle to axle; mass weight, 4¼ lbs.; peak draw weight, 50 lbs.; 50% letoff; moulded grip in wood-grain finish, checkered grip; drilled, tapped for sight; threaded accessory inserts; window-mounted arrow rest; nylon-coated cables. **$99.95**

INDIAN COMANCHE
Length is 36¾", axle to axle; mass weight, 2-9/16 lbs.; peak draw weight, 50 lbs.; 50% letoff; moulded contour grip for both left and right-handed shooters; 3 adjustable sight pins; lightweight aluminum brackets, pulley system; window-mounted arrow rest; nylon-coated cables; forest green fiberglass limbs. **$72.50**

JENNINGS TWINSTAR HUNTER
Length is 48-3/8", axle to axle; draw weights, 35/45 lbs., 40/50 lbs., 50/60 lbs., 55/70 lbs.; draw lengths, 24 to 33"; 40% to 50% letoff; textured black custom riser, interchangeable wood-grained grip; adjustable arrow rest carriage with custom plunger, arrow rest; laminated wood, Magna-Ply black limbs; drilled, tapped for sight, stabilizer, cushion plunger, bow quiver. .... **Does not .... release retail prices.**

B JENNINGS SUPER T TARGET
Length is 43¾", axle to axle; draw weights, 25/35 lbs., 35/45 lbs., 40/50 lbs., 45/55 lbs.; draw lengths, 24 to 31"; 40% to 50% letoff; white riser; chromed hardware; laminated wood, white Magna-Ply limbs; arrow rest; drilled, tapped for sight, stabilizer, cushion plunger. .... **Does not release retail prices.**

JENNINGS SUPER T HUNTER
Length is 43¾", axle to axle; draw weights, 25/35 lbs., 35/45 lbs., 45/60 lbs., 55/70 lbs.; draw lengths, 25, 27, 29, 31" maximums; 40% to 50% letoff; textured black riser; laminated wood, black Magna-Ply limbs; drilled, tapped for sight, stabilizer, bow quiver, cushion plunger; arrow rest, center-shot adjustment screw. .... **Does not release retail prices.**

JENNINGS MODEL T HUNTER
Length is 43¾", axle to axle; draw weights, 30, 35, 40, 45, 50, 55, 60, 65, 70 lbs.; 40% to 50% letoff; draw lengths, 27, 28, 29, 31" maximums; textured black riser; laminated wood, black Magna-Ply limbs; center-shot adjustment screw; arrow rest; drilled, tapped for sight, stabilizer, cushion plunger, bow quiver. .... **Does not .... release retail prices.**

JENNINGS SIDEKICK II
Length is 39½", axle to axle; adjustable draw weights, 40 to 60 lbs.; draw lengths, 29 to 31" maximums; 40% to 50% letoff; textured black riser; laminated black Magna-Ply limbs; center-shot adjustment screw; arrow rest; drilled, tapped for sight, stabilizer, cushion plunger, bow quiver. ...... **Does not release retail prices.**

C JENNINGS TWINSTAR TARGET
Length is 48-3/8", axle to axle; draw weights, 25/35 lbs., 30/40 lbs., 35/45 lbs., 45/55 lbs.; draw lengths, 24 to 33"; 40% to 50% letoff; white custom riser; chromed hardware; laminated wood, white Magna-Ply limbs; interchangeable black grip; adjustable arrow rest carriage, spring arrow rest; drilled, tapped for sight, stabilizer, cushion plunger. .... **Does not release retail prices.**

D JENNINGS ARROWSTAR TARGET
Length is 47-5/8", axle to axle; draw weights, 25/35 lbs., 30/40 lbs., 35/45 lbs., 40/50 lbs.; draw lengths, 23 to 33"; 40% letoff; with low letoff eccentrics, 25%; custom riser in white, black, red, banner, blue or astro; interchangeable black grip; chromed hardware; laminated limbs of wood, white Magna-Ply; magnesium eccentrics; aluminum idler wheels, dorsal pylons; adjustable arrow rest carriage, spring arrow rest; drilled, tapped for sight, stabilizer, cushion plunger. .... **Does not release retail prices.**

JENNINGS ARROWSTAR HUNTER

Length is 47-5/8", axle to axle; draw weights, 35/45 lbs., 40/50 lbs., 50/60 lbs., 55/70 lbs.; draw lengths, 23 to 33"; 40% letoff; with low letoff eccentrics, 25%; textured black custom riser; interchangeable wood-grained grip; magnesium eccentrics; aluminum idler wheel, dorsal pylons; limbs of laminated wood, black Magna-Ply; adjustable arrow rest carriage, cushion plunger, arrow rest; drilled, tapped for sight, stabilizer, cushion plunger, bow quiver.
.... **Does not release retail prices.**

E MARTIN M-10 CHEETAH DYNABO

Length is 51" overall; mass weight, 3 lbs.; draw weights, 25 to 55 lbs.; 50% letoff; draw lengths, 24 to 33"; laminated wood handle; wood/fiberglass laminated upper limb; quick takedown; stabilizer, bow weight inserts; lower limb mechanized of alloy; SFX Posi-Flit rest; Martin pro string; right or left-hand models. **$225**

MARTIN MT-3 OCELOT

Length is 44½", axle to axle; mass weight, 2½ lbs.; draw weights, 30 to 65 lbs.; 50% letoff; simple wood handle design; fiberglass laminated limbs; hardened steel axles; stabilizer insert; rest; pro bowstring; right or left-hand models. **$129.95**

F MARTIN MT-6 COUGAR II

Length is 45¾", axle to axle; mass weight, 3-7/8 lbs.; Hunter model draw weights, 40 to 55 lbs.; competition model, 20/30, 35/50 lbs.; draw lengths, 24 to 32"; new design magnesium handle in black or white finish; drilled, tapped for sight, stabilizer, pressure button; rest; Martin pro string; right or left-hand models. ... **$160**

MARTIN M-7 LYNX

Length is 40½", axle to axle; mass weight, 2¼ lbs.; draw weights from 45 to 65 lbs.; hardened steel axles; draw lengths, 26 to 31"; hard shedua handle; stabilizer insert; rest; pro string; right or left-hand models. **$139.95**

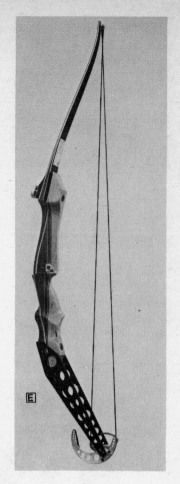

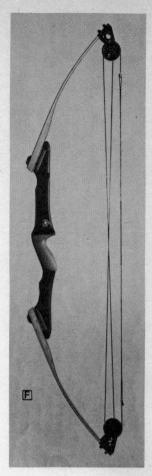

G PEARSON PRO STAFF 6000

Length is 49", axle to axle; mass weight, 3-15/16 lbs.; adjustable draw weights, 45/55 lbs., 55/65 lbs.; 28% to 31% letoff; draw lengths, 28/29", 30/31", plus short draws to 27"; die-cast magnesium riser; polyester powder-coated finish; moulded vinyl grip; laminated limbs of maple, glass; micarta tips; 7" sight window; drilled, tapped for stabilizers, bow quiver, bow sights, cushion plunger; right or left-hand models. **$215**

Pro Staff 6001 has same general specifications as 6000, except designed for target archery; draw weight, 30/40 lbs.; platinum magnesium riser; white Hyper-Flex laminated limbs. **$225**

H PEARSON PRO STAFF 4000

Length is 49¼", axle to axle; mass weight, 3-15/16 lbs.; adjustable draw weights, 45/55 lbs., 55/65 lbs.; 28% to 31% letoff; draw lengths, 28/29", 30/31", plus short draws to 27"; die-cast magnesium riser, polyester powder-coated finish; moulded vinyl handle; laminated Hyper-Flex limbs; tapered maple cores, micarta tips; 7" sight window; tapped for stabilizers, bow quivers, bow sight, cushion plunger; right or left-hand models. **$215**

Pro Staff 4001 has same general specifications as 4000, except designed for target archery; draw weight, 30/40 lbs.; platinum magnesium riser; white limb laminations. **$225**

I PEARSON PRO STAFF 2000

Length is 45½", axle to axle; adjustable draw weights, 50/60 lbs.; 45% letoff; draw lengths, 27/29", 29/31", plus 27" short draw; die-cast magnesium riser; polyester powder-coated finish; contoured moulded vinyl handle; 7" sight window; drilled, tapped for stabilizers, bowquiver, sight, cushion plunger; adjustable arrow pressure plate; right or left-hand models. **$135**

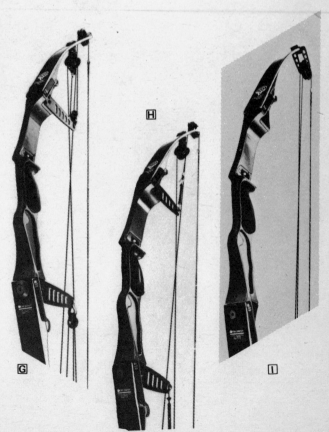

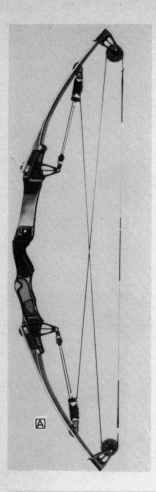

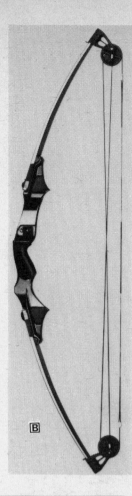

PEARSON PRO STAFF 1000

Length is 41¾", axle to axle; adjustable draw weights, 40/60 lbs.; 45% letoff; draw lengths, 27/29", 29/31", plus 27" short draw; die-cast magnesium riser, polyester powder-coated finish; 4½" sight window; drilled, tapped for stabilizer, cushion plunger; moulded vinyl contoured grip; Pearsonite reinforced fiberglass limbs. .. **$90**

Ⓐ PEARSON SHADOW 600

Length is 44", axle to axle; adjustable draw weights, 45/55 lbs., 55/65 lbs.; 30% letoff; draw lengths, 28/29", 30/31"; die-cast magnesium riser, polyester powder-coated finish; moulded vinyl contoured handle; interchangeable laminated limbs with maple cores, black fiberglass; 7" center-shot sight window; tapped for stabilizers, bow quiver, sight, cushion plunger. **$175**

Ⓑ PEARSON SHADOW 300

Length is 41¾", axle to axle; adjustable draw weights, 50/60 lbs.; 45% letoff; draw lengths, 28/29", 30/31"; die-cast magnesium riser, polyester powder-coated finish; moulded vinyl contoured grip; 4½" sight window; interchangeable Hyper-Flex limbs, tapered maple cores; drilled, tapped for stabilizer, cushion plunger. **$135**

PEARSON SHADOW 100

Length is 41¾", axle to axle; adjustable draw weights 50/60 lbs.; 45% letoff; draw lengths, 28/29", 30/31"; die-cast magnesium riser, polyester powder-coated finish; moulded vinyl contoured grip; 4½" sight window; interchangeable fiberglass limbs; drilled, tapped for stabilizer, cushion plunger. **$87.50**

PEARSON MODEL 210

Length is 42½", axle to axle; adjustable draw weights, 45/60 lbs.; 45% letoff; draw lengths, 27/29", 29/31"; 6½" sight window; laminated Hyper-Flex limbs; marblewood handle; flexible arrow rest. **$152.50**

Model 200 has same general design as Model 210, except has fixed peak weights of 45, 50, 55, 60 lbs. **$130**

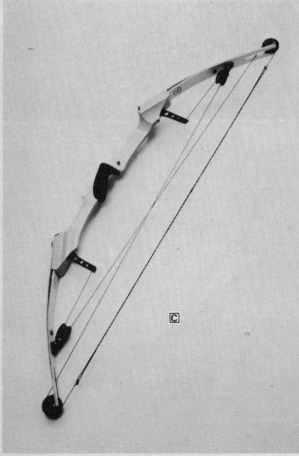

Ⓒ PSE CITATION TARGET

Length is 51"; draw weights, 15 to 60 lbs., in 10-lb. adjustment ranges; draw length, 23 to 34"; die-cast magnesium handle; integrally moulded limb sockets; tension lock system; spring rest; speed brackets; handle available in blue, black, white; laminated limbs, with white fiberglass face, back; nonslip replaceable grip; right and left-hand models. **$295.50**

Citation Hunter model has the same general specifications as Target version, with draw weights from 35 to 70 lbs.; black fiberglass face, back on limbs, black handle only. **$249.50**

PSE PROFICIENCY

Length is 48"; six adjustable draw weights, 35/40 lbs., 40/50 lbs., 45/55 lbs., 50/60 lbs., 55/66 lbs., 60/70 lbs.; draw lengths, 26 to 32"; magnesium handle; black finish only; laminated limbs with black fiberglass face, back; spring rest; drilled, tapped for stabilizer, arrow rest, hunting sight. **$194.50**

PSE PACER TARGET

Length is 48"; six adjustable draw weights, 35/45 lbs., 40/50 lbs., 45/55 lbs., 50/60 lbs., 55/65 lbs., 60/70 lbs.; laminated limbs, black fiberglass face, back; magnesium handle; white, blue or black finish; extra-wide eccentric wheels; spring rest; drilled, tapped for stabilizer, arrow rest, hunting sight. **$185**

Pacer hunter has the same general specifications as target model, except that it is available in black and camouflage finish only. **$169**

PSE SIZZLER

Length is 51"; draw weights, 40, 50, 60 lbs.; draw lengths, 27/28", 28/29", 29/30", 30/31"; alloy handle, Hammertone finish; limbs are blackwood/fiberglass laminations; drilled, tapped for standard sight pattern, stabilizer; accepts all PSE accessories. **$139**

D RIGID TARGET MODEL

Length is 50", axle to axle; four-wheel model; target draw weights and draw lengths; laminated wood, fiberglass riser, black-crackle finish; limbs adjusted with knurled nut; drilled, tapped for stabilizer. $265

RIGID HUNTER

Length is 34", axle to axle; four-wheel model; all-metal frame; green, black or blue anodized frame; adjustable draw weights, 35 to 70 lbs.; 47% letoff; draw lengths, 26 to 32"; drilled, tapped for sight mounts, bow quiver, cushion plungers; 5" sight window; left or right-hand models. $174.95

WESTERN DIRECT SALES 1050 TARGET

Length is 47½", axle to axle; draw weight, 20 to 50 lbs.; 24 to 32" draw length; 35% to 50% letoff; alloy pistol grip handle; composite maple/fiberglass limbs; stabilizer insert; drilled for target sight; handle available in candy apple colors, black or white; black or white limbs. $136.85

WESTERN DIRECT SALES 850 HUNTER

Length is 47½", axle to axle; draw weight, 20 to 65 lbs.; 23 to 31" draw length; weight tuning and draw length adjustments; 35% to 50% letoff; alloy pistol grip handle; all black; camouflage finish at additional cost. $119.50

E WESTERN DIRECT SALES 700 HUNTER

Length is 39½", axle to axle; draw weight, 20 to 60 lbs.; 22 to 29" draw length; 20% to 30% letoff; alloy pistol grip handle; composite maple/fiberglass limbs; drilled for sight, rest, bow quiver; all-black finish; camo at added cost. $166.32

WING PRESENTATION TARGET

Length is 48", axle to axle; draw weights, 25/40 lbs., 35/50 lbs.; 15/20-lb. weight adjustment range; draw length, 25 to 32"; new 2-step eccentric wheel; die-cast magnesium handle; replaceable grip; adjustable tuning arms; self-aligning cable attachment; cushion plunger; needle bearings; drilled, tapped for stabilizer, bowsight, quiver; white with white limbs, chrome fixtures. $310

Presentation Hunter model has same general specifications as target model, except draw weights are 45/60 lbs., 55/70 lbs.; black riser and limbs. $275

WING THUNDERBIRD

Length is 48", axle to axle; draw lengths, 26/27", 28/29", 30/31", 32/33"; black riser, limbs; die-cast magnesium handle; three-step eccentric wheels; same draw weights as Presentation models; hunting rest; drilled, tapped for stabilizer, cushion plunger, bowsight, quiver. $190

WING CHAPARRAL

Length is 46", axle to axle; draw lengths, 25/27", 27/29", 29/31"; brown riser, limbs; die-cast magnesium handle; three-step eccentric wheels; same draw weights as Presentation models; hunting rest; drilled, tapped for stabilizer, cushion plunger, bowsight, quiver. $140

F WING IMPACT II

Length is 48", axle to axle; adjustable draw weights, 40 to 70 lbs.; draw lengths, 26/27", 28/29", 30/31", 32/33"; takedown features; black Wingwood handle; decorative riser overlays; stabilizer insert, quiver inserts, hunting rest. $250

YORK CORONET

Length is 43", axle to axle; draw weights, 50, 55, 60 lbs.; draw lengths, 26 to 31"; aluminum alloy handle; solid epoxy fiberglass limbs; 50% letoff; available in right-hand style only. $88.80

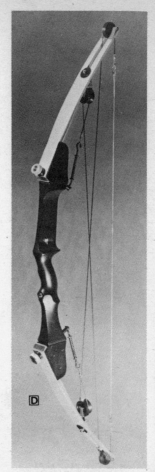

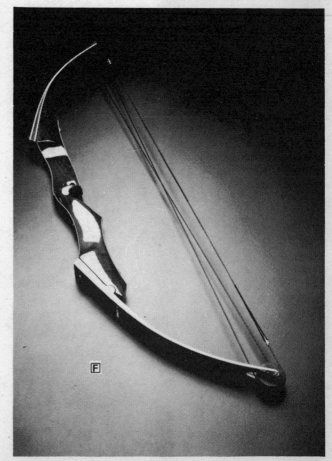

Recurves

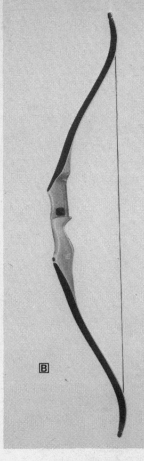

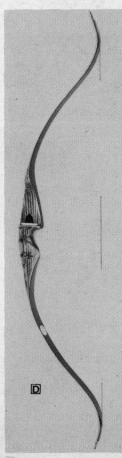

AMERICAN HUNTER
Length is 56"; draw limit, 32"; draw weight, 35 to 70 lbs.; dark glass limbs; hardwood riser, capped overlay; super-slim taper core, reminder grip. **$59.95**

A AMERICAN SHORTIE X-48
Length is 48"; draw limit, 32"; draw weight, 40, 45, 50, 55 lbs.; hardwood riser, capped overlay; dark glass; super-slim taper core, reminder grip. **$59.95**

B BEAR VICTOR TIGERCAT
Length is 56"; draw weights, 40, 45, 50, 55 lbs.; draw length, unlimited; hardwood handle; hand-contoured grip with thumb rest; tip overlays; laminated limbs, fiberglass back, face; camouflage finish at no added cost; left or right-hand models. **$60**

BEAR BLACK BEAR HUNTER
Length is 58"; draw weights, 40, 45, 50 lbs.; draw length, unlimited; hardwood handle; laminated limbs, fiberglass back, face; drilled, tapped for accessories; arrow rest; camouflage finish at no added cost; right or left-hand models. **$52.50**

C BEAR BLACK BEAR MAGNUM
Length is 52"; draw weights, 40, 45, 50 lbs.; draw length, unlimited; hardwood handle; laminated limbs, dark fiberglass back, face; drilled, tapped for accesories; arrow rest; camouflage finish at no added cost; right or left-hand models. **$52.50**

BEAR VICTOR PATRIOT
Length is 66"; draw weights, 25, 30, 35 lbs.; draw length, unlimited; Futurewood handle with red stripe; laminated limbs, white fiberglass back, face; Futurewood tip overlays; drilled, tapped for accessories; arrow rest; designed for Junior Olympic competition; right or left-hand models. **$102.50**

BEAR WHITE BEAR
Length is 62"; draw weights 25/30, 30/35 lbs.; draw length, unlimited; hardwood handle; arrow rest; laminated limbs; white fiberglass back, face; white dacron bowstring; right or left-hand models. **$52.50**

CRAVOTTA BLACK HAWK SHORT BEE-B6
Length is 60, 62"; mass weight, 1¾ lbs.; 8" fistmele; standard draw lengths; hardwood handle, laminated limbs; comes with rug rest, leather plate for quiet shooting. **$60**

D CRAVOTTA BLACK HAWK AVENGER-B13
Length is 52"; mass weight, 1¾ lbs.; 7" fistmele; standard draw lengths; compact hunting-bow design; hardwood handle, maple laminated limbs; rug rest, leather plate. **$55**

DARTON VALIANT 58F
Length is 58"; draw weight at 28", 35 to 60 lbs.; string length, 54"; imported wood riser; laminated limbs; center-shot sight window; string grooves with overlays; stabilizer insert; stringer. **$110**

DARTON SCHOLAR 66B
Length is 66"; draw weight at 28", 20 to 40 lbs.; string length, 62"; imported wood riser; laminated limbs; arrow rest; stabilizer insert; for beginning target shooter. **$55**

HERTER'S PERFECTION PREMIER MAGNUM HUNTER
Lengths are 62, 60, 58"; draw weights, 35/39 lbs.; 40/44 lbs., 40/44 lbs., 45/49 lbs., 50/54 lbs., 55/59 lbs., 60/65 lbs.; center-shot handle of imported hardwood; urethane finish; arrow rest, fiberglass backing and facing laminated to hardwood core; fiberglass tip overlays; right or left-hand models. **$56.95**

HERTER'S PERFECTION HUNTER

Lengths are 56, 52, 46''; draw weights, 30/34 lbs., 35/39 lbs., 40/44 lbs., 45/49 lbs., 50/54 lbs., 55/59 lbs., 60/65 lbs.; center-shot bow handle of exotic hardwood; fiberglass backing, facing; International Match arrow rest; fiberglass top overlays; right or left-hand models. .... **$41.97 to $47.69**

HERTER'S PERFECTION SITKA

Lengths are 72, 66''; draw weights, 25/29 lbs., 30/34 lbs., 35/39 lbs., 40/45 lbs. in 72'' length; 66'' length available in draw weights from 25 to 60 lbs.; center-shot handle of imported wood; International Match arrow rest; glass backing, facing; urethane finish; three laminations; fiberglass tip overlays; right or left-hand models.

Perfection Sitka Magnum Hunter has same general specifications as standard model, except for 62'' or 58'' limbs; left or right-hand models. .... **$52.73 to $63.83**

E HOWARD GAMEMASTER JET

Length is 66''; draw weights to 65 lbs. at standard draw lengths; laminated Brazilian rosewood pistol grip handle; laminated wood/fiberglass limbs, white face, black backing; recurves designed for quietness, no silencers needed for hunting; uses Howard's exclusive glass spine method; features controlled limb recovery. **$247.75**

F HOYT PRO SPECIAL

Length is 66''; draw weights to 50 lbs. at 28'' draw; stylized handle of dark exotic wood; stabilizer bushing; pro rest; wood, white fiberglass laminated limbs; Ply-O-String bowstring. . **$109.50**

HOYT XPERT

Length is 65''; draw weights to 50 lbs. at 28'' draw; contoured shedua hardwood handle; fiberglass tip overlays; arrow rest. **$59.94**

HOYT SCOUT

Length is 62''; draw weights to 50 lbs. at 28'' draw; contoured handle of hardwood; fiberglass tip overlays; arrow rest. **$49.95**

G HOYT PRO HUNTER

Length is 58''; draw weights to 70 lbs. at 28'' draw; exotic hardwood handle; two stabilizer bushings for mounting bow quiver or bow reel; limbs of laminated wood, olive-colored fiberglass; Ply-O-String bowstring. **$82.50**

INDIAN DEERSLAYER

Length is 60''; draw weight at 28'', 40 to 55 lbs.; imported hardwood handle with integral stabilizers; contoured grip, thumb rest; laminated maple, fiberglass limbs; tip overlays; arrow rest, plate; right or left-hand models. **$67.95**

INDIAN BIGHORN

Length is 58''; draw weight at 28'', 40 to 50 lbs.; imported hardwood handle; hand-finished sculpted grip, thumb rest; laminated maple, fiberglass limbs; tip overlays; arrow rest. **$45.95**

Bighorn R model has same basic design as standard Bighorn, except draw weights at 28'' are 25 to 35 lbs.; designed for archer instruction. **$45.95**

PEARSON PRO STAFF 3000

Length is 30''; draw weights, 30, 35, 40, 45 lbs.; die-cast magnesium riser; interchangeable recurve limbs with tapered maple cores,; 7'' sight window; drilled, tapped for stabilizers, bow sights, cushion plunger. **$140**

H PEARSON BPH 60

Length is 50''; draw weight at 28'', 45/50 lbs.; draw limit, 31''; die-cast magnesium handle; 4½'' sight window; 3-piece takedown; interchangeable maple/fiberglass limbs; drilled, tapped for stabilizer, cushion plunger. **$55**

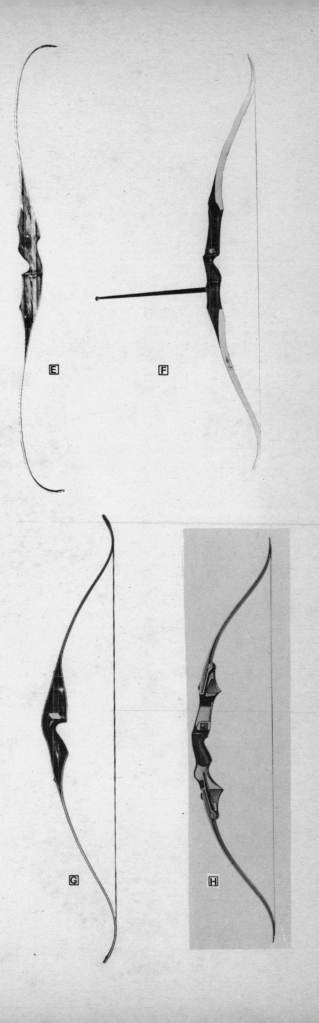

E   F

G   H

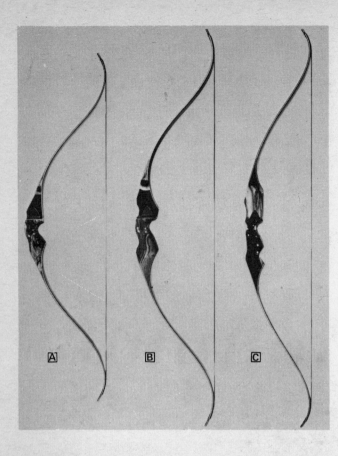

PEARSON RENEGADE

Length is 60"; draw weight at 28", 40 to 55 lbs.; unlimited draw length; pistol-grip marblewood handle; mohair carpet arrow rest; 5½" sight window; recurve fiberglass limbs; reinforced tips; prestretched, prewaxed bowstring; right or left-hand models. $65

A PEARSON EQUALIZER

Length is 48"; draw weight at 28", 40 to 55 lbs.; draw limit, 31"; marblewood pistol grip handle; mohair carpet arrow rest; 4" sight window; black fiberglass limbs, reinforced tips; prestretched, prewaxed string; right or left-hand models. $55

B PEARSON SPOILER

Length is 52"; draw weight at 28", 40 to 55 lbs.; unlimited draw length; marblewood pistol grip handle; mohair carpet arrow rest; 4½" sight window; black fiberglass limbs; reinforced tips; prestretched, prewaxed string; right or left-hand models. $55

C PEARSON ROGUE

Length is 58"; draw weight at 28", 40 to 55 lbs.; unlimited draw length; marblewood/hardwood pistol grip handle; mohair arrow rest; 5½" sight window; black figerglass limbs; reinforced tips; prestretched, prewaxed string; right or left-hand models. $65

WING COMPETITION II

Length is 66, 68, 70"; draw weights, 25 to 50 lbs.; interchangeable limb capability; magnesium high-wrist riser; aluminum limb wedges; stabilizer, counterbalance inserts; cushion plunger; flip rest; bowstringer; white riser, glass laminated limbs. $225

D WING FALCON

Length is 66"; draw weight at 28"; 20, 25, 30, 35, 40 lbs.; exotic hardwood riser; laminated fiberglass limbs; stabilizer adaptor; built-in stabilizer insert; padded arrow rest. $75

Falcon Hunter has same general specifications as Falcon 66, but is 60" in length; target weights of 25, 30, 35 lbs.; hunting weights, 40, 45, 50 lbs. $60

E WING NIGHTHAWK

Length is 60"; draw weight at 28", 15, 25, 30, 35 lbs.; maple riser; laminated maple/fiberglass limbs; padded shelf arrow rest; designed for beginning target archer. $50

RED WING HUNTER

Length is 52, 58, 62"; draw weights, 40, 45, 50, 55 lbs.; custom draw weights, 35, 50, 65, 70 lbs.; Wingwood riser; laminated limbs; brown fiberglass face, back; inserts for hunting stabilizer, bowfishing reel, quiver. $82.95

WING LITTLE WING

Length is 48"; draw weight at 24", 20 lbs.; draw limit, 28"; tropical hardwood riser; laminated wood; fiberglass limbs; for young beginning archers. $41.75

F YORK TROPHY

Length is 60"; draw weights, 40, 45, 50, 55 lbs.; unlimited draw length; brace height, 8½"; pistol grip handle of laminated hardwoods; laminated fiberglass, hardwood limbs; arrow rest, plate; stabilizer bushing; right or left-hand models; designed for hunting. $75.50

YORK CREST

Length is 68"; draw weights, 20, 25, 30, 35, 40 lbs.; unlimited draw length; brace height, 9"; hardwood pistol grip handle; laminated fiberglass, hardwood limbs; arrow rest, plate; stabilizer bushing; right or left-hand models; designed as target bow. $71

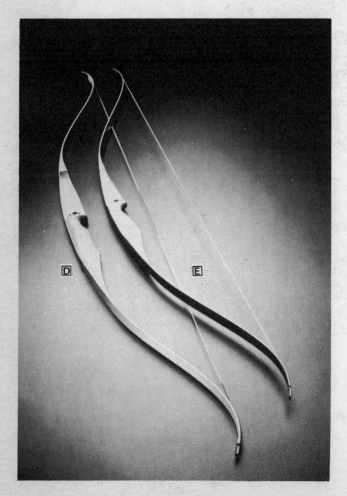

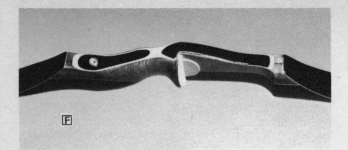

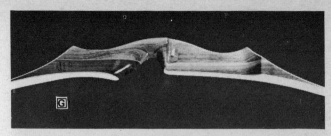

G YORK THUNDERBOLT

Length is 54"; draw weights, 40, 45, 50, 55 lbs.; unlimited draw length; brace height, 8½"; pistol grip handle of laminated hardwoods; laminated fiberglass, hardwood limbs; arrow rest, plate; available in right or left-hand models; designed for hunting. .. $62

H YORK CRESCENT

Length is 66"; draw weights, 20, 25, 30, 35, 40 lbs.; unlimited draw length; brace height, 9"; one-piece hardwood pistol grip handle; laminated fiberglass, hardwood limbs; arrow rest, plate; available in right or left-hand models; designed for targets. . $57.70

I YORK CADET

Length is 62"; 20, 25, 30, 35, 40 lbs.; unlimited draw length; brace height, 9"; semi-pistol grip hardwood handle; laminated hardwood, fiberglass limbs; arrow rest, plate; right or left-hand models; for schools, camps, beginning archers. $43.30

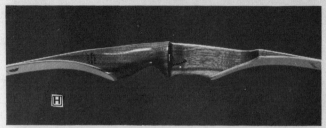

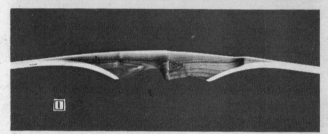

Takedowns

J BEAR BEARCAT TAKE-DOWN HUNTER

Length is 60"; draw weights, 20 to 55 lbs.; draw length, unlimited; magnesium pistol grip handle; silver vein metallic epoxy finish; laminated limbs, white or dark fiberglass face, back; arrow rest; sight platform; drilled, tapped for bow quiver, other accessories; right or left-hand models. $59.50

K BEAR '76er TAKE-DOWN HUNTER

Length is 58"; draw weights. light, medium heavy, extra-heavy; draw length, unlimited; magnesium handle; black standard grip; fiberglass limbs; tip overlays; sight stage; rest; drilled, tapped for accessories; right or left-hand models. $37.50

Bear '76er Take-Down has same general design specifications as Hunter model, except length is 64"; limbs are white fiberglass only; right or left-hand models. $37.50

BEAR BEARCAT TAKE-DOWN

Length is 66"; draw weights, 18, 23, 28, 33, 38, 43, 48, 53 lbs.; draw length, unlimited; glass laminated composite limbs; magnesium handle; glacier vein metallic epoxy finish; standard pistol grip handle; rest; sight stage; drilled, tapped for accessories; right or left-hand models. $59.95

HERTER'S MODEL 62 MAGNUM T/D

Lengths are 62, 58"; choice of Amaloy aluminum handle or rosewood; laminated recurve limbs with tan fiberglass backing, black facing; spring-tempered steel takedown brackets; spring rest; fiberglass bow tip overlays; 4½" sight window; right or left-hand models; with alloy handle. $66.97
With rosewood handle. $77.97

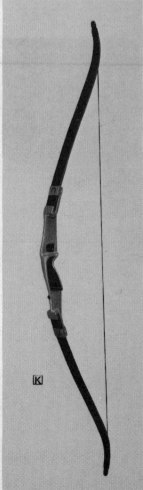

HERTER'S PERFECTION UTOPIAN T/D

Lengths are 75, 70"; Amaloy aluminum handle; laminated recurve limbs with white fiberglass backing, facing; 8" sight window; spring arrow rest; spring-tempered steel takedown brackets; draw weights, 25/29 lbs., 30/34 lbs., 35/39 lbs. and 40/45 lbs.; telescope stabilizer; three-lamination bow tip overlays; right or left-hand models. $88.25

HOYT PRO MEDALIST T/D 24

Lengths are 66, 68, 70"; has long takedown handle; with white glass, draw weights to 50 lbs. at 28"; with olive glass, draw weights to 60 lbs. at 28"; 7½" sight window; action-core powered limbs, teardrop tip overlays; standard interchangeable thumb rest pistol grip. dual stabilizers; two additional bushings for optional counterweights; microrest with Super-Rest sight mounting surfaces adaptable to face, back or side-mounted sights; black or white handle. $222

Pro Medalist T/D 20 has same general specifications, except for medium handle, lengths of 63, 65, 67"; draw weights of 55 lbs.; at 28" with white glass, 65 lbs. with olive glass; 6" sight window. $222

Ⓐ WING SWIFT WING TAKEDOWN

Length is 66, 70"; draw weights, 25 to 50 lbs.; magnesium riser; sight adaptor; 3 stabilizer inserts; hole for cushion plunger; riser, laminated glass limbs finished in ivory color. $141.75

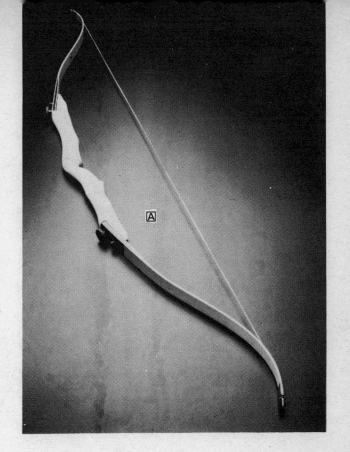

Longbows

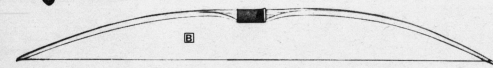

HERTER'S PERFECTION ITASCA

Length is 70"; draw weights, 40 to 80 lbs.; imported hardwood handle; limbs have rock maple tapered cores; laminated with fiberglass backing, facing; 5" sight window; Herter's International Match arrow rest; high-gloss urethane finish; left or right-hand models. $53.49

HOWARD HILL TEMBO

Length is 66 to 70"; draw weights to 100 lbs.; Oregon myrtlewood handle; leather-covered grip; laminated heat-tempered bamboo limbs; may be ordered with recurve handle; price given is to 75-lb. draw weight; over that add $1 per pound. $125

HOWARD HILL BIG FIVE

Length is 66 to 70"; draw weights to 100 lbs.; rosewood or bubinga hardwood handle; leather covering; limbs of four select bamboo laminations, fiberglass; price given is to 75-lb. draw weight; over that add $1.07 per pound. $136.95

HOWARD HILL HALF BREED

Length is 60 to 66"; draw weights to 100 lbs.; bubinga hardwood riser; recurve-style pistol grip handle, thumb rest available; limbs are laminated bamboo with yew core; price given is to 75-lb. draw weight; over that add $1 per pound. $125.95

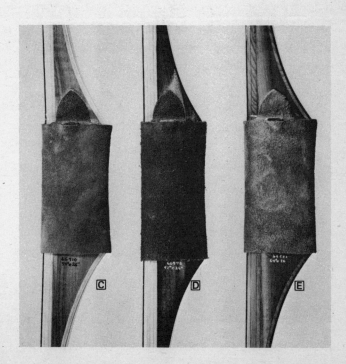

HOWARD HILL REDMAN

Length is 66 to 70"; draw weights to 100 lbs.; laminated yew wood; leather grip cover; recurve handle at no added cost; price given is to 75-lb. draw weight; over that add $1 per pound. **$109.95**

B HOWARD HILL MOUNTAIN MAN

Length is 66 to 70"; draw weights to 100 lbs.; laminated hard rock maple; leather grip cover; recurve handle at no added cost; price given is to 75-lb. draw weight; over that add $1 per pound. **$92.95**

C LONGBOW HUNTER

Length is 60 to 70"; draw weight at 28" to 100 lbs.; hardwood riser; laminated split bamboo, fiberglass limbs; three laminations; roughout leather-covered handle; arrow rest. **$124.50**

D LONGBOW TROPHY HUNTER

Length is 60 to 70 inches; draw weight at 28" to 100 lbs.; hardwood handle riser; four lamination limbs of split bamboo, fiberglass; roughout leather-covered handle; arrow rest. **$135.50**

E LONGBOW GAZELLE

Length is 60 to 70 inches; draw weight at 28" to 100 lbs.; hardwood handle riser; limbs laminated of fiberglass yew wood; roughout leather-covered handle; arrow rest. **$118.50**

LONGBOW CHEETAH

Length is 60 to 66"; draw weight at 28" to 100 lbs.; recurve-style handle; two-thirds center-shot pistol grip, thumb rest; laminated hardwood, fiberglass limbs; arrow rest. **$120.50**

F MARTIN ML-12

Length is 70"; draw weight at 28", 70 to 100 lbs.; made of assorted hardwoods; glass laminated face, back; brown, black or green fiberglass; handle is set forward slightly for smoothness; unstrung, limbs have forward flex; arrow shelf, small sight window area; right or left-hand models. **$130**

ML-17 longbow has the same specifications as the ML-12, except in draw weights of 40 to 60 lbs. **$110**

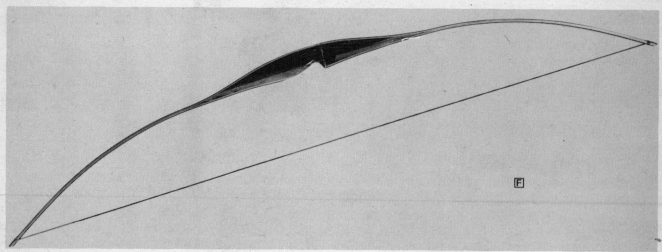

Budget Bows

AMERICAN YOUNG AMERICAN

Length is 56"; draw length 28"; draw weight, 20 lbs. to 50 lbs.; hardwood riser; dark glass; sure grip; recurve design; for the beginner or for instruction at schools and camps. **$39.95**

G BEAR LITTLE BEAR

Length is 48"; draw weight at 24", 20 lbs.; handle of selected hardwoods; laminated limbs; dark fiberglass face, back; arrow rest; designed for youngsters. **$31.75**

H BROWNING ROVER

Length is 64"; draw weight, 25 to 60 lbs.; draw lengths, 24 to 30"; custom white dacron string; 6¼" full center-shot sight window; laminated hardwood pistol grip handle; twin accessory insert bushings; black back, white face. **$27**

I BROWNING WASP

Length is 56"; draw weight, 35 to 70 lbs.; draw lengths, 26 to 30"; custom black dacron string; 5" full center-shot sight window; hardwood handle, maple/glass limbs; accessory insert bushings; charcoal face, back; designed primarily for hunting. **$22**

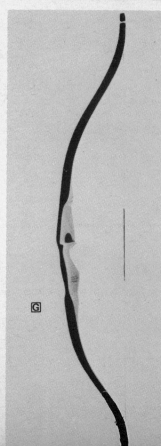

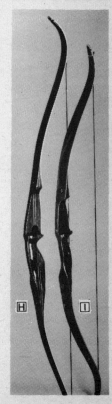

BROWNING PREP

Length is 62"; draw weight, 20 to 42 lbs.; draw lengths, 24 to 30"; 5" full center-shot sight window; light maple handle riser; semi-pistol grip; laminated maple limbs; white back, face; designed for beginning archery programs. $18.50

BROWNING MOHAWK

Length is 54", 25, 30, 35-lb. draw weights; draw lengths, 26 to 29"; 4½" full center-shot sight window; semi-pistol grip; light maple handle riser; laminated maple, glass limbs; designed for junior archers. $17.25

BROWNING SUPERGLASS

Lengths are 54, 58, 60"; draw weights, 20/26 lbs., 25/30 lbs., 30/35 lbs.; custom white dacron string; available in assorted colors; constructed entirely of fiberglass; handle designed for either left or right-handed shooter. $21.50

Superglass Hunter has same specifications as standard model, in 54" length, except for draw weight of 40/54 lbs.; available only in black fiberglass. $21.50

Ⓐ CRAVOTTA BLACK HAWK FIREBOLT — B7

Length is 56"; mass weight, 1¾ lbs.; standard draw lengths; center-shot hardwood handle; maple laminated limbs; rug rest, plate; designed for beginning hunter, bowfishing, schools and camps. $40

DARTON RANGER 58

Length is 58"; draw weight at 28", 20 to 50 lbs.; string length, 54"; imported wood handle riser; laminated limbs. $40

DARTON SCOUT 50A

Length is 50"; string length, 46"; maple riser; laminated limbs; center-shot sight window; full grip. $30

HERTER'S INTERNATIONAL MATCH 17

Length is 63½"; draw weights, 25/29 lbs., 30/34 lbs., 35/39 lbs., 40/44 lbs., 45/49 lbs., 50/54 lbs., 55/60 lbs.; center-shot handle of imported hardwood; fiberglass backing, facing on limbs; 5" sight window; high-gloss urethane finish; fiberglass bow tip overlays; right or left-hand models. $27.95

PEARSON HUNTER II

Length is 58"; draw weight at 28", 45/50 lbs.; unlimited draw length; selected hardwood handle; mohair carpet arrow rest; 4½" sight window; black fiberglass limbs; custom dacron string. ... $40

PEARSON MUSTANG

Length is 58"; draw weights at 28", 40 to 50 lbs.; unlimited draw length; selected hardwood semi-pistol grip handle; mohair carpet arrow rest; 4½" sight window; black fiberglass limbs; custom dacron string. $40

PEARSON COUGAR

Length is 62"; draw weights at 28", 30 to 55 lbs.; unlimited draw length; select hardwood semi-pistol grip handle; mohair carpet arrow rest; 6½" sight window; black fiberglass limbs; custom dacron string. $38.50

Ⓑ PLAS/STEEL BUSHWHACKER

Length is 60"; draw weight, 25 to 65 lbs.; draw limit, 30"; aluminum alloy pistol grip handle, thumb rest; center-shot sight window; wide arrow shelf; interchangeable recurve laminated fiberglass limbs; takedown capability; right-hand model only. ... $29.95

Ⓒ PLAS/STEEL STINGER

Length is 50"; draw weight, 15 to 40 lbs.; draw limit, 28"; aluminum alloy semi-pistol grip handle; dual arrow shelf; interchangeable recurve laminated fiberglass limbs; takedown capability; left or right-hand models. $18.95

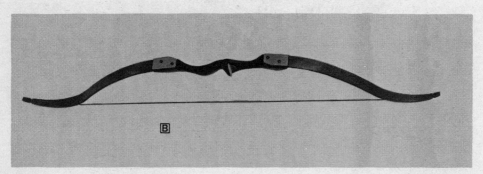

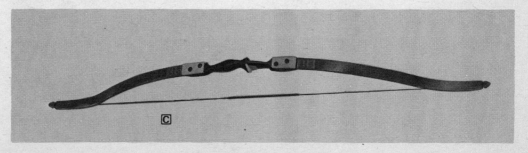

Glossary Of Archery Terms

Arm guard: This shaped leather protector is worn on the inside of the forearm of the bow hand. Purpose is to protect this section of the arm from the bowstring.

Arrow plate: This is a protector, often inlaid, just above the bow handle, on the side where the arrow passes as it is launched in flight.

Back: This is the surface of the bow that is farthest away from the shooter, when the bow is held ready to shoot.

Backing: This can be any one of a number of materials that are glued or affixed to the back of the bow to improve cast. Included have been such materials as fiberglass, rawhide, sinew and various synthetics of modern manufacture.

Backed bow: This is a bow which has had some type of backing material glued to it.

Barb: Part of the hunting arrowhead or broadhead that is fashioned to keep it from being shaken out or pulled from the wound.

Barreled arrow: One, the shaft of which is tapered, starting in the middle and becoming smaller at the ends. The greatest cross-sectional area is in the middle.

Bast: This is the coil of twisted straw that is behind the target and to which the target face is attached.

Boss: The same as bast.

Bow stave: This is the billet of wood from which a bow is made.

Bowyer: One who makes bows; in this era, more often used in connection with one who builds custom bows to order.

Brace: To string the bow, using any of the accepted methods.

Belly: The side that one sees, closest to him, when the bow is held in the standard shooting position.

Bend: Bracing or placing the bowstring in the nocks of the bow.

Bobtail arrow: One that has the greatest cross-section at the pyle and tapers toward the nock.

Bolt: The missile-like shaft that is shot from a crossbow.

Broadhead: A hunting head, usually made of steel, that is triangular in shape. Originally, it had only two blades, hence the name, but the same term is used to describe more complicated heads now.

Butt: A backstop, such as straw bales, to which the target can be attached.

Cast: The ability of the bow to propel an arrow and the degree of efficiency with which this is achieved.

Chested arrows: One that has its greatest cross-section area near the nock, tapering both toward the nock and pyle.

Clout target: A standard target of four feet, which has been enlarged twelve times and is laid out on the ground for clout shooting.

Cock feather: Fletching feather on the arrow at right angles to the nock. In commercially made arrows, this usually is the bright-colored feather.

Crest: This incorporates bands of varying colors and widths, which are painted around the arrows, often by the individual shooter, for identification.

Crossbow: A short bow set on a stock, which usually must be drawn by a mechanical device. It was used primarily for warfare during the Middle Ages. It discharges a bolt by means of a trigger. Numerous sporting models are built today.

Curl: This is a natural swirl in the grain of the wooden bow stave.

Draw: To pull the bowstring the full length of the arrow, ready to shoot.

Draw fingers: Normally the first three fingers of the hand. These are used in pulling the string to full draw.

Draw weight: The force — measured in pounds — required to pull the bow to a full draw.

Drift: The movement to one side or the other of the arrow in its flight, caused by a crosswind.

End: The number of arrows used in scoring a particular

target event. In most instances, and end is considered to be six arrows.

Eye: The loop in the end of the bowstring.

Field captain: The official in charge of a target archery tournament.

Finger tips: Sewn leather finger stalls that are worn over the tips of the shooting or drawing fingers to protect them against the string.

Fistmele: This is the distance from the base of the clenched fist to the tip of the extended thumb. This distance is used as a measurement of the proper distance from the bow handle to the string, when the bow is braced.

Fletch: A verb, often confused with a noun; it concerns actual placement of the feathers on the arrow shaft.

Fletching: This is the noun that often is confused. It is the term to describe the feathers that guide the arrow in flight — after they have been fletched — as in the verb — to attach them.

Flight arrow: This is a light and lengthy arrow with little in the way of fletching that is used in the distance shooting event.

Flirt: A jerky or jumping movement of an arrow in its normal line of flight. This also is decribed by some shooters as "porpoising."

Floo-floo: An arrow that is used in shooting birds, usually on the wing. It usually is fletched with a complete spiral and, in recent years, rabbit fur has been tried rather than feathers. The size and shape of the fletching are determined in such a way that the arrows travel only a short distance and can be retrieved easily. Also: flu-flu.

Footing: Little used except in special instances today, this is a spliced section of hardwood at the pile end of a wooden arrow.

Gold: This is the bullseye in the four-foot regulation circular target. The actual circle is 9-3/5ths inches in diameter.

Grip: The section of the bow, which is held in the shooting hand. It also is called the handle; however, grip also can refer to the manner in which the bow is held.

Hen feathers: Usually of the same color, these are the two feathers that are not at a right angle to the arrow nock.

High brace: According to the Archery Manufacturers Organization, this is when the fistmele distance is more than seven inches. It generally is accepted that it is better to high brace a bow, than to use a low brace.

Hold: This is a pause by the archer, while at full draw, and is just prior to release of the arrow, aligning the arrow with the target.

Lady paramount: Assistant to the field captain, this is a woman who is charged with the women's shooting segment of a tournament.

Laminated bow: A bow that is created from super imposed layers of materials. This can be different types of wood; wood in combination with other materials such as fiberglass or even metal.

Limb: This is the section of the bow from the handle to the tip. Each bow has an upper and a lower limb; these usually cannot be interchanged in the more custom type of bows.

Longbow: The type of bow, without recurve, that usually was fashioned of a single piece of wood without laminations. It gained its reputation during the Middle Ages, but has been replaced almost entirely by bows of more modern design and efficiency.

NAA: This abbreviation refers to the National Archery Association, which is made up entirely of target archers. It also controls United States' participation in all international competitions, insofar as archery is concerned.

NFAA: This abbreviation refers to the National Field Archery Association. Its members, primarily bow-hunters, sought a course on which they could compete, using animal targets at varying distances. Although much younger than the NAA, it also has become much larger in membership.

Nocks: This has a double meaning in archery. First it is the slot behind the fletch into which the bowstring fits. It also is used to denote the groove at the tip of each bow limb into which the loop of the bowstring fits, when the bow is strung.

Nocking point: This is the section of the bowstring, where the nock of the arrow rests. There is a specific point on the string at which efficiency of the arrow is best when shot.

Over-bowed: This term is used to indicate the instance wherein the draw of the bow is more than an individual archer can draw and shoot with any degree of comfort and efficiency.

PAA: These initials refer to the Professional Archery Association, an organization made up primarily of those who compete in contests for money, but the competition must be recognized by the membership; it also includes others who make their livelihood from archery, including qualified instructors and others. It is a young, but aggressive organization.

Petticoat: This is that section outside of the last ring of the target, which has no value in scoring.

Pile: This also is spelled "pyle" in Old English references. It is metal tip attached to the head of the arrow shaft; the arrow point. It comes from the Anglo-Saxon term meaning dart, which is "pil."

Pinch: To squeeze the arrow between the fingers, when drawing.

Pinhole: The exact center of the gold ring in the target used in competitive events.

Point of aim: This is the point or the object at which the archer aims, when he sights over the tip of his arrow.

Quiver: The size, shape and style varies considerably, but this is a holder for arrows so that they may be transported, ready for quick use. The quiver may be slung over the shoulder on the back, hung from the waist, or special designs attached to the bow. In target archery, a device called a ground quiver often is used on the shooting line. This is a rod about twenty inches in length with a loop at the top. The sharp end is stuck into the ground, then arrows are dropped through the loop, standing ready to be withdrawn as they are used.

Recurved bow: This is a bow that is bent back from the straight line at the ends of the limbs.

Reflexed bow: If the recurve bit, didn't throw you, watch out for this one: According to the Archery Manufacturers Organization, "when the bow is unstrung and is held in the shooting position, the limbs curve outward, away from the shooter."

Release: This is an artificial device that is about as old as archery, but recently has been rediscovered in sundry forms. It is used to draw and release the bowstring without the fingers actually doing the work. It has been responsible for higher scores in many cases, since it tends to afford more consistent shots. It is considered illegal in some types of competition.

Round: This designates the number of shots taken at a give distance or standardized series of distances.

Run: When one of the strings in a bowstring frays, stretches or even breaks, this string is said to have a run much as one might refer to a similar situation in hosery.

Self: This refers to a bow or arrow that is made from a single piece of wood, thus they are called self bows and self arrows.

Serving: The wrapping around the bowstring at the nocking points, which protects the string from normal wear at these stress points.

Shaft: This is the body of the arrow — wood, fiberglass or aluminum — to which the fletching and arrowhead are attached.

Shaftment: The section at the rear of the shaft to which the fletching or feathers are attached.

Shake: A crack running with the grain in a bow stave.

Shooting glove: The partial glove with three fingers used to protect the fingers in shooting.

Spiral: The curved manner in which the fletch is attached to the shaft of the arrow.

Spine: The bending quality of an arrow that allows it to spring out as it passes the bow upon being shot, then return to its original straightness, when free in flight.

Stacked bow: A bow in which the thickness of the limbs is little greater than the width; this type of bow usually is oval in cross-section.

Tab: A piece of leather, which is worn across the shooting fingers for protection much as is the shooting glove.

Tackle: A collective phrase to cover all of the archer's equipment, including bow, arrows, strings and accessories.

Take-down: The type of bow that has limbs that can be removed for transportation or even to change the weight of the bow by a switch in limbs.

Tiller: This involves shaping the bow, usually in the limb sections.

Under-bowed: The situation wherein an archer has a bow that is too light in draw weight.

Unit: The fourteen targets on a roving field archery course.

Upshot: The final shot in an archery competition.

Vane: This originally referred to the flat expanded segment of the feather fletching. In recent years, however, it has come to be used more in connection with the flat pieces of plastic that are cemented to shafts in place of feathers. These are used primarily in target archery.

Wand: A piece of wood, six feet long and two inches in width. It is driven into the ground and serves as a shooting mark.

Whip-ended: Description of a bow of which the limbs are too weak in the tip area.